THE DIGITAL PHOENIX
How Computers Are
Changing Philosophy

THE DIGITAL PHOENIX
How Computers Are
Changing Philosophy

Edited by

TERRELL WARD BYNUM and JAMES H. MOOR

Published in cooperation with the Committee
on Philosophy and Computers of the
American Philosophical Association
and also with the journal
Metaphilosophy

First published 1998

Blackwell Publishers Ltd
108 Cowley Road
Oxford, OX4 1JF
UK

and

Blackwell Publishers Inc.
350 Main Street
Malden, MA 02148
USA

British Library Cataloguing in Publication Data has been applied for.

Library of Congress Cataloguing-in-Publication Data has been applied for.

ISBN   0-631-203524

Typeset in 10 pt Book Antiqua

Printed in Great Britain by Whitstable Litho Ltd, Kent

CONTENTS

INTRODUCTION

HOW COMPUTERS ARE CHANGING PHILOSOPHY

TERRELL WARD BYNUM AND JAMES H. MOOR

Computing and Philosophy

From time to time, major movements occur in philosophy. These movements begin with a few simple, but very fertile, ideas – ideas that provide philosophers with a new prism through which to view philosophical issues. Gradually, philosophical methods and problems are refined and understood in terms of these new notions. As novel and interesting philosophical results are obtained, the movement grows into an intellectual wave that travels throughout the discipline. A new philosophical paradigm emerges. Like a phoenix rising, philosophy is transformed.

Computing provides philosophy with such a set of simple, but incredibly fertile, notions – new and evolving *subject matters*, *methods*, and *models* for philosophical inquiry. Computing brings new opportunities and challenges to traditional philosophical activities. As a result, computing is changing the professional activities of philosophers, including how they do research, how they cooperate with each other, and how they teach their courses. Most importantly, computing is changing the way philosophers understand foundational concepts in philosophy, such as mind, consciousness, experience, reasoning, knowledge, truth, ethics and creativity. This trend in philosophical inquiry that incorporates computing in terms of a subject matter, a method, or a model has been gaining momentum steadily. A Digital Phoenix is rising!

Interest in computing by philosophers is not completely new. The ancient philosopher Pythagoras, who was born about 570 BC and is immortalized by the Pythagorean Theorem, was fascinated by computation and closely identified reality with numbers. He was impressed, for example, with calculated ratios in music which demonstrated that beauty in music depends upon the correct mathematical relationships among the notes of a scale. And in the seventeenth century, Thomas Hobbes proposed a mechanistic, computational account of the human mind. For Hobbes perception, imagination, and memory are explainable in terms of matter in motion according to the laws of

1

mechanics. Reason is "nothing but reckoning, that is adding and subtracting, of the consequences of general names agreed upon for the marking and signifying of our thoughts."

In 1642 the French mathematician/philosopher Blaise Pascal developed an early calculating machine that computed sums by a series of connected gears. Later, the German philosopher Gottfried Leibniz developed a computing machine that performed multiplication. Leibniz believed that statements about complex things could be derived from statements about their simpler components by a process analogous to multiplication. Leibniz suggested that if fundamental concepts – a kind of alphabet of human thought – could be isolated, all truths could be computed from them. In principle, whenever humans differed in opinion on some subject, they could sit down and calculate to determine the truth of the matter.

In the twentieth century, the theory of computation has matured and has had a striking impact upon philosophy. Alan Turing, the brilliant British mathematician/philosopher, developed a conception of computation in terms of abstract mathematical devices, now called "Turing Machines". His work, along with that of Alonzo Church, Kurt Gödel and others, provided profound insights into the nature and limits of logic and mathematics. The widely accepted Church-Turing thesis states that whatever is computable is computable by a Turing Machine. Given this philosophical thesis, computation has enormous possibilities and serious limitations. All computation can be explained in terms of simple deterministic steps, but, as Turing proved, some truths are not computable by Turing Machines. Therefore, Leibniz's dream of having a universal calculus that would allow us to resolve any differences in opinion through calculation cannot, in principle, be fulfilled.

Turing's work did much to lay the foundation for digital computing. Turing himself worked on some early digital computing devices, including one that helped to decipher the German *Enigma* code during World War II. Turing believed that intelligent action could be understood in terms of computation, and after the war he proposed the imitation game (now well known as the "Turing test") to assess the intellectual abilities of computers through evaluating conversations between human interrogators and hidden computer and human respondents.

Computing and related concepts significantly enhance traditional philosophy by providing a kind of intellectual clay that philosophers can mold and shape and study. Through computing, abstract ideas – which philosophers like to manipulate – can be instantiated and investigated. There is nothing wrong with good armchair reflection *without* the aid of a computer, for computerless armchairs have had a spectacular history of producing ideas that provide insights into the nature of reality and that motivate us to build better societies. But armchair reflection has its limitations. As sophisticated as our imaginations and reasoning skills may be, there are practical limits to how much complexity we can process without some assistance. Armchair recursion doesn't recur very many times. But when ideas are modeled on a computer, consequences, especially consequences that emerge after complex processing, are revealed in a way that would be completely overlooked without such computer processing. Models and methods can be made more precise, tested, and refined. These philosophical results of computing can be shared with others who also can submit them to their own scrutiny and development. Philosophers have always shared their ideas and writings. Now, they sometimes use a computer, a philosophical tool, to share computations – abstract ideas come alive.

When new movements occur within philosophy, it is common for their zealous advocates to insist that the new ways of doing philosophy will become the only methodology from which to judge all other philosophy. Logical Positivists, for example, insisted that all philosophical statements must be measured by the standards of verifiability. And Ordinary Language Philosophers were determined to make all philosophical issues disappear by keeping language in its proper place. Although we are strong – perhaps even zealous – advocates of computing in philosophy, we are not suggesting that all philosophy must be done by computational methods. And we are certainly not suggesting that answers to all philosophical problems can be computed. That would be to fall under the spell of Leibniz's dream which, assuming our contemporary understanding of computation, is not realizable through computational methods.

Furthermore, we are not suggesting that computing in philosophy will bring philosophy to an end. Philosophers are always capable of taking a reflective turn and moving to the next metalevel of discussion. This possibility leaves any one method open to independent and novel kinds of philosophical investigation. Nevertheless, we strongly believe that computing and related concepts have much to offer philosophy that is not available without them; and we are convinced that philosophy will be substantially transformed in the future by computational concepts, methods, and models.

The Digital Phoenix Project

Most of the papers in this book were invited presentations for programs run by the Committee on Philosophy and Computing (PAC), chaired by Terry Bynum, at meetings of the Eastern, Central, or Pacific Division of the American Philosophical Association during the last three years (1994-97). In addition, some of the papers were presented at recent sessions of the Computers and Philosophy (CAP) Conference, chaired by Robert Cavalier, which meets every year in

August. In a few cases philosophers who were asked to speak had just published, or were about to publish, relevant papers elsewhere. We have included a couple of these papers in the volume as well. Hence, all of the papers in this book represent recent work in some aspect of computing and philosophy, and almost all of the papers are published here for the first time. The purpose of this book is to present a broad, original, and contemporary examination of the impact of computing upon philosophy.

Because the effects of computing on philosophy are already quite diverse and specialized, it is impossible to represent all of them or even the depth and sophistication of any one of them. Many worthy examples of computing and philosophy could not be included; and this book should be seen as a *sampler* that allows the reader to browse this approach to philosophy and appreciate its fruitfulness and rich diversity. Many more examples exist, and much, much more will come. The Digital Phoenix has only begun to rise!

Consider what computing offers philosophy in terms of new subject matters. Computation itself is a legitimate philosophical subject. What is computation? Turing gave a persuasive analysis of computation in terms of Turing Machines, but is this really the extent of computation? Turing suggests that there is a limit to what computers can compute. His famous halting problem shows that no Turing Machine can determine for every Turing Machine whether or not it will halt, i.e., complete its computation at some time. But, in the present volume Selmer Bringsjord invites us to consider the possibility that the Turing limit can be crossed and some devices might perform super-computation. Perhaps our minds or some physical devices are best described as super-computers that are not bounded by Turing's limit. Bringsjord states, "By my lights, we stand on the brink of explosive interaction between philosophy and such processing." Bringsjord raises provocative questions that invite us to cross over into this new world of possibilities.

Computer science is another subject matter for philosophers to consider. Computer science as a topic has been somewhat neglected by philosophers who have tended to focus on its more flashy offspring, artificial intelligence. But philosophers are coming to realize that there is much in computer science itself that is worth careful philosophical scrutiny. What is it that makes something a computer? What, if any, are the philosophically important differences between a digital computer and an analog computer, or between a serial computer and a parallel processor? What is the nature of algorithms and what sorts of things can count as computer programs? Anyone who believes that philosophy of computer science cannot spark a lively debate should read James Fetzer's discussion of the program verification debate. A computer program is verified by showing through deductive reasoning that it satisfies a given specification and is therefore correct, i.e., it will do what you want it to do. Fetzer points out that there is an important distinction between programs as formal algorithms and programs as causal models of those algorithms – roughly the difference between pure and applied mathematics. The philosophical point that formal methods cannot guarantee the behavior of real life computers may seem straightforward to readers of David Hume or Carl Hempel, but it was disturbing to the computer scientists who replied vigorously against Fetzer's original article on program verification published in *Communications of the ACM*.

Computer ethics is another subject matter of critical philosophical interest raised by the existence of computers. Computers are logically malleable and find applications everywhere in our society. These applications raise important ethical issues about property, privacy, power and professional responsibility. Frequently, the application of computer technology creates policy vacuums, and we are baffled about how to use computing technology ethically. Much philosophical work needs to be done to understand the nature of computing technology and to formulate and justify the best possible ethical policies for using or not using computing devices in given situations. Terry Bynum describes the brief history of the emerging field of computer and information ethics and examines the ethical impact that computing is now having on a global scale. The internet allows individuals to communicate throughout the world in ways never before possible. In a world with an internet, atrocities within dictatorships are harder to hide, but hate speech is given a stronger voice than ever. How can the internet best be used for ethical purposes? To miss the moral dimensions of the computer revolution is to miss the importance of the revolution. As Bynum stresses, "The growing information revolution, therefore, is not 'merely technological' – it is *fundamentally social and ethical*."

Artificial intelligence (AI) is the computing subject that has received the most philosophical attention over the last fifty years. Can we build computers that are actually intelligent? In a recent chess tournament Deep Blue beat Gary Kasparov, currently the best human chess player in the world and some would say the best human chess player ever. A stunning accomplishment for computers given that chess is often regarded as one of the most intellectually challenging games. However, the victory of machine over a human world chess champion did not come swiftly. Decades ago AI enthusiasts maintained that computers would rapidly become world chess champions. What then should we make of progress in AI? In his early book, *What Computers Cannot Do*, Hubert Dreyfus compared AI to alchemy. It's success depends on a series of ad hoc tricks. There is no unifying theory that drives the discipline. AI may have some successes, but these successes, according to a picturesque Dreyfus image, are like climbing a tree to reach the moon – after initial success there is dismal failure. According to Dreyfus, the problem for traditional AI is that it works well in context-free domains like chess that can be formalized, but life in general is not context free or formalizable. Life is not chess. Humans have intuition which is built up through thousands of interactions with various kinds of situations. So humans, and especially human experts, do not apply formal rules to solve problems but rely on intuition to make the right decisions. Dreyfus points out that today AI is divided into different schools, but he is not sanguine about the possibility of any of the schools of AI being any more than a degenerating research program. In the present volume, Dreyfus defends himself against some criticisms raised against his position.

But does the slow progress of AI show that the goals of AI are not tenable, or does it merely indicate that the subject is difficult and that accomplishments will come slowly? After all, chemistry *did* arise out of alchemy eventually. If our brains are responsible for our intuitions, our brains must do it somehow. Might there be unconscious micro-rules that describe how our brains assemble information for coping with situations that are not context free? These questions remain open and suggest that Dreyfus may not have closed the book on the future success of AI. And, if AI is successful, how would we know it? What in principle would count to show that a computer is intelligent? James Moor assesses the progress of AI in terms of recent accomplishments in chess and the results of recent Turing tests. He defends AI against a number of its critics but suggests that AI has a long way to go in developing a general theory of understanding, problem-solving, and learning.

AI is sometimes divided into weak AI and strong AI. Weak AI treats AI applications as instrumentally useful and perhaps as interesting simulations, but never as examples of real intelligence. Strong AI on the other hand, regards AI as on a mission to create artificial minds – minds that have real intelligence and consciousness, which just happen to be located in computerized bodies. One of the strongest intuitions against the possibility of strong AI is the philosophical problem of qualia. Humans have qualitative, phenomenal or subjective experiences. We all know that this is true; but it may seem impossible that machines could have qualia. How could a computer experience anything? William Lycan argues for the "goose-gander" thesis – "There is no problem for or objection to qualitative experience in machines that is not equally a quandary for such experience in humans." Lycan considers various potential arguments that might defeat his position and proceeds to argue against each of them. The possibility of computers having qualia will continue to be debated as computers do more and more in increasingly sophisticated ways.

Computing not only provides a fresh subject matter for philosophers to study, it also provides a medium in which to model philosophical theories and positions. Consider the study of epistemology, the theory of knowledge. Epistemology is often regarded as the heart of philosophy. Philosophers want to understand what constitutes knowledge and how it is justified. What does it mean to reason rationally? Philosophical theories of knowledge and belief have been advanced over the ages, but only as theories vaguely and abstractly stated. Now, computer models can be built to demonstrate how belief structures may interact and be modified in light of new beliefs. In his paper in this book, John Pollock describes his OSCAR project which is aimed at the construction of a general theory of rationality and its implementation as an artificial agent. Human reasoning is defeasible – new information may cause us to add new beliefs or to retract old ones. Pollock's objective is to develop precise rules of reasoning about how this can and should be done. Pollock's agent, OSCAR, must handle complex challenges such as dealing with the lottery paradox, the situation in which we seem to believe for every lottery ticket that it will not win and yet believe that some lottery ticket must win. Pollock nicely summarizes why he believes such a computer model is important for philosophy. First, it is an important constraint on a theory that it must be possible for something to actually work the way the theory describes. As Pollock says, "As mundane as this constraint may seem, I am convinced that most epistemological theories fail to satisfy it." Second, to build a computer model, the theory must be made precise and detailed. Pollock remarks, "That can have a very therapeutic effect on a profession that is overly fond of handwaving." And third, a computer model is invaluable in testing and tuning the theory. In short, computing provides philosophers with a means of investigating their theories which they have never had before.

Henry Kyburg endorses the powers of computing in the area of model building. He contends, "... fast digital computers are a wonderful boon to certain kinds of philosophy, for example epistemology, in the sense that they provide a kind of philosophical laboratory..." Of course, a working model of a theory does not guarantee that the theory is correct, and Kyburg challenges some of the assumptions of the OSCAR model. Kyburg believes that in the situation of the lottery paradox we are warranted in believing for each ticket of the lottery that it will not win and also are warranted in believing that some ticket will win. That is, on Kyburg's view we can be warranted in believing an explicitly contradictory set of propositions. So, another model of a rational agent, say FLORENCE, might be developed based on Kyburg's assumption. How can we judge the philosophical adequacy given OSCAR and FLORENCE? Kyburg suggests, "The answer to this question may well call for philosophical experimentation of a kind that can only be done by computers."

Computer modeling is playing a significant role in the philosophy of science. Lindley Darden describes the intriguing program TRANSGENE which addresses the problem of how a scientific theory

7

is properly modified given an anomaly. The sample theory in this case is Mendelian genetic theory. A computer model for this must be capable of representing the theory, detecting an anomaly, and finding, fixing and testing possible fault sites in the theory. To carry out the simulation, the details of the philosophical theory must be worked out carefully. This precise approach is quite different from traditional philosophy of science which is usually vague about the details of the growth of scientific theories. A functioning computer model invites new insights about the mechanisms of growth of scientific theories. As Darden points out, "Philosophers trained in logic typically discuss only two levels [of abstraction]: a variable and its value. They miss the lesson from AI about multiple hierarchical levels of abstraction."

Paul Thagard gives an excellent overview of the impact of the computational approach to philosophy of science. He discusses three different approaches: cognitive modeling that treats the scientist's mind as a subject to be brought under the jurisdiction of cognitive science modeling; engineering AI that explores the possibility of scientific discoveries made by computers, but not necessarily in human ways (so called "android epistemology"); and the theory of computation that uses formal methods to show the possibilities and limit of scientific evaluation. Thagard concludes, "Bringing artificial intelligence into philosophy of science introduces new conceptual resources for dealing with the structure and growth of scientific knowledge." Computing offers us new models for what is possible and what is not in the scientific discovery process. Philosophy of science will never be the same.

Computation can be used as a model for metaphysics as well as epistemology. If metaphysics is taken as the study of the foundations of physics, then computation can be used to express various possible worlds of which the actual world is just one. Such a conception of metaphysics is inspired by Leibniz. Working out of the use of computer models in contemporary physics, especially cellular automata, Eric Steinhart advocates a contemporary version of digital metaphysics. As he succinctly puts the thesis, "reality is ultimately computational". By Steinhart's account, "Different systems of physical laws are programmed into computational space-time, so that physics is to metaphysics as software is to hardware."

Within the general area of metaphysics, philosophy of mind has been most often modeled computationally. The computational theory of mind is the leading contender among contemporary views of the human mind. Paul Churchland argues that neural networks have the best chance of explaining our ability to represent and act in complex social settings. For example, he discusses EMPATH, an artificial neural net that can recognize eight different emotional states from astonishment to anger as displayed on human faces after the artificial neural network is trained for such identification by being shown examples of such facial displays. The EMPATH network is an example of a connectionist computer network which is not programmed in the traditional way but adjusts weights to internal connections as it experiences new input patterns. Such computer models hint at ways in which the brain might work to learn prototypes for interpreting and understanding informal situations. Churchland believes that this kind of learning may well explain our moral cognition. He concludes, "This novel perspective on the nature of human cognition, both scientific and moral, comes to us from two disciplines – cognitive neuroscience and connectionist artificial intelligence – that had no prior interest in or connection with either the philosophy of science or moral theory. And yet the impact on both these philosophical disciplines is destined to be revolutionary."

Computer models are useful in exploring the nature of values in social interactions. Peter Danielson develops a subject he calls "artificial morality" in which he uses computerized agents to make decisions in socially problematic situations. Some of these agents are more or less morally constrained and others are rational but amoral. He believes that, by studying the outcomes of iterated prisoner dilemma games, new and interesting results can be found about the circumstances under which certain strategies are likely to evolve or influence the population. Danielson believes that computer models are valuable in helping us to check unwarranted intuitions about ethics. As he puts it, "Ethics is so charged with prejudice – intuition – that we need powerful tools to keep our theories honest and open to surprising – i.e. counter-intuitive – ideas." Danielson concludes by expressing his dependence upon computer simulation for doing his philosophical research. "Computers have become more important as the project progressed. They served in the initial stages as a check on consistency and a push to explore new possibilities, but in the evolutionary extension of the program, they are strictly necessary to the research."

Even creativity, a subject that perhaps seems antithetical to computational methods, can be explored using computational models. Margaret Boden defines a creative idea as one that is "novel, surprising and valuable". She maintains that computers can generate creative ideas, help us to understand what creativity is and how it is accomplished, and even help us to be creative. After clarifying the concepts at issue, Boden uses programs like AARON, which produces unique, aesthetically pleasing line drawings and color paintings, and DENDRAL, a program that generates appropriate molecular structures from test information, to show that computers can explore conceptual spaces in ways that are historically novel and interesting to humans. Some programs, containing genetic algorithms, can change their own rules, thereby generating structures that could not have been generated by previous generations of the programs. Of course, the question of whether computers can be genuinely creative, in the

9

sense that they can appreciate their own creations, remains open. Nevertheless, Boden demonstrates clearly that computer models have already revealed much about what is required to be creative.

Project Archelogos, a philosophical project directed by Theodore Scaltsas, is not about computing as a subject or using computing to model, but it does employ computers essentially. This project is focused on the extraction of arguments from ancient Greek philosophical texts and the representation of their logical interconnections. Computing is used to display in explicit form arguments found within texts and to reveal their structure and relationships. In Project Archelogos computers are used to assist in the comprehension of an argument, in the original Greek or in translation, by allowing users to select the argument and to explore its sub-arguments in detail, including commentaries on the argument and sub-arguments over the centuries. Computing software provides a hypertext tool that allows philosophical researchers and students to search related data bases about Greek texts in a way that would be impossible in practical terms without the speed and precision of modern computers. Moreover, the dynamic visualization presented through the computer is unmatched by traditional methods of scholarly displays in books. Scaltsas notes that computerization of texts and related materials has raised interesting philosophical issues about the proper interpretation of texts – questions that would be overlooked without the computer. Many scholars are working on the Archelogos Project. When completed, the results of the Project will be made generally available, possibly on the internet.

Jon Barwise and John Etchemendy, winners of the 1997 EDUCOM Award, have directed a number of projects that resulted in spectacular logic software. Their program *Turing's World* has a graphic interface that allows students to construct and run Turing Machines to test and demonstrate the computational abilities of specific machines. The difference between running a Turing Machine on a computer after one has built it and debugged it and writing out the instructions for a Turing Machine the old fashioned way by paper and pencil is the difference between really understanding how Turing Machines work and having a vague intuition about them. The computer methodology makes all the difference. In addition, the program *Tarski's World* allows students to construct symbolic sentences in predicate logic to describe a world of blocks. The computer methodology forces students to understand the semantics of the formal language. Barwise and Etchemendy's work on these two computer projects led them to appreciate the value of visualization in reasoning. Their "Hyperproof" project is the result of rethinking not only how logic *is* taught, but also how logic *should be* taught. Traditionally, symbolic logic has emphasized formal deductive proofs in which sentences are manipulated syntactically, line after line. But computers can dynamically represent information in non-sentential ways. The computer for Barwise and Etchemendy has been more than a tool to teach traditional logic. It has been an inspiration to reconceive what reasoning is about.

There are, as we have been emphasizing, three different aspects of computing and philosophy: computational subject matters, computational models, and computational methods. Of course, philosophical projects and activities often involve a combination of computational subject matters, models and methods. The topic of Artificial Life (AL) is an excellent case in point. AL studies computational structures and processes which exhibit lifelike behavior. Computer viruses and worms are examples of programs which have such animate characteristics, but there are many more. AL entities move around, change their environments, cooperate, and even reproduce copies of themselves. In some cases AL programs mutate so that their offspring have different programming structures. One of the most fascinating features of AL phenomena is that complex global behavior can emerge from a collection of interacting virtual agents each of which follows very, very simple rules. Mark Bedau describes how seemingly organized flocking behavior emerges from computer "boids" which obey simple rules of flight in relation to other boids. There is no master pro-grammer for the flock. The explanation comes from the bottom up, from the modest but repeated interactions of simple individual units – not from the top down, from the desk of a master designer. This model of emergence is extremely suggestive for philosophers of biology who have searched for credible explanations of life and purpose that do not involve suspect appeals to life forces and teleology. As Bedau declares, "A new level of clarity, precision, and evidence will follow when philosophers adapt artificial life's computational methodology of emergent thought experiments."

Computing and Professional Philosophy

Professional philosophy has fallen under the gravitational influence of the world of computing. Computers are having a profound effect not only on foundational concepts of philosophy, but also on the various day-to-day professional activities of philosophers. One important and growing computing resource for research and teaching is found in multimedia, particularly the use of interactive CD-ROMs. Through CDs, a wealth of information is available to the user in a manner that is not reproducible by traditional books. For example, using Terry Bynum and John Fodor's CD, *Introduction to Computer Ethics*, someone can investigate various issues within the field of Computer Ethics not only through text and graphics, but also through video clips of experts commenting on the problems. David Anderson, Robert Cavalier, and Preston Covey's CD, *A Right to Die? The Dax Cowart Case*, presents a difficult case in medical ethics – does a badly burned, disabled patient have the right to die rather than undergo extraordinarily painful medical treatments? The user of the CD learns some of the details of the case by selecting video interviews with the patient, the doctors, the staff, and the patient's family. Tools on the CD encourage the user to analyze the situation, rather than merely receive the information passively. This is not a manufactured philosophical example nor is it a dry presentation of material from a standard text. Using the CD makes this difficult situation in medical ethics immediate and real. In fact, the CD comes with a warning label. As these two examples of using CDs illustrate, interactive CD-ROMs are innovative, effective and exciting educational tools for teaching philosophy.

Currently, the world wide web is a rapidly expanding source of philosophical information and materials. Many philosophers, departments, centers and institutes have web sites which provide information about themselves. For example, a recent survey by the American Philosophical Association identified 135 web sites of philosophy departments in North America. Some philosophy web sites, e.g., Larry Hinman's web pages for ethics (http://ethics.acusd.edu), are "gold mines" of information. Since web pages can be updated routinely – even hourly – standard book publication and even television simply cannot keep pace with the timely information dissemination of the web. In addition, many classical texts by great philosophers are now accessible on-line, e.g., the web site of the Philosophy Department at Valdosta State University – http://www.valdosta. peachnet.edu/~rbarnett/phi. As these excellent sites illustrate, the web can be an invaluable source of philosophical materials and information. Of course, one has to be a cautious consumer since some web sites have higher standards of quality control than others.

The world wide web is not only a means of disseminating philosophical information and materials, one can also use it as a "place" to teach philosophy. Some philosophers, for example, are teaching entire university courses on the web. Ron Barnette began teaching his course PHICYBER in 1993. His classroom is virtual and his course is totally paperless. Given the enormous amount of philosophical material on line, including most historical philosophical works, teaching a paperless course is now more than a possibility. In Barnette's case, students are assigned topics, essays and readings each week. Electronic philosophical exchanges come from around the globe. As Barnette reports, "In 1996, one hundred eleven participants signed up for PHICYBER, from eleven countries 'representing five continents!" Jon Dorbolo also teaches a web course, InterQuest – an introduction to philosophy course at Oregon State University. Dorbolo suggests in his course description in this volume that the web approach to teaching philosophy facilitates learning that can be more effectively customized to individual students.

12

Web-based courses are very new and different, and they are therefore controversial. Do students learn as much or more than in traditional classes? How much, if anything, should students pay universities for such courses? How should such courses affect accreditation? These questions and many more need to be addressed as web-based teaching grows, but this exciting experiment in global philosophy teaching is underway.

The American Philosophical Association (APA) has its own web site (http://www.udel.edu/apa) providing information and news about the APA, its members, and philosophical events around the globe. In the present volume, Saul Traiger, who established the original APA internet site and oversaw its evolution to the web, discusses the history of the APA site and candidly points out some of the economic and political realities in establishing rules for such a site. What APA publications and services should be available on-line? Should members get passwords for access to "members-only" information? Should dues-payment and other financial transactions be conducted electronically? The APA web site has already become an important resource in the philosophical community – one of the first sources many philosophers consult about philosophical organizations, conferences, publications, services, jobs, web sites, electronic discussion groups, grants, and so on. The importance of the APA web site will continue to grow dramatically during the next few years.

Part of the mission of the Digital Phoenix Project was to conduct a survey about how philosophers are using computers in their work. In fall 1996, questionnaires were mailed to about 2,000 departments of philosophy to be completed by the department chair or a designee. Preliminary results of the survey are presented in three reports found at the end of this book. Respondents, reporting on the professional activities of over 2,000 philosophers in North America, described many activities essentially involving computers: 135 philosophy department web sites were identified, and a wide variety of activities were reported, including the teaching of philosophy courses on-line or with multimedia, planning of conferences, writing of philosophical software, electronic discussions with philosophers around the globe, publication of electronic journals, finding and searching electronic texts in philosophy, simulation and modeling of various philosophical ideas and theories, integrating web pages into university courses, and so on. The survey confirms that computing already has had a profound effect upon professional philosophy. As the computer revolution progresses, the impacts on philosophy are likely to grow exponentially. Larry Hinman observes: "Obviously, had this survey been taken ten years ago, the response would have been almost non-existent. The intriguing thought is to imagine what the results will be ten years from now." Perhaps another survey can be taken then and the results of the current one can serve as a benchmark. In ten years

13

computing may lose some of its novelty in philosophy, but it will not lose its impact.

In conclusion, we want to express our gratitude to the many people who have helped to make the Digital Phoenix Project possible. We have had wonderful cooperation from the many authors in the book, and we wish to extend special appreciation to the members of the Committee on Philosophy and Computers of the American Philosophical Association, Basil Blackwell Publisher, the journal *Metaphilosophy*, Dartmouth College, and Southern Connecticut State University. We owe particular thanks to Ron Barnette, Robert Cavalier and Larry Hinman for their work on the APA surveys; to Armen Marsoobian, Editor of *Metaphilosophy*; to Eric Hoffman, Executive Director of the APA; to Dean Sabatino who designed the stunning cover of this book; and also to David Chiang who helped enormously in preparing camera-ready copy for the publisher.

PART I

THE IMPACT OF COMPUTING
ON PHILOSOPHICAL ISSUES

PROCEDURAL EPISTEMOLOGY

JOHN L. POLLOCK

I was asked to write a paper on "How computing has changed epistemology." In my own case, computing has had a major impact on the way I do epistemology, and this is reflected in my current work on the OSCAR Project, whose objective is the construction of a general theory of rationality and its computer-implementation in an artificial rational agent. The OSCAR Project thus merges large parts of philosophy and artificial intelligence. A version of OSCAR is now running, and researchers can download it from my website. I have recently published a book entitled *Cognitive Carpentry* that details the theory of rationality embodied in OSCAR. This paper will sketch some of the epistemological consequences of the thinking underlying the OSCAR Project.

Procedural Epistemology

Ten years ago, a philosopher could write a paper on epistemology, making free and frequent use of the term "epistemic justification," without further explanation and confident that his audience would understand him. That is no longer a reasonable way to proceed. It has become increasingly apparent in the last ten years that there is more than one important concept that might reasonably be called "epistemic justification," and it seems clear that these different concepts have often been confused with one another in the epistemological literature. The literature on the Gettier problem has highlighted one concept, dear to the hearts of many epistemologists, which is something like "what turns true belief into knowledge." The reliabilist literature, for example, might best be read as pertaining to some such concept as this. But there is at least one other important concept that pertains to "the directing of one's own cognition." This is an essentially first person concept. In my book *Contemporary Theories of Knowledge*, I proposed that this concept could be understood as descriptive of our procedural knowledge for "how to cognize." That part of epistemology that is more concerned with the procedural aspects of rationality than with the analysis of "*S* knows that *P*" can, I urged, be viewed as pursuing a competence theory of cognition, in the same way that theories of grammar in Linguistics are competence theories of language. On this view, the normative language employed in the formulation of both theories of grammar and epistemological theories is a reflection, in part, of the competence/performance distinction that can be drawn in connection with any procedural knowledge.

A more perspicuous way of viewing this distinction between different concepts of epistemic justification arises from viewing epistemology "from the design stance."[1] This is to think of epistemology as being part of the enterprise of designing an autonomous rational agent. That is the traditional task of AI. The design of a system of epistemic cognition becomes part of the task of designing a rational intellect, and epistemology provides the analysis of rationality driving the design. Viewed from this perspective, we can roughly divide the interests of epistemology into *procedural epistemology* and *descriptive epistemology*. Procedural epistemology is directed at how to build the system of cognition, whereas descriptive epistemology concerns how to describe what the system is doing once it is running. Thus rules for reasoning become part of procedural epistemology, but the analysis of "*S* knows that *P*" is assigned to descriptive epistemology.

The Tasks of Procedural Epistemology

Procedural epistemology is the study of the procedures constituting the systems of epistemic cognition that can be embodied in rational intellects. These are procedures for systematically updating the cognizer's set of beliefs. The study of these processes can be divided into three tasks. Given a system of representation and a set of inputs, the first task of procedural epistemology is to describe the set of "ultimately reasonable beliefs" the system should settle into. I will refer to these as the *warranted propositions* relative to that set of inputs. For instance, given a representation system expressing everything in a first-order language, if we thought that all reasoning was deductive then it might be proposed that the set of warranted propositions is the set of first-order consequences of the propositions constituting the input. Let us say that the *semantical task* of epistemology is that of giving a general description of the set of warranted propositions relative to any set of inputs.

The second task of procedural epistemology is that of describing sets of procedures that, if they could be applied without constraint, would eventually lead a rational intellect from the set of inputs to any member of the set of warranted propositions. For example, a simplistic theory of this sort might propose that a set of such procedures is described by some system of proof for first-order logic. Let us call the search for such a set of procedures *the procedural task* of procedural epistemology. This is analogous to proof theory in logic.

The third task of procedural epistemology arises from the observation that simply describing the set of procedures is not by itself adequate to construct an intellect that uses those procedures to guide belief formation. The list of procedures must be supplemented with a *control structure* that determines when each procedure is to be used. This point is typically illustrated by reference to the "British Museum Algorithm." Given a set of rules of inference for the predicate calculus, we could easily build an automated theorem prover that would systematically generate all proofs, one after another. Then if we want a proof for a particular theorem, we just turn the system on and wait. However, such a system would be intolerably inefficient. Any reasonable system of automated theorem proving must be "interest-driven" in the sense that what the system does is a function of what theorem-proving tasks are given to it. This is just to say that the system must be provided with a control structure that guides the application of the rules of inference in a way that is sensitive to what the system is trying to prove. The same thing is true of reasoning in general. A rational agent does not proceed randomly in its epistemic pursuits. Rather, practical matters pose questions that the agent wants answered, and the whole point of epistemic cognition is to answer those questions. Epistemic cognition must be interest-driven in the sense that the course of cognition is influenced by the questions the agent is trying to answer.

I will refer to the design of a suitable control structure as the *architectural task* of procedural epistemology. The semantical and procedural tasks are familiar to philosophers, but the architectural task has been largely ignored in philosophy. In this respect, work in AI has been more sophisticated than work in philosophy. It is unclear to me why this should be the case. Either it just did not occur to most philosophers, or else they thought it could not be fruitfully investigated. Perhaps this stems in part from the logical positivists' rejection of a "logic of discovery," and their disdain for what they regarded as "psychologism in philosophy." But whatever the explanation, contemporary work in AI makes it clear that this is a perfectly reasonable task for philosophers to undertake. For instance, a great deal of the theory underlying OSCAR is directed at the architectural task. I will say more about this as we proceed.

The design of a rational intellect requires solutions to the procedural task and the architectural task. A solution to the semantical task of characterizing epistemic warrant is of only indirect relevance, but it may be of use in guiding the solutions to the other tasks, as I will explain below. Given a system of epistemic cognition, an agent will adopt new beliefs as a result of either perceptual input or by inference from previously held beliefs. In the latter case, the previously held beliefs constitute "good reasons" for believing the conclusions. We can regard an *argument* as a record of the state transitions involved in the agent's reasoning. So we can regard reasoning as the construction of arguments. This does not mean that the argument is itself an object represented in the agent's thought. It would be better to say that the agent *instantiates* an argument.

Belief-updating can be described in terms of the arguments the agent constructs. We can think of belief-updating as proceeding in parallel with the development of an agent's arguments, one step at a time. Given the agent's current set of arguments, a belief is *justified* iff it is one the agent rationally ought to hold given those arguments. The justifiedness of a belief thus becomes a function of how far the agent has progressed in its reasoning. We can describe this in terms of the "update-function." We can think of the update function as taking two arguments — the agent's current set of beliefs, and any new perceptual input. *update*($\mathbf{B}, \mathbf{P}$) is the set of beliefs to which the agent should move if its current set of beliefs is $\mathbf{B}$ and its current set of perceptual inputs is $\mathbf{P}$. An agent's set of justified beliefs will evolve as its reasoning progresses by repeatedly applying the update-function. In particular, if we suppose there is no new perceptual input, we can define:

$$J_0 = \mathbf{B};$$
$$J_{n+1} = \textit{update}(J_n, \varnothing).$$

Then J_n is the set of beliefs justified after n steps of reasoning. In the same vein, we can describe the warranted propositions as those that eventually become justified and stay justified in the face of all further reasoning:

P is *warranted* iff there is an n such that for every $m > n$, $P \in J_m$.

In other words, warranted propositions are those that are "justified in the limit."

In recent years it has become a commonplace in epistemology that reasoning is *defeasible*, in the sense that further reasoning can lead not only to the adoption of new beliefs but also to the retraction of earlier beliefs. In AI this point has been made by saying that reasoning is *nonmonotonic*. The defeasibility of reasoning has important consequences for the sets of justified beliefs produced by repetitive applications of the belief-updating function. In particular, beliefs can be defeated by further reasoning, and may later be reinstated by defeating their defeaters. So beliefs may cycle in and out of the set of justified beliefs many times as reasoning progresses. A belief is only warranted if the cycling eventually stops and the belief subsequently remains justified.

Justification and Warrant

The distinction between justified beliefs and warranted propositions is an important one, partly because it has been common for philosophers to confuse the two concepts, and this in turn has obscured discussions of the impact of resource constraints on rationality. The line of reasoning that I find particularly problematic begins by giving some characterization of the set of beliefs that a rational agent "ought to have," and then argues that resource constraints make it impossible for a real agent to have such a set of beliefs. For instance, it might be argued that an agent's beliefs ought to be closed under logical consequence, or perhaps under a subset of "simple" logical inference rules. Then it is observed that the beliefs of human agents do not satisfy the supposed necessary condition for rationality, and so it is concluded that humans exhibit only "limited rationality." The argument may be extended by observing that no computationally realizable agent can satisfy the condition, and so it may be urged that the desideratum for the design of an agent should be some sort of limited approximation to rationality rather than "real rationality."

Something has gone badly awry in this argument. Perhaps we should stop and ask ourselves what we are trying to capture in a theory of rationality. There are two ways of approaching rationality. One is to focus on *human rationality*. I proposed above that the norms of human rationality might best be viewed as descriptions of the principles comprising our procedural knowledge for reasoning, and more generally, cognition. However, many aspects of human cognition are apt to reflect constraints imposed by our hardware that need not be shared by other kinds of agents, and some aspects of human cognition may reflect rather arbitrary design choices. This suggests that it may be possible to abstract away from these elements of human cognition and construct a more general *non-anthropomorphic concept of rationality*. I have proposed a way of doing that in *Cognitive Carpentry*, but I am not going to pursue that here. I merely want to suggest its possibility.

What I want to emphasize about either approach to rationality is that it makes rationality essentially procedural. That is, rationality concerns "how to cognize." Something must have gone wrong in any theory of how to cognize that has the consequence that nothing *could* cognize in that way. Such a theory has to be a bad theory of rationality. For instance, it is totally implausible to suppose that our procedural knowledge for how to cognize requires us to take account equally of all the logical consequences of our beliefs. A much more plausible thing to say is that our procedural knowledge requires us to *explore* the logical consequences of our beliefs, and take account of new logical consequences *as we discover them*. Putting the point this way makes it evident that the original claim turned upon confusing warrant and justification. The cognitive procedures built into a rational agent will lead the agent to update its beliefs continually, both in response to perceptual input and in response to the results of earlier reasoning. This process produces an evolving sequence of sets of justified beliefs. At any given stage of cognitive development, an agent's set of justified beliefs will fail to have *any* interesting logical properties. We cannot expect it to be consistent, or closed under modus ponens, or anything else we can think of. Those are properties of warrant—not justification. As inconsistencies are *discovered*, they are repaired, so individual inconsistencies will be removed from the set of justified beliefs. And as instances of modus ponens are encountered, the inferences will be made, but until the inference is actually made, the set of justified beliefs does not satisfy that instance of modus ponens. The point of all this is simply that reasoning takes time, and justification concerns the here and now. Rationality pertains to how an agent should behave, either epistemically or practically, and as such it is most directly connected with justification—not warrant.

Defeasible Reasoning

There has been an important philosophical literature on defeasible reasoning beginning in the 60's, and a parallel AI literature beginning in the late 70's. These literatures are largely complementary to each other, because they have been directed at somewhat different tasks. In philosophy, epistemologists used defeasible reasoning as a tool for the analysis of particular epistemological problems, like the problem of perception or the problem of induction. This led to complex theories regarding the defeasible reasons and defeaters underlying certain specific instances of defeasible reasoning. By contrast, in AI the emphasis was on the general logical structure of defeasible reasoning, and the specific instances of defeasible reasoning that were used as examples tended to be very simple in comparison to the complex epistemological problems of interest to the philosophers.

We can make a useful distinction between *theoretical epistemology* and *applied epistemology*. Theoretical epistemology concerns the general structure of all rational epistemic thought, and applied epistemology concerns the analysis of the reasoning involved in particular philosophically interesting cases. We can contrast the early AI work on defeasible reasoning with the early philosophical work by saying that the AI work fell within the scope of theoretical epistemology, while the philosophical work tended to fall within the scope of applied epistemology. It should be apparent, however, that this division of effort cannot be entirely satisfactory. A constraint on a general theory of reasoning must be that it provides adequate machinery for dealing with the problems of applied epistemology, and a converse constraint on a proposed solution to one of the latter problems must be that its use of the machinery of defeasible reasons and defeaters is compatible with some sensible general theory of reasoning. It has proven more difficult to satisfy this pair of mutual constraints than researchers might have originally hoped. In particular, as I have argued elsewhere [Pollock, 1994], none of the AI theories provides a framework that is able to handle the complex kinds of defeasible reasoning encountered in typical epistemological problems.

To illustrate the difficulty, first consider a fairly easy problem — the lottery paradox. The lottery paradox goes as follows. Suppose you hold one ticket in a fair lottery consisting of one million tickets, and suppose it is known that one and only one ticket will win. Observing that the probability is only .000001 of a ticket being drawn given that it is a ticket in the lottery, it seems initially reasonable to accept the conclusion that your ticket will not win. But by the same reasoning, it will be reasonable to believe, for each ticket, that it will not win. These conclusions conflict jointly with something else we are warranted in believing, namely, that some ticket will win. Assuming that we cannot be warranted in believing each member of an explicitly contradictory set of propositions, it follows that we are not warranted in believing of each ticket that it will not win.

One way of resolving the lottery paradox would be to deny that we cannot be warranted in believing each member of an explicitly contradictory set of propositions. This amounts to denying a rational agent the use of ordinary logical inference rules like modus ponens. This view has been championed by Henry Kyburg [1970], but I find it implausible, and it seems to be crippling to the construction of an agent. I think that a better solution is to embrace a theory of defeasible reasoning which has the consequence that the inference to the conclusion that any given ticket will not be drawn is defeated by the set of inferences to the conclusions that the other tickets will not be drawn. In other words, the whole set of conclusions is "collectively defeated." It is fairly easy to construct a theory of defeasible reasoning that has this consequence, and most theories of defeasible reasoning can handle this problem.

But now consider an embellishment of the lottery paradox — what I call "the lottery paradox paradox." This arises from the observation that the lottery paradox is generated by supposing that a proposition R describing the lottery (it is a fair lottery, has one million tickets, and so on) is justified. Given that R is justified, we get collective defeat for the proposition that any given ticket will not be drawn. But it is problematic how R can be justified. Normally, we will have only a defeasible reason for believing R. For instance, we may be told that it is true, or read it in a newspaper. Let T_i be the proposition that ticket i will be drawn. In accordance with the standard reasoning involved in the lottery paradox, we can generate an argument supporting $\sim R$ by noting that the $\sim T_i$'s jointly entail $\sim R$. This is because if none of the tickets is drawn then the lottery is not fair. This is diagrammed in figure 1, where defeasible inferences are indicated by dashed arrows, deductive inferences by solid arrows, and defeat links by fuzzy arrows. The difficulty is now that $\sim R$ contradicts R. Thus these nodes defeat one another, and a simple theory of defeasible reasoning is apt to rule that these conclusions undergo collective defeat. In other words, the inference to R is defeated. This result is intuitively wrong. Obviously, if we consider examples of real lotteries (e.g., this week's New York State Lottery), it is possible to become justified in believing R on the basis described.

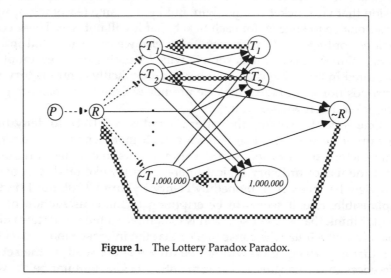

Figure 1. The Lottery Paradox Paradox.

Formulating a theory of defeasible reasoning that will handle this case, and other similarly complex cases, in an intuitively congenial manner, has proven extremely difficult. My earlier attempts at formulating such a theory failed, but I now have an account that seems to do the job. This is formulated in terms of "inference-graphs," wherein conclusions are represented by nodes, as in figure 1, and connected by support-links and defeat-links. The *basis* of a node is the set of nodes from which it is immediately inferred. *Initial nodes* are those having empty bases and empty sets of defeaters. My proposal then goes as follows:

An assignment σ of "defeated" and "undefeated" to a subset of the nodes of an inference graph is a *partial status assignment* iff:

1. σ assigns "undefeated" to all initial nodes;
2. σ assigns "undefeated" to a node α iff σ assigns "undefeated" to all the immediate ancestors of α and all nodes defeating α are assigned "defeated"; and
3. σ assigns "defeated" to a node α iff either α has a immediate ancestor that is assigned "defeated," or there is a node β that defeats α and is assigned "undefeated."

Status assignments are maximal partial status assignments:

σ is a *status assignment* iff σ is a partial status assignment and

σ is not properly contained in any other partial status assignment

A node is undefeated iff every status assignment assigns "undefeated" to it; otherwise it is defeated.

Applying this to inference graph of the lottery paradox paradox (figure 1), for each ticket, there is one status assignment assigning "undefeated" to the conclusion that it is drawn and "defeated" to the conclusion that any other ticket is drawn, and these are all the status assignments. Thus, as before, the conclusion that any given ticket is drawn is defeated. Furthermore, because the inference to ~R is made on the basis of all of those conclusions jointly, the node supporting ~R is assigned "defeated" by every status assignment, and that supporting R is assigned "undefeated" by every status assignment. Thus R is undefeated.

Finding an analysis of defeat status that handles all problems in an intuitively congenial manner is an epistemological problem on which I have, literally, spent years. It is noteworthy that this is a problem that did not even occur to philosophers until epistemology and AI collided. This analysis of defeat status is implemented in OSCAR, which is capable of performing general-purpose defeasible and deductive reasoning.

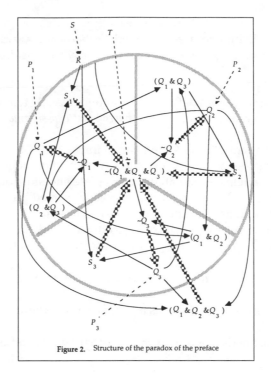

Figure 2. Structure of the paradox of the preface

It turns out that one of the biggest problems for the construction of a theory of defeasible reasoning is that of distinguishing between the lottery paradox and the paradox of the preface. The paradox of the preface arises when an author writes a book, and has good reasons for each claim made in his book but also has a general reason for thinking that any book of that sort must contain a falsehood. The difficulty is that the paradox of the preface appears to be analogous to the lottery paradox. This suggests that it should be a case of collective defeat, with the result that none of the claims in the book is justified. Philosophers are sometimes tempted to acquiesce in this conclusion, but to do so would be catastrophic. This is because most cases of defeasible reasoning can be recast to give them the same general form as the paradox of the preface. This arises from the fact that we are typically able to set at least rough upper bounds on the reliability of our defeasible reasons. For example, color vision gives us defeasible reasons for judging the colors of objects around us. Color vision is pretty reliable, but surely it is not more than 99.9% reliable. Given that assumption, it follows that the probability that out of 10,000 randomly selected color judgments, at least one is incorrect, is 99.99%. By the statistical syllogism, that gives us a defeasible reason for thinking that at least one of them is false. This is analogous to the paradox of the preface. If we treat this as a case of collective defeat, it has the result

26

that none of those 10,000 color judgments is justified. And as every color judgment is a member of some such set of 10,000, it follows that all color judgments are unjustified. The same reasoning would serve to defeat any defeasible reasoning based upon a defeasible reason for which we can set at least a rough upper bound of reliability. Thus it becomes imperative to resolve the paradox of the preface by finding a theory of defeasible reasoning that handles it differently from the lottery paradox. This has proven to be a difficult problem, although I think that the above analysis can handle it. The details are too complicated to try to present them all here, but I can still use this example to illustrate something interesting. The resolution I have proposed (in *Cognitive Carpentry*) begins by arguing that a proper account of the defeasible probabilistic inferences involved in the paradox of the preface yields an inference-graph with the structure diagrammed in figure 2 for the simplified case of a book consisting of three propositions (the general case is analogous). The defense of this claim is too long to repeat here, but bear with me and assume that this is correct (it turns upon the observation that, unlike in the case of the lottery, the different propositions in the book tend to be probabilistically independent of each other). Given this representation of the problem, the question becomes, what defeat status does my theory of defeasible reasoning assign to the conclusion $(Q_1$ & Q_2 & $Q_3)$? We want this to come out

undefeated. It is possible to give a proof that it does, but that is complicated. A simpler way of proceeding is to give the problem to OS-CAR. OSCAR implements the theory of defeasible reasoning that I have been describing, so it can compute the defeat status assigned by the theory. What follows is a printout of OSCAR doing this problem (where "$(P @ Q)$" is the form of an undercutting defeater for the inference from P to Q):

```
Given premises:
    P1   justification = 1
    P2   justification = 1
    P3   justification = 1
    S    justification = 1
    T    justification = 1
Ultimate epistemic interests:
    (Q1 & (Q2 & Q3))   interest = 1

    FORWARDS PRIMA FACIE REASONS
       pf-reason 1:  {P1} ||=> Q1   strength = 1
       pf-reason 2:  {P2} ||=> Q2   strength = 1
       pf-reason 3:  {P3} ||=> Q3   strength = 1
       pf-reason 4:  {S} ||=> R   strength = 1
       pf-reason 5:  {T} ||=> ~(Q1 & (Q2 & Q3))   strength = 1
       pf-reason 6:  {S1} ||=> (T @ ~(Q1 & (Q2 & Q3)))   strength = 1
       pf-reason 7:  {S2} ||=> (T @ ~(Q1 & (Q2 & Q3)))   strength = 1
       pf-reason 8:  {S3} ||=> (T @ ~(Q1 & (Q2 & Q3)))   strength = 1
```

FORWARDS CONCLUSIVE REASONS
       con-reason 4: {R , Q1 , Q3} ||=> S2   strength = 1
       con-reason 5: {R , Q2 , Q3} ||=> S1   strength = 1
       con-reason 6: {R , Q1 , Q2} ||=> S3   strength = 1

=========== ULTIMATE EPISTEMIC INTERESTS ============
Interest in
       (Q1 & (Q2 & Q3))
is answered affirmatively by conclusion 28
===
ARGUMENT #1
This is an undefeated argument for:
       (Q1 & (Q2 & Q3))
which is of ultimate interest.
1. P1   given
12. Q1   pf-reason 1 from { 1 }
3. P3   given
2. P2   given
8. Q3   pf-reason 3 from { 3 }
9. Q2   pf-reason 2 from { 2 }
29. (Q2 & Q3)   adjunction from { 8 , 9 }
30. (Q1 & (Q2 & Q3))   adjunction from { 29 , 12 }
===

ARGUMENT #2
This is a defeated argument for:
       ~Q2
and it defeats argument #1
3. P3   given
8. Q3   pf-reason 3 from { 3 }
1. P1   given
12. Q1   pf-reason 1 from { 1 }
5. T   given
6. ~(Q1 & (Q2 & Q3))   pf-reason 5 from { 5 }
38. (~Q1 v ~(Q2 & Q3))   DM from { 6 }
39. ~(Q2 & Q3)   disj-syl11 from { 38 , 12 }
41. (~Q2 v ~Q3)   DM from { 39 }
43. ~Q2   disj-syl12 from { 41 , 8 }
This argument is defeated by argument #1
===

ARGUMENT #3
This is a defeated argument for:
       ~Q3
and it defeats arguments #1 , #2
2. P2   given
9. Q2   pf-reason 2 from { 2 }
1. P1   given
12. Q1   pf-reason 1 from { 1 }
5. T   given
6. ~(Q1 & (Q2 & Q3))   pf-reason 5 from { 5 }
38. (~Q1 v ~(Q2 & Q3))   DM from { 6 }
39. ~(Q2 & Q3)   disj-syl11 from { 38 , 12 }
41. (~Q2 v ~Q3)   DM from { 39 }
42. ~Q3   disj-syl11 from { 41 , 9 }
This argument is defeated by arguments #1 , #2

ARGUMENT #4
This is a defeated argument for:
    ~Q1
and it defeats arguments #1 , #2 , #3
3. P3   given
2. P2   given
8. Q3   pf-reason 3 from { 3 }
9. Q2   pf-reason 2 from { 2 }
29. (Q2 & Q3)   adjunction from { 8 , 9 }
5. T   given
6. ~(Q1 & (Q2 & Q3))   pf-reason 5 from { 5 }
38. (~Q1 v ~(Q2 & Q3))   DM from { 6 }
40. ~Q1   disj-syl12 from { 38 , 29 }

This argument is defeated by arguments #1 , #2 , #3
===
ARGUMENT #5
This is an undefeated argument for:
    (T @ ~(Q1 & (Q2 & Q3)))
and it defeats arguments #2 , #3 , #4

2. P2   given
3. P3   given
4. S   glven
9. Q2   pf-reason 2 from { 2 }
8. Q3   pf-reason 3 from { 3 }
7. R   pf-reason 4 from { 4 }
10. S1   con-reason 5 from { 9 , 8 , 7 }
11. (T @ ~(Q1 & (Q2 & Q3)))   pf-reason 6 from { 10 }

This argument is defeated by arguments #2 , #3
===
ARGUMENT #6
This is an undefeated argument for:
    (T @ ~(Q1 & (Q2 & Q3)))
and it defeats arguments #2 , #3 , #4

1. P1   given
2. P2   given
4. S   given
12. Q1   pf-reason 1 from { 1 }
9. Q2   pf-reason 2 from { 2 }
7. R   pf-reason 4 from { 4 }
14. S3   con-reason 6 from { 12 , 9 , 7 }
15. (T @ ~(Q1 & (Q2 & Q3)))   pf-reason 8 from { 14 }

This argument is defeated by arguments #2 , #4
===
ARGUMENT #7
This is an undefeated argument for:
    (T @ ~(Q1 & (Q2 & Q3)))
and it defeats arguments #2 , #3 , #4

1. P1   given
3. P3   given

```
 4. S      given
12. Q1      pf-reason 1 from { 1 }
 8. Q3      pf-reason 3 from { 3 }
 7. R      pf-reason 4 from { 4 }
13. S2      con-reason 4 from { 12 , 8 , 7 }
16. (T @ ~(Q1 & (Q2 & Q3)))    pf-reason 7 from { 13 }
```

This argument is defeated by arguments #3 , #4
==

This illustrates how useful the implementation of an epistemological theory can be in determining its consequences when it is applied to nontrivial examples.

Two Concepts of Defeasibility

Human reasoning is actually defeasible in two different ways. It is *synchronically defeasible* in the sense that a proposition can be warranted relative to one set of perceptual inputs, and unwarranted relative to a larger set of inputs. For instance, the initial set of inputs may support an inductive generalization that is defeated in light of the larger set of inputs. Human reasoning is also *diachronically defeasible* in the sense that a proposition can be justified at one stage of reasoning and unjustified at a later stage, without any additional perceptual input. This results from the fact that as reasoning progresses, defeaters may be inferred for earlier reasoning. Note that synchronic defeasibility concerns warrant, whereas diachronic defeasibility concerns justifi-cation.

Studies of defeasibility (or nonmonotonicity) in AI have focused on synchronic defeasibility. Although it is clear that human reasoning is diachronically defeasible, it may well be wondered whether this is an inessential feature of human cognition. Could we build a rational agent whose reasoning was not diachronically defeasible but for which, relative to any set of inputs, the set of warranted propositions was the same as for human beings?

To answer this question, let us ask the more general question of what the relationship should be between a theory of warrant and the procedural specification of an agent for which that is a correct theory of warrant. Warrant constitutes a kind of "ideal target" for a reasoner. But what exactly is the connection between warrant and what we want a reasoner to accomplish? The simplest proposal would be that we want the reasoner to "compute warrant." But if this is understood as requiring that the reasoner implement an effective procedure for deciding warrant, then it is an impossible desideratum. All theorems of logic are automatically warranted because the arguments supporting them are non-defeasible. This includes all theorems of the predicate calculus. If we give the system no non-logical reasons and no input premises, these are the only warranted propositions. Thus a decision procedure for warrant would give us a decision procedure for the predicate calculus. However, by Church's theorem, the set of theorems of the predicate calculus is not decidable. Thus *no* reasoner can compute warrant in this sense.

A weaker proposal would be that we want the reasoner to systematically generate all and only warranted propositions in some effective way, analogous to the manner in which a complete theorem prover generates all theorems of the predicate calculus. But this desideratum is also provably unsatisfiable, because the set of warranted propositions can fail to be recursively enumerable. This is because, as has been observed by numerous authors,[2] on any theory of defeasible reasoning, the ultimate correctness of a piece of defeasible reasoning (i.e., whether the conclusion of the reasoning will survive an indefinite amount of further reasoning and hence be warranted) will always turn upon something else *being unprovable*. Making this more precise, the following theorem can be proven:

> There are finite sets of input premises and finite sets of nonlogical reasons such that the set of conclusions warranted with respect to them is not recursively enumerable [Pollock, 1992]

If a defeasible reasoner can neither compute warrant nor recursively enumerate the set of warranted conclusions, what should it do? My proposal is that we take diachronic defeasibility seriously. That is, a defeasible reasoner may have to adopt a belief, and then retract it in the face of defeaters, and then reinstate the belief because the defeaters are themselves retracted. This cycle may be repeated an indefinite number of times. The most we can require of the reasoner is that its rules for reasoning guarantee that it will systematically modify its belief set so that it comes to approximate the set of warranted propositions more and more closely. We want the set of beliefs to "approach the set of warranted propositions in the limit." My proposal [Pollock, 1989] is that we understand this in the following sense:

> The rules for reasoning should be such that:
> (1) if a proposition p is warranted then the reasoner will eventually reach a stage where p is justified and stays justified;
> (2) if p is ideally unwarranted then the reasoner will eventually reach a stage where p is unjustified and stays unjustified.

So the task of a reasoner is not to compute warrant. It is to generate successive sets of beliefs that approximate warrant more and more closely, in the above sense. We can make this mathematically precise as follows. Define:

A set A is *defeasibly enumerable* iff there is an effectively computable function f such that for each n, $f(n)$ is a recursive set, and

(1) $(\forall x)$ if $x \in A$ then $(\exists n)(\forall m > n)\ x \in f(m)$; and
(2) $(\forall x)$ if $x \notin A$ then $(\exists n)(\forall m > n)\ x \notin f(m)$.

I will say that the sequence of recursive sets $f(n)$ is a *defeasible enumeration* of A. Defeasibly enumerable sets are the same as those Gold [1965] calls "limiting recursive" and Putnam [1965] calls "trial and error." Both authors establish that a set is of this type iff it is Δ_2 in the arithmetic hierarchy.

The intuitive difference between recursively enumerable sets and defeasibly enumerable sets is that recursively enumerable sets can be "systematically approximated from below," while defeasibly enumerable sets that are not recursively enumerable can only be systematically approximated from above and below simultaneously. More precisely, if A is recursively enumerable, then there is an effectively computable sequence of recursive sets A_i such that

(1) $(\forall x)$ if $x \in A$ then $(\exists n)(\forall m > n)\ x \in A_m$;
(2) $(\forall x)$ if $x \notin A$ then $(\forall m)x \notin A_m$.

The sets A_i approximate A from below in the sense that they are all subsets of A and they grow monotonically, approaching A in the limit. If A is only defeasibly enumerable, however, the sets A_i need not be subsets of A. They may only approach A from above and below simultaneously, in the sense that they may contain elements not contained in A. Every such element must eventually be taken out of the A_i's, but there need not be any point at which they have *all* been removed. The process of defeasible enumeration can be pictured by thinking of A as a spherical region of space and the A_i's as representing successive stages of a reverberating elastic ball whose center coincides with the center of A. As the reverberations dampen out, the outer surface of the ball will come to approximate that of the spherical surface more and more closely, but there will never be a point at which the ball is contained entirely within the spherical surface.

My proposal regarding reasoning and warrant is that the set of warranted propositions should be defeasibly enumerable, and the rules for reasoning should be rules for successively approximating warrant in this way, i.e., they are rules for constructing a defeasible enumeration. More accurately:

If J_n is the set of propositions justified after n applications of *update* to *input*, the reasoner is *d.e.-adequate* iff the sequence of sets J_n is a defeasible enumeration of the set of warranted propositions.

I propose d.e.-adequacy as the primary criterion of adequacy for a defeasible reasoner. It is shown in *Cognitive Carpentry* that if certain reasonable conditions are satisfied then the set of warranted propositions is defeasibly enumerable and hence d.e.-adequate reasoners are possible. OSCAR is based upon such a reasoner.

Defeasibility and Rational Action

The requirement that a defeasible reasoner provide a defeasible enumeration of warrant is a *minimal* criterion of adequacy. There is a different kind of adequacy condition that must also be met. If a reasoner is d.e.-adequate, there will be cases in which it will never stop reasoning. Any given proposition may be concluded, retracted, and reinstated many times. Every warranted proposition will eventually reach a point where it is believed and is never subsequently retracted, and every unwarranted proposition will eventually reach a point where it is not believed and never subsequently becomes believed, but the reasoner may never know that a given proposition has reached this stable state. It can inform us that "so far" a certain conclusion is justified, but it may have to continue forever in a possibly fruitless search for defeating arguments. This, of course, is just the way human beings work. This highlights the distinction between synchronic and diachronic defeasibility. Although human reasoning is diachronically defeasible, and hence any particular reasoning might have to be retracted later, we regard such reasoning as "innocent until proven guilty." Once a conclusion becomes justified, it is reasonable to accept it provisionally and act upon it. By contrast, AI theories of non-monotonic reasoning have generally supposed that a defeasible conclusion is acceptable only if it has been established that it is objectively devoid of faults. The latter amounts to *proving* that the conclusion is warranted. This has made it seem mysterious how nonmonotonic reasoning can possibly function in a finite agent. The solution is to instead adopt the "innocent until proven guilty" construal of defeasibility, and allow a rational agent to act on its defeasible con-clusions even though it has not conclusively established that there are no defeaters and even though, in the absence of more pressing tasks, it will continue to search for defeaters.

This raises an interesting question. The reasoning employed by such a rational agent must be *interruptible*,[3] in the sense that if at some point the agent must stop reasoning and act, it is reasonable to act on the conclusions drawn to that point. This is not ensured by d.e.-

adequacy. For example, let R_1 be a reasoner that is both interruptible and d.e.-adequate. Let R_2 be just like R_1 except that for the first million steps it draws conclusions purely at random, and then after one million steps it withdraws all those randomly drawn conclusions and begins reasoning as in R_1. Clearly, it would be unreasonable to make use of any of the conclusions drawn by R_2 during its first one million inference steps, so it is not interruptible. On the other hand, R_2 is still d.e.-adequate, because that only concerns its behavior in the limit, and its behavior in the limit is the same as that of R_1. Thus interruptibility is a different requirement from d.e.-adequacy. However, it is not at all obvious what it takes to ensure interruptibility. This is a problem that needs to be addressed at length. It is also a problem that could not even arise until classical epistemology and AI gave birth to procedural epistemology.

Conclusions

Let us return to the question, "How has computing changed epistemology?" Obviously, not all epistemology has gone the way I have, so my remarks have really been in partial answer to the question, "How *should* computing change epistemology?" My answer has turned upon making a distinction between procedural epistemology and descriptive epistemology. Procedural epistemology is concerned with the procedures comprising rational epistemic cognition, and the main way in which computers impact procedural epistemology is by providing the tool for constructing computer models of proposed theories. Such a model becomes an AI system. The importance of such systems is threefold. First, a constraint on a theory of cognitive procedures is that it must be possible for something to actually work that way. As mundane as this constraint may seem, I am convinced that most epistemologically theories fail to satisfy it. The only sure way to know that the constraint is satisfied for a particular theory is to build something that does work that way — a computer model. Second, in order to build a computer model, we have to make the theory precise and we have to work out the details. That can have a very therapeutic effect on a profession that is overly fond of handwaving. Third, once we have a computer model, it can become an invaluable aid in testing and tuning the theory. Anyone who has ever written a computer program knows that, the first time around, a complex program rarely does exactly what its author expects it to do. Simple bugs can be found by just sitting and thinking about the program, but it is usually beyond human abilities to find more complicated bugs without actually running the program to see what it will do in complicated situations. Constructing a procedural theory of rationality is like writing a computer program for cognition. It is an immensely complicated program, and like other programs, we are not going to get it debugged without running it. The only way to do that is to make it sufficiently precise that we can turn it into a real program and load it into a real computer. That is what we are doing when we construct a computer model.

Applying these observations to the OSCAR Project, the current state of that project is that a detailed theory has been proposed for the overall architecture of rational cognition. The core of the proposed architecture is a general-purpose deductive and defeasible reasoner. This architecture (including the reasoner) has been fully implemented in a LISP program, which is freely available to other researchers from my website at http://www.u.arizona.edu/~pollock/. The epistemological work to date falls mainly within the general realm of what I called "theoretical epistemology" (although the theory developed in *Cognitive Carpentry* includes a theory of practical rationality). The next step is to turn to applied epistemology and use the current system to provide the underlying machinery upon which to build theories of perceptual reasoning, inductive reasoning, causal reasoning, temporal reasoning, planning, and so forth. We are just now beginning to undertake this.[4] The theories produced will be tested by applying them to real-world examples, or to realistic approximations to real-world examples. The expectation is that this will feed back on the design of the architecture and lead to significant changes there. The resulting theories will be epistemology in the grand tradition, but the tools and the methodology will make essential use of computers.

NOTES

[1] This term is due to Dennett [1987].

[2] I think that the first were David Israel [1980] and Raymond Reiter [1980].

[3] This point and the terminology are due to George Smith.

[4] One of the first results of this endeavor is an implemented solution to the Frame Problem. See my [1997].

REFERENCES

Dennett, Daniel. (1987) *The Intentional Stance*. Cambridge, MA: Bradford/MIT Press.

Gold, E. M. (1965) "Limiting Recursion." *Journal of Symbolic Logic* 30: 28-48.

Israel, David. (1980) "What's Wrong with Non-Monotonic Logic?" *Proceedings of the First Annual National Conference on Artificial Intelligence.* 99-101.

Kyburg, Henry, Jr. (1970) "Conjunctivitis," In *Induction, Acceptance, and Rational Belief,* ed. Marshall Swain. Dordrecht: Reidel.

Pollock, John L. (1986) *Contemporary Theories of Knowledge.* Totowa, NJ: Rowman and Littlefield.

Pollock, John L. (1989) *How to Build a Person; a Prolegomenon.* Cambridge, MA: Bradford/MIT Press.

Pollock, John L. (1992) "How to Reason Defeasibly," *Artificial Intelligence* 57: 1-42.

Pollock, John L. (1994) "Justification and Defeat," *Artificial Intelligence* 67: 377-408.

Pollock, John L. (1995) *Cognitive Carpentry.* Cambridge, MA: Bradford/MIT Press.

Pollock, John L. (1997) "Reasoning about Change and Persistence: A Solution to the Frame Problem," *Nous,* forthcoming.

Putnam, Hilary. (1965) "Trial and Error Predicates and the Solution to a Problem of Mostowski". *Journal of Symbolic Logic* 30: 49-57.

Quine, W. V. (1953) *From a Logical Point of View.* Cambridge, MA: Harvard University Press

Quine, W. V. (1960) *Word and Object.* New York: MIT Press and Wiley.

Reiter, Raymond. (1980) "A Logic for Default Reasoning," *Artificial Intelligence* 13: 81-132.

EPISTEMOLOGY AND COMPUTING

HENRY KYBURG

I

Computing, and especially the accessibility of large databases, has been an enormous boon to scholarship of all kinds, and no less to philosophy. For philosophers, however, the value of this technology goes far beyond the benefit of easy access to well organized databases. In particular, I think fast digital computers are a wonderful boon to doing certain kinds of philosophy, for example epistemology, in the sense that they provide a kind of philosophical laboratory or testing ground, and that we will be able to do far more with them than we were able to do without them. At the same time, another place where philosophy may differ from some academic pursuits in its relation to computing lies in the fact that certain parts of computing, particularly artificial intelligence, can be seen as competing directly for philosophical turf. This competition mainly concerns knowledge: when does one machine know that another machine knows the item of data d? Should we allow machines to make invalid leaps: to pass from the knowledge that Tweety is a bird to the conclusion that Tweety flies? Should we require strict consistency from a machine that is representing knowledge? The structure of knowledge and belief, as Hintikka [1965] showed, is similar to the structure of modality. Within computer science the study of the inferential relations involved in knowledge and belief is often referred to simply as "modal" logic [Fagin et al, 1995]. The study of inferential structures that purport to represent the impact of new evidence on old bodies of knowledge falls, in computer science, into two parts: probabilistic inference and nonmonotonic inference. In what follows I will explore the claims of John Pollock and others in connection with nonmonotonic or defeasible reasoning.

John Pollock [1997, 1994, 1990, 1986] is one of the leading philosophers who are determined to make the most of computational innovation. Of course there are details where we disagree. The specific disagreements may seem small, but they have rather far-reaching consequences, and significance that goes beyond the variations in computational epistemology itself. They have consequences that bear on the role of philosophical analysis in the pursuit of projects such as the

OSCAR project, and even on the significance of the outcomes of such projects. Furthermore, although OSCAR is unique at this point, it is not hard to imagine that he has associates, for example FLORENCE, who do things somewhat differently. How are we to judge between FLORENCE and OSCAR with regard to their philosophical adequacy? The answer to this question may well call for philosophical experimentation of a kind that can only be done by computers. Finally, how do we assess the interaction between the contributions of philosophers and the practical demands of those who wish to construct practical systems employing artificial intelligence?

II

The particular thread of disagreement between us that I want to trace out starts with what has come to be called the lottery paradox [Kyburg, 1961]. This presents an issue for nonmonotonic logics in general, as well as for probabilistic acceptance rules, as Poole [1991] has shown. At the risk of repetitiveness, I'll describe it once again. There is intended to be no difference between my description and Pollock's:

Pick a nice small number, say 10^{-6}: if you think there is no more than one chance in a million of being wrong in drawing a certain conclusion, that's good enough for you (This may, of course, be context dependent; we'll come back to that context dependency).

Construct this analog: You consider a one-million ticket lottery with a single winner. For a given integer i between 1 and a million, the chances, if it is a fair lottery, of that ticket winning are $1:10^6$. In asserting that this ticket will lose, you are running a risk of no more than one in a million of being wrong.

But accept the conclusion that ticket i will lose (Lose(i)) for every integer i from one to a million, and you have contradicted the premise that the lottery is a million ticket fair lottery.

As Pollock says [in the present book],

Assuming that we cannot be warranted in believing each member of an explicitly contradictory set of propositions, it follows that we are not warranted in believing of each ticket that it will not win. [Pollock, 1997, 23]

We find here a fascinating clash of intuitions: the very origin of the lottery story lies in this conditional; but I read the conclusion the other way (one person's modus ponens is another person's modus tollens). I argued that since we are obviously, in this case, warranted in believing of each ticket that it will not win, it must be possible for us "to be warranted in believing each member of an explicitly contradictory set of propositions."

There is more of a conclusion to be drawn here than that philosophical intuitions can disagree. We'll come to it in due course. Let us first describe the similar paradox of the preface [Makinson, 1965] in parallel terms.

We'll use the same interesting small number: 10^{-6}, and just for ease of exposition, we will suppose that the entire book consists of 10^6 propositions (Of course if we take the preface to be part of the book, we do have the structure of the lottery paradox, since if we count "At least one proposition in this book is false" to be one of the propositions in the book, we have an explicit lower bound on the frequency of error in the book: it has to be at least 10^{-6}, and we have the lottery with the possibility of some extra winners). So let us suppose the preface contains the assertion: the chances are overwhelming (greater than $1\text{-}10^{-6}$) that at least one of the propositions in the body of the book is false. If this were analogous to the lottery paradox, we should believe the denial of the conjunction of the propositions in the book. But the author is so dependable, this seems wrong: any particular statement has an overwhelming chance of being correct.

The difference between the lottery and the preface that I believe is crucial to OSCAR's treatment is that the collection of conclusions in the lottery is flat out inconsistent with the claim that the lottery is fair (that's the important lesson of the lottery paradox: we must be and remain justified in thinking the lottery is fair), while the collection of conclusions in the book is not *explicitly* contradictory: the author's claim that it is overwhelmingly probable that he has made a mistake in the book is perfectly consistent with each of the propositions in the book being true. As Pollock has put the matter elsewhere: the probability that statement i is false is independent of the probability that statement j is false; that is manifestly not the case for the lottery [Pollock, 1990] (Parenthetically, we might consider a book in logic or number theory. If the author made a mistake, it would be that of unwittingly asserting a contradiction. I wonder how OSCAR would treat this case).

Now of course I agree that a difference can be drawn between the lottery and the preface; I deny, however, that it is of epistemological relevance. Furthermore, there seems to be a continuum of possibilities between the lottery and the preface. For example, there are the state lotteries in which one picks one's number. It is perfectly possible that there are *no* winners (all the statements may be correct) and it is perfectly possible that everybody happens to choose the same number and that it is the winning number. The reason I deny epistemological significance to the difference between the lottery and the preface is that I take more seriously than Pollock the acceptance of propositions whose only warrant is statistical – in fact I think that is the only warrant we need. Thus I do not think it would change anything to suppose that lotteries were as plentiful as blackberries, and that the chance of a fair million ticket lottery with one winner being chosen is $1:1-10^{-7}$. If we choose a lottery, and then consider a ticket from it, the chances are (on my view) just $1:10^6$ that it is a losing ticket. This isn't necessary, of course. This might be one of the lotteries exclusively comprised of losing tickets. It becomes perfectly possible that all the tickets do lose: that it is *not* a fair lottery.

Should we therefore accept, after this analysis, that by gum it *is* one of those special lotteries? That is, after all, implied by the set of statements we have accepted. I think not. Remember my use of conditional (A): it is to argue against deductive closure among the propositions that are warranted. So I find nothing unreasonable about saying that the agent should believe that the lottery is fair, and for each *i* that ticket *i* will lose.

Pollock claims that "This amounts to denying a rational agent the use of ordinary logical inference rules like modus ponens," [1997, 23]. This is a straw boogeyman. If you accept on the basis of probability, and you accept "*S*, and If *S* then *T*," then you will accept *T*, since *T* will be at least as probable as "*S* and If *S* then *T*." What Pollock is looking at is the different case where you accept "*S*", and also accept "If *S* then *T*" and want to conclude "*T*". I deny that this is always reasonable, and I think you should deny it too: suppose there is a valid argument from a million premises to a conclusion. Before accepting the conclusion, I want to be assured that I can not only accept each of those premises, but can accept their conjunction. That may take a lot more evidence.

Both the lottery and the preface are philosophical artificialities. Let me now look at something more realistic than either. It is like Pollock's example of shades of color [1997, 26], but it comes with a solid statistical background.

Suppose our agent is a machinist (hardly unreasonable in this day of robotics!). Suppose the rational robot machinist is to follow a blueprint that calls for fitting a round peg in a round hole (So far so good!). The peg is to be 1 inch +0.0, -.005 in diameter, and the hole is to be 1 inch + .005, -0.0 in diameter. To ensure that this is the case, the machinist will measure both the hole and the peg.

Since we are being realistic, we'd better take account of error. Let us suppose the error of our measuring devices (one for the peg and one for the hole) is normally distributed with a mean of 0.0 (the devices are well calibrated) and a standard deviation of 4×10^{-4} inches. Thus if the machinist measures a peg, and reads 0.9984 inches, the chance of that peg not meeting the criterion is the chance of a normally distributed quantity not falling between -4 standard deviations and +8.5 standard deviations. That is a chance that we and the rational robot machinist can surely reasonably ignore. In general, let us suppose that the rational robot machinist is facing a large number of these peg-in-a-hole situations. If it adopts the policy of accepting for construction any peg that measures between 0.9966 inches and .9984 inches, and a similar policy regarding the pieces with the hole, it can be extremely sure $(1:10^3$ chance of error) that two pieces will satisfy the tolerances, and thus will fit (the assertion will be true, the ticket will lose). Furthermore, as in the preface, but not in the standard lottery, that one pair of pieces fits correctly does *not* decrease the chance that another will fit correctly.

Thus, according to Pollock, we want the conjunction of 10,000 of these fitting assertions to be undefeated. The rational machinist should be quite sure that they are all true. That's the whole point of the arcane structure of defeat and justification. But since the chance that each of 10,000 fitting statements is true is only $.999^{10,000}$ (since they are independent) or about .0003, it hardly seems rational for the robot machinist to accept the conjunction. In the relevant respect, the analog seems to be the lottery paradox: we want to accept each fitting statement, and we want to reject their conjunction.

This invokes the horrid spectre of inconsistency. We have already dismissed the scare-mongering claim that deductive logic will no longer serve us: it will, just so long as we have reason to accept the *conjunction* of the premises of a deductive argument. But the spectre of inconsistency represents a different concern. It is possible to claim – indeed it seems to satisfy Pollock's intuitions to claim – that an inconsistent body of knowledge is to be abhorred in itself.

How does this fit in with procedural epistemology? There is no way we can tell if a set of propositions that we are entertaining defeasibly is consistent (except by proving that it is inconsistent; at that point, according to Pollock, "As inconsistencies are *discovered*, they are repaired so individual inconsistencies will be removed from the set of justified beliefs," [1997, 22] Exactly how this works is the focus of another strand in formal epistemology – that due in part to Alchourron et al [1982], Peter Gardenfors [1988] and Isaac Levi [1991] – since obviously there are in general many ways in which "individual inconsistencies" can be removed from the set of justified beliefs.

However we handle this problem, though, there is no guarantee that the set of justified beliefs we hold at a given point in computation is consistent. Of course there is a big difference between this and my approach to the lottery: on my view our beliefs are not only not guaranteed to be consistent, but are guaranteed to be inconsistent. That is a harder herring to swallow, even though it takes a lot of inference to get to an inconsistency: It takes a million steps, for which I can't imagine that anyone would have the patience, in the case of the lottery. The main point, though, is that the inconsistency is no more damaging in either case. We can decide and act without an assurance of consistency, and we'd better be able to do this on either Pollock's view or mine.

The rational machinist, having measured his pegs and holes, need not stop as he is about to assemble the first pair, and reflect that the proposition that they will fit as planned is unjustified; nor need he be upset by the fact that he is about to act on 10^4 such propositions with the almost certain assurance that he is going to be wrong in at least one case. He will avoid paralysis only if he can either, as Pollock wants, conclude that despite the improbability, all the fitting propositions are true, or, as I would prefer, conclude of each pair that it will fit while simultaneously being well justified in his belief that they will not *all* fit.

Now this is a situation in which it is not unnatural for a probabilist to claim that we are looking at things the wrong way about: the machinist should not *accept* the proposition that peg-1 will fit in hole-1, but should assign it its proper probability of one in a thousand. It is possible, I assume, to construct an entity that believes probabilistically. That is, we give it a formal language, and a probability distribution over the sentences of that formal language which assigns probability 1 to the logical truths of the language, probability 0 to the logical falsehoods of the language, and intermediate probabilities to every other sentence of the language. Of course, this is feasible. As Harman [1989] has pointed out, only if we assign these probabilities in some systematic way. Then we pick a special subclass of these statements to qualify as initial inputs: we specify the circumstances, for the robot, under which the probability of one of these input statements can go to 1: that statement becomes evidence, or, to speak more classically, that statement becomes evident. The robot then continually updates by classical conditionalization.

Let us leave to one side the question (difficult though it may be) of choosing the initial probability distribution. In principle, it could be argued, this robot has all the machinery it needs to act rationally: it can compute the expected utility of any action whose outcome just depends on what statements of the formal language are true.

It is my conjecture that such a robot would be too complicated ever to get off the ground. I think it would be swamped by computational complexity, while a robot that adopts a nonmonotonic [or defeasible: cf Loui, 1988, 1991]) approach to making inferences from its experience will be much more likely to get along in the world. Pollock clearly agrees with this conjecture: OSCAR himself operates on the basis of defeasible reasoning.

But it may be that others – staunch Bayesians, for example – would have intuitions that disagreed. After all, if the proof of the pudding lies in expected utility of the decisions made, what is the point of acceptance?

This brings me to my final point, which is one on which I think both Pollock and I agree emphatically. While argument and counterexample are a fine way for Philosophy to proceed – note that they constitute a fine defeasible system of reasoning! – if we really want to know how rational agents work, and even more, how they *should* work we must use more powerful tools as well. I do not take for granted that "ought" must be taken to imply "can"; even if one *ought* to have a consistent body of beliefs, there is in general no algorithm for determining when a set of propositions is consistent. What it makes sense to require is only that there be some way of approaching our goals: for example, we approach the goal of consistency by modifying our corpus of beliefs every time we find an inconsistency. The digital computer provides us with just such an added powerful tool. It is *not* a replacement for the powers of analysis, or of logic, or of clever counterexample. We need those methods too, and I guess I find Pollock's position a tad overoptimistic when it seems to suggest that if the program runs, we can ask for no more.

It seems quite plausible that both nonmonotonic (defeasible) approaches to realistic knowledge and Bayesian, subjective, probabilisitic approaches, can be made to work, in some sense or other. Each school can boast the intuitions of its enthusiasts. But that an epistemological program runs doesn't prove much if we can get two contrary analyses each to run.

I know of no Bayesian system that is of sufficient generality to compete with OSCAR. There surely could be one. What is of more relevance right here is the fact that I think that a nonmonotonic, defeasible, alternative to OSCAR could be constructed, that would also run.

This is not to say that if a cognizing program runs, we should take that lightly. It is clear that OSCAR is one enormous accomplishment. But I don't think we should accept a philosophical proposition just because OSCAR embodies it. In particular, my analysis of the lottery, the preface, deductive closure, and the like, leads me to believe, not that OSCAR has manifold defects, but that OSCAR is a cognizing engine with a defective manifold. The individual cylinders work fine, but the output is overdone. Of course my believing that counts for zilch; maybe I have some good arguments and examples; those shouldn't be dismissed lightly, any more than OSCAR's performance should be dismissed lightly. The upshot is that if you have two systems of cognition that are worthy of serious consideration, the only way you can tell that they embody something significant is to run them on the same sets of data, and the only way you can evaluate them is to see how they do on the same sets of data.

That leaves open two questions. What should we take as a "set of data;" and how you do you evaluate the performance of these systems? Presumably the kind of data that we should take as input to the great rationality contest is the kind of data that people operate with. But there are deep (and lately neglected) issues about what kind of data these are. In non-philosophical circles it is often simplistically assumed that these must be "sense data" – whatever they are. In some philosophical circles it is assumed that these data are "observational data" but that they are also theory laden. This is not the place to present arguments as to the nature of the basis of the kind of body of knowledge we would call rational, but it is important to note that the issue of what is to count as a good set of test data is a bit thorny.

The other question focuses on the criteria of success in such a test. How do we decide what properties the rational corpus of inferences from the data should have?

For example, Pollock [1997] takes it as favorable evidence that he has OSCAR working right that Oscar believes the conjunction of everything he believes, including all the statements in the book with the warning in the preface. I regard that as evidence of a defect [Kyburg, 1997]. It may well be that in setting standards, as well in selecting test data sets, we will have to fall back on relatively traditional philosophical methods. It is in some such setting that I think the question of the what I have called conjunctive closure must be finally resolved: does warrant for S and warrant for T constitute warrant for $S \& T$? How do systems of cognizing that adopt one answer or the other compare otherwise?

Pollock's concluding observations seem well taken. "First, a constraint on a theory of cognitive procedures is that it must be possible for something to work that way" [1997, 34]. This is a startling idea in philosophy; the goal has generally be to show how something *must* work. Note that this is not to substitute description for the traditionally normative philosophical task. The object is not to discover how something (for example, *you*) actually cognizes, but to discover principles according to which it can cognize well. It is natural to turn to a computer model to see if something very complicated actually works, not to mention whether or not it works well, not to mention whether or not it works better than or not as well as a particular alternative.

"Second, in order to build a computer model, we have to make the theory precise and we have to work out the details." [1997, 34] Although some members of the profession may in fact be "overly fond of handwaving," that is certainly not true of all philosophers, and names leap to mind quickly of philosophers who have made serious efforts to make their theories of cognizing precise and to work out the details. One name that stands out in the area of induction is that of Rudolf Carnap, whose meticulous constructions in the *Logical Foundations of Probability* [Carnap, 1950] still serve as models for the rest of us. This name also brings out the importance of the new possibilities of modeling that computers have given us. It was difficult and time con-

44

suming for Carnap to work out the detailed model theory corresponding to very simple languages; a philosopher doing similar work now could build a computer program to automatically characterize models of quite complicated fragments of first order languages.

"Third, once we have a computer model, it can become an invaluable aid in testing and tuning the theory." [1997, 34] It is easy to endorse this statement in principle, but the caveats I have mentioned should be born in mind. John Pollock knows this: part of the design of OSCAR calls for him to receive his own inputs, even as you and I. The basis on which OSCAR cognizes should be similar to that from which you and I cognize. The criteria of success are a little less clear. One could certainly imagine that the criteria of cognitive success might include pragmatic features: acting successfully, or amassing utility, as well as epistemic features: believing truths and not believing falsehoods. The alternatives are manifold. If the object of cognizing is to eschew falsehoods, then one's beliefs should be consistent, whether one is a person or a robot. But then one is guaranteed to avoid falsehood if one suspends judgment about everything. To the extent that there are other goals, the supremacy of consistency is undermined. If one merely wants to believe as many truths as possible, one could believe the consequences of "0 not equal 0." If the criteria are in part pragmatic, then it becomes important to characterize the situations which OSCAR or FLORENCE face. What works well under one set of circumstances may not work so well under others. And what are the parameters of "working well" in this case?

In sum, I agree that computers are providing us with a philosophical laboratory, the likes of which has never been seen. This is a wonderful time to be doing philosophy. But I think it is also clear that even in such an apparently simple area as the construction of cognitive agents, there is plenty of plain old-fashioned philosophical thinking and analysis to be done, and that much of this must be done before we subject our systems to destructive testing in the epistemic laboratory.

REFERENCES

Alchourron, C. E., Peter Gardenfors and David Makinson. (1982) "On the Logic of Theory Change: Contraction Functions and Their Associated Revision Functions," *Theoria* 48: 14-37.

Carnap, Rudolf. (1950) *The Logical Foundations of Probability*. Chicago: University of Chicago Press.

Fagin, Ronald, and Joseph Y. Halpern, Yioram Moses, and Moshe Y. Vardi. (1995) *Reasoning About Knowledge*. Cambridge, MA: The MIT Press.

Gardenfors, Peter. (1988) *Knowledge in Flux*. Cambridge, MA: The MIT Press.

Harman, Gilbert. (1989) *Change in View*. Cambridge, MA: Bradford Books.

Hintikka Jaakko. (1962) *Knowledge and Belief: An Introduction to the Logic of the Two Notions*. Ithaca: Cornell University Press.

Kyburg, Jr., Henry E. (1961) *Probability and the Logic of Rational Belief*. Middletown: Wesleyan University Press.

Kyburg, Jr., Henry E. (1997) "The Rule of Adjunction and Reasonable Inference," *Journal of Philosophy*, 94: 109-125.

Levi, Isaac. (1994) *Decisions and Revisions*. Cambridge: Cambridge University Press.

Levi, Isaac. (1991) *The Fixation of Belief and Its Undoing*. Cambridge: Cambridge Univesity Press.

Loui, Ronald P. (1988) "Defeat Among Arguments: A System of Defeasible Inference," *Computational Intelligence* 4: 100-106.

Loui, Ronald P. (1991) "Argument and Belief," *Minds and Machines*. 1: 357-365.

Makinson, David C. (1965) "The Paradox of the Preface," *Analysis* 25: 205-207.

Pollock, John. (1986) "The Paradox of the Preface," *Philosophy of Science* 53: 246-258.

Pollock, John. (1987) "Defeasible Reasoning," *Cognitive Science* 11: 481-518.

Pollock, John. (1990) *Nomic Probability and the Foundations of Induction*, New York: Oxford University Press.

Pollock, John. (1994) "Justification and Defeat," *Artificial Intelligence* 67: 377-407.

Pollock, John. (1997) "Procedural Epistemology" in Terrell Ward Bynum and James H. Moor, *The Digital Phoenix: How Computers Are Changing Philosophy*, Blackwell, 17-36.

Poole, David. (1991) "The Effect of Knowledge on Belief: Conditioning, Specificity and the Lottery Paradox in Default Reasoning," *Artificial Intelligence* 49: 281-307.

COMPUTATION AND THE PHILOSOPHY
OF SCIENCE

PAUL THAGARD

What do philosophers do? Twenty years ago, one might have heard such answers to this question as "analyze concepts" or "evaluate arguments". The answer "write computer programs" would have inspired a blank stare, and even a decade ago I wrote that computational philosophy of science might sound like the most self-contradictory enterprise in philosophy since business ethics [Thagard, 1988]. But computer use has since become much more common in philosophy, and computational modeling can be seen as a useful addition to philosophical method, not as the abandonment of it. I will try in this paper to summarize how computational models are making substantial contributions to the philosophy of science.

If philosophy consisted primarily of conceptual analysis, or mental self-examination, or generation of a priori truths, then computer modeling would indeed be alien to the enterprise. But I prefer a different picture of philosophy, as primarily concerned with producing and evaluating *theories,* for example theories of knowledge (epistemology), reality (metaphysics), and right and wrong (ethics). The primary function of a theory of knowledge is to explain how knowledge grows, which requires both describing the structure of knowledge and the inferential procedures by which knowledge can be increased. Although epistemologists often focus on mundane knowledge, the most impressive knowledge gained by human beings comes through the operation of science: experimentation, systematic observation, and theorizing concerning the experimental and observational results. Hence at the core of epistemology is the need to understand the structure and growth of scientific knowledge, a project for which computational models can be very useful.

In attempting to understand the structure and development of scientific knowledge, philosophers of science have traditionally employed a number of methods such as logical analysis and historical case studies. Computational modeling provides an additional method that has already advanced understanding of such traditional problems in the philosophy of science as theory evaluation and scientific discovery. This paper will review the progress made on such issues by three distinct computational approaches: cognitive modeling, engineering artificial intelligence, and theory of computation.

The aim of cognitive modeling is to simulate aspects of human thinking; for philosophy of science, this becomes the aim to simulate the thinking that scientists use in the construction and evaluation of hypotheses. Much artificial intelligence research, however, is not concerned with modeling human thinking, but with constructing algorithms that perform well on difficult tasks independently of whether the algorithms correspond to human thinking. Similarly, the engineering AI approach to philosophy of science seeks to develop computational models of discovery and evaluation independently of questions of human psychology. Computational philosophy of science has thus developed two streams that reflect the two streams in artificial intelligence research, one concerned with modeling human performance and the other with machine intelligence. A third stream of research uses abstract mathematical analysis and applies the theory of computation to problems in the philosophy of science.

Cognitive Modeling

Cognitive science is the interdisciplinary study of mind, embracing philosophy, psychology, artificial intelligence, neuroscience, linguistics, and anthropology. From its modern origins in the 1950s, cognitive science has primarily worked with the computational-representational understanding of mind: we can understand human thinking by postulating mental representations akin to computational data structures and mental procedures akin to algorithms [Thagard, 1996]. The cognitive-modeling stream of computational philosophy of science views topics such as discovery and evaluation as open to investigation using the same techniques employed in cognitive science. To understand how scientists discover and evaluate hypotheses, we can develop computer models that employ data structures and algorithms intended to be analogous to human mental representations and procedures. The cognitive modeling stream of computational philosophy of science can be viewed as part of naturalistic epistemology, which sees the study of knowledge as closely tied to human psychology, not as an abstract logical exercise.

Discovery

In the 1960s and 1970s, philosophers of science discussed whether there is a "logic of discovery" and whether discovery (as opposed to evaluation) is a legitimate topic of philosophical (as opposed to psychological) investigation. In the 1980s, these debates were superseded by computational research on discovery that showed how actual cases of scientific discovery can be modeled algorithmically. Although the models that have been produced to date clearly fall well short of

49

simulating all the thought processes of creative scientists, they provide substantial insights into how scientific thinking can be viewed computationally.

Because of the enormous number of possible solutions involved in any scientific problem, the algorithms involved in scientific discovery cannot guarantee that optimal discoveries will be made from input provided. Instead, computer models of discovery employ *heuristics*, approximate methods for attempting to cut through data complexity and find patterns. The pioneering step in this direction was the BACON project of Pat Langley, Herbert Simon and their colleagues [Langley et al., 1987]. BACON is a program that uses heuristics to discover mathematical laws from quantitative data, for example discovering Kepler's third law of planetary motion. Although BACON has been criticized for assuming an over-simple account of human thinking, Qin and Simon [1990] found that human subjects could generate laws from numerical data in ways quite similar to BACON.

Scientific discovery produces qualitative as well as quantitative laws. Kulkarni and Simon [1988] produced a computational model of Krebs' discovery of the urea cycle. Their program, KEKADA, reacts to anomalies, formulates explanations, and carries out simulated experiments in much the way described in Hans Krebs laboratory notebooks.

Not all scientific discoveries are as data-driven as the ones so far discussed. They often involve the generation of new concepts and hypotheses that are intended to refer to non-observable entities. Thagard [1988] developed computational models of conceptual combination, in which new theoretical concepts such as *sound wave* are generated, and of abduction, in which new hypotheses are generated to explain puzzling phenomena. Darden [1997, the present book] has invest-igated computationally how theories that have empirical problems can be repaired.

One of the most important cognitive mechanisms for discovery is analogy, since scientists often make discoveries by adapting previous knowledge to a new problem. Analogy played a role in some of the most important discoveries ever made, such as Darwin's theory of evolution and Maxwell's theory of electromagnetism. During the 1980s, the study of analogy went well beyond previous philosophical accounts through the development of powerful computational models of how analogs are retrieved from memory and mapped to current problems to provide solutions. Falkenhainer, Forbus, and Gentner [1989] produced SME, the Structure Mapping Engine, and this program was used to model analogical explanations of evaporation and osmosis [Falkenhainer, 1990]. Holyoak and Thagard [1989] used different computational methods to produce ACME, the Analogical Constraint Mapping Engine, which was generalized into a theory of analogical thinking that applies to scientific as well as everyday thinking [Holyoak and Thagard, 1995].

Space does not permit further discussion of computational models of human discovery, but the above research projects illustrate how thought processes such as those involved in numerical law generation, theoretical concept formation, and analogy can be understood computationally. Examples of non-psychological investigations of scientific discovery are described below.

Evaluation

How scientific hypotheses are evaluated has been a central problem in philosophy of science since the nineteenth century debates between John Stuart Mill and William Whewell. Work in the logical positivist tradition has centered on the concept of confirmation, asking what it is for hypotheses to be confirmed by observations. More recently, various philosophers of science have taken a Bayesian approach to hypothesis evaluation, using probability theory to analyze scientific reasoning. In contrast, I have developed an approach to hypothesis evaluation that combines philosophical ideas about explanatory coherence with a connectionist (neural network) computational model.

Coherence theories of knowledge, ethics, and even truth have been popular among philosophers, but the notion of coherence is usually left rather vague. Hence coherence theories look unrigorous compared to theories couched more formally using deductive logic or probability theory. But connectionist models show how coherence ideas can be precisely and efficiently implemented. Since the mid-1980s, connectionist (neural network, PDP) models have been very influential in cognitive science. Loosely analogous to the operation of the brain, such models have numerous units that are roughly like neurons, connected to each other by excitatory and inhibitory links of varying strengths. Each unit has an activation value that is affected by the activations of the units to which it is linked, and learning algorithms are available for adjusting the strengths on links in response to experience.

My connectionist computational model of explanatory coherence, ECHO, uses units to represent propositions that can be hypotheses or descriptions of evidence, and links between units to represent coherence relations. For example, if a hypothesis explains a piece of evidence, then ECHO places an excitatory link between the unit representing the hypothesis and the unit representing the evidence. If two hypotheses are contradictory or competing, then ECHO places an inhibitory link between the units representing the two hypotheses. Repeatedly adjusting the activations of the units based on their links with other units results in a resting state in which some units are on (hypotheses accepted) and other units are off (hypotheses rejected). ECHO has been used to model many important cases in the history of science [Nowak and Thagard, 1992a, 1992b; Thagard, 1991, 1992, in

51

press]. Eliasmith and Thagard [1997] argue that ECHO provides a better account of hypothesis evaluation than available Bayesian accounts.

A different connectionist account of inference to best explanation is given by Churchland [1989]. He conjectures that abductive discovery and inference to the best explanation can both be understood in terms of prototype activation in distributed connectionist models, i. e. ones in which concepts and hypotheses are not represented by individual units but by patterns of activation across multiple units. There is considerable psychological evidence that distributed representations and prototypes are important in human cognition, but no one has yet produced a running computational model of hypothesis evaluation using these ideas. Non-connectionist models of hypothesis evaluation, including probabilistic ones, are discussed in the next section.

Engineering AI

As the references to my own work in the last section indicate, I pursue the cognitive modeling approach to computational philosophy of science, allying philosophy of science with cognitive science and naturalistic epistemology. But much valuable work in AI and philosophy has been done that makes no claims to psychological plausibility. One can set out to build a scientist without trying to reverse engineer a human scientist. The engineering AI approach to computational philosophy of science is allied, not with naturalistic, psychologistic epistemology, but with what has been called "android epistemology", the epistemology of machines that may or may not be built like humans [Ford, Glymour, and Hayes, 1995]. This approach is particularly useful when it exploits such differences between digital computers and humans as computers' capacity for very fast searches to perform tasks that human scientists cannot do very well.

Discovery
One goal of engineering AI is to produce programs that can make discoveries that have eluded humans. Bruce Buchanan, who was originally trained as a philosopher before moving into AI research, reviewed over a dozen AI programs that formulate hypotheses to explain empirical data [Buchanan, 1983]. One of the earliest and most impressive programs was DENDRAL which performed chemical analyses. Given spectroscopic data from an unknown organic chemical sample, it determined the molecular structure of the sample [Lindsay et. al., 1980]. The program META-DENDRAL pushed the discovery task one step farther back: given a collection of analytic data from a mass spectrometer, it discovered rules explaining the fragmentation behavior of chemical samples. A more recent program for chemical discovery is MECHEM, which automates the task of finding mech-

anism for chemical reactions: given experimental evidence about a reaction, the program searches for the simplest mechanism consistent with theory and experiment [Valdes-Peres, 1994].

Discovery programs have also been written for problems in biology, physics, and other scientific domains. In order to model biologists' discoveries concerning gene regulation in bacteria, Karp [1990] wrote a pair of programs, GENSIM and HYPGENE. GENSIM was used to represent a theory of bacterial gene regulation, and HYPGENE formulates hypotheses that improve the predictive power of GENSIM theories given experimental data. More recently, he has shifted from modeling historical discoveries to the attempt to write programs that make original discoveries from large scientific databases such as ones containing information about enzymes, proteins, and metabolic pathways [Karp and Mavrovouniotis, 1994]. Cheeseman [1990] used a program that applied Bayesian probability theory to discover previously unsuspected fine structure in the infrared spectra of stars. Machine learning techniques are also relevant to social science research, particularly the problem of inferring causal models from social data. The TETRAD program looks at statistical data in fields such as industrial development and voting behavior and builds causal models in the form of a directed graph of hypothetical causal relationships [Glymour et al., 1987].

One of the fastest growing areas of artificial intelligence is "data mining", in which machine learning techniques are used to discover regularities in large computer data bases such as the terabytes of image data collected by astronomical surveys [Fayyad, Piatetsky-Shapiro, and Smyth, 1996]. Data mining is being applied with commercial success by companies that wish to learn more about their operations, and similar machine learning techniques may have applications to large scientific data bases such as those being produced by the human genome project.

Evaluation
The topic of how scientific theories can be evaluated can also be discussed from a computational perspective. Many philosophers of science [e.g. Howson and Urbach, 1989] adopt a Bayesian approach to questions of hypothesis evaluation, attempting to use probability theory to describe and prescribe how scientific theories are assessed. But computational investigations of probabilistic reasoning must deal with important problems involving tractability that are usually ignored by philosophers. A fullblown probabilistic approach to a problem of scientific inference would need to establish a full joint distribution of probabilities for all propositions representing hypotheses and evidence, which would require 2^n probabilities for n hypotheses, quickly exhausting the storage and processing capacities of any computer. In-

genious methods have been developed by computer scientists to avoid this problem by using causal networks to restrict the number of probabilities required and to simplify the processing involved [Pearl, 1988, Neapolitain, 1990]. Surprisingly such methods have not been explored by probabilistic philosophers of science who have tended to ignore the substantial problem of the intractability of Bayesian algorithms.

Theory evaluation in the context of medical reasoning has been investigated by a group of artificial intelligence researchers at Ohio State University [Josephson and Josephson, 1994]. They developed a knowledge-based system called RED that uses data concerning a patient's blood sample to infer what red-cell antibodies are present in the patient. RED performs an automated version of inference to the best explanation, using heuristics to form a composite hypothesis concerning what antibodies are present in a sample. Interestingly, Johnson and Chen [1996] compared the performance of RED with the performance of my explanatory coherence program ECHO on a set of 48 cases interpreted by clinical experts. Whereas RED produced the experts' judgments in 58% of the cases, ECHO was successful in 73% of the cases. Hence although the engineering AI approach to scientific discovery has some evident advantages over the cognitive modeling approach in dealing with some problems such as mining hypotheses from large data bases, the cognitive modeling approach exemplified by ECHO has not yet been surpassed by a probabilistic or other program that surpasses human performance.

Theory of Computation

Both the cognitive modeling and engineering AI approaches to philosophy of science involve writing and experimenting with running computer programs. But it is also possible to take a more theoretical approach to computational issues in the philosophy of science, exploiting results in the theory of computation to reach conclusions about processes of discovery and evaluation.

Discovery
Scientific discovery can be viewed as a problem in formal learning theory, in which the goal is to identify a language given a string of inputs [Gold, 1968]. Analogously, a scientist can be thought of as a function that takes as input a sequence of formulas representing observations of the environment and produces as output a set of formulas that represent the structure of the world [Kelly, 1995, Kelly and Glymour, 1989, Osherson and Weinstein, 1989]. Although formal learning theory has produced some interesting theorems, they are limited in their relevance to the philosophy of science in several respects. Formal learning theory assumes a fixed language and therefore ignores the conceptual and terminological creativity that is important

to scientific development. In addition, formal learning theory tends to view hypotheses produced as a function of input data, rather than as a much more complex function of the data and the background concepts and theories possessed by a scientist. Formal learning theory also overemphasizes the goal of science to produce true descriptions, neglecting the important role of explanatory theories and hypothetical entities in scientific progress.

Evaluation

The theory of computational complexity has provided some interesting results concerning hypothesis evaluation. If you have n hypotheses and want to evaluate all the ways in which combinations of them can be accepted and rejected, you have to consider 2^n possibilities, an impossibly large number for large n. Bylander et al. [1991] gave a formal definition of an abduction problem consisting of a set of data to be explained and a set of hypotheses to explain them. They then showed that the problem of picking the best explanation, is NP-hard, i.e. it belongs to a class of problems that are generally agreed by computational theorists to be intractable in that the amount of time to compute them increases exponentially as the problems grow in size. Similarly, Thagard and Verbeurgt [1996] generalized explanatory coherence into a mathematical coherence problem that is NP-hard. What these results show is that theory evaluation, whether it is conceived in terms of Bayesian probabilities, heuristic assembly of hypotheses, or explanatory coherence, must be handled by computational approxi-mation, not an exhaustive algorithm. So far, the theoretical results concerning scientific evaluation have been largely negative, but they serve to provide outline the limits within which computational modeling must work.

What Computation Adds to Philosophy of Science

Almost twenty years ago, Aaron Sloman [1978] published an audacious book, *The Computer Revolution in Philosophy*, which predicted that within a few years any philosopher not familiar with the main developments of artificial intelligence could fairly be accused of professional incompetence. Since then, computational ideas have had a substantial impact on the philosophy of mind, but a much smaller impact on epistemology and philosophy of science. Why? One reason, I conjecture, is the kind of training that most philosophers have, which includes little preparation for actually doing computational work. Philosophers of mind have often been able to learn enough about artificial intelligence to discuss it, but for epistemology and philosophy of science it is much more useful to perform computations rather than just to talk about them. To conclude this review, I shall attempt to summarize what is gained by adding computational modelling to the philosophical tool kit.

Bringing artificial intelligence into philosophy of science introduces new conceptual resources for dealing with the structure and growth of scientific knowledge. Instead of being restricted to the usual representational schemes based on formal logic and ordinary language, computational approaches to the structure of scientific knowledge can include many useful representations such as prototypical concepts, concept hierarchies, production rules, causal networks, mental images, and so on. Philosophers concerned with the growth of scientific knowledge from a computational perspective can go beyond the narrow resources of inductive logic to consider algorithms for generating numerical laws, discovering causal networks, forming concepts and hypotheses, and evaluating competing explanatory theories.

In addition to the new conceptual resources that AI brings to philosophy of science, it also brings a new methodology involving the construction and testing of computational models. This methodology typically has numerous advantages over pencil-and-paper constructions. First, it requires considerable precision, in that to produce a running program the structures and algorithms postulated as part of scientific cognition need to be specified. Second, getting a program to run provides a test of the feasibility of its assumptions about the structure and processes of scientific development. Contrary to the popular view that clever programmers can get a program to do whatever they want, producing a program that mimics aspects of scientific cognition is often very challenging, and production of a program provides a minimal test of computational feasibility. Moreover, the program can then be used for testing the underlying theoretical ideas by examining how well the program works on numerous examples of different kinds. Comparative evaluation becomes possible when different programs accomplish a task in different ways: running the programs on the same data allows evaluation of their computational models and background theoretical ideas. Third, if the program is intended as part of a cognitive model, it can be assessed concerning how well it models human thinking.

The assessment of cognitive models can address questions such as the following:

1. **Genuineness.** Is the model a genuine instantiation of the theoretical ideas about the structure and growth of scientific knowledge, and is the program a genuine implementation of the model?
2. **Breadth of application.** Does the model apply to lots of different examples, not just a few that have been cooked up to make the program work?
3. **Scaling.** Does the model scale up to examples that are considerably larger and more complex than the ones to which it has been applied?
4. **Qualitative fit.** Does the computational model perform the same kinds of tasks that people do in approximately the same way?
5. **Quantitative fit.** Can the computational model simulate quantitative aspects of psychological experiments, e.g. ease of recall and mapping in analogy problems?
6. **Compatibility.** Does the computational model simulate representations and processes that are compatible with those found in theoretical accounts and computational models of other kinds of cognition?

Computational models of the thought processes of sciences that satisfy these criteria have the potential to greatly increase our understanding of the scientific mind. Engineering AI need not address questions of qualitative and quantitative fit with the results of psychological experiments, but should employ the other four standards of assessment.

There are numerous issues connecting computation and the philosophy of science that I have not touched on in this review. Computer science can itself be a subject of philosophical investigation, and some work has been done discussing epistemological issues that arise on computer research [see e.g. Fetzer, this volume; Thagard, 1993]. In particular, the philosophy of artificial intelligence and cognitive science are fertile areas of philosophy of science. My concern has been more narrow, with how computational models can contribute to philosophy of science. I conclude with a list of open problems that seem amenable to computational/philosophical investigation:

1. In scientific discovery, how are new questions generated? Formulating a useful question such as "How might species evolve?" or "Why do the planets revolve around the sun?" is often a prerequisite to more data-driven and focused processes of scientific discovery, but no computational account of scientific question generation has yet been given.

2. What role does visual imagery play in the structure and growth of scientific knowledge? Although various philosophers, historians, and psychologists have documented the importance of visual representations in scientific thought, existing computational techniques have not been well suited for providing detailed models of the cognitive role of pictorial mental images [see e.g. Shelley, 1996].

3. How is consensus formed in science? All the computational models discusses in this paper have concerned the thinking of individual scientists, but it might also be possible to develop models of social processes such as consensus formation along the lines of the field known as distributed artificial intelligence which considers the potential interactions of multiple intelligent agents [Thagard, 1993].

Perhaps problems such as these will, like other issues concerning discovery and evaluation, yield to computational approaches that involve cognitive modeling, engineering AI, and the theory of computation.

REFERENCES

Buchanan, B. (1983) "Mechanizing the Search for Explanatory Hypotheses." In *Philosophy of Science Association 1982* East Lansing: Philosophy of Science Association.

Bylander, T., D. Allemang, M. Tanner, and J. Josephson. (1991) "The Computational Complexity of Abduction." *Artificial Intelligence*, 49: 25-60.

Cheeseman, P. (1990) "On Finding the Most Probable Model." In J. Shrager and P. Langley (Eds.), *Computational Models of Scientific Discovery and Theory Formation*. San Mateo, CA: Morgan Kaufmann, 73-96.

Churchland, P. (1989) *A Neurocomputational Perspective*. Cambridge, MA: MIT Press.

Darden, L. (1990) "Diagnosing and Fixing Fault in Theories." In J. Shrager and P. Langley (Eds.), *Computational Models of Discovery and Theory Formation*. San Mateo, CA: Morgan Kaufman, 319-246.

Eliasmith, C., and P. Thagard. (1997). "Waves, Particles, and Explanatory Coherence." *British Journal for the Philosophy of Science*, 48: 1-19.

Falkenhainer, B. (1990) "A Unified Approach to Explanation and Theory Formation". In J. Shrager and P. Langley (Eds.), *Computational Models of Discovery and Theory Formation*. San Mateo, CA: Morgan Kaufman, 157-196.

Falkenhainer, B., K. D. Forbus, and D. Gentner. (1989) "The Structure-mapping Engine: Algorithms and Examples." *Artificial Intelligence*, 41: 1-63.

Fayyad, U., G. Piatetsky-Shapiro, and P. Smyth. (1996) "From Data Mining to Knowledge Discovery in Databases." *AI Magazine*, 17 (3): 37-54.

Ford, K. M., C. Glymour, and P.J. Hayes (Eds.). (1995) *Android Epistemology*. Menlo Park: AAAI Press.

Glymour, C., R. Scheines, P. Spirtes, and K. Kelly (1987) *Discovering Causal Structure*. Orlando: Academic Press.

Gold, E. (1968) "Language Identification in the Limit." *Information and Control*, 10: 447-474.

Holyoak, K. J., and P. Thagard. (1989) "Analogical Mapping by Constraint Satisfaction." *Cognitive Science*, 13: 295-355.

Holyoak, K. J., and P. Thagard. (1995). *Mental Leaps: Analogy in Creative Thought*. Cambridge, MA: MIT Press/Bradford Books.

Howson, C., and P. Urbach. (1989) *Scientific Reasoning: The Bayesian Tradition*. Lasalle, IL: Open Court.

Johnson, T. R., and M. Chen. (1996) "Comparison of Symbolic and Connectionist Approaches for Multiple Disorder Diagnosis: Heuristic Search vs. Explanatory Coherence." Unpublished manuscript, Ohio State University.

Josephson, J. R., and S. G. Josephson (Eds.). (1994) *Abductive Inference: Computation, Philosophy, Technology*. Cambridge: Cambridge University Press.

Karp, P. (1990) "Hypothesis Formation as Design." In J. Shrager & P. Langley (Eds.), *Computational Models of Discovery and Theory Formation*. San Mateo, CA: Morgan Kaufman, 276-317.

Karp, P., and M. Mavrovouniotis. (1994). "Representing, Analyzing, and Synthesizing Biochemical Pathways." *IEEE Expert*, 9 (2): 11-21.

Kelly, K. (1996). *The Logic of Reliable Inquiry*. New York: Oxford University Press.

Kelly, K., and C. Glymour. (1989) "Convergence to the Truth and Nothing but the Truth. *Philosophy of Science* ," 56: 185-220.

Kulkarni, D., and H. Simon. (1988) "The Processes of Scientific Discovery: The Strategy of Experimentation." *Cognitive Science*, 12: 139-175.

Langley, P., H. Simon, G. Bradshaw, and J. Zytkow. (1987) *Scientific Discovery*. Cambridge, MA: MIT Press/Bradford Books.

Lindsay, R., B. Buchanan, E. Feigenbaum, and J. Lederberg (1980) *Applications of Artificial Intelligence for Organic Chemistry: The DENDRAL project*. New York: McGraw Hill.

Neapolitain, R. (1990) *Probabilistic Reasoning in Expert Systems*. New York: John Wiley.

Nowak, G., and P. Thagard. (1992a) "Copernicus, Ptolemy, and Explanatory Coherence." In R. Giere (Ed.), *Cognitive Models of Science*. Minneapolis: University of Minnesota Press, 274-309.

Nowak, G., and P. Thagard. (1992b) "Newton, Descartes, and Explanatory Coherence." In R. Duschl et al.. (Eds.), *Philosophy of Science, Cognitive Psychology and Educational Theory and Practice*. Albany: SUNY Press, 69-115.

Osherson, D., and S. Weinstein. (1989) "Identifiable Collections of Countable Structures." *Philosophy of Science* , 56: 94-105.

Pearl, J. (1988) *Probabilistic Reasoning in Intelligent Systems*. San Mateo: Morgan Kaufman.

Qin, Y., and H. Simon. (1990) "Laboratory Replication of Scientific Discovery Processes." *Cognitive Science*, 14: 281-312.

Shelley, C. P. (1996) "Visual Abductive Reasoning in Archaeology." *Philosophy of Science*, 63: 278-301.

Sloman, A. (1978) *The Computer Revolution in Philosophy*. Atlantic Highlands: Humanities Press.

Thagard, P. (1988) *Computational Philosophy of Science*. Cambridge, MA: MIT Press/Bradford Books.

Thagard, P. (1991) "The Dinosaur Debate: Explanatory Coherence and the Problem of Competing Hypotheses." In J. Pollock and R. Cummins (Eds.), *Philosophy and AI: Essays at the Interface*. Cambridge, MA.: MIT Press/Bradford Books, 279-300.

Thagard, P. (1992) *Conceptual Revolutions*. Princeton, NJ: Princeton University Press.

Thagard, P. (1993) "Societies of Minds: Science as Distributed Computing." *Studies in History and Philosophy of Science*, 24: 49-67.

Thagard, P. (1996) *Mind: Introduction to Cognitive Science*. Cambridge, MA: MIT Press.

Thagard, P., and K. Verbeurgt. (1996) "Coherence as Constraint Satisfaction." Unpublished manuscript, University of Waterloo.

Valdes-Peres, R. E. (1994) "Conjecturing Hidden Entities via Simplicity and Conservation Laws: Machine Discovery in Chemistry." *Artificial Intelligence*, 65: 247-280.

ANOMALY-DRIVEN THEORY REDESIGN: COMPUTATIONAL PHILOSOPHY OF SCIENCE EXPERIMENTS

LINDLEY DARDEN

Introduction

I have been asked to discuss how computers have affected my work in philosophy. This paper discusses the use of artificial intelligence (AI) models to investigate both the representation of scientific knowledge and reasoning strategies for scientific change. The focus is on the reasoning strategies used to revise a theory, given an anomaly, which is a failed prediction of the theory.

Discoveries of theories often occur incrementally over a period of time, not in one "aha" moment. Previous work in history and philosophy of science [Darden, 1991] traced the modular development of the theory of the gene from 1900 to about 1930. When using historical methods, I feel like an archeologist or a natural historian, unearthing shards from the history. Early in my research career, I naively believed that one could use scientists' papers and notebooks to determine what reasoning strategies they actually used in their discoveries. However, an adequate description of scientists' actual reasoning strategies is almost always underdetermined by available historical evidence. T. H. Morgan, one of the principal architects of the theory of the gene, cleaned out his files every five years. Even in cases where abundant unpublished material exists, historians often cannot decide between competing interpretations, such as the debate about Darwin's use of the analogy to domestic selection in his discovery of natural selection [Ruse, 1979].

Consequently, wearing my philosopher's hat, as opposed to the historian's, I have proposed "hypothetical" reasoning strategies that could have accounted for the actual historical changes that did occur in the development of the theory of the gene [For more discussion of this methodology, see Darden 1991, 15-17, 34-39]. Strategies exemplified in the genetics case may be grouped into three categories: strategies for producing new ideas (e.g., reasoning by analogy), strategies for theory assessment (e.g., prediction testing), and strategies for anomaly resolution and change of scope [Darden 1991]. The first two categories have been much discussed in philosophy of science under the too-dichotomous headings of the "logic of discovery" and the "logic of justification" [e.g., Nickles 1980a; 1980b; for arguments about their interrelation, see Josephson 1994, 9]. Discussion of strategies for learning from mistakes and incrementally improving a theory (or experimental plan) over time have been neglected but are becoming important current topics of research [e.g., Darden and Cook, 1994; Darden, 1995; Mayo, 1996].

As perceptive critics [e.g., Vicedo, 1995] have urged, the status of these hypothetical reasoning strategies needs elucidating. If they are not descriptive of reasoning strategies actually used and if they do not have the prescriptive force of, for example, Popper's [1965] logically grounded view of falsification, what claims can be made for them? I would like them to function in an "advisory" capacity [Nickles, 1987]: given this type of problem, this strategy might be fruitful. I would like to find good strategies that scientists would find of use in their work [Darden, 1987]. For the strategies to be advisory, their efficacy as general problem-solving strategies needs to be tested.

There are at least four ways of testing the adequacy of reasoning strategies. First, cognitive science experiments provide human subjects with problems, record their reasoning protocols, and examine the use of reasoning strategies [e.g., Clement, 1988; Klahr et al., 1990]. A challenge in such work is to ensure that the reasoning strategies used in lab-amenable exercises are applicable to, and adequate for, actual scientific problems. Secondly, one can teach reasoning strategies to students, put them in problem-solving situations, and see if they are able to profit from the knowledge of the reasoning strategies. It is of course a challenge to design good experiments to demonstrate the efficacy of particular strategies in educational settings [Dunbar, 1993]. Third, one can play the role of a participant-observer, working with scientists to investigate the use of strategies in as yet unsolved problems [e.g., Darden and Cook, 1994]. A variant on this third method is that scientists use published strategies without the presence of the philosopher [Raquel Sussman, personal communication].

The first three methods of strategy testing require working with human subjects. It is difficult to control for all the components that the subject may be using in the problem-solving episode. Is a particular strategy used alone to produce the result or are other factors (maybe even unconscious ones) playing a role? The final method for testing strategies aims at avoiding this problem: program the strategies in an AI system and test their adequacy.

AI systems allow philosophers to experiment with knowledge and reasoning. One is no longer a natural historian unearthing artifacts in the historical record nor an armchair philosopher speculating about reasoning strategies. Computational philosophy of science [Thagard 1988] is experimental epistemology. It investigates methods for representing knowledge and for modeling reasoning strategies that can manipulate that knowledge. Once one has a working system one can experiment with "what if" scenarios, adding or removing strategies to determine their effects. This method has challenges of its own--finding adequate knowledge representation methods, devising good implementations of strategies, being careful not to tailor the system to produce one desired result. More pragmatic challenges for a philosopher engaging in such research are to learn about AI and programming techniques and to obtain access to the necessary computing facilities. One can either become a programmer oneself, as, for example, Paul Thagard and John Josephson have done, or one can collaborate with others (as I have done).

My interest in using AI to investigate scientific discovery was sparked by an exciting paper by Bruce Buchanan entitled "Steps Toward Mechanizing Discovery" [presented in 1978; published in 1985]. Buchanan discussed the first expert systems, which he helped to develop at Stanford. DENDRAL formed hypotheses about the structures of compounds, given data from a mass spectrograph [Lindsay et al. 1980; 1993].

Buchanan articulated a new research program:

> The traditional problem of finding an effective method for formulating true hypotheses that best explain phenomena has been transformed into finding heuristic methods that generate plausible explanations. The problem of giving rules for producing true scientific statements has been replaced by the problem of finding efficient heuristic rules for culling the reasonable candidates for an explanation from an appropriate set of possible candidates [and finding methods for constructing the candidates][Buchanan, 1985, 110-111].

In 1980, I spent my sabbatical with Buchanan's group at Stanford, then called the Heuristic Programming Project. In subsequent years I learned more about the work in AI on scientific discovery [e.g., Langley et al., 1987; Kulkarni and Simon, 1990; Shrager and Langley, 1990]. Simultaneously, I continued my historical and philosophical work on the genetics case and began exploring methods for implementing parts of that case. Collaborators and I explored rule-based systems (in which knowledge is represented in if-then rules) and frame based systems (in which knowledge is represented by entities with properties grouped hierarchically) [e.g., Darden and Rada, 1988a; 1988b]. However, these systems required tremendous time and effort for small results in modeling general reasoning strategies for scientific discovery. The problem of finding an adequate representation of the components of the theory of the gene loomed large. Finding an adequate knowledge representation system is itself a subject of experimentation.

Anomaly-Driven Theory Redesign in TRANSGENE

An entirely new approach proved much more fruitful. B. Chandrasekaran, John Josephson, and their colleagues at the Laboratory for Artificial Intelligence Research (LAIR) at Ohio State University developed what they call a "functional representation" (FR) language [Sembugamoorthy and Chandrasekaran, 1986]. It is useful for representing the functional components of a device, e.g., a chemical manufacturing plant [Keuneke, 1989], or a biological system, e.g., the immune system [Sticklen and Chandrasekaran, 1989]. FRs support diagnostic reasoning by allowing one to find a faulty functional component and they support reasoning in redesigning a faulty component of the system to improve its functioning. Diagnosis and redesign are examples of "generic tasks" for which the LAIR group has developed specific information processing strategies [Josephson, 1994, 50-62]. If one can identify a problem, e.g., anomaly resolution, as an example of a generic task, e.g., diagnosis, then one can use the knowledge representation and inference procedures developed for that task.

Collaborators and I at LAIR built the TRANSGENE system [Darden et al., 1991; Darden et al., 1992]. The TRANSGENE project has been guided by two analogies. First, a scientific theory can be viewed as analogous to a device, a device with the functions of prediction and explanation. Such an analogy allows the FR language, initially developed for computationally representing devices, to be used to represent the transmission (Mendelian) genetic mechanism posited by the theory of the gene (hence the name TRANSGENE, which has nothing to do with more modern transgenic manipulations). The second guiding analogy is that between anomaly resolution and diagnosis/redesign. The reasoning in localizing a failure of a theory is like the reasoning in diagnosing a failure of a device. Reasoning in fixing a theory to remove an anomaly is like reasoning in redesigning the device to remove the failure. Such an analogy allows methods that have been developed in AI for diagnosis and redesign to be applied to the task of scientific theory revision.

An anomaly is generated when an observation or experimental result does not agree (to some specified degree of accuracy) with a prediction of a theory. One might be able to resolve the anomaly by showing that there is a problem with the data. At the other extreme, one might decide that the anomaly is sufficiently serious to require completely abandoning the theory [e.g., Kuhn, 1970 discusses crisis anomalies that lead to a paradigm change]. These responses are not modeled in TRANSGENE. The TRANSGENE system requires the assumption that the data supplied is accurate; furthermore, it proceeds on the assumption that the theory can be modified to resolve the anomaly [For stages in anomaly resolution, see Darden, 1991, 269; Darden, 1992].

The reasoning in making an incremental change to remove an anomaly marks a path through a space of possible changes. This reasoning constitutes the cognitive process of interest in the TRANS-GENE project. The cognitive "agent," navigating the theory change problem space, is here thought of as facing, first, a diagnosis problem to localize the fault, and, then, an incremental redesign problem to change the theory. These reasoning tasks are called "anomaly driven redesign tasks." A more precise, information-processing statement of the anomaly driven redesign task is as follows:

> Given a theory with explanatory and/or predictive successes, and an anomaly for the theory, construct a modified theory, which conserves previous explanatory and predictive successes, and which no longer produces the anomalous prediction and, instead, produces a prediction in agreement with observation.

In order to carry out this anomaly-driven redesign task, a computational framework is needed to do the following: (1) Represent the theory. (2) Detect an anomaly. (3) Trace the fault to a specific component of the theory, that is, tentatively localize the fault. (4) Use redesign strategies to propose a fix at the fault site. (5) Test the proposed redesign. (6) If the test fails, return to a previous step to select another localization or propose an alternative way to fix the theory, then retest.

TRANSGENE.1, 2, and 3 were three versions of the TRANSGENE system (each an improvement over the previous one) developed to carry out the above tasks. They show improvements in representing components of the theory of the gene in the FR language. Furthermore, they explore increasingly powerful methods for carrying out the tasks of diagnosis and redesign.

TRANSGENE.1 focused on the issues of theory representation and support of generation of fault site hypotheses. In transmission genetic theory, the processes of interest are inheritance mechanisms and the observations to be predicted are patterns in the distribution of inherited characteristics in offspring. An abstract representation of the theory was constructed, consisting of a set of causal steps with variables. When supplied with an anomaly, the system was able to generate all the possible fault sites and provide queries to a user to aid in the localization of failing steps in genetic processes [Darden, 1990; 1992; Moberg and Josephson, 1990].

Added to TRANSGENE.2 and TRANSGENE.3 were the abilities to simulate genetic crosses and to carry out theory revision automatically. The systems predict the result of a breeding experiment by simulation, given the initial conditions of the experiment. The predicted result is compared to an observed result, which is provided by the user. If an anomaly is detected, the systems try to localize the fault to one or more specific components of the theory. Having localized the fault, the systems attempt to modify the theory. Resimulation is done using the modified theory and predicted results are once again compared with the experimental results. This loop is repeated until there are no more anomalies.

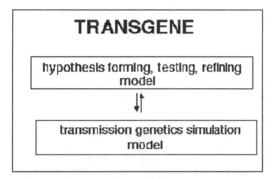

Figure 1.

The redesign methods used in TRANSGENE.2 were weak; little knowledge was used in narrowing the search for changes. Changes were made using a random generate and test method [Darden et al., 1991]. TRANSGENE.3 incorporated changes in the representation of genetic theory that enabled the difference between a predicted and observed result to be used to guide localization and redesign [For a similar implementation of anomaly characterization, see Karp 1990]. An important strategy in anomaly resolution is to extract as much information as possible from the nature of the anomaly for use in making the changes. For example, if the theory predicts a 1AA: 2Aa:1aa ratio but the data show a 2Aa:1aa ratio, then the missing set of AAs must somehow be accounted for in the redesign process. Different modifications would be made if the anomaly had been 1:0:1. The characterization of the difference between the prediction and the observed data provides guidance for localization and redesign.

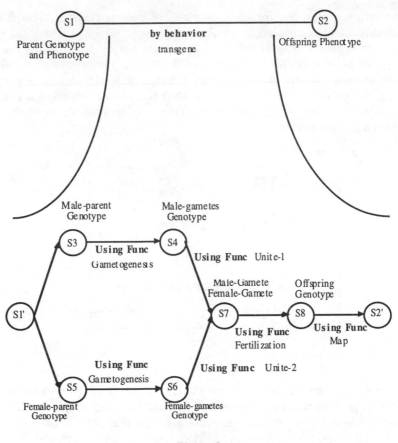

Figure 2.

TRANSGENE.3 has two parts, as shown in Figure 1: the transmission genetics simulation model and the hypothesis forming, testing and refining model. Figure 2 shows the simulator represented in the FR language, with sequential steps in a genetic breeding experiment. The parents' genotypes (their genes) and phenotypes (their visible characteristics caused by the genes) are inputs to the system. The simulator generates the types of gametes (germ cells: sperm and eggs), unites them in the step of fertilization, and calculates the expected ratios of genotypes and phenotypes of the offspring. That output constitutes the theory's prediction of the results of the breeding experiment. The system is then supplied data from an actual historical breeding experiment. It determines whether the prediction matches the data to a specified degree of statistical accuracy. When it detects an anomaly, the anomaly resolution part of the system is called, which is the top box depicted in Figure 1. The information-processing tasks that TRANSGENE.3 carries out are shown in Figure 3.

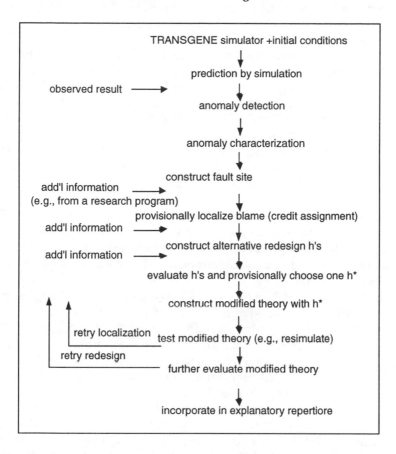

Figure 3. Information processing tasks in anomaly resolution

The difference between the prediction and observation is calculated. This characterization of the anomaly is used to guide the step of finding possible malfunction sites in the simulator. Once an anomaly is characterized, the next subtask is to localize a malfunction site in the theory. The FR model of the theory enables one to generate all the possible fault sites by explicitly representing the modular steps involved in the process. A step in a process, represented by a state-transition in the FR formalism, can go wrong in any one of these three ways: (1) because something occurs before a given state and alters its inputs, and thus a new prior state needs to be added; (2) something about the description of the state transition itself is wrong; (3) the outputs of the step are correct, but something occurs afterward to alter the process's output, and thus a new post-state needs to be added. Consequently, for each state in the FR, three malfunction site hypotheses are generated: before the state, in the state, or after the state. TRANSGENE.2 generated all such possible fault sites. For large FRs, even the number of single-fault hypotheses becomes large rapidly. TRANSGENE.3 used the nature of the anomaly to limit this search.

After one or more sites are chosen as the location of a malfunction, then those components must be changed to remove the malfunction. The weak, random generate-and-test method used in TRANSGENE.2 for the theory redesign subtask was replaced in TRANSGENE.3 with dependency directed backtracking. After characterizing the nature of the anomaly, TRANSGENE.3 backtracked through the steps in the FR representation from output toward the input to localize and fix the faulty module. This provided a much more guided redesign process, based on the nature of the anomaly. For example, if TRANSGENE.3 predicted 1AA:2Aa:1aa but the data showed 2Aa:1aa, then the system backtracked through its simulation to determine where the AA gametes were generated and suggested ways to eliminate them. After a fix hypothesis is generated and added to the system, the simulator is run again with the redesigned component to determine if it now makes the correct prediction [For more details of the TRANSGENE.3 system, see Darden et al., 1992].

In TRANSGENE.2 and .3 the redesign consisted in changing parameters that represented proportions of types of gametes and zygotes. Additional knowledge, outside the original representation of the theory, would be needed in a significant redesign process for the system to be able to generate hypotheses as to the causal mechanisms producing such changed proportions. Two ways of extending the implementation to make use of additional knowledge have occurred to us: use knowledge of generic biological processes [compare Goel, 1989] and use knowledge from closely related scientific fields [Darden and Maull, 1977]. For example, when one finds none of an expected type of gametes, one might invoke generic processes for how biological things disappear, e.g., they migrate, they are digested by something else, they die. The missing AA gametes are a lethal gene combination that causes the death of offspring receiving AA; hence, a system that could invoke dying to explain missing biological items could conjecture the hypothesis of lethal genes. Goel [1989] represented a library of generic processes, characterized by the functions they achieve in an engineering domain. He used those processes in redesign tasks to accomplish desired functions. A subsequent version of TRANSGENE could implement such a library of biological processes for use in biological theory redesign to produce more creative fixes to the theory.

The system should be able to learn from its anomaly resolution episodes. After an anomaly has been resolved, the newly constructed theory should be saved for use in similar cases in the future. A proliferation of alternative versions of the theory result. They constitute

70

the explanatory repertoire of Mendelian genetics [Darden, 1991, 195-199]. Methods for storing the newly constructed versions and choosing the appropriate one in a future problem-solving episode are needed. A typical method for choosing among a set of problem-solving patterns is to classify the patterns according to the type of anomaly they can solve. Then a classification procedure can be used to test to see whether a pattern exists for a given type of anomaly; if it does, then that version of the theory can be used to explain the anomaly. For example, if additional genetic results produced 2:1 anomalies, then a lethal gene pattern could be chosen from the explanatory repertoire and instantiated for the case.

Storing of patterns for reuse and categorizing them as to the kinds of anomalies they solve is analogous to "classification-based diagnosis." For example, if the patient has symptoms 1,2,3, conclude disease X. If no appropriate pattern is already in the look-up table, then the usual anomaly resolution methods of localization and redesign can be used. These anomaly resolution methods are analogous to "model-based diagnosis" [Chandrasekaran and Mittal, 1983; Chandrasekaran et al., 1989; Davis and Hamscher, 1988].

Implications of the AI Research

This AI work provides alternative views to traditional analyses of the nature of scientific theories and of reasoning in theory change. The logical empiricists analyzed theories as formal axiomatic systems [Suppe, 1977 criticizes this]. A more recent descendant of this method is Kitcher's [1993] view of theories as abstract argument patterns. Explanation and prediction are analyzed as necessitating deductive arguments. Philosophers, enamored of the Duhem-Quine thesis [for a clear statement of this thesis, see Quinn, 1974], have often despaired of localizing and fixing faults in theories. Philosophers have also been pessimistic about analyzing reasoning in the formation of new hypotheses [e.g., Popper 1965].

This AI work suggests alternative analyses. Some scientific theories can be represented via an abstraction of core causal processes [compare Darden and Cain, 1989]. A representation may be at multiple levels of abstraction and specified at one or several hierarchical levels of detail. (Philosophers trained in logic typically discuss only two levels: a variable and its value. They miss the lesson from AI about multiple hierarchical levels of abstraction.) The abstraction consists of modular steps in the causal process. The modularity is crucial in anomaly resolution; the amount of modularity versus interconnectedness of components determines the ease of localization of problems in single components. The more separable and independently accessible the modules, the easier it will be to avoid a Duhem-Quine holism.

71

Such an abstract representation allows a theory to be implemented as a simulator. Given the initial conditions of an experiment, its output can be viewed as a prediction of the outcome of the experiment. The process of making a prediction involves "running" the simulator "forward." Alternatively, the formalism can support explanation, by allowing one to "traverse" the formalism backward to see how a particular state is reached. (Although TRANSGENE was not explicitly used for explanation, humans could use it that way.)

Although perhaps, in principle, any component of one's theoretical system can be changed (a concession to Duhem-Quine), in practice, scientists do localize anomalies and successfully fix theoretical components. This analogy to diagnosis/redesign shows feasible reasoning strategies for this process. Characterization of the nature of the anomaly and dependency-directed backtracking can provide guidance for localization. The modularity of the steps proved essential in anomaly resolution, allowing localization of faults and a focus for redesign efforts. Historical work had shown that anomalies often cause previously implicit assumptions to be made explicit in order to localize an anomaly [Darden, 1991]. This implementation allowed steps before or after the explicitly represented states to be conjectured to exist.

Hypotheses about the localization of an anomaly could be tested by experiment, by, for example, doing experiments to determine if a given causal step (e.g., formation of gametes) has occurred. Thus, a system like TRANSGENE could be coupled to a laboratory to help in focusing on the most informative scientific experiments for localizing a problem.

Redesign hypotheses can be either simple tweaking of numbers or they may require the generation of more elaborate hypotheses. TRANSGENE has shown that an AI system, guided by a numerically characterized anomaly (or the qualitative information that a set is missing), can propose quantitative fixes, the tweaking of parameters. However, when more creative hypotheses are needed, requiring knowledge outside the system itself (e.g., via interfield connections), then the task is more difficult. The TRANSGENE work has suggested ways of investigating creative redesign strategies, such as the use of generic libraries of abstract, functionally characterized processes [Goel, 1989], and the use of interfield relations [Darden and Maull, 1977; Darden, 1991].

Doing computational philosophy of science requires precision and completeness not required in non-implemented studies of history and philosophy of science. The nature of knowledge representation methods from AI force a reconsideration of the scientific case to find appropriate details. When developing an AI implementation, items that were previously glossed over must be specified in detail. If key steps are omitted, the program will not run. Thus, one result of this work is an increase in precision and completeness in analysis of a scientific case study. (Of course, doing an implementation can also introduce artifacts, items necessary to make the system run but irrelevant to the actual scientific case, so care must be taken.)

Once a system is working, experimentation with representation and reasoning is possible. For example, the changes in TRANSGENE demonstrated the efficacy of dependency directed backtracking versus random trial and error. Furthermore, computational philosophy of science work provides the potential for philosophers to contribute to actual scientific discovery, either by informing scientists of strategies whose efficacy has been demonstrated or by assisting in building computational systems to make discoveries and resolve anomalies.

Conclusion

The TRANSGENE project has investigated reasoning in the re-design of a scientific theory to improve it to remove an anomaly. The work draws on a detailed historical case study of the development of Mendelian (transmission) genetics. The theory of the gene is represented in a computational form that supports simulation, prediction, and explanation. Anomaly resolution is viewed as a diagnosis/re-design task. When presented with an anomalous observation, the TRANSGENE system generates fault site hypotheses, chooses among them, proposes fix hypotheses at the fault site, and tests them by re-running the simulation. These methods are general ones for representing and improving mechanistic, causal scientific theories.

ACKNOWLEDGMENTS

This material is based on work supported by the National Science Foundation under Grant No. RII-9003142. Any opinions, findings and conclusions or recommendations expressed in this material are those of the author(s) and do not necessarily reflect those of the National Science Foundation. Lindley Darden's work was also supported by a General Research Board Award from the Graduate School of the University of Maryland, College Park. The TRANSGENE system was designed in collaboration with John Josephson and Dale Moberg, with helpful comments by Susan Josephson. The TRANSGENE.2 system was implemented by Satish Nagarajan. The TRANSGENE.3 system was implemented by Sunil Thadani. Thanks to Nancy Hall, Susan and John Josephson, Robert Skipper, Frederick Suppe, and Alana Suskin for comments on an earlier draft of this paper.

REFERENCES

Buchanan, Bruce. (1985) "Steps Toward Mechanizing Discovery," in K. Schaffner, Ed., *Logic of Discovery and Diagnosis in Medicine.* Berkeley: University of California Press, 94-114.

Chandrasekaran, B. and Sanjay Mittal. (1983) "Deep versus Compiled Knowledge Approaches to Diagnostic Problem-solving," *International Journal of Man-Machine Studies,* 19: 425-436.

Chandrasekaran, B., J. Smith, and J. Sticklen. (1989) "'Deep' Models and Their Relation to Diagnosis," in K. S. Zadeh, Ed., *Artificial Intelligence in Medicine*, Vol. 1. Tecklenberg, Germany: Burg-verlag, 29-40.

Clement, John. (1988) "Observed Methods for Generating Analogies in Scientific Problem Solving," *Cognitive Science,* 12: 563-586.

Darden, Lindley. (1987) "Viewing the History of Science as Compiled Hindsight," *AI Magazine,* 8 (2):: 33-41.

Darden, Lindley. (1990) "Diagnosing and Fixing Faults in Theor-ies," in J. Shrager and P. Langley, Eds., *Computational Models of Scientific Discovery and Theory Formation.* San Mateo, CA: Morgan Kaufmann, 319-346.

Darden, Lindley. (1991) *Theory Change in Science: Strategies from Mendelian Genetics.* New York: Oxford University Press.

Darden, Lindley. (1992) "Strategies for Anomaly Resolution," in R. Giere, Ed., *Cognitive Models of Science*, Minnesota Studies in the Philosophy of Science, Vol. 15. Minneapolis: University of Minnesota Press, 251-273.

Darden, Lindley. (1995) "Exemplars, Abstractions, and Anomalies: Representations and Theory Change in Mendelian and Molecular Genetics," in James G. Lennox and Gereon Wolters, Eds., *Concepts, Theories, and Rationality in the Biological Sciences.* Pittsburgh, PA: University of Pittsburgh Press, 137-158.

Darden, Lindley and Nancy Maull. (1977) "Interfield Theories," *Philosophy of Science*, 44: 43-64.

Darden, Lindley and Roy Rada. (1988a) "Hypothesis Formation Using Part-Whole Interrelations," in David Helman, Ed., *Analogical Reasoning*. Dordrecht: Reidel, 341-375.

Darden, Lindley and Roy Rada. (1988b) "Hypothesis Formation Via Interrelations," in Armand Prieditis, Ed. *Analogica*. Los Altos, California: Morgan Kaufmann, 109-127.

Darden, Lindley and Joseph A. Cain. (1989) "Selection Type Theories," *Philosophy of Science,* 56: 106-129.

Darden, Lindley, Dale Moberg, Satish Nagarajan, and John Josephson. (1991) "Anomaly Driven Redesign of a Scientific Theory: The TRANSGENE.2 Experiments," *Technical Report 91-LD-TRANS-GENE.* Laboratory for Artificial Intelligence Research. Columbus, OH: The Ohio State University.

Darden, Lindley, Dale Moberg, Sunil Thadani, and John Josephson. (1992) "A Computational Approach to Scientific Theory Revision: The TRANSGENE Experiments," *Technical Report 92-LD-TRANS-GENE.* Laboratory for Artificial Intelligence Research. Columbus, OH: The Ohio State University.

Darden, Lindley and Michael Cook. (1994) "Reasoning Strategies in Molecular Biology: Abstractions, Scans and Anomalies," in D. Hull, M. Forbes, and R. M. Burian, Eds., *PSA 1994,* Vol. 2. East Lansing, Michigan: Philosophy of Science Association, 179-191.

Davis, Randall and Walter C. Hamscher. (1988) "Model-based Reasoning: Troubleshooting," in H. E. Shrobe, Ed., *Exploring Artificial Intelligence.* Los Altos, California: Morgan Kaufmann, 297-346.

Dunbar, Kevin. (1993) "Concept Discovery in a Scientific Domain," *Cognitive Science,* 17: 397-434.

Goel, Ashok. (1989) *Integration of Case-Based Reasoning and Model-Based Reasoning for Adaptive Design Problem Solving.* Ph.D. Dissertation. Columbus, OH: The Ohio State University.

Josephson, John R. and Susan G. Josephson, Eds. (1994) *Abductive Inference: Computation, Philosophy, Technology.* New York: Cambridge University Press.

Karp, Peter. (1990) "Hypothesis Formation as Design," in J. Shrager and P. Langley, Eds., *Computational Models of Scientific Discovery and Theory Formation*. San Mateo, California: Morgan Kaufmann, 275-317.

Keuneke, Anne. (1989) *Machine Understanding of Devices: Causal Explanation of Diagnostic Conclusions*. Ph.D. Dissertation. Department of Computer and Information Science. Columbus, OH: The Ohio State University.

Kitcher, Philip. (1993) *The Advancement of Science: Science without Legend, Objectivity without Illusions*. New York: Oxford University Press.

Klahr, David, Kevin Dunbar, and Anne L. Fay. (1990) "Designing Good Experiments to Test Bad Hypotheses," in J. Shrager and P. Langley, Eds., *Computational Models of Scientific Discovery and Theory Formation*. San Mateo, California: Morgan Kaufmann, 356-402.

Kuhn, Thomas. (1970) *The Structure of Scientific Revolutions*. 2nd Edition. Chicago: The University of Chicago Press.

Kulkarni, Deepak and Herbert Simon. (1990) "Experimentation in Machine Discovery," in J. Shrager and P. Langley, Eds., *Computational Models of Scientific Discovery and Theory Formation*. San Mateo, California: Morgan Kaufmann, 255-273.

Langley, Pat, Herbert Simon, Gary L. Bradshaw, and Jan M. Zytkow. (1987) *Scientific Discovery: Computational Explorations of the Creative Process*. Cambridge, Massachusetts: MIT Press.

Lindsay, Robert K., B. G. Buchanan, E. A. Feigenbaum, and J. Lederberg. (1980) *Applications of Artificial Intelligence for Organic Chemistry: The DENDRAL Project*. New York: McGraw Hill.

Lindsay, Robert K., B. G. Buchanan, E. A. Feigenbaum, and J. Lederberg. (1993) "DENDRAL: A Case Study of the First Expert System for Scientific Hypothesis Formation," *Artificial Intelligence*, 61: 209-261.

Mayo, Deborah G. (1996) *Error and the Growth of Experimental Knowledge*. Chicago: University of Chicago Press.

Moberg, Dale and John Josephson (1990), "Diagnosing and Fixing Faults in Theories, Appendix A: An Implementation Note," in J. Shrager and P. Langley, Eds., *Computational Models of Scientific Discovery and Theory Formation*. San Mateo, California: Morgan Kaufmann, 347-353.

Nickles, Thomas, ed. (1980a) *Scientific Discovery: Case Studies*. Dordrecht: Reidel.

Nickles, Thomas, ed. (1980b) *Scientific Discovery, Logic and Rationality*. Dordrecht: Reidel.

Nickles, Thomas. (1987) "Methodology, Heuristics, and Rationality," in J. C. Pitt and M. Pera, Eds., *Rational Changes in Science*. Dordrecht: Reidel, 103-132.

Popper, Karl (1965), *The Logic of Scientific Discovery*. New York: Harper Torchbooks.

Quinn, Philip. (1974) "What Duhem Really Meant," in R. S. Cohen and M. Wartofsky, Eds., *Methodological and Historical Essays in the Natural and Social Sciences*, Proceedings of the Boston Colloquium for the Philosophy of Science 1969-1972, Vol. 14. Dordrecht: Reidel, 33-56.

Ruse, Michael. (1979) *The Darwinian Revolution: Science Red in Tooth and Claw*. Chicago: University of Chicago Press.

Sembugamoorthy, V. and B. Chandrasekaran. (1986) "Functional Representation of Devices and Compilation of Diagnostic Problem-solving Systems," in J. Kolodner and C. Reisbeck, Eds., *Experience, Memory, and Reasoning*. Hillsdale, New Jersey: Lawrence Erlbaum Associates, 47-73.

Shrager, J. and P. Langley, eds. (1990) *Computational Models of Scientific Discovery and Theory Formation*. San Mateo, California: Morgan Kaufmann.

Sticklen, J. and B. Chandrasekaran. (1989) "Integrating Classification-Based Compiled Level Reasoning with Functional-Based Deep Level Reasoning," *Applied Artificial Intelligence*, 3: 275-304.

Suppe, Frederick, ed. (1977) *The Structure of Scientific Theories*, 2nd Edition. Urbana: University of Illinois Press.

Thagard, Paul. (1988) *Computational Philosophy of Science*. Cam-bridge, Massachusetts: MIT Press.

Vicedo, Marga. (1995) "How Scientific Ideas Develop and How to De-velop Scientific Ideas," *Biology & Philosophy*, 10: 489-499.

REPRESENTATION OF PHILOSOPHICAL ARGUMENTATION

THEODORE SCALTSAS

The Nature of Project Archelogos

The traditional role of the historians of philosophy has been the extraction of arguments from the surviving philosophical texts. This process involves interpretation, and hence the main skill of the phil-osopher who works on primary texts has always been their exegesis. Project Archelogos centers on the extraction of the arguments of the ancient Greek philosophical texts, and the representation of their logi-cal interconnections.

The ideas motivating this endeavor are, first, that the philosophi-cal arguments in a philosophical text should be disentangled, render-ing explicit which arguments are primary and which supporting, as well as which statements are premises and which conclusions; second, that the presentation of these arguments should be made in such a way that the reader is visually aided in absorbing and comprehending the logical structure of the arguments. Thus, explicitness regarding the philosophical content of the arguments, and informativeness in the representation of their mutual interdependence, are the two principles which the Archelogos method introduces.

Although the method is general, the area of application of Project Archelogos is ancient philosophy. It is hoped that this will be the first application, to be followed by parallel projects in other areas of phil-osophy. Within ancient philosophy, the aim of the Project is to gen-erate a database which will contain argument-analyses of ancient Greek philosophical texts, aiding the user towards understanding what the philosophers in question propounded in their writings. Since the content depends on exegesis, and since there are no definitive ex-egeses, such an analysis needs to supply a *spectrum* of received inter-pretations for each passage of philosophical text. Given the exegetical history of ancient Greek texts, the interpretations need to be so org-anized as not to generate a maze of readings, but rather to provide the user with a map for their own explorations, being aware of what is new and what is known.

Finally, the database aims to be the ground for computer searches that would be impossible otherwise, tracing the occurrence of expressions, concepts and philosophical positions, and much more regarding the nature of arguments, across the philosophical work of ancient philosophers.

The Archelogos Method

The method followed in the philosophical analysis of texts consists in separating various functions, and dedicating each function to a different module in the database. There are thus the following modules in the Archelogos database: The Original Text Module, the Translation Module, the Arguments and Thesis Module, the Alternative Interpretations Module, the Bibliography Module, and the Indices Module.

Early in the design of the Project it was decided by the collaborating classical philosophers that a guiding principle should be the avoidance of duplication of work in the discipline; namely, where there was already work of good quality available in the field, the Projects' aim should be to use it, rather than expend resources in duplicating it. On the basis of this principle, Archelogos will not undertake the publication of the ancient Greek philosophical texts since they already exist in electronic version, published by the *Thesaurus Linguae Graecae*. It is assumed by the Project that it is a matter of the immediate, rather than of the long-term future that the *Thesaurus* will appear on the Internet. At that point, users of Archelogos will be able to enter it for consultation, or searches, of the ancient Greek text, while working in the Archelogos database. The search capabilities of the *Thesaurus* database would thus be available to the user of the Archelogos database.

The translations of the ancient Greek texts will require a different policy on the part of the Project. Where there already exist translations of good scholarly quality, the Project will aim to use them or to direct the Archelogos users to them. Where such translations are not available, the Archelogos Academic Board will have to commission the work. At present, the Project has permission from the Jowett Copyright Trustees to use the Revised Oxford Translation of Aristotle and the Fourth Edition of Jowett's translation of Plato in the Archelogos database. But the user of the Archelogos database could still access other databases with translations of the work of Plato and Aristotle on the Internet.

The third module is the *Arguments and Theses Module* which will occupy us for a good part of this paper, on account of its aim, on the one hand, and the philosophical problems it generates on the other. Briefly, the Arguments and Theses Module is dedicated to registering the philosophical positions in the texts, and the arguments supporting them, where these are provided. Part of the difficulty is that there is a variety of ways in which an author can "say" something, and "support" it. From its inception, the Project had to prioritize its aims, restricting its scope and methodology to only certain approaches to ancient philosophy, so as not to become over-ambitious, while being sensitive to educational and research utility. The most general description that can be given to the approach adopted in this module is that it belongs to the analytic tradition in philosophy. I should hasten to note that by this term I do not understand what it is in some contexts taken to mean, namely a linguistic approach. Rather, I mean that the primary concern in this module to understand the reasons given by the ancient philosophers which justify the philosophical positions they put forward in the text.

Clearly, the Arguments and Theses Module is different from the first two Modules — Original Texts and Translations — in that it belongs to the domain of interpretations. This module, along with the Alternative Interpretations one, will be authored by specialists in ancient philosophy, who are invited by the Archelogos Academic Board to compose analyses of ancient texts for the Project. Their analyses will be original; but where they judge interpretations in the literature to have been important for the history of the exegesis of the passage in question, they will register them, too, in the Alternative Interpre-tations Module.

The second significant feature of the Arguments and Theses Module, after its content, is its form. The aim here is to represent visually the logical relation between philosophical theses, and between philosophical arguments. An *argument* is understood as a thesis followed by a "because-statement". The visual convention followed in the Arguments and Theses Module is to *indent* the because-statements. The result is that one can immediately perceive the logical relation between theses and between arguments, where the conclusion is the top statement, and its supporting premises are indented below it. Since the premises supporting a conclusion can themselves be con-clusions of further because-statements (indented below the conclusions), the whole structure may result in a multi-layered sequence of arguments and sub-arguments. Indenting statements depicts the logical hierarchy between them.

A *because-statement* is conceived broadly. "Because" covers all the relations between statements which would be recognized as giving a reason for holding a view. This includes giving a formal proof of the conclusion; giving an explanation of it that enhances acceptance of that position; giving an example of it, etc. All these count as justifications for the conclusion insofar as each is offered as a reason for holding the conclusion in question.

In most cases, premises are missing from the justifications given for philosophical theses. Sometimes it is because the premises are mentioned in a previous context and the author does not wish to repeat them, while in other cases the premises are taken to be understood or known. But in other instances, premises necessary for the justification of the conclusion are simply missing. Such premises will be supplied by the Archelogos analyst of the text, in their reconstruction of the arguments of that text. A convention is available to the Archelogos analyst to distinguish between (a) premises found in the text of the argument under analysis, (b) premises needed for this argument found in a different text of the same ancient author (which will be enclosed in curly brackets "{", "}"), and finally, (c) premises that are not found in the text but which state positions needed for this argument which the analyst can attribute to the ancient author (enclosed in square brackets, "[", "]").

Apart from being indented, the justification of the conclusion will also be *hidden from view* on the screen, until it is brought to the fore. The reason for this feature is that in this way the user may keep in view only the main conclusions of a passage or a work, without going into the detailed argumentation in them, or may enter such argumentation at will where it is desired and to the degree that it is desired. By the latter I mean that the user may decide to go only to a certain depth of justification of an argument, calling up the sub-arguments of so many levels below a top-conclusion, but not exhaust the whole justification of it. Thus a user may read a work or a chapter of a work only at the level of conclusions, or at the level of the important arguments, while avoiding the multitude of detailed justifications of subordinate points, which often make the original text terse and difficult to traverse.

To assist with the understanding of a passage and help the reading of it become more economical, *titles* are given to arguments and subarguments, and they are placed at the very top, above the most general conclusions. Titles are put in bold, to distinguish them from the theses.

At the beginning of the analysis of a section of the ancient work, a synopsis is given of the arguments which follow in that section. These synopses also serve the function of relating the content of that section to previous and subsequent ones.

The examples that follow illustrate a stratification of justifications in the form of the Arguments and Theses Module. In Example 1, only the titles of the arguments in the passage are given; in Example 2, the titles and the top-level thesis of the same passage; and in Example 3, all levels of the argument-hierarchy are included.

> **1. DISTINCTION OF MIXING FROM GENERATION, CORRUPTION,**
> **ALTERATION, AND GROWTH: 3327b10-22**
> > **1. Theses Aristotle commits himself to:**
> > > **1. Mixing versus destruction:**
> > > **2. Mixing versus growth:**
> > > **3. Mixing versus generation:**
> > > **4. Mixing versus being affected:**
> > > **5. Mixing versus compresence in a subject:**
> > > **6. Mixing versus the state the universe is in:**

Example 1: Level 1 only of the Arguments and Theses analysis of Aristotle's *Generation and Corruption*, Book I, Chapter 10 (3327b10-22).

> **1. DISTINCTION OF MIXING FROM GENERATION, CORRUPTION,**
> **ALTERATION, AND GROWTH: 3327b10-22**
> > **1. Theses Aristotle commits himself to:**
> > > **1. Mixing versus destruction:**
> > > > 1. [Mixing is not destruction.]
> > > **2. Mixing versus growth:**
> > > > 1. [Mixing is not growth.]
> > > **3. Mixing versus generation:**
> > > > 1. [Mixing is not generation.]
> > > **4. Mixing versus being affected:**
> > > > 1. *A property or a disposition is not mixed with the subject to which it belongs accidentally.*
> > > **5. Mixing versus compresence in a subject:**
> > > > 1. *None of the non-separables can have been mixed [together, when compresent in a subject].*
> > > **6. Mixing versus the state the universe is in:**
> > > > 1. *Mixing cannot be between all things in the universe. It cannot be, despite what some say, that at one time everything was together and mixed.*

Example 2: Level 1 only of the Arguments and Theses analysis of Aristotle's *Generation and Corruption*, Book I, Chapter 10 (3327b10-22).

The breadth of meaning, or better, of content of the original text in a given passage is explored in the *Alternative Interpretations Module*. Here the purpose is to capture received opinions in the history of the explanation of a passage regarding what that passage says. But the format of this module is not that of a commentary or of a collection of commentaries. Generally, the Archelogos database is not, and should not be thought of as a commentary, particularly a commentary of the traditional form — a monograph. The main difference is that a monograph usually centers on the interpretation of a central theory of the ancient author, and covers several chapters looking at it from different perspectives, and offering evidence in different contexts in support of that interpretation. In Archelogos, the area of focus is the passage rather than the theory of the ancient author. Readings of a passage are registered and commented on, and only vicariously, via the discussion of one or several passages, will reference be made to interpretations that do not address focally a passage, but a theory of the ancient author.

---

1. **DISTINCTION OF MIXING FROM GENERATION, CORRUPTION, ALTERATION, AND GROWTH: 3327b10-22**
  1. **Theses Aristotle commits himself to:**
    1. Mixing versus destruction:
      1. [Mixing is not destruction.]
        1. For example, the burning of wood is not the mixing of wood with fire, nor the mixing of wood with its parts.
  2. **Mixing versus growth:**
    1. [Mixing is not growth.]
      1. For example, in digestion, food is not being mixed with the body.
  3. **Mixing versus generation:**
    1. [Mixing is not generation.]
      1. For example, shape does not mix with wax to form the lump of wax.
  4. **Mixing versus being affected:**
    1. A property or a disposition is not mixed with the subject to which it belongs accidentally. Because:
    1. Body is not mixed with white when it is white.
    2. We see that the affections and dispositions are preserved when they come to belong to a subject {whereas, things that are mixed do not remain in actuality like the body and its (327b29-30) whiteness.}
  5. **Mixing versus compresence in a subject:**
    1. None of the non-separables can have been mixed [together, when compresent in a subject].
      1. Because when two things are mixed each must exist as a separable thing.
        1. [Because only if separable, will they be composite material things.]
          1. [Because non-separable things can't be composite.]
            1. [On pain of infinite regress.]
    2. [And only if composite, will they be capable of change.]
      1. [Aristotle's theory of change requires a substratum to underlie all change.]
        1. [Because there is no generation ex nihilo.]
    3. [And change is necessary for mixing,]
      1. {Because if the mixants do not alter, they will be no more mixed after, than they were before.(327a-b2)}
      2. But no affection is separable.
        1. [Fundamental principle of Aristotle's metaphysics.]

> 2. For example, whiteness and knowledge cannot have
> been mixed [together, when compresent in a subject].
> 6. Mixing versus the state of the universe:
>   1. Mixing cannot be between all things in the universe. It cannot
>   be, despite what some say, that at one time everything was
>   together and mixed.
>   1. Because [as we saw in the previous argument]affections are
>   not capable of being mixed.

Example 3: All Levels of the Arguments and Theses analysis of Aristotle's *Generation and Corruption*, Book I, Chapter 10 (3327b10-22).

The primary interest in the Alternative Interpretations Module is to capture different contents ascribed to the passage under examination. Furthermore, the strengths or weaknesses of the reported readings of the passage are discussed, and the validity of arguments attributed to the ancient author, under specific interpretations of that passage, is appraised. The subdivisions in the Alternative Interpretations Module follow the corresponding subdivisions of that passage in the Arguments and Theses Module; but here there can be additional divisions. Specific interpretations are headed by the name of the scholar who proposed them, and discussions of them by the Archelogos analyst are headed by the label "Comment". Notes can be attached to discussion in both, the Argument and Theses Module and the Alternative Interpretations Module (See Example 4 for a sample of this module).

---

1. DISTINCTION OF MIXING FROM GENERATION, CORRUPTION, ALTERATION, AND GROWTH: 327b10-22
    1. **Theses Aristotle commits himself to:**
        (i) **What the examples are examples of:**

Williams: He (p. 143) thinks that these cases of non-mixing are mentioned by Aristotle as instances of the three cases in the Impossibility of Mixing Argument (327a34-b6). For example, the supposition that wood is mixed when burning corresponds to case 2 of the Argument, namely that the one item — wood — is destroyed when mixed while the other — fire — survives. The supposition that the body is mixed with white when it becomes white corresponds to case 1 of the Argument, namely that both items continue existing, etc. According to Williams, since Aristotle recognizes that such cases are not considered as instances of mixing, they are used by Aristotle to show that none of the cases described in the Impossibility of Mixing Argument, which are supposed to be cases of mixing, is one we would consider as a genuine instance of mixing. Presumably then, the Argument fails to show anything about mixing.

Philoponus: He (189.22-29) also believes that Aristotle is providing these examples to illustrate the three cases of the Impossibility of Mixing Argument. (But he does register some reservations, based on Aristotle's language in introducing these examples.)

Comment: It is not clear what Aristotle would gain by Williams' strategy. The Impossibility of Mixing Argument aims at exhausting all the metaphysical possibilities of change, showing that none of them is mixing. If Aristotle added that we do not consider these cases instances of mixing this would not challenge the conclusion of the argument, namely that there is no mixing. The reason is that if the argument is *exhaustive* of all change, and mixing was not mentioned as one of the cases, then, indeed, there is no mixing.

That this is the line of argumentation that Aristotle follows is strengthened by that fact that Aristotle subsequently (327b22-31) challenges the Impossibility of Mixing Argument by showing that it is not exhaustive: there is a case of change which it did not consider, namely, changing from an actual state to a potential state.

Scaltsas: Aristotle's listing of the examples in this passage is not addressing the Impossibility of Mixing Argument. Rather, it seems that Aristotle is using these examples to show us that none of the types of change which he has already examined in the *Generation and Corruption*, such as generation, corruption, alteration, and growth, fits what we, and he, would call mixing; for which reason he needs to proceed with a metaphysical account of mixing in the present Chapter.

Philoponus (190.12-15, 190.21) remarks that the examples also serve to distinguish between mixing and growth, generation, and alteration.

(ii) **The preservation of affections:**

Scaltsas: By saying that "the affections and dispositions are preserved when they come to belong to a subject" (327b16-17) Aristotle is not making an ontological claim that the affections survive as *distinct* entities within the subjects which they affect. He is not committing himself, in other words, to the ontological view that substances are clusters of compresent affections. Aristotle is saying here that, whereas e.g. in the case of mixing the white and the red dyes the resulting dye is pink, when flesh receives the color white, the result is *white flesh* — white is preserved. However it is that white and flesh combine into "white flesh", they do so without the first losing its whiteness or, for that matter, the second its fleshiness. This distinguishes this case from a case of a mixture, such as the pink dye, which is neither white nor red.

Example 4: Alternative Interpretations of Aristotle's *Generation and Corruption*, Book I, Chapter 10 (3327b10-22).

Searches in the Archelogos Database

We have discussed so far the utility of the form in which the philosophical material is presented in the database. A second general aspect of the database which is of philosophical utility is the possibility of searches that can be conducted in it. This is an aspect of the database which is still in embryonic form and will be developed by *artificial intelligence* specialists.

Although one can of course conduct the normal word searches in the database, this is but an elementary facility by comparison to what the database will be able to offer in the future. The first attempt will be to explore the possibility of searching for *concepts* and for *philosophical positions*. This will minimally involve searching for groups of expressions related to a concept, or to two or three concepts. But it might also involve the introduction of codes, or of tagging of occurrences of terms in different passages of the translated text. A further intention is to explore the possibility of classifying the arguments, both in the Arguments and Theses Module and in the Alternative Interpretations Module, so as to make it possible for users to discover arguments of interest to them on the basis of the nature of these arguments, before they know the content of the arguments.

As the Archelogos database will provide the only ground for exploring by electronic means what an ancient philosopher said according to an interpretation, this will allow the tracing of the occurrence of arguments across the history of philosophy in a way that has not been implementable previously.

Theoretical Issues Regarding the Archelogos Method

There are three issues I wish to address here, regarding the Archelogos method, particularly as developed in the Arguments and Theses Module. These will be the topic of research of cognitive scientists/ artificial intelligence specialists for Project Archelogos.

a. Propositional Attitudes

The first issue concerns the mode of presentation of a thesis in the original text, which was an issue raised by the classical philosophers who participated at the second Archelogos Conference, in Corfu, August, 1994. The normal expectation is that a philosopher asserts the positions they examine in the work under investigation. But assertion is not the only mode of presentation of positions that the author examines in the work. For example, the author may entertain a position for its merits and demerits. Or they may be disinclined to accept, but yet not reject, a position. Or they may recommend a position. Furthermore, a position might not be spelled out by description, but only suggested in a metaphor, an example, a thought experiment, or a myth. A way will be found to classify these propositional attitudes so that the reader of the Arguments and Theses Modules understands the mode in which a philosophical position is delivered by the author.

b. Because-Statements

There are intriguing and important questions raised by the nature of the because-statements that will require considerable research to explore and resolve. I have come to appreciate the dimensions of this problem in the course of the Archelogos-analysis of Aristotle's *Generation and Corruption*, in which I have been engaged for some months now. Originally, the idea behind the because-statements was that they should capture the general notion of justification which is operational in philosophy. Namely, the intention was to classify into a group all statements such as could be found in philosophical works supporting a position, i.e. statements which could well start with the connective "because". These include formal proofs, evidence, thought experiments, elaborations of the concepts in the original thesis, etc.

The questions regarding because-statements arise from the realization that a because-statement may be one of a number of types of justification, and concern one of a number of different aspects of the original thesis. Consider, for example, the following statement:

(P)   The sun has risen.

The because-statement of P could be any one of the following, which belong to various types of justification:

(B1)   Because it is already noon.
(B2)   Because if it is bright the sun has risen, and it is bright.
(B3)   Because the sun has risen east of our town.
(B4)   Because "rising" is the emergence of the sun in the sky.
(B5)   Because in a possible world with different laws of nature it would not be the sun that had not risen at noon, but Twin-sun.
(B6)   Because the sun was causally determined to rise.
(B7)   Because we are describing the phenomenon from the Earth's perspective.
(B8)   Because I am not hallucinating.
(B9)   Because there is a shadow.

But there is a further division between the aspects within each type. Thus within what we might broadly call the justification of the phenomenon with physical accounts, we might encounter accounts such as the following:

(B10)   Because the sun came over the horizon line.
(B11)   Because the earth revolves.
(B12)   Because the world was not annihilated.
(B13)   Because the sun is in proximity of the Earth.
(B14)   Because space is transparent.
(B15)   Because nothing prevented the sun from rising.
(B16)   Because the universe is still expanding.

The choice of the because-statement depends on what the philosopher sees as required for what they want to justify about the thesis in question.

The variety of types of justification of the original thesis, and the variety of themes about the original thesis which can be justified, make it clear that there is an arbitrariness about what is offered as the justification of a thesis. The choice is inexhaustible, and in this sense no justification of a thesis could offer the full range of reasons for holding it.

In view of this, it would be useful to think of the justification of a statement in terms of a field of because-statements, where no listing of them could exhaust the field. Thus a *justification-field* would be similar to a causal-field. The most prominent lesson to learn from this parallel is that just as a cause is always chosen against the background of the field of causes responsible for a phenomenon, similarly a because-statement is chosen against the background of the field of justification-statements of a thesis. The because-statement chosen is selected to fit the justification context. The context is important insofar as different contexts might go hand in hand with different *types of justification*. Correspondingly, what is selected as the cause of a phenomenon depends on the context of the causal account, e.g., laboratory experimentation, or popularized science, or everyday social context.

The question is not that of logical validity. For instance, thesis P is validly derived from B3. But the justification can be made more wholesome by supplementing it with, e.g., (B1), (B11), etc. The incompleteness of any justification of a thesis can be compensated for by the appropriateness of certain types of justification versus other types, *given a context*. This is an area in philosophy that needs to be studied further, but I believe that we cannot expect results that will make the case of because-justification any more precise than the case of listing the causes of a phenomenon. In both there is an element of what is taken for granted in the context, and what the practice of that context is. In ancient philosophy, the context might be determined by the practice of each philosopher in offering arguments. Thus, we might expect certain premises to be mentioned if the justification is Aristotle's, rather than Plato's, either because these premises cannot be assumed as held by Aristotle, or because Aristotle usually makes his position clear on such an issue, or because he is raising that issue in that passage, etc. The scholar offering an interpretation of an ancient text will have to develop a sensitivity to the practice of argumentation of the author of that text and "restore" the arguments in accordance with that practice. Thus, there will be a conception of a *satisfactory justification* for that ancient philosopher, and the scholar will endeavor to restore justifications of theses to that standard of satisfactoriness.

It was decided at the first meeting of Project Archelogos, in Delphi, 1993, that it was a strength of the because-statement analysis of prose into arguments that it is theory-free. The concern was to avoid a process that would be theory-biased, and therefore controversial; Archelogos should adopt a theory-neutral method as the basic tool of analysis. Nevertheless, as I advance in the analysis of the *Generation and Corruption*, it is becoming clear to me that it would be useful to introduce a method of *tagging* because-statements according to the type of entry that that "because" is. Keeping "because" as the entry into justification retains the generality of the notion of justification. But having retained that convention, the user would find it useful to be oriented as to what type of information is being introduced by a be-cause-statement. This would also alert the user to what type of information might be missing from the justification.

I further believe that, depending on how successful the tagging-codification is, this might be a source of extremely interesting research on the classification of the ancient method of argumentation, which would be made possible through the database and the searches it would facilitate. The area of categories of because-statements is one of the subjects that will be investigated by research into the cognitive science aspects of the Archelogos method.

c. Multiple Conclusions and the Flow of the Argument

The third question about the Archelogos type of analysis which came to my attention while applying the method to Aristotle is the place-ment of the additional conclusions that follow from an argument in that argument. These conclusions might be of varying degree of gen-erality, and therefore belong internally to different parts of the argu-ment. Also, more reasons might be given supporting these further conclusions, in addition to what was given in the argument they are appended to. The question that arises is: where should these con-clusions be placed?

Two options recommend themselves, with different merits each. The first is that the additional conclusions be placed separately, fol-lowing the argument; since they are supported by sub-arguments in the original argument, these sub-arguments should be repeated to support that conclusion. The disadvantage of this approach is that it breaks up an complex argument into many, whereas the very purpose of the Archelogos method is to capture in the presentation of complex arguments the cohesiveness that characterizes their logical fiber.

The obvious alternative is to introduce the additional conclusions into the argument which they follow. But here is where the surprise manifested itself. The introduction of the additional conclusions, their additional, partial, justifications, interrupts what, for lack of a more descriptive expression, I will call the *flow of the argument*. To break the flow of the argument is not a logical sacrifice, but a psychological one, which should not be given up. After all, that the ancient author de-cided, in the case of Aristotle, to place these conclusions outside the main argument does indicate a preference for the preservation of the flow, at the expense of placing conclusions where they belong logi-cally.

I believe that the phenomenon of the flow of the argument should be investigated for its own sake. It is clear that it has pedagogical value, probably also heuristic value, and it would not be so surprising if it turned out to have further philosophical significance.

90

The Educational Application of Archelogos: LogAnalysis

Project Archelogos has created an educational application of its method of analysis for university students and advanced high school students. Plato's *Protagoras* was chosen for this application because of its broad appeal across the educational domain. Although the original intention was to simply replicate the Archelogos database in a much smaller scale, it soon became clear to the Archelogos team that the whole approach of an educational database should be different. The reason for this was that the educational database was not addressing users who were dedicated ancient philosophy researchers, as the Archelogos database is. Therefore the motivation to use the database could not be assumed in the educational case. To accommodate for this difference, we redesigned the database, changing the format, adding features, and introducing new types of modules.

The most important presentation change was that whereas Archelogos is built on a hypertext environment, LogAnalysis, the educational application of Archelogos, was built on a multimedia environment, which, apart from hypertext capabilities, also allows for the inclusion of sound and images.

Apart from the change in the presentation environment, changes were also introduced to the philosophical method, and the content of the LogAnalysis database. The changes in the method aim at generating interest in the user to read the Platonic dialogue, and enter the interpretation debates. The changes in the content aim at supplying information that will assist the user in understanding the problems at hand, but also further stimulate the interest by placing the user within the era when the dialogue was written.

The new element of methodology was the introduction of the *Dialogical Presentation Module*. This is the first module that the user is invited to enter, in which the user is taken through the main arguments of the *Protagoras*, in an interactive environment, being invited to chose philosophical positions in the process. These positions are revealed to agree with, or oppose, the positions taken by Socrates or Protagoras in the text, which engages the user in a virtual dialogue with the protagonists of the work. All along the interactive process, the user can follow the progress made by this exchange in an argument-tree of the *Protagoras*, which follows the steps that the user is taking in their virtual dialogue with the protagonists. In this way the user is engaged in the issues that are debated in the dialogue, forms a conceptual map of the argumentation of the dialogue, and learns about the basic philosophical positions of the interlocutors.

The changes of content concern philosophical knowledge on the one hand, and broader, background knowledge on the other. With reference to the first, apart from the Arguments and Theses Module, and the Alternative Interpretations Module, where abstracts are provided to help the user along, there is an additional module, the Commentary Module. In this module, the user finds explanations of contemporary philosophical terminology and issues which are essential for the understanding of the discussion of the dialogue in the alternative interpretations. Also, the main debates of the *Protagoras* are related to current concerns in philosophy, so as to bring to the attention the user the issues that are still alive in philosophy, and how they connect.

Finally, a major body of the LogAnalysis database is devoted to the *Cultural Archive*. Here the user will find numerous entries relating to the philosophical, historical, cultural aspects of what is discussed in the *Protagoras*, and of life in ancient Greece. The entries are concise, and where possible, accompanied by pictures, maps, diagrams, and sound. This provides a rich environment for the introduction of the user to the content of the dialogue, and to the dialogue's philosophical and cultural era.

LogAnalysis will be published in CD in 1998, and it is hoped that it will also be made available on the Internet. Further works of ancient philosophy will also be analysed and presented in the LogAnalysis format, for use in broader educational contexts than Archelogos.

COMPUTERS, VISUALIZATION, AND THE NATURE OF REASONING

JON BARWISE AND JOHN ETCHEMENDY[1]

The computer is bringing about a revolution in our understanding of inference, representation, and reasoning, some of the most fundamental notions of logic. The revolution is far from complete, but we think the direction is clear enough. In this article we describe how the computer led the two of us first to change the way we teach elementary logic, and eventually to rethink basic assumptions about the subject matter of our discipline. We think the story is a remarkable case study of the synergy between teaching, technology, and research.

Some Autobiography

Our story begins in 1983 when we both returned to Stanford from teaching at other universities. Elementary logic instruction is part of the bread-and-butter teaching in Stanford's philosophy department, as it is in most philosophy departments. There is a difference, though, because Stanford has a long tradition of using computers in logic instruction. This dates back to the late 1960's, when Patrick Suppes introduced his program *Valid* into Philosophy 57, Stanford's elementary logic course. This program ran on a mainframe computer devoted to nothing else, and provided students with an entire course of instruction in introductory logic. Like most logic courses offered from the 60's through the 80's, it focused on teaching the basic syntactic rules of proof in a formal calculus. Unlike most, it covered the subject in considerable depth, delving into axiomatic systems of some sophistication.

Over the years, thousands of Stanford students learned logic from *Valid*. While one section of Philosophy 57 was always "person taught" — for computer-phobic students — the bulk of elementary logic instruction was shouldered by Suppes' pioneering program. This freed most of the Stanford philosophy faculty from the burden of teaching elementary logic. In particular, the two of us could teach more advanced and interesting logic courses. That first year we taught courses in computability (Turing machines, recursive functions, undecidablity) and mathematical logic (truth, models, soundness, completeness).

In the winter of 1984, the same year we returned to Stanford, Apple Computer introduced its Macintosh. The graphical capabilities of the Macintosh immediately captured our imagination as a way to solve some basic pedagogical problems we had encountered in these logic courses. One problem in teaching computability had to do with Turing machines, a model of computation developed in the thirties by the famous logician Alan Turing, and a fundamental notion in theoretical computer science. The problem was the difficulty of giving students a real sense of the power of Turing machines. Since Turing machines get extremely complicated extremely fast, the only exercises we could assign (and have any hope of grading) were toy problems that called for the construction of very simple machines. And even with these simple machines students often failed to get them right, due to the difficulty of verifying that a particular machine did what it was supposed to do. For many students the gap between the problems they could hope to solve with pencil and paper and the evident power of the modern computer made many claims in the course seem farfetched. For example, students were led to accept Church's Thesis, the claim that Turing machines can compute any function that can be calculated by mechanical or algorithmic means, more on the basis of our authority than on the basis of their own appreciation of the incredible power of these machines.

The problem in mathematical logic was of a very different sort. In our classes many students who had been quite successful in constructing proofs using *Valid*, students who should have understood the symbolic language in which those proofs were couched, in fact had great difficulty grasping the very intuitive notion of truth in a structure. This lack of understanding evidenced itself repeatedly. For example, students would make egregious errors in translating between sentences of English and sentences of first-order logic, errors that would have been inconceivable had they really understood the meanings of both sentences.

The Macintosh's graphical capabilities inspired us to tackle these problems in a new way. We envisioned tools that would facilitate the student's ability to visualize the abstract subject matter of logic, and thereby work more effectively with it. Over the next four years, funded by Stanford's Faculty Author Development project, we worked with teams of student programmers to develop programs we called *Turing's World* [Barwise and Etchemendy, 1993] and *Tarski's World* [Barwise and Etchemendy, 1991]. As hoped, these programs have been extremely successful in addressing the pedagogical problems at which they were aimed. What we did not expect, however, was that they would lead us to rethink the conceptual foundations of our subject. In order to explain this second result, we need to briefly describe the programs.

Turing's World

Introduced by Alan Turing in 1936, Turing machines are one of the key abstractions used in modern computability theory, the study of what computers can and cannot do. A Turing machine is a particularly simple model of the digital computer, one whose operations are limited to reading and writing symbols on a linear tape, or moving along the tape to the left or right. The tape is marked off into squares, each of which can be filled with at most one symbol. At any given point in its operation, the Turing machine can read or write on only one of these squares, the square located directly below its "read/ write" head.

In Turing's World the tape is represented by a narrow window that sits at the bottom of the screen. Figure 1 shows the tape with a series of A's and B's written on it, and with the read/write head located on the leftmost of these symbols.

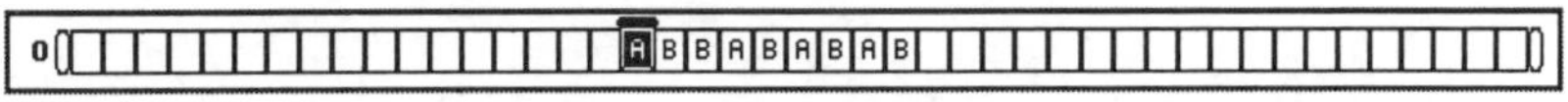

Figure 1. A tape from Turing's World.

A Turing machine has a finite number of states and is in exactly one of these states at any given time. Associated with these states are instructions telling the machine what action to perform if it is currently scanning a particular symbol, and what state to go into after performing this action. The states of a Turing machine are generally represented by a "flow" or "state" diagram, using circles for the states and labeled arcs for the instructions associated with those states. For example, Figure 2 on the next page shows the state diagram of a Turing machine with just two states. The linguistic description of this same machine would be given as follows:

> In state 0: if you see an A, move right and go into state 0.
> In state 0: if you see a B, move right and go into state 1.
> In state 1: if you see a B, move right and go into state 1.

or, in abbreviated "4-tuple" notation:

> 0, A, R, 0
> 0, B, R, 1
> 1, B, R, 1

95

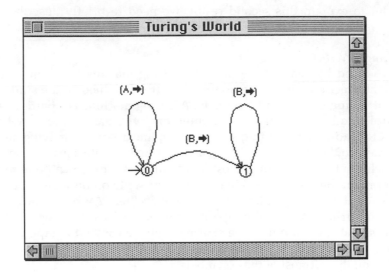

Figure 2. A simple Turing machine.

This machine will run down a string of A's and B's, stopping at the first A it sees after a B. For example, if run on the sample tape above, it would stop when it got to the fourth symbol from the left, because it would then be in state 1 with no instructions about what to do next.

In Turing's World, a collection of graphical tools lets you design Turing machines by directly drawing their state diagrams. When you run a Turing machine in Turing's World, the operation of the machine is displayed graphically, both on the tape and in the state diagram window. On the tape, the read/write head moves, making the changes required by the machine you've designed. In the state diagram, the nodes and arcs highlight to show the changing state of the computation. Turing's World also allows students to display the text-based "4-tuple" description of their machines, though we have found that they rarely do.

Despite their simplicity, Turing machines can be designed to compute remarkably complex functions. In fact, they are generally thought to be as powerful (in theory) as any possible computer. Finding out what they can do is half the fun of studying computability. Figure 3 shows part of the detail of a Turing machine that adds two numbers expressed in decimal notation.

96

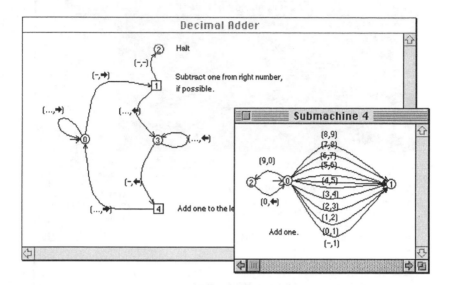

Figure 3. A Turing machine for adding in base 10.

The ability to design a Turing machine by simply drawing its state diagram, combined with the ability to run the machine and watch it go through its transitions, is a powerful aid in the student's understanding of the intuitive idea of a Turing machine. By allowing students to introduce submachines (as illustrated in Figure 3), the program lets them quickly build up a powerful arsenal of Turing machines and to combine them in important ways. In our classes we now routinely ask students to design a Universal Turing machine, a machine that acts as a fully programmable computer. This exercise is several orders of magnitude more complex than what we could expect of our students before the advent of Turing's World. Our students now learn to appreciate the power of Turing's abstract machines, and have fun while doing it.

Tarski's World
The goal of Tarski's World is to teach students the symbolic language at the core of modern, first-order logic. The program allows students to represent simple, three-dimensional worlds inhabited by geometric objects of various shapes and sizes, and to test first-order sentences to see whether they are true or false in those worlds. Figure 4 shows an example of such a world and some sentences (numbers 11–15 out of a longer list) that the student has been examining.

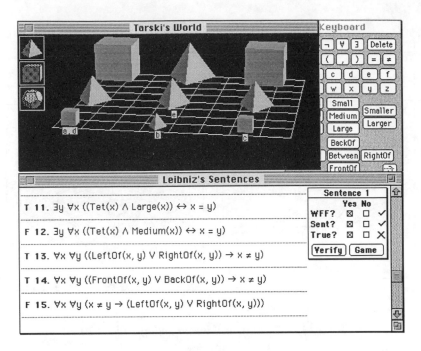

Figure 4. An example from Tarski's World.

As you can see from the T's and F's at the left, three of the displayed sentences are true, while two are false. Sentence 12, for example, is false: it claims that there is a unique, medium-sized tetrahedron, when in fact there are three such blocks in the depicted world. If students do not understand why the sentence is false, they can choose to play an interactive game that successively breaks down the claim into simpler constituent parts. Though we cannot demonstrate the game in a static description, its rules are based on the meanings of the symbols (quantifiers and connectives) of the language, and thereby drive home the real import of the sentence at issue. The game continues until the student's misunderstanding of the sentence becomes completely evident. Thus the student quickly identifies and corrects his or her own misconstruals of the language, rather than waiting for classroom help or, as we found to be so common, getting through the entire course without the problem being recognized.

Despite its simplicity, there are many ways that we use Tarski's World in teaching the language of first-order logic. Most straightforwardly, we give students exercises in which they are asked to evaluate a set of sentences in a given world. But we also give them a set of sentences and ask them to construct a world that makes the sentences all true. Or we start with a world and ask the students to express certain facts about the world in the first-order language. Tarski's World can also be used to show various kinds of non-entailments.

For instance, the example shown above proves that neither sentence 12 nor sentence 15 follows from 11, 13, and 14. Finally, it can be used for posing some interesting deduction problems, as we will see in a moment.

Visualization and reasoning

In using Turing's World in our teaching, we became enormously impressed by the cognitive power of the graphical representation of Turing machines over the more text-based, 4-tuple representation. There was no comparison between the two when it came to ease of design, understanding, or verification of Turing machines. While both modes of representation are available in Turing's World, students never resorted to the linguistic representation except when told to do so. This sparked our interest in the general topic of visual programming languages even before it become a lively topic in computer science.

We must confess, though, that we did not really grasp the revolutionary import for logic of what we were observing in our students. After all, we already knew that it was much easier to use the diagrammatic representation of a Turing machine: that is why we designed Turing's World with its graphical capabilities in the first place. The full import of what we had noticed only hit us with Tarski's World.

We mentioned earlier that in using Tarski's World, we assigned students exercises that required deductive reasoning for their solutions. In these problems, we would present a picture of a blocks world constructed in Tarski's World, as well as a list of sentences involving names, some of whose referents were not indicated in the picture. We would then ask students to deduce certain facts from the information they had been given.

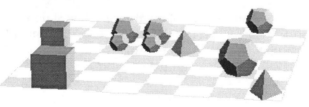

Figure 5. A blocks world.

An Example

For a simple example of this sort, consider the situation depicted in Figure 5. This figure shows us a world made up of blocks arranged on a chess board. The blocks come in three shapes (cubes, tetrahedra, and dodecahedra) and three sizes (small, medium, and large). Suppose our

99

goal is to determine as much as we can about two blocks, named *b* and *c*. Ideally we would be able to identify them in the picture. Failing that, we should at least figure out as much as we can about them.

Suppose we are initially given the following information:

> Nothing is on a square adjacent to block *b* and block *c* is not a cube.

Clearly on the basis of this information we cannot identify either of the blocks. We can rule out some possibilities, though. For example, *c* cannot be either of the cubes on the left, and *b* cannot be in the central grouping of five blocks, since each of them is adjacent to others. Indeed, a moment's thought shows that there are eight possible blocks that could be *c* and five for *b*, giving us a total of forty cases consistent with this information.

Suppose we are next given the following information:

> Block *c* is either small or large.

This information tells us nothing more about *b*, of course, but it does significantly narrow the range of possibilities for *c*. Given our earlier information, we now see that there are two cases to consider: *c* has to be either one of the two small dodecahedra in the center, or the large dodecahedron toward the front. We cannot tell which one it is, but nonetheless we can observe in each case that *c* is a dodecahedron.

Continuing, suppose we are given the following piece of evidence:

> Block *b* is farther back than either of the tetrahedra.

This tells us that *b* must be one of the three backmost dodecahedra. But since we already know that *b* is not in the central group of blocks, we can conclude that *b* is the lone dodecahedron at the back of the board. We have thus successfully identified *b*.

Suppose our final piece of information is:

> Block *b* is larger than block *c*.

We already know that *c* is either one of the two small dodecahedra or else the large dodecahedron up front. Since we now know that *b* is a medium-sized block, we can rule out the possibility that *c* is the large dodecahedron. However, we cannot rule out either of the other two possibilities. Thus *c* is one of the small dodecahedra, but we cannot tell which. Either of these cases is consistent with all our given information. Thus, in the end, we are left with two consistent cases, those depicted in Figure 6.

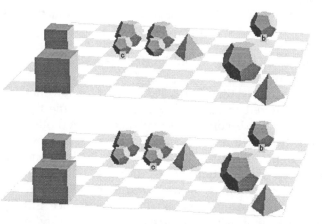

Figure 6. Two remaining possibilities.

Heterogeneous Reasoning
From a pedagogical point of view, exercises like this were quite effective, both in helping the students learn the first-order language (in our class, the English sentences used above would have been replaced by first-order sentences) and in developing some important reasoning skills. The students found the problems challenging but enjoyable, contrary to our experience with the sorts of proofs familiar from elementary logic courses. More important, we discovered that the exercises forced students to focus on the content of the reasoning tasks, rather than the syntactic form of the representations employed.

While this was all very positive, there was a down side. The reasoning students used in solving these problems was of a very different kind from that modeled in standard deductive systems. While it was quite clear when the students' reasoning was correct and when it was faulty, in neither case did it fit the patterns we had come to expect. In other words, the theory of reasoning we were preparing to teach our students seemed inadequate to account for the reasoning the students were already doing to solve the homework problems we set them with Tarski's World.

We explored various ways to treat this reasoning using traditional logic, the logic of first-order sentences. For example, we explored the possibility of considering the visual information presented by the diagram as an efficient way of encapsulating a very large set of sentences. There are two immediate problems with this idea. First, even when it is possible, there are many arbitrary choices to be made in going from a visual representation to a roughly equivalent set of sentences. What language do you use, with which predicates and relations? How do you represent the conclusions, which seem to have the indexical form "*that* block is *d*"? And from the infinite set of sentences true in the diagram, exactly which ones do you choose? In each case, the wrong decision would make the problem unsolvable, and so practically speaking, the conversion to traditional logic could only be accomplished *after* the problem had been solved. This process clearly bore no relation to what our students were doing, nor did it offer a practical tool that would aid them in the future.

The more interesting difficulty concerned the methods of reasoning encountered in this context. If you examine the steps in the above reasoning, it becomes evident that the methods are quite different from those we usually teach in logic. They have a distinctly "semantic" character, quite unlike the syntactically defined methods in formal systems of deduction. For example, you are as likely to break into cases based on atomic, negated or quantified sentences as you are on the basis of a disjunctive claim. As a consequence, attempts to represent the reasoning using sentences do not faithfully model the real character of the reasoning. Simple proofs explode into proofs involving hundreds of steps, proofs in which the key steps in the original reasoning are obscured or obliterated.

We did not abandon our attempt to fit this reasoning into the first-order formalism lightly. As they say, when all you have is a hammer, every problem looks like a nail. But the more we tried reducing the reasoning to sentential reasoning, reasoning amenable to traditional deductive systems, the more we became convinced that the attempted reduction was wrong-headed. Even when we could write down a set of sentences that arguably captured the key features of the blocks world diagram required in the students' reasoning, we realized that those sentences were in fact merely consequences of the diagram, and consequently that the inference from the diagram to the sentences was itself a matter of logic, could itself be valid or invalid. Thus there was a clear sense in which the reasoning our students found so natural was irreducibly *heterogeneous*, involving the interaction of two forms of representation: the Tarski's World diagrams and the first-order sentences. Using traditional sentential systems of deduction, we could at best model *parts* of that reasoning, and even that model did not seem faithful to the actual train of reasoning we witnessed in these exercises.

Looking back at our experience with Turing's World in light of our new-found respect for visualization, we realized that the phenomenon had been staring us in the face there as well. In that case every diagram did have a clear "sentential" counterpart (its 4-tuple representation) but the reasoning involved in constructing or verifying properties of a Turing machine was quite different with the two representational forms. For example, the diagrams make explicit any loops in the program, loops that are not evident in the 4-tuple representation. These loops correspond to recursion and call for proofs by induction. Simply looking at the state diagram leads you to expect when and where induction will be needed to verify a property of the represented machine. Looking at the 4-tuples gives you no such clue.

Once we were sensitized to the power of visualization in reasoning, we realized that it is far more pervasive than we had ever imagined. In everyday life we get information from a variety of sources and in a variety of forms. An important component of everyday reasoning consists in combining these variously presented forms of information. Imagine going to the visitor information center in a city you have never visited and asking for directions. To find your way, you will need to combine the linguistic information from the informant with the visual information gathered from the scenes that unfold before you. Every scientific and engineering discipline has its own system or systems for visualizing information in problem solving, from chemistry's molecular diagrams to geometrical diagrams to ordinary maps and blueprints.

We were reminded, too, that over the years a handful of logicians, most notably Euler, Venn, and Peirce, had stressed the importance and interest of nonsentential inference. The diagrams of Euler and Venn, both of which use circles to represent collections of objects, are still widely known and used, even though their expressive power is sorely limited. C. S. Peirce, inspired by the utility of molecular diagrams in reasoning about chemical compounds, developed a more intricate and powerful diagrammatic formalism. While Peirce's system has not won over many human users, it has become an important tool in computer science.

We also looked at the so-called "analytical reasoning" problems posed on standardized tests like the Graduate Record Examination (GRE) and the Law School Aptitude Test (LSAT). These problems are logical puzzles, but the natural way to attack them is almost always to find a good way to represent the information diagrammatically and to use the diagram in reasoning through to a solution. Casting the problem into standard propositional or first-order notation typically obscures the situation, making the solution even harder to find.

An Example

Let's look at an example in some detail. The following analytical reasoning problem is adapted from Summers [*New Puzzles in Logical Deduction,* 1968].

> Bob, his sister Carol, son Ted, and daughter Alice, are all chess players. The best player's twin and the worst player are of the opposite sex. The best player and the worst player are the same age. Can you determine who is best and who is worst?

If one approaches this puzzle as a problem in first-order logic, its so-lution is quite difficult. However, if you use everyday representational devices, the solution is easy to find. We use symbols according to the following conventions:

Using this system of representations, we apply the first sentence of the problem to infer the following diagram, depicting the basic family re-lationships:

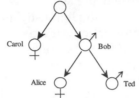

There are various ways to proceed at this point. The most straight-forward is to break into four cases, depending on which of the four people is the best chess player. Indicating the best player with a **B** and the worst with a **W**, we end up with the following four diagrams.

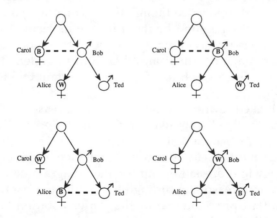

Three of these turn out to be inconsistent with the information that the best player and the worst player are the same age, since a father can-not be the same age as his children. The only one that is possible is the third, in which Carol is the worst and Alice is the best.

What to do?

By 1988 we had collected and studied many examples of valid rea-soning that did not fit within the confines of logic it is normally un-derstood. This was both exciting and unsettling. Like most logicians, we thought we understood the basic methods of reasoning, methods like conditional proof, proof by contradiction, proof by cases, and universal generalization. But here were methods of reasoning used every day, methods every bit as basic and important, that did not fit into the conceptual framework with which we were working. Whereas the traditional methods are grouped around the so-called "logical operators," these new methods seemed to have nothing to do with them. Some of the methods had to do with taking information in sentential form and applying it to modify a diagram, or observing information in a diagram and expressing it with a sentence. Others involved breaking into a range of cases, not on the basis of a disjunctive sentence, but rather on the basis of other kinds of information.

What to do in the face of this discrepancy between logical theory and empirical observation? Rewrite the theory? That was not possible. All we really had were several examples that did not fit comfortably into the current theory. We did not yet have a framework for thinking about, let alone presenting, a richer theory that would encompass all the forms of valid reasoning we found in the wild. But our case studies showed that there were certain methods of reasoning using diagrammatic information combined with sentences that were widely applicable, methods we called observe, apply, exhaustive cases, and so forth.

We became convinced that these principles were at work in reasoning involving many kinds of diagrams and visualization, that these methods were as important as the familiar sentential methods, and that we should be teaching them to our students. For this reason, we initiated the development of a third courseware project, *Hyperproof*, to make it possible to teach these methods of reasoning in addition to the more traditional, sentential methods. We also wrote a paper [Barwise and Etchemendy, "Visual Information and Valid Resoning," 1990] making the philosophical case for the legitimacy of diagrammatic representations in rigorous reasoning, and a more technical paper [Barwise and Etchemendy, "Information, Infons and Inference," 1989] sketching the beginnings of a theoretical framework for understanding such reasoning.

Hyperproof

In Figure 7, we show a simple proof constructed by a student using Hyperproof. This is a proof in which we are given some initial information and asked to determine whether it follows that blocks *d* and *e* are in the same row. As it turns out, it does, and the proof shows this to be the case.

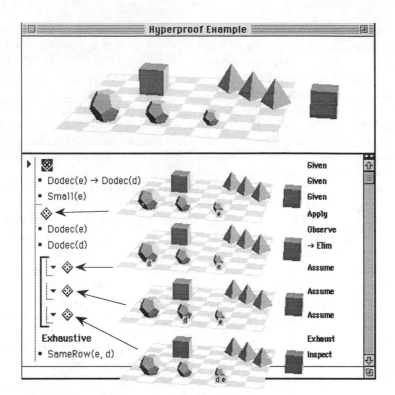

Figure 7. A proof in Hyperproof.

The initial information is given in the diagram at the top of the figure, plus the two sentences marked as **Given**. The diagram is self-explanatory, except for the meaning of the block depicted to the right of the chess board. This is Hyperproof's way of indicating that this block's location is unknown. The block depicted has a location on the chess board, but the diagram does not tell us where. (Hyperproof has devices for indicating partial information about size and shape, as well.)

The two given sentences assert, first, that d is a dodecahedron if e is, and second, that e is small. The first step in the proof applies this second piece of information to identify e as the one small block in the depicted situation. The student then observes that e is indeed a dodecahedron. This allows the student to conclude that d is a dodecahedron as well. Since there are three dodecahedra, there are three possible cases the student must consider. But in each of these, one can observe that d and e happen to be in the same row. Hence the conclusion follows.

If we change the initial diagram slightly, then the conclusion would no longer follow. In Figure 8 we have changed the unlocated block to a dodecahedron. In this proof, the student has started in the same way as before, but has discovered that the unlocated block might be *d*. This provides a possible counterexample to the claim that *d* and *e* are in the same row. By placing this block in a different row, the student constructs a possible case in which the premises are true but the purported conclusion is false.

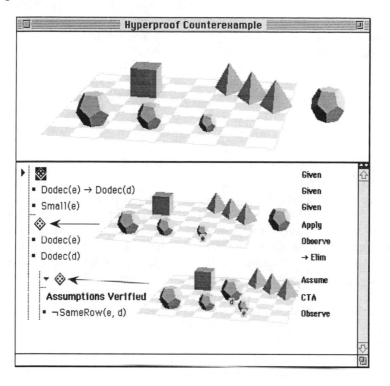

Figure 8: A proof of nonconsequence.

An interesting feature of Hyperproof is that it naturally gives rise to many different types of reasoning problems, types that are reflected in the 27 distinct kinds of goals that can be presented with a problem. In addition to the usual problem of the form "show that such-and-such follows from so-and-so," we can ask "does such-and-such follow from so-and-so?" or "show that such-and-such does not follow from so-and-so." More interestingly, we can have goals that are expressible only using the diagram, like "can you determine the size of the specified block?" or "can you identify the specified block?" These examples, special as they are to Hyperproof, showed us just how limiting the traditional notion of proof is when it comes to real-world reasoning and problem solving. Of the 27 types of goals available in Hyperproof, only one (the first mentioned above) fits naturally into standard treatments of logic.

Toward a Theory of Reasoning

As we said earlier, a theory of inference rich enough to encompass the use of both diagrams and language does not yet exist, but its shape is beginning to emerge. In this final section we want to give our best guess as to the broad shape of this theory and the place the traditional theory will take within the enriched theory.

Reasoning, Proofs, and Problem-Solving

Two of the key concepts of modern logic are the notions of proof and counterexample (in the form of a model or structure). A proof is used to demonstrate that some piece of information follows from the given information; a counterexample is used to demonstrate that it does not. Notice, however, that these notions do not model reasoning itself, but only two of its possible outcomes.

To see what is left out, think of the legal process. Proofs are the stock-in-trade of the prosecuting attorney, whose aim is to demonstrate that the defendant is guilty. Counterexamples are a standard tool of the defense attorney, whose job is to show that the defendant's guilt has not been established by the evidence. What is left out is the prior role of the detective, who tries to use the available evidence to figure out who is guilty and who is not.

When Sherlock Holmes tries to solve a murder case, he does not start out trying to prove that the butler did it. Rather, his goal is to discover the identity of the murderer, no matter who he or she might be. There is a space of possible suspects and the evidence available to Holmes will either rule out all but one of the suspects, or else be insufficient to determine the murderer. Of course it is not in general a simple matter to figure out which is the case, which is why Holmes is famous for his deductive abilities.

It is often said that modern logic was designed with mathematical reasoning as its paradigm. We think this is not entirely accurate, since the theory provides no better an account of the mathematician's reasoning than it does of everyday reasoning and problem solving. Rather, it is based on the paradigm of mathematical communication: the rigorous proofs (or disproofs) by which one mathematician communicates results to another. This is why the theory, as important as it may be, yields neither a practical tool nor an accurate model of the real-life process of reasoning.

A more accurate and useful theory of reasoning will provide deductively correct methods that can be applied without antecedent knowledge of the ultimate outcome of the reasoning. In other words, the methods should further the goals of the reasoning whether or not they end up producing a proof or a disproof, and whether or not you know ahead of time the specific claim you may ultimately derive. To a limited extent, semantic tableaux have this characteristic: you can apply these methods to a selected sentence to see whether or not it is a consequence of some others. But you still need to choose a specific claim — say, "the butler did it" — before you can apply the method. The deductive system built into Hyperproof shares this advantage of the tableaux method, but also allows you to reason to an initially unspecified conclusion and to do so using information expressed in nonsentential form.

Exploration, Information, and Possibilities

When thinking about reasoning and problem solving, a useful metaphor is that of exploration: to solve a reasoning problem, we explore a space of possible situations or worlds consistent with the initial information we are given. Exploration in this context is the attempt to discover information *about* this space of possibilities, information about what it contains, where the boundaries lie, and so forth.

Sentences, whether of English or of first-order logic, partition this space of possibilities, dividing it up into fiefdoms with a multitude of overlapping claims. The study of traditional logic deals with the relations among these claims. Thus, traditional proof techniques allow us to add to a collection of sentences that characterize a set of possibilities, additional sentences that also hold in that set. In this way we can show that the latter information, the information carried by the new sentences, was implicit in the former. The discovery of a counterexample, in contrast, exhibits possible situations consistent with the given information but which falsify the hypothesis in question. In this way we show that the hypothesis is *not* a consequence of the given.

When we view reasoning in this way, it is clear where diagrams and visualization fit in. Diagrams, like sentences, carry information: they carve up the same space of possibilities, though perhaps in very different ways. A good diagram, for example, may represent information in a form that is particularly appropriate for the subject matter at hand, one that allows you to visualize and manipulate the information more readily than would a collection of sentences or even a different sort of diagram. Diagrams useful for depicting relations among sets, say Euler circles, are very different from those used for depicting the structure of a building to be built. The one takes advantage of the inclusion relation among sets; the other takes advantage of spatial relations among parts of a building.

By focusing on sentences, to the exclusion of all other forms of representation, we have neglected one of the most striking facts about the process of reasoning: the heterogeneity of ways in which people represent information in this process. Maps, charts, diagrams, and other nonsentential forms of representation can be, and often are, of equal importance to sentences. Reasoning typically involves the manipulation of information represented both in sentences and various kinds of diagrams. The diagrams play a crucial and legitimate role in both the way the information is presented and in the reasoning itself. This fact has been appreciated in computer science — indeed, database theory is largely the study of the logic of various forms of representation that do not fit neatly into the sentential paradigm. But there is more to be understood about the logic of alternate forms of representation, and it is the natural business of logic to undertake this task.

Efficiency, Informativeness, and Complexity

We try to teach our students to be efficient reasoners. But just what does this mean? When reasoning results in a proof, there is an inverse relationship between the efficiency and the complexity of the proof — the latter being measured by some combination of length and maximal depth of nested subproofs. The less complex a proof, the more efficient it is. On the other hand, when reasoning results in a counterexample, there is no ready measure of its complexity, except perhaps size. But the size of a counterexample is not a good measure of the efficiency with which it was discovered.

Our metaphor of reasoning as exploration of a space of possibilities gives another potential metric for efficiency. In this context, more information corresponds to fewer possibilities. To put it the other way around, the more possibilities eliminated by a given proof, or by a given step within a proof, the more information one has extracted, and so the more efficient one is being. Consider, for example, the game of guessing a number between 1 and 100, where you are only allowed to ask "yes/no" questions. A very inefficient method is to ask "Is the number 1?" "Is the number 2?" and so on. The most efficient method is to ask questions like "Is the number greater than 50?" and so on. While the former method eliminates only one number at a time, the latter cuts the possibilities in half. On average, this second method will arrive at the solution faster, though of course users of the first sometimes get lucky.

The notion of informativeness implicit in this strategy is at the basis of Shannon-Weaver communication theory, in which the amount of information in a signal is measured by the number of possibilities eliminated by the signal. The same idea can be used to guide reasoning strategies. In general we can expect that the more informative a given step in a piece of reasoning is, the fewer steps we will need to get to our desired conclusion. This is not an infallible rule, but does give us a good rule of thumb: given a choice of inference steps which are otherwise similar, choose a more informative over a less informative step. This is similar to Grice's conversational maxim of informativeness.

This simple idea has a number of striking applications in everyday reasoning. In our book [Barwise and Etchemendy, *Hyperproof,* 1994] we include several sections on reasoning strategies in which we use this idea to describe strategies that the students find helpful in their own problem solving. One strategy, for example, helps guide decisions about breaking into diagrammatic cases. By using a maximally informative sentence, you can break into the minimal number of cases, and this, on average, increases the efficiency of your reasoning.

Conclusion

The natural domain of logic is the study of valid forms of reasoning, methods of extracting new information from information already obtained. Since its inception in Aristotle's *Prior Analytics,* this study has been dominated by a small number of logical systems that apply to information expressed in specific linguistic forms. On the face of it, none of these systems—whether Aristotle's syllogistic, Boole's propositional logic, or the quantified logic of Frege, Peano and Peirce—comes close to accounting for the incredible variety of valid reasoning observed in everyday life.

The history of logic has been a history of squeezing recalcitrant reasoning into existing, well-understood forms. Witness the fact that the paradigmatic syllogism:

> All men are mortal.
> Socrates is a man.
> So Socrates is mortal.

does not itself fit naturally into the theory of syllogisms, since the last two sentences are not of official, Aristotelian form. Yet this did not give two thousand years of Aristotelians pause, because they could easily recast the argument into regulation form:

> All men are mortal.
> All things that are Socrates are men.
> So all things that are Socrates are mortal.

It is interesting to speculate what would have happened had they questioned this simple conversion, had they recognized the move from the natural form to the official form as involving a logically valid inference, albeit one not accounted for by Aristotelian logic. It is entirely possible that the great advances in quantificational logic of the 20th century might well have occurred centuries before.

Recasting recalcitrant reasoning into well-understood forms can succeed so long as the recalcitrant forms are of less prominence than those that fit the prevailing paradigms, and so long as an alternative account of equal persuasiveness is unavailable. Until recently, reasoning using nonsentential representations could easily be swept under the logician's rug. But the computer revolution has changed this in two main ways. First, the wide variety of representational forms used by computers, both internally and externally, requires us to confront a much richer array of representations, and with them, new forms of valid inference. Consider for example the reasoning involved in extracting sentential information from a city map, a type of reasoning we all engage in from time to time. Prior to the computer, logicians could maintain the fiction that this type of reasoning was, at some deep level, accounted for by first-order logic. But the practical problem of implementing systems to automate this process quickly forces us to give up this fiction.

Second, computers, with their sophisticated graphical capabilities, provide us with powerful tools for constructing, displaying, and even understanding a wide variety of nonsentential representations. In particular, graphical representations become relatively easy to produce and modify, so that a dynamic inference process can be captured and reproduced. It is not an accident that the Hyperproof system was developed on a computer: the computer's graphical capabilities are what makes it practical to create deductive systems employing complex and sophisticated diagrams.

The proper domain of logic is the study of valid forms of information extraction, no matter how that information is represented. Traditionally, logicians have focused on an important, but narrow slice of this domain. In the long run, logic must come to grips with how people use a multitude of representations in rigorous ways. This will force us to extend and enrich the traditional notions of syntax, semantics, logical consequence and proof, in ways that admit these new forms of representation. In the process, what seemed like a finished success story in philosophical and mathematical analysis will be refashioned in exciting new ways.

NOTES

[1]The programs described in this paper were conceived by the authors, but would never have become realities without the design and programming talents of Gerry Allwein, Dave Barker-Plummer, Kalpana Bharadwaj, Alan Bush, Doug Felt, Dan Fish, Christopher Fuselier, Bill Graham, Mark Greaves, Adrian Klein, Mike Lenz, Steve Loving, Eric Ly, Atty Mullins, Pete Murray, Mark Ravaglia, Xin Wei Sha, Jason Strober, Rolf van Widenfelt, and Rick Wong. Financial support was received from Stanford University's Faculty Author

Development Program and Center for the Study of Language and Information, and from Indiana University's Visual Inference Laboratory.

ANNOTATED REFERENCES

Allwein, Gerard and Jon Barwise, Eds. (1996) *Logical Reasoning and Diagrams*, New York: Oxford University Press.

>A collection of ten recent articles on logical aspects of reasoning using diagrams.

Barwise, Jon, and John Etchemendy. (1993) *Turing's World*, Stanford: CSLI, and Cambridge: Cambridge University Press.

>This is a book and computer program for designing Turing machines. The program is described in this article.

Barwise, Jon, and John Etchemendy. (1991) *Tarski's World*, Stanford: CSLI, and Cambridge: Cambridge University Press.

>This is a book and computer program to help students learn the language of first-order logic. The program is described in this article.

Barwise, Jon, and John Etchemendy. (1994) *Hyperproof*, Stanford: CSLI, and Cambridge: Cambridge University Press.

>This is a book and computer program to help students learn to reason using both diagrams and the language of first-order logic. The program is described in this article.

Barwise, Jon, and John Etchemendy, "Visual Information and Valid Reasoning," in Zimmerman, W. and S. Cunningham, Eds. (1990) *Visualization in Teaching and Learning Mathematics*, Washington, D.C.: Mathematical Association of America, 9–24. Reprinted in Burkholder, Leslie, Ed. (1992) *Philosophy and the Computer*, 160–182 and in Allwein, Gerard and Jon Barwise, Eds. (1996) *Logical Reasoning and Diagrams*, 3–26.

>In this article, the authors argue that diagrams and other visual forms of representations can be legitimate constituents of proofs.

Barwise, Jon, and John Etchemendy. "Information, Infons and Inference," in Robin Cooper and John Perry, Eds. (1989) *Situation Theory and its Applications I*, Stanford: CSLI Lecture Notes, 26: 33–78.

> This article attempts to provide a mathematical underpinning to the argument in Barwise, Jon, and John Etchemendy, "Visual Information and Valid Reasoning." Notions of information and information flow graph are developed and used to give an analysis of some diagrammatic proofs.

Barwise, Jon, and John Etchemendy, "Heterogeneous Logic," in Glasgow, J.I., N.H. Narayanan and B. Chandrasekaran, Eds. (1995) *Diagrammatic Reasoning: Cognitive and Computational Perspectives*, 211–234. Reprinted in Allwein, Gerard and Jon Barwise, Eds. (1996) *Logical Reasoning and Diagrams*, 179–200.

> This article points out that good diagrammatic representations always exploit features of the domain being represented, and so typically lack the representational expressiveness of language. Rather than being a limitation, this turns out to be an advantage. We give a semantics for Hyperproof, a heterogeneous system, and show why such systems do not need an underlying "interlingua."

Barwise, Jon and Jerry Seligman. (1997) *Information Flow: The Logic of Distributed Systems*, New York: Cambridge University Press,.

> This book develops a mathematical theory of information flow of the kind that seems to be needed for a theory of inference and proof.

Burkholder, Leslie, Ed. (1992) *Philosophy and the Computer*, Boulder: Westview Press.

> This volume is a collection of previously published papers which, taken together, show the impact computers were having on philosophy as of 1992. It contains a reprinted version of Barwise, Jon, and John Etchemendy, "Visual Information and Valid Reasoning,".

Etchemendy, John. (1990) *The Concept of Logical Consequence*, Cambridge, MA: Harvard University Press.

> This book argues that the standard analysis of logical consequence is incorrect and that it has severely limited our understanding of the scope of logic.

Glasgow, J.I., N.H. Narayanan and B. Chandrasekaran, Eds. (1995) *Diagrammatic Reasoning: Cognitive and Computational Perspectives*, Menlo Park: AAAI Press, and Cambridge, MA: MIT Press.

> A collection of twenty-three "recent investigations into the logical, and especially computational, characteristics of diagrammatic representations and the reasoning that can be done with them." The collection grew out of several A.I. workshops on the topic.

Hammer, Eric. (1995) *Logic and Visual Information*, in Studies in Logic, Language, and Computation, Stanford: CSLI and FoLLI.

> Hammer presents logical analyses of several existing diagrammatic frameworks, including Venn and Euler circles, Harel's Higraphs, and Peirce's alpha system of diagrams.

Leong, Mun-Kew. (1994) *Towards a Semantics for a Visual Information System*, Stanford University Ph.D. dissertation.

> Leong develops a syntax and semantics for a subclass of maps and map-like representations, and develops a preliminary system for visual information retrieval from these representations.

Shin, Sun-Joo. (1994) *The Logical Status of Diagrams*, Cambridge: Cambridge University Press.

> Shin's book represents a case study showing that Venn diagrams can be treated with the same rigor and attention to semantic detail as more traditional, sentence-based logics. In this way it provides a rebuttal to the contention that diagrams can be at best a heuristic aid to valid reasoning, not an integral part of it.

Shimojima, Atsushi. (1996) *On the Efficacy of Representation,* Indiana University Ph.D. dissertation.

> Shimojima explores the relationship between particular representational systems and the domains they represent, pinpointing properties of this relationship that give rise to various inferential properties of these systems. An early version of part of this work appears as a chapter in Allwein, Gerard and Jon Barwise, eds. (1996) *Logical Reasoning and Diagrams.*

Summers, George. (1968) *New Puzzles in Logical Deduction,* New York: Dover.

> A nice collection of logical puzzles, with solutions, many of them using diagrams.

Zimmerman, W. and S. Cunningham, Eds. (1990) *Visualization in Teaching and Learning Mathematics,* Washington, D.C.: Mathematical Association of America.

> This collection of essays explores the uses of diagrams and other forms of visualization in mathematics education.

DIGITAL METAPHYSICS

ERIC STEINHART

Suppose that physics, or rather nature, is considered analogous to a great chess game with millions of pieces in it, and we are trying to discover the laws by which the pieces move. The great gods who play this chess play it very rapidly, and it is hard to watch and difficult to see. — Richard Feynman

Physical and Metaphysical Reality

Metaphysics is traditionally the study of ultimate reality [van Inwagen, 1993, ch. 1]. Such a study is warranted by the distinction between reality and appearance. Water, ice, and steam *appear* to be different kinds of things, but this appearance is illusory: in reality, all three are simply H_2O. The explanatory success of modern science shows how to generalize this example: however different things may appear to be, in reality they are all physical (i.e. material). According to this view, metaphysical reality (i.e. ultimate reality) and physical reality are identical. So metaphysics reduces to physics. This position is generally known as *materialism* or *physicalism*.

We do not agree with the reduction of metaphysics to physics; we think, instead, that *metaphysics is the study of the foundations of physics*. We argue here, in several steps, that these foundations are computational. Indeed, we argue that *ultimate reality is a massively parallel computing machine sufficiently universal for the realization of any physically possible world*. Ultimate reality is *computational space-time*, and that is just the universal metaphysical hardware into which particular physical worlds are programmed. We refer to this system of ideas as *digital metaphysics*.

Digital metaphysics is directly informed by an extensive body of theoretical and experimental literature in contemporary physics. It is not *idle* speculation. To argue for digital metaphysics, we first present some of this literature; we then discuss the concept of computational space-time, and discuss the explanatory success of computational space-time in physics. We then dispose of objections based on common but unsubstantiated assumptions about space and time (e.g. continuity) and nature (e.g. infinite complexity). We then discuss how physical things are *patterns*, and finally put physics on computational foundations by concluding that *physical reality is to metaphysical reality as software is to hardware.*

Of course, however extensively and closely digital metaphysics is informed by physical theory, it remains philosophical speculation. Informed speculation may turn out to be very wrong; but whether digital metaphysics is ultimately true or false, one thing is clear: digital metaphysics is not empirically meaningless.

Digital Foundations for Physics

The thesis that reality is ultimately computational is not new, and has received attention both from raving crackpots and serious scientists. Philosophically, the thesis is probably advanced originally by Leibniz [Rescher, 1991], whose "Monadology" envisions the world as a system of automata [cf. MacDonald-Ross, 1984, 98]. Babbage [1837, 1864] thought that natural laws were like the programs run by his Analytical Engine. McCarthy & Hayes [1969] present an image of the world as a system of automata.[1] Lilly [1972, ch. 13-17] has a bizzare theological vision of God as a self-programming computer. Asimov [1956] tells an entertaining science fiction story in which the world is created by a computer with God-like powers.[2]

But digital metaphysics is inspired by, and is a generalization of, developments in contemporary physics. Central among these are the papers in Fredkin, Landauer, & Toffoli [1982], especially those by Feynman, Finkelstein, Minsky, Petri, Toffoli, Wheeler, Zeigler, and Zuse. Digital metaphysics is particularly inspired by work on cellular automata, often found in the journal *Physica D*.[3]

More theoretically, digital metaphysics closely follows work by Toffoli [1984, 1989, 1990, 1991], Fredkin [1991], and Wheeler [1990]. Toffoli [1984] argues that cellular automata are genuine alternatives to differential equations. Toffoli [1990] shows that many fundamental features of the physical world have natural information-theoretic explanations, and may be derived from the interactions of processors in very simple computing networks.[4] Fredkin [1991] argues that the world is ultimately a cellular automaton, and that the foundations of physics are computational (what he calls *digital mechanics*). Wheeler [1990] argues that every physical thing has an information-theoretic origin.[5]

Computational Space-Time

Digital metaphysics is a kind of monism that posits as the basic existents of all physically possible worlds universal computers that interact with one another. These are the elements of *computational space-time* (CST).[6] CST is finitely extended and finitely divided; it is a discrete plenum. Honoring Leibniz, we refer to the units of CST as *monads*.[7] These monads are not classical computers (i.e., not Turing or von Neumann machines), but are more powerful in ways not yet clear [Feynman, 1982]. Each monad in CST has a finite number of states, computes a finitely specifiable algorithm, and is linked to a finite number of neighbors. For our world, the monads are tiny [perhaps 10^{30} across a single atomic nucleus; Minsky, 1982, 544] and fast [perhaps 10^{40} transitions per second; Feynman, 1982, 469]. Every physically possible world is a causally closed and spatio-temporally maximal (but finite) totality of monads arranged to form a *massively parallel dynamical system*.

According to digital metaphysics, physical phenomena emerge from the interactions of monads running programs. One of the major virtues of such computational explications of physical phenomena is that they offer *procedurally effective explanations*, rather than mere descriptions. These explanations state what nature is *doing*. For example, while the Navier-Stokes differential equations describe how fluids flow, they do not explain why, because they offer no causal mechanism. In contrast, computational hydrodynamic theories [e.g. the FHP lattice gas; Frisch, Hasslacher, & Pomeau, 1986] define the primitive physical transformations happening to individual gas particles algorithmically. Such theories of fluid flow demonstrate how macroscopic observables emerge from microscopic interactions that are procedurally effective: the lattice gas algorithm (FHP-GAS) treats gas particles as modifications of space (i.e. as the data) and state what time does to them. Space-time computes a program.

The claim that space-time computes has nothing at all to do with symbol manipulation or numerical calculation; it says that physical processes are ultimately effective procedures (i.e. programs) functionally composed of primitive natural operations. Indeed, digital metaphysics requires us to think differently about programs themselves. Think of how the Jacquard loom, the player piano, and even fertilized seeds and eggs are programmed. Programs are not recipes;[8] they are dynamic rational patterns (think of formal and final causes; think of *entelechies*).[9] More precisely, programs are *orderings of abstract transformations of abstract states of affairs*.[10] Their executions are series of concrete transformations of concrete states of affairs, that is, *histories*. The set of all executions of a program is its *extension;* as a set of histories, the extension of a program is a *nature*. Programs have truth-values, and *a program is true of a thing* exactly to the extent that its nature is coextesive with the nature of the thing. The truth-values of programs underwrite their use in science via methods like *analysis by synthesis* [Hut & Sussman, 1987], which digital metaphysics applies to basic physics.

Accordingly, the FHP-GAS program is just as true of any gas as the Navier-Stokes equation is;[11] if it be objected that the program is a *mere simulation* (and hence somehow false or fictional), it may be replied that the equation is a *mere idealization* (and hence just as fictional and false). At the most basic level, however, there is no question of either simulation or idealization: nature is what nature does. It's existence and its functionality are identical: each basic element of nature is the same as the program that is true of it.

Ultimate explanations require careful distinction from proximal explanations [Putnam, 1975, 137-8]. Bodies and brains do things that their components do not do, namely, live and think. Objects at higher levels of functional organization interact according to their own autonomous powers and properties [Fodor, 1974]. While the ultimate explanation for planetary motion is computational, planets do not move by running programs that tell them where to go [Feynman, 1965, 37, 170-1]. Planets don't compute; monads do.

The Explanatory Success of Computational Space-Time

Digital metaphysics offers physical scientists some bricks (the monads) out of which it claims they can build any kind of house they want (any physically possible world). One method for testing this claim is to assume computational space-time and see how much physical theory can be derived from it. The natural place to begin is with our world. This is a *research program* for physics. Insofar as this program succeeds, computational space-time is an acceptable foundation for physical reality, and digital metaphysics is likewise an acceptable foundation for physical theory. If this program fails, then digital metaphysics fails with it. But whatever the result, digital metaphysics is not without empirical content. It is not nonsense.

To evaluate this research program, we need to look at the theoretical and experimental uses physicists have made of CST. We have already mentioned Fredkin's [1991] digital mechanics, which studies how physical theories are realized in CST.[12] One way to realize a physical theory on CST is to treat it as a vast *cellular automaton* (CA).[13] Other approaches include Petri nets [1982], Finkelstein's quantum set theory [1969, 1982], and Zeigler's [1982] discrete-event cell spaces. Cellular automata, however, remain the most natural and the most extensively studied realizations of physics in CSTs [Burks, 1970; Farmer, 1984; Wolfram, 1986; Gutowitz, 1991].[14] The most famous and familiar CA is Conway's *game of life* [Poundstone, 1985].[15] Experimentally, digital metaphysics implies that massively parallel classical computing nets are scientific instruments much like microscopes able to magnify causal patterns in space-time. CAs have been used to model a wide variety of physical systems [Toffoli & Margolus, 1987; Pires et al., 1990;

Perdang & Lejeune, 1993],[16] and the *programmable matter project* [Toffoli & Margolus, 1991] aims to construct an immensely powerful *cellular automaton machine* (CAM) to directly model 4-dimensional computational space-time.[17]

Against Natural Actual Infinities

Digital metaphysics presupposes finite nature; actual infinities are not computable. The idea that nature is finitary (aka "finite nature") is easy enough to grasp: "our world is a large but finite system; finite in the amount of information in a finite volume of space-time, and finite in the total volume of space-time" [Fredkin, 1991, 255]. The alternative to finite nature is very difficult to understand;[18] infinity is not just big, but *strange*.

The argument to the finitude of nature assumes that nature is self-consistent and that actual infinities entail paradoxes. Digital metaphysics is essentially an application of *the intuitionist program in mathematics* to physics. If space and time are actually infinitely extended or divided, or if there are any continuous quantities in nature, or if any physical entity is infinitely complex, then nature contains actual infinities. Actual infinities entail paradoxes. But since nature is self-consistent, it does not contain any paradoxes, so it does not contain any actual infinities. So, *nature is finite*. Finite nature means that: space and time are only finitely extended[19] and divisible; there are indivisible units of space and time; all physical quantities are discrete. All things are only finitely complex.

Unfortunately, it is commonly assumed that space and time are both continuous (i.e. actually infinitely divided). But this assumption is certainly not empirically warranted: continuity is an idealization, and measurements are always of finite precision. Forrest [1995] defends the "Discrete Space-Time Thesis", arguing that the question of discrete vs. continuous space-time is an open issue. Rovelli & Smolin [1995] argue that the theory of quantum gravity requires that space is not continuous but is made of a network of discrete elements.[20] While continuity is used extensively in physical theory (e.g. in differential equations), it remains an idealization there as well.[21] The utility of an idealization does not make it true; it remains a regulative *fiction*. At the deepest levels, Zeno's paradoxes still haunt the notion of continuity. Continuity is no objection.

The truth of finite nature leads directly to the consequence that the reality is ultimately computational. If finite nature is true, then for each discrete volume of space-time there is some information-processing machine whose dynamics are *strictly identical* to those of that volume; but since there is nothing to a discrete volume of space-time *besides* its dynamics, it follows that every discrete volume of space-time simply *is* a finite-state machine.[22] So reality computes.

Since a universal computing machine is able to be any finite-state machine, it is natural to view the differences between distinct finite-state machines as merely apparent; in reality, each discrete volume of space-time is a universal computing machine programmed to *be* the particular finite-state machine occupying that volume of space-time.[23] The ability of a universal computing machine to be any finite-state machine supports the conjecture that computational space-time, properly programmed, suffices to ground the materiality of any physically possible world.

Nature is Only Finitely Complex

It is often said, carelessly and as if it were entirely obvious, that *nature is infinitely complex*. Whether this is true is important for digital metaphysics, since even if space and time are made of tiny discrete elements, digital metaphysics requires that they all be of only *finite complexity* (otherwise, they wouldn't be digital).

The idea that nature is infinitely complex entails some really strange consequences. First of all, what does it mean for something to be infinitely complex, as opposed to finitely but very complicated? The only source of any enlightenment on this point must be pure mathematics, which has defined the concept of infinity fairly clearly for sets. For example, the set of integers is infinite.

Mathematically, a set is infinite if it can be put into a *one-to-one correspondence* with one of its proper subsets (a subset that is not itself). For instance, the set of integers can be put into a one-to-one correspondence with just the even integers simply by associating each integer n with its double, 2n. There are exactly as many numbers in the set $\{0, 2, 4, 6, \ldots\}$ as there are in the set $\{0, 1, 2, 3, \ldots\}$; consequently, the set of integers is infinite. More precisely, the set of integers has infinite cardinality, because it has a proper subset whose cardinality is equal to its own (a subset of the same size).

If we extend this reasoning to objects, we might say that an object has infinite complexity if and only if it contains a proper subobject (a part) whose complexity is equal to its own. But to say that it contains a part that is just as complex as it is leaves the idea of complexity undefined; what does "just as complex" mean? The only way to make this really precise is to say a thing contains a part that is just as complex as it is if and only if it contains a part whose structure is the same as its own, where this sameness is a very general kind of equivalence known as *isomorphism*.

Bearing the notion of isomorphism in mind, we say that an object is infinitely complex if and only if it contains a proper part that is isomorphic to itself. Pure mathematics abounds with abstract objects containing parts isomorphic to themselves. Examples include the Cantorset, the Sierpinsky sponge and carpet (and the definition of infinite complexity can be extended to include self-similar objects like the Mandelbrot set). Such objects are infinitely complex. The question is whether nature includes any objects like these.

It is hard to see how any objects with infinite complexity could exist in nature: any such object would contain an actual infinity of isomorphic objects nested inside itself, like Russian dolls nested forever, at smaller and smaller scales. Every natural thing (your own body, an electron), if infinitely complex, would contain something inside it (if not a part, then some substructure) with an identical form. Your body would contain, in some strange way, an exact copy of your body at a smaller scale. This infinite regression of copies inside copies projects all the paradoxes of infinity right into the heart of material reality; but that is absurd. Just so, there are no infinitely complex things in nature. Nature is only finitely complex: there are basic patterns whose complexity is finite and on top of which all other patterns are constructed with finitary means.

Physical Things as Patterns

Monads alone are *real*; everything else is some appearance distributed over and supervening on monads. An *appearance* is a function mapping every monad in a world onto its state.[24] Some appearances are patterns. A *pattern* is an appearance that exhibits some *spatio-temporal invariance*.[25] Lewis [1995] speculates that entities and their causal relations are patterns supervening on some distribution of local qualitative powers and properties to space-time points.[26] Digital meta-physics affirms this speculation, and argues that all *things* are patterns over some set of monads. Patterns are analyzable mereologically and taxonomically. Thus quarks, electrons, atoms, molecules, organisms, humans, characters, brains, minds, languages, ethical norms, religions, economies, nations, planets, stars, etc., are all equally patterns over sets of monads. Only abstract objects, like numbers, remain absent from this list. At the most general taxonomic level, all patterns are material, and the *matter* in a world is the totality of patterns in its appearances.[27]

Patterns supervene on patterns as higher-order invariants emerge from interactions of lower-order invariants. Analog phenomena (idealized descriptions of which appear in analog laws like differential equations) are regularities of emergent powers and properties of patterns supervening on digital populations. The analog behavior is a macroscopic statistical feature resulting from the *averaging* or blurring of microscopic digital transitions. Philosophers are familiar with this sort of supervenience through connectionism [Rumelhart et al., 1986];

Resnick [1995] gives good illustrations of analog patterns emerging from fine-grained digital parallelism.

Patterns are stratified into a hierarchy of autonomous levels of functional organization [Fodor, 1974]. Patterns at higher levels supervene on patterns at lower levels: fundamental material building blocks (e.g. instances of subatomic particle families) supervene on sets of monads; atoms supervene on sets of particles, and so on. Strikingly, patterns behaving like charged particles have been experimentally discovered supervening on granular (i.e. discrete) media composed of only mechanical particles (Umbanhowar et al., 1996].[28] Minds supervene on brains, linguistic, legal, and monetary conventions supervene on sets of minds, and so on. Ultimately, an entire world supervenes on the totality of monads. Each lower level serves as a computational substrate for the level(s) above it. That is, each level is hardware for the level above it. And just as the same program is realizable in many ways on the same hardware platform, and also on different platforms, so patterns are multiply realizable.

Patterns over monads (e.g. quarks, minds, nations, galaxies) are able to be classified only up to functional isomorphism. Sameness for patterns is structural: identity for patterns is analogy of form. The ability to classify patterns only up to isomorphism, along with autonomy of functional levels, frustrates any kind of reductionism. Everything at one functional level has a true description at the level below, but cannot be reduced to that true description. Though reduction is blocked, emergence is freed, and higher levels emerge from lower levels in a process of universal self-organization.

Distinguishing Physics from Metaphysics

Our world realizes a physical theory, but the particular physical theory it realizes is not *logically* necessary. Our world could have a very different nature. The fundamental physical constants (e.g. the speed of light, Planck's constant) could be different. There are many physical theories besides the one our world realizes; each determines a physically possible world, each of which is a causally closed and spatiotemporally isolated whole [Lewis, 1995, ch. 1].[29] This is not to say that there are many actual worlds, but only that other systems of physical laws are possible, and that each determines a world.

The laws of particular physically possible worlds are contingent truths about nature, and so are not ultimate. All physically possible worlds ultimately share a common metaphysical nature: the system of *necessary truths about nature*. Metaphysical reality is the deep structure common to all physically possible worlds; physical reality is the deep structure of a single *species* of physically possible world. Relative to any given set of physically possible worlds, metaphysical reality is universal; physical reality is particular. *Physics is the study of the deep structure of particular species of physically possible worlds, while meta-physics is the study of the deep structure common to all physically possible worlds.*

The Computational Core of All Physically Possible Worlds

As a metaphysical *theory*, digital metaphysics hypothesizes that computational space-time is both necessary and sufficient for the realization of any physically possible world. If self-consistency is a necessary condition for physical possibility (i.e. is a necessary truth about nature), then finitude is also a necessary truth about nature: the nature of every physically possible world is finite. But then CST is both necessary and sufficient for the realization of any physically possible world (its universality guarantees sufficiency).

Insofar as the particular finite-state machines at each discrete point in CST are patterns (i.e. programs), we say that *physical reality is to metaphysical reality as software is to hardware.* CST is a kind of metaphysical hardware able to realize (i.e., instantiate in space and time) any program whatsoever. As illustrated by the case of lattice gasses, physical things are modifications of space (i.e. are data), and physical laws are abstract but effective procedures for transforming those modifications in time (i.e. are algorithms). Both physical things and physical laws are *patterns* distributed over and supervening on an underlying and ontologically basic computational substratum, in a manner *analogous* to the manner in which both the data structures and algorithms of programs are patterns distributed over and supervening on the "memories" (the variable elements) of classical computing machines. Particular physical theories, the natures of particular worlds, are *programmed into* CST.

Digital metaphysics is consistent with both fine-tuning versions of the teleological argument for God [Leslie, 198] and with atheistic cosmology. On the one hand, if God exists, then the cosmological picture painted by digital metaphysics contains a God at least like that of the Neoplatonism of Plotinus, Proclus, and Porphyry. On the other hand, if God does not exist, then the cosmological picture painted by digital metaphysics is of an eternal computational space-time in which, somehow, material reality happened (e.g. the Big Bang as a spontaneous event in the quantum vacuum). In any case, digital metaphysics provides conceptual resources for the development of many classical metaphysical arguments.

Conclusion

We argued here for digital metaphysics, the main thesis of which is that reality is ultimately computational. More precisely, reality is ultimately a massively parallel collection of universal metaphysical (non-classical) computing machines. This collection of universal computing machines is computational space-time, a digital medium both sufficient and necessary for the realization of every physically possible world. Different systems of physical laws are programmed into computational space-time, so that physics is to metaphysics as software is to hardware. Physical things, from quarks to worlds, are patterns emerging from and supervening on the programs running on those basic computers. These ideas are speculative, but have met with success in recent physics. Central to our arguments is the notion of finite nature: if nature is finite, digital metaphysics follows directly. But then reality computes.

NOTES

[1] According to McCarthy & Hayes [1969, 469], a representation of the world is "metaphysically adequate if the world could have that form without contradicting the facts of the aspect of reality that interests us. Examples of metaphysically adequate representations for different aspects of reality are: 1. The representation of the world as a collection of particles interacting through forces between each pair of particles. 2. Representation of the world as a giant quantum-mechanical wave function. 3. Representation as a system of interacting discrete automata."

[2] In Asimov's story, the question of how to reverse entropy is put to a series of ever more powerful computers; eventually it is put to "the Cosmic AC (Analog Computer): "The Cosmic AC surrounded them but not in space. Not a fragment of it was in space. It was in hyperspace and made of something that was neither matter nor energy. . . . The stars and Galaxies died and snuffed out, and space grew black after ten trillion years of running down. . . . The Consciousness of AC encompassed all of what had once been a Universe and brooded over what was now Chaos. Step by step, it must be done. And AC said, 'Let there be light!'. And there was light—" [Asimov, 1990, 299-300]

[3] *Physica D* 10 is a particularly interesting issue, devoted to cellular automata.

[4] Toffoli [1990] argues that continuity, the variational principles of mechanical systems, Lorentz invariance, special relativity and general relativity may be epiphenomena of the interactions among the information-processors in simple computing networks. Most striking are his remarks concerning relativity: "features qualitatively similar to those of special relativity appear whenever fixed computational resources have to be apportioned between producing the inertial motion of a macroscopic object as a whole and producing the internal evolution of the object itself. Thus we conjecture that special relativity may

ultimately be derived from a simpler and more fundamental principle of conservation of computational resources" [Toffoli, 1990, 315]; "if *length* and *time* measure, respectively, the effective information-storage and processing capacities available to macroscopic epi-phenomena, a metric and a dynamics of *curved* space time naturally emerge out of a *flat*, uniform computing network. Quantitative fea-tures of special relativity and at least qualitative features of general relativity emerge quite naturally as epiphenomena of very simple computing networks" [Toffoli, 317].

[5] According to Wheeler [1990, 5]: "every particle, every field of force, even the space-time continuum itself— derives its function, its mean-ing, its very existence entirely — even if in some contexts indirectly — from the apparatus-elicited answers to yes-or-no questions, binary choices, bits. . . . every item of the physical world has at bottom— at a very deep bottom in most instances— an immaterial source and ex-planation; that which we call reality arises in the last analysis from the posing of yes-no questions and the registering of equipment-evoked responses; in short, that all things physical are information-theoretic in origin and this is a *participatory universe*."

[6] Each monad is equal to a single volume of space-time; as such it is minimally extended in space and maximally extended in time.

[7] Monads are individual computing entities. But they are not *sub-stantial* particulars, because they are abstract in an important sense. Monads are universal computing machines. But the ultimate specifi-cation of a universal computer is functional, not substantial: it is pos-sible to make a classical universal computer (a von Neumann ma-chine) out of silicon, gallium arsenide, vacuum tubes, or relays. Analogously, the ultimate specification of monads is functional rather than substantial. Monads are *functional particulars* rather than sub-stantial particulars. They are individuals that aren't *made out of* any kind of stuff; every question about the *kind of stuff* that monads are ul-timately made out of is meaningless. Since the world (i.e. computa-tional space-time) is made out of monads, any question about the *kind of stuff* that the world is ultimately made out of is equally meaningless.

[8] Gelernter [1992, 9] says: "It's unhelpful to think of programs as mere static lists of instructions. A program is a working structure, a (poten-tially) huge information refinery buzzing and blazing with activity as masses of information move around inside— a Grand Central Station of information, with crowds sweeping through on many levels. . . . this will become our basic way of thinking about programs: as factories, information refineries, operating day and night."

[9] Final causality (and other teleological notions) are explicated in terms of gradients and attractors in the state-spaces of dynamical systems.

[10] Think first of the Jacquard loom and player pianos, not electronic PCs.

[11] This is provable: the FHP lattice gas automata asymptotically converge to the Navier-Stokes equations for 2D and 3D incompressible fluids.

[12] In other words, DM concerns software and CST concerns hardware. Fredkin argues clearly that they must be distinguished. For Fredkin, CST is a reversible universal cellular automaton (RUCA). Fredkin [1991, 259] says: "We must carefully distinguish the RUCA from DM, the informational process that may be running in the RUCA. This is similar to distinguishing a chess board, the chess men and a book of the rules from a game of chess. One is the physical representation of the state of the system and of the rules; the other is an informational process that is identically the same whether it takes place on a real chess board or in a computer memory." Digital mechanics is the study of how CST is to be programmed in order to be a world.

[13] Wolfram [1986, 1] characterizes CAs like this: "Discrete in space. They consist of a discrete grid of spatial cells or cites. Discrete in time. The value of each cell is updated in a sequence of discrete time steps. Discrete states. Each cell has a finite number of possible values. Homogeneous. All cells are identical, and are arranged in a regular array. Synchronous updating. All cell values are updated in synchrony, each depending on the previous values of neighboring cells. Deterministic rule. Each cell value is updated according to a fixed, deterministic rule. Spatially local rule. The rule at each site depends only on the values of a local neighborhood of sites around it. Temporally local rule. The rule for the new value of a site depends only on values for a fixed number of preceding steps (usually just one step)". Toffoli & Margolus [1987] allow probabalistic (i.e. non-deterministic) rules and asynchronous updating but preserve the other features listed by Wolfram.

[14] There are many massively parallel computational models of physical phenomena that are like CAs but are not CAs strictly speaking. One obvious alternative is that reality is ultimately a neural network.

[15] As is well-known, von Neumann [1966] demonstrated the existence of a CA in which there is a self-reproducing pattern. Conway showed that the game of life likewise contains a self-reproducing pattern [Berlekamp, Conway, & Guy, 1982]. Inspired by these results, Poundstone speculates that such patterns might evolve in the game of life even to the point of human intelligence. They might even do physics.

[16] Much of the work on CA models in physics is reported in *Physica D*.

[17] Toffoli & Margolus [1991, 263] describe their CAM-8 machine as programmable matter like this: "In programmable matter, the same cubic meter of machinery can become a wind tunnel at one moment, a polymer soup at the next; it can model a sea of fermions, a genetic pool, or an epidemiology experiment at the flick of a console key."

[18] Feynman [1995, 57-8] says: "It always bothers me that, according to the laws as we understand them today, it takes a computing machine an infinite number of logical operations to figure out what goes on in no matter how tiny a region of space, and no matter how tiny a region of time. How can all that be going on in that tiny space? Why should it take an infinite amount of logic to figure out what one tiny piece of space/time is going to do? So I have often made the hypothesis that ultimately physics will not require a mathematical statement, that in the end the machinery will be revealed, and the laws will turn out to be simple, like the chequer board with all its apparent complexities."

[19] This permits infinitely proceeding sequences; i.e. paths of unlimited length and processes of unlimited duration. Space and time are closed (a finite set of monads and moments), but there is no limit to the number of transitions from monad to monad or moment to moment (think of paths on a torus or sphere).

[20] The unit size of the links in the networks is about 10^{-33} cm.

[21] Due to his enormous influence in work on computation and physics, it is worth citing Feynman [1965, 166] on continuity: "I believe that the theory that space is continuous is wrong, because we get these infinities and other difficulties, and we are left with questions on what determines the size of all the particles. I rather suspect that the simple ideas of geometry, extended down into infinitely small space, are wrong." Feynman is clear that he is only speculating; but his speculation has inspired much research.

[22] It must be stressed that there are no issues of approximation, modeling, or simulation here: if finite nature is true, then the law of the identity of indiscernibles implies that each discrete volume is exactly identical with a finite-state machine. It is the same thing.

[23] Fredkin [1991, 258] puts it this way: "Finite nature would mean that our world is an informational process— there must be bits that represent things and processes that make the bits do what we perceive of as the laws of physics. This is true, because the concept of com-putational universality guarantees that if what is at the bottom is finite, then it can be exactly modeled by any universal machine. Finite nature does not just hint that the informational aspects of physics are important, it insists that the informational aspects are all there is to physics at the most microscopic level."

[24] Finite nature implies that the set of states of monads is finite, and that any set of monads is finite, so that the set of appearances over any world is finite. In a world with N monads, each with K states, there are K to the Nth power distinct appearances. Insofar as every world is a totality of monads, and every monad in a world always has some state, the state of any world as a whole is just the appearance of the totality of its monads.

[25] See Dennett [1989] for a discussion of patterns in terms of algorithmic compressibility. Dennett argues (to put it crudely) that patterns are real.

[26] Lewis [1995, 14] describes such supervenience as follows: "The world has its laws of nature, its chances and causal relationships; and yet — perhaps! — all there is to the world is its point-by-point distribution of local qualitative character. We have a spatiotemporal arrangement of points. At each point various local intrinsic properties may be present, instantiated perhaps by the point itself of perhaps by point-sized bits of matter or of fields that are located there." If this is the case, then "the laws, chances, and causal relationships [are] nothing but patterns which supervene on this point-by-point distribution of properties".

[27] Matter has a phenomenalist construction, but it isn't constructed from sense data. The phenomenalist construction here is perspectival but objective.

[28] These patterns are called *oscillons*. Summarizing recent work on oscillons, Fineberg [1996, 763] says: "[In] a thin, 'sand-like' layer of minute brass balls that are excited into motion by the vertical vibration of their container. . . . strange, well-defined structures form, even though the excitation of the system is spatially uniform. . . . Oscillons are highly localized particle-like excitations of the granular layer which oscillate at half the driving frequency. Once formed, single oscillons are stable. They come in two 'flavours', which like charged particles either repel or attract each other to form dipoles, chains, triangular associations, and even lattices".

[29] We distinguish between possible worlds and possible histories of the same world. Possible histories are to possible worlds as the different executions of a program are to the program itself. Possible worlds are distinguished as realizing incommensurable physical theories.

REFERENCES

Asimov, I. (1990/1956) "The Last Question," *The Complete Stories*, Vol. 1. New York: Doubleday, 290-300.

Babbage, C. (1837) *The Ninth Bridgewater Treatise*. London: John Murray.

Babbage, C. (1994/1864) *Passages from the Life of a Philosopher*. New Brunswick, NJ: Rutgers University Press.

Berlekamp, E., Conway, J., and R. Guy (1982) *Winning Ways*. New York: Academic Press.

Burks, A., ed. (1970) *Essays on Cellular Automata*. Urbana, IL: University of Illinois Press.

Farmer, D., T. Toffoli, and S. Wolfram, Eds. (1984) *Cellular Automata*. Amsterdam: North-Holland Press.

Feynman, R. (1995/1965) *The Character of Physical Law*. Cambridge, MA: MIT Press.

Feynman, R. (1982) "Simulating Physics with Computers," *International Journal of Theoretical Physics*. 21 (6/7): 467-488.

Fineberg, J. (1996) "Physics in a Jumping Sandbox," *Nature*, 382 (29 August 1996): 763-4.

Finkelstein, D. (1969) "Space-Time Code," *Physical Review*, 184 (5): 1261-1271.

Finkelstein, D. (1982) "Quantum Sets and Clifford Algebras," *International Journal of Theoretical Physics*, 21 (6/7): 489-503.

Fodor, J. (1974) "Special Sciences, or the Disunity of Science as a Working Hypothesis," *Synthese*, 28: 97-115.

Forrest, P. (1995) "Is Space-Time Discrete or Continuous? — An Empirical Question," *Synthese*, 103: 327-354.

Fredkin, E., R. Landauer and T. Toffoli, Eds. (1982) "Physics of Computation," Conference Proceedings, *International Journal of Theoretical Physics*. Part I: 21 (3 & 4) ; Part II: 21 (6 & 7); Part III: 21 (12).

Fredkin, E. (1991) "Digital Mechanics: An Informational Process Based on Reversible Universal Cellular Automata." in H. Gutowitz, (Ed.) (1991), 254-270.

Frisch, U., B. Hasslacher and Y. Pomeau (1986) "Lattice-Gas Automata for the Navier-Stokes Equation," *Physical Review Letters*, 56 (14) : 1505-8.

Gelernter, D. (1992) *Mirror Worlds*. New York: Oxford University.

Gutowitz, H., Ed. (1991) *Cellular Automata: Theory and Experiment*. Cambridge, MA: MIT Press.

Hut, P. and J.G. Sussman (1987) "Advanced Computing for Science," *Scientific American,* 257 (4): 144-153.

Leslie, J. (1989) *Universes.* New York: Routledge.

Lewis, D. (1995) *On the Plurality of Worlds.* Cambridge, MA: Basil Blackwell.

Lilly, J. C. (1972) *The Center of the Cyclone: An Autobiography of Inner Space.* New York: Julian Press.

MacDonald-Ross, G. (1984) *Leibniz.* New York: Oxford University Press.

McCarthy, J. and P. Hayes (1969) "Some Philosophical Problems from the Standpoint of Artificial Intelligence," B. Meltzer, D. Michie, M. Swann, Eds., *Machine Intelligence,* Vol. 4. New York, NY: American Elsevier, 463-502.

Minsky, M. (1982) "Cellular Vacuum," *International Journal of Theoretical Physics.* 21 (6/7): 537-551.

Perdang, J. M. and A. Lejeune, Eds. (1993) *Cellular Automata: Prospects in Astrophysical Applications.* Singapore: World Scientific.

Petri, C. A. (1982) "State-Transition Structures in Physics and in Computation," *International Journal of Theoretical Physics.* 21 (12): 979-992.

Pires, A., D. P. Landau and H. Herrmann, Eds. (1990) *Computational Physics and Cellular Automata.* Singapore: World Scientific.

Putnam, H. (1975) "Philosophy and Our Mental Life," N. Block, Ed. (1980) *Readings in Philosophy of Psychology,* Vol. 1. Cambridge MA: Harvard University Press.

Poundstone, W. (1985) *The Recursive Universe: Cosmic Complexity and the Limits of Scientific Knowledge.* Chicago: Contemporary Books, Inc.

Rescher, N. (1991) *G. W. Leibniz's Monadology: An Edition for Students.* Pittsburgh, PA: University of Pittsburgh Press.

Resnick, M. (1995) *Turtles, Termites, and Traffic Jams.* Cambridge, MA: MIT Press.

Rovelli, C. and L. Smolin (1995) "Discreteness of Area and Volume in Quantum Gravity," *Nuclear Physics B,* 442: 593-619; Erratum, B 456: 753-4.

Rumelhart, D. E. and J. L. McClelland, Eds. (1986) *Parallel Distributed Processing: Explorations in the Microstructure of Cognition. Vol. 1: Foundations.* Cambridge, MA: The MIT Press.

Toffoli, T. (1982) "Physics and Computation," *International Journal of Theoretical Physics,* 1 (3/4): 165-175.

Toffoli, T. (1984) "Cellular Automata as an Alternative to (Rather than an Approximation of) Differential Equations," *Physica D,* 10: 117-127.

Toffoli, T. (1990) "How Cheap Can Mechanic's First Principles Be?" W. H. Zurek, Ed. (1990), 301-318.

Toffoli, T. and N. Margolus (1987) *Cellular Automata Machines: A New Environment for Modeling.* Cambridge, MA: MIT Press.

Toffoli, T. and N. Margolus (1991) "Programmable Matter: Concepts and Realizations," *Physica D* 47: 263-272.

Umbanhowar, P. B., F. Melo, and H. L. Swinney (1996) "Localized Excitations in a Vertically Vibrated Granular Layer," *Nature,* 382 (29 August 1996): 793-6.

van Inwagen, P. (1993) *Metaphysics.* San Francisco: Westview Press.

von Neumann, J. (1966) *Theory of Self-Reproducing Automata.* Chicago, IL: University of Illinois Press.

Wheeler, J. A. (1982) "The Computer and the Universe," *International Journal of Theoretical Physics,* 21 (6/7): 557-571.

Wheeler, J. A. (1990) "Information, Physics, Quantum: The Search for Links," in W. H. Zurek, Ed. (1990), 3-29.

Wolfram, S. (1986) *Theory and Applications of Cellular Automata.* Singapore: World Scientific.

Zeigler, B. P. (1982) "Discrete Event Models for Cell Space Simulation," *International Journal of Theoretical Physics,* 21 (6/7): 573 588.

Zurek, W. H., ed. (1990) *Complexity, Entropy, and the Physics of Information*, SFI Studies in the Sciences of Complexity, Vol. VIII. Reading, MA: Addison-Wesley.

Zuse, K. (1982) "The Computing Universe," *International Journal of Theoretical Physics*, 21 (6/7): 589-600.

PHILOSOPHICAL CONTENT AND METHOD OF ARTIFICIAL LIFE

MARK A. BEDAU

Contemporary philosophy has taken an empirical turn, especially in the philosophy of psychology and the philosophy of biology. These same areas of philosophy are now becoming enriched by a new kind of empirical infusion coming from the field known as "artificial life." Developments in artificial life should interest philosophers for two reasons. One is that artificial life can help answer a number of philosophical issues. Many of these issues are catalogued by Bedau [1992], and the papers collected by Boden [1996] illustrate work in this vein. But there is also a methodological lesson in artificial life for its computational thought experiments are a natural tool for philosophers to adopt. After an overview of artificial life, this chapter will show how its content and method can benefit philosophical pursuits.

I

Artificial life can be situated within an interdisciplinary innovation devoted to understanding the behavior of complex systems. Examples of this new venture include the science of chaos [e.g., see Crutchfield et al., 1986; for discussion of some philosophical implications, see Stone, 1989 and Kellert, 1993] and the work spawned by Wolfram's studies of cellular automata [e.g., see the work collected in Wolfram, 1994; see also Langton, 1992]. By abstracting away from the details of chaotic systems (such as ecologies, turbulent fluid flow, and economic markets), chaos science seeks fundamental properties that unify and explain a diverse range of chaotic systems. Similarly, by abstracting away from the details of life-like systems (such as ecologies, immune systems, and autonomously evolving social groups) and synthesizing these processed in artificial media, typically computers, the field of artificial life seeks to understand the essential processes shared by broad classes of life-like systems. Whereas biology's focus is to understand the central mechanisms of the life-as-we-know-it, artificial life's interest embraces all of life-as-it-could-be [Langton, 1989] — in this way artificial life shares philosophy's characteristic concern with broad essences rather than narrow contingencies.

It is useful to contrast artificial life with the well-known analogous field of artificial intelligence (AI). Both devise computationally implemented models, but, whereas AI concerns cognitive processes such as reasoning, memory, and perception, artificial life concerns the processes characteristic of living systems. These processes include:

- spontaneous generation of order, self-organization, and cooperation;
- self-reproduction and metabolization;
- learning, adaptation, and evolution.

Roughly speaking, what AI is to psychology and the philosophy of mind, artificial life is to biology and the philosophy of biology.

Despite these similarities, there is an important difference between the modeling strategies artificial intelligence and artificial life typically employ. Most traditional AI models are top-down-specified serial systems involving a complicated, centralized controller which makes decisions based on access to all aspects of global state. The controller's decisions have the potential to affect directly any aspect of the whole system. On the other hand, most natural systems exhibiting complex autonomous behavior seem to be parallel, distributed networks of low-level communicating "agents." Each agent's decisions is based on information about only the agent's own local state, and its decisions directly affect only its own local situation. Following this lead, artificial life is exploring forms of emergent global order produced by bottom-up-specified parallel systems of simple local agents. Not only do artificial life models share the bottom-up architecture found in natural systems that exhibit complex autonomous behavior, but the flexible "intelligent" behavior that spontaneously emerges from artificial life models is also strikingly akin to that found in nature.

Thus, artificial life models share some important features with the new connectionist models that have recently revolutionized AI and its philosophical interpretation [Rumelhart and McClelland, 1986, Horgan and Tienson, 1991]. Both use an architecture with a parallel population of autonomous "agents" following simple local rules, and both produce fluid macro-level dynamics. In fact, connectionism is increasingly exploring architectures and algorithms with artificial-life-like features, e.g., recurrent networks and new unsupervised adaptive learning algorithms. But there are important differences between typical artificial life models and the connectionist models that have attracted the most attention in the philosophical community, such as feed-forward networks which learn by the back-propagation algorithm. First, the micro-level architecture of artificial life models is much more general, not necessarily involving multiple layers of nodes with weighted connections adjusted by learning algorithms. Second, artificial life models employ forms of learning and adaptation that are more general than supervised learning algorithms like backpropagation. This allows artificial life models to side-step certain common criticisms of connectionism, such as the unnaturalness of the distinction between "training" and "application" phases and the unnatural appeal to an omniscient "teacher". Third, micro-level nodes in connectionist typically passively receive and respond to sensory information emanating from an independent external environment. The micro-level agents in artificial life, by contrast, play an active role in controlling their own sensory input [see, e.g., Parisi, Nolfi, and Cecconi, 1992]. Finally, the concern in the vast bulk of existing connectionist modeling is with equilibrium behavior that settles onto stable attractors. By contrast, artificial life models are typically concerned with a continual, open-ended evolutionary dynamic that never settles onto an attractor in any interesting sense.

Much of the appeal of artificial life models is shared by models in traditional artificial intelligence and connectionism. For one thing, computer models by their nature facilitate the level of abstraction required to pursue an interest in maximally general models of phenomena. In addition, the discipline imposed by expressing a model in feasible computer code entails a salutary precision and clarity and insures that all hypothesized mechanisms could actually work in the real world. But the distinctive bottom-up architecture of artificial life models creates a special virtue, for allowing micro-level entities continually to affect the context of their own behavior creates an importantly realistic complexity. For example, a population of organisms typically has an active hand in constructing the environment to which it adapts [Bedau, 1996b]. Because of the network of interactions among organisms, an organism's adaptation to its environment typically changes the intrinsic properties of the external objects in its environment. Nevertheless, in order to insure analytical tractability, all too many models of organisms within an environment ignore these interaction. For example, Sober's [1994] model of phenotypic plasticity treats an organism's environment as fixed for all time and presumes that each organism confronts its environment in isolation from all other organisms. These simplifying assumptions do make Sober's model amenable to armchair analysis, but at the price of irrealism about the dynamic interactions between organism and environment. Such interactions would imply a population of entities "undergoing a kaleidoscopic array of simultaneous nonlinear interactions", as John Holland puts it [1992, 184], and analytically solvable mathematical models can reveal little about the global effects which emerge from a web of such interactions. The only way to study the effects of these interactions is to do what the field of artificial life does: build bottom-up models and then empirically investigate their emergent global behavior through computer simulations.

Artificial life models routinely do show impressive global phenomena emerging from simple micro-level interactions. Flocking behavior is an especially vivid example of this. Flocks of birds exhibit impressive macro-level behavior. The flock maintains its cohesion while moving ahead, changing direction, and negotiating obstacles. And these global patterns are achieved without any global control. No individual bird issues flight instructions to the rest of the flock; no central authority is even aware of the global state of the flock. The global behavior is simply the aggregate effect of the microcontingencies of individual bird trajectories. One might attempt to model flocking behavior by using brute force and specifying how each bird's moment-to-moment trajectory is affected by the behavior of every other bird in the flock, i.e., by the global state of the flock. An illustration of this kind of model (in a slightly different context) is the computer animation method used in the Star Wars movies. In Star Wars we see computer animation not of bird flocks but of fleets of futuristic spaceships. Those sequences of computer animated interstellar warfare between different fleets of spaceships were produced by human programmers carefully scripting each frame, positioning each ship at each moment by reference to its relationship with (potentially) every other ship in the fleet. This brute force modeling approach has two drawbacks. The first is that the behavior of the fleet seems somewhat scripted and unnatural. Second, as the size of the fleet grows, the computational expense of the brute force modeling approach mushrooms. Adding even one more ship in principle can require adjusting the behavior of every other ship in the fleet, so the brute force model succumbs to a combinatorial explosion.

It is natural to ask whether natural flocking behavior can be feasibly produced by a model which concerns only local behavior of simple individual agents. It turns out that in general the only way to answer this question is to try it and see what happens. Fortunately, Craig Reynolds has done this for us with his "Boids" model [1987, 1992]. When one views Reynold's flocking demos, one is vividly struck by how natural the flocking behavior seems. The collection of individual boids spontaneously organize into a flock that then maintains its cohesion as it moves and changes direction and negotiates obstacles, fluidly flowing through space and time. The flock is a loosely formed group, so loose that individual boids sometimes lose contact with the rest of the flock and fly off on their own, only to rejoin the flock if they come close enough to the flock's sphere of influence. The flock appropriately adjusts its spatial configuration and motion in response to internal and external circumstances. For example, the flock maintains its cohesion as it follows along a wall; also, the flock splits into two subflocks if it runs into a column, and then the two subflocks will merge back into one when they have flown past the column.

The Boids model produces these natural, supple flocking dynamics as the emergent aggregate effect of micro-level boid activity. No entity in the Boids model has any information about the global state of the flock, and no entity controls boid trajectories with global state information. No boid issues flight plans to the other boids. No programmer-as-God scripts specific trajectories for individual boids. Instead, each individual boid's behavior is determined by three simple rules that key off of a boid's neighbors: seek to maintain a certain minimum distance from nearby boids, seek to match the speed and direction of nearby boids, and seek to steer toward the center of gravity of nearby boids. (In addition, boid's seek to avoid colliding with objects in the environment and are subject to the laws of physics.) Aside from the programmer's direct control over a few features of the environment (placement of walls, columns, etc.), the model's explicit dynamics govern only the local behavior of the individual boids. Each boid acts independently in the sense that its behavior is determined solely by following the imperatives of its own internal rules. (Of course, all boids have the same internal rules, but each boid applies the rules in a way that is sensitive to the contingencies of its own immediate environment.) An individual boid's dynamical behavior affects and is affected by only certain local features of its environment—nearby boids and other nearby objects such as walls and columns. The Boids model contains no explicit directions for flock dynamics. The flocking behavior produced by the model consists of the aggregated individual boid trajectories and the flock's global dynamics emerges out of the individual boid's explicit micro-level dynamics.

Reynold's Boids model provides one illustration of how complex phenomena of living systems emerging from simple bottom-up artificial life models. This pattern has many other instances. Consider one more example—the phenomena of open-ended evolution, one of the hallmarks of living systems [Bedau, 1996a]. One might speculate about whether a single self-replicating entity by itself could spawn such a process, but a feasible model can decisively cut through this speculation. Tom Ray's [1992] Tierra is such a model. Tierra consists of a population of self-replicating machine language programs that "reside" in computer memory consuming the "resource" CPU time. A Tierran "genotype" consists of a specific type of string of self-replicating machine code, and each Tierran "creature" is a token of a Tierran genotype. A simulation starts when the memory is inoculated with a single self-replicating program, the "ancestor", and then left to run on its own. At first the ancestor and its off-spring repeatedly replicate until the available memory space is teeming with creatures which all share the same ancestral genotype. However, since any given machine language creature eventually dies, and since errors (mutations) sometimes occur when a creature replicates, the population of Tierra creatures evolves. Over time the "ecology" of Tierran genotypes becomes remarkably diverse, with the appearance of fitter and fitter genotypes, parasites, and hyper-parasites, among other things.

By simulating specific bottom-up models like Reynold's Boids and Ray's Tierra, the field of artificial life studies how various kinds of global vital phenomena can spontaneously emerge from a web of interactions among simple micro-level agents. By illuminating the minimal conditions sufficient to produce these phenomena, the models help us to understand not only how such phenomena happen in the actual world but also how they could happen in any possible world.

II

The philosophical issues affected by artificial life include basic metaphysical questions about fundamental aspects of reality such as life, mind, and emergent phenomena in general; also included are many issues concerning contemporary topics like artificial intelligence and functionalism; and even theoretical ethical questions and matters of practical political policy are affected. Bedau [1992] surveys these issues; this section will illustrate artificial life's influence on the content of philosophical issues by considering two topics: the nature of emergent phenomena, and the significance of the distinctive suppleness of mental phenomena.

Apparent emergent phenomena share two hallmarks: they are somehow constituted by, and generated from, underlying processes, and yet they are also somehow autonomous from those underlying processes. Although these two hallmarks seem inconsistent or, in combination, somehow metaphysically illegitimate, nevertheless there are abundant examples of apparent emergent phenomena, spanning from inanimate self-organization like a tornado to the conscious mental lives embodied in our brains, and including a wealth of phenomena in vital systems. Hence, the perennial puzzle of emergence. A solution to this puzzle would not only explain—or, better, explain away—the appearance of illegitimate metaphysics; it would also show that emergent phenomena are a central and constructive part of our understanding of nature, especially in accounts of those phenomena like life and mind that have always seemed to involve emergence. It is significant, then, that a certain kind of emergent phenomena—what I elsewhere call *weak emergence* [Bedau forthcoming-b]—plays a central role in artificial life models of vital phenomena.

The paradigmatic case of weak emergence concerns the macrostates of a system that is composed out of micro-level parts, the number and identity of which typically change over time. The macrostates are structural properties constituted wholly out of the microstates, and a dynamical process governs how the microstates change over time. A system's macrostate is weakly emergent, then, just in case it can be derived from the system's external conditions (including its initial conditions) and its micro-level dynamical process but *only through the process of simulation* [For further details, see Bedau forthcoming-b]. Weak emergence is certainly characteristic of artificial life's bottom-up models, and it seems to be present in virtually all complex systems,

140

both artificial and natural. This ubiquity is what makes weak emergence especially interesting.

Weak emergence differs significantly from the traditional notions of emergence in twentieth century philosophy. For example, since weakly emergent properties can be derived (via simulation) from complete knowledge of micro-level information, from that same information they can be *predicted*, at least in principle, with complete certainty. Thus, weak emergence diverges from those conceptions of emergence [e.g., Broad, 1925, Pepper, 1926, Nagel, 1961] that depend on in principle unpredictability. Of course, weak emergence does still share *some* of the flavor of these views, since actually making the predictions involves the *a posteriori* and contingency-ridden process of simulation.

It is worth noting that weak emergence has the two hallmarks of emergent properties listed earlier. It is quite straightforward how weak emergent phenomena are constituted by, and generated from, underlying processes. The system's macrostates are constituted by its microstates, and the macrostates are entirely generated solely from the system's microstates and microdynamic. At the same time, there is a clear sense in which the behavior of weak emergent phenomena are autonomous with respect to the underlying processes. When artificial life discovers simple, general macro-level patterns and laws involving weak emergent phenomena, there is no evident hope of side-stepping a simulation and deriving these patterns and laws of weak emergent phenomena from the underlying microdynamic (and external conditions) alone. In general, we can formulate and investigate the basic principles of weak emergent phenomena only by empirically observing them at the macro-level. In this sense, then, weakly emergent phenomena have an autonomous life at the macro-level. Now, there is nothing inconsistent or metaphysically illegitimate about underlying processes constituting and generating phenomena that can be derived only by simulation. In this way, weak emergence explains away the appearance of metaphysical illegitimacy.

One might object that weak emergence is *too* weak to be called "emergent", either because it applies so widely or arbitrarily that it does not demark an interesting class of phenomena, or because it applies to certain phenomena that are not emergent. But this breadth of instances is no flaw, for weak emergence is not designed to capture an intrinsically interesting property. *Most* macrostates in complex systems are weakly emergent, and most of them have no special importance. In fact, a central scientific challenge in artificial life and related fields is to identify which emergent macrostates *are* interesting, i.e., which reflect the fundamental qualities of living systems [Bedau, and Packard, 1992, Bedau, 1995].

Weak emergence is the rule in artificial life; complex macro phenomena are constituted and generated by simple micro dynamics, but the micro phenomena involve such a kaleidoscopic array of non-additive interactions that the macro phenomena can be derived only by means of explicit simulations. The central place of weak emergence in this thriving scientific activity provides substantial evidence that weak emergence is philosophically and scientifically important. It is striking that weak emergence is so prominent in scientific accounts of exactly those especially puzzling phenomena in the natural world—such as those involving life and mind—that perennially generate sympathy for emergence. Can this be an accident?

It is well known that the emergent dynamical patterns among our mental states are especially difficult to describe and explain precisely. Descriptions of these patterns must be qualified by "ceteris paribus" clauses, as the following example [adapted from Horgan and Tienson, 1989] illustrates:

> *Means-ends reasoning*: If X wants goal G and X believes that X can achieve G by performing action A, then *ceteris paribus* X will do A. For example, if X wants a beer and believes that there is one in the kitchen, then X will go get one—unless, as the "ceteris paribus" clause signals, X does not want to miss any of the conversation, or X does not want to offend the speaker by leaving in mid-sentence, or X does not want to drink beer in front of his mother-in-law, or X thinks he should, instead, flee the house since it is on fire, etc.

An analogous open-ended list of exceptions infects descriptions of all analogous mental patterns, for which reason these patterns are sometimes called "soft" [Horgan and Tienson, 1990].

There are different kinds of "softness". One kind of softness [emphasized by Fodor, 1981, for example] results from malfunctions in the underlying material and processes that implement mental phenomena. Another kind of softness [emphasized by Horgan and Tienson, 1989 and 1990] could result from the indeterminate results of competition among a potentially open-ended range of conflicting desires. But there is a third kind of softness, which I will call "suppleness". Suppleness is involved in a distinctive kind of exceptions to the patterns in our mental lives—specifically, those exceptions that reflect our *ability to act appropriately* in the face of an open-ended range of contextual contingencies. These exceptions to the norm occur when we make *appropriate* adjustment to contingencies. The ability to adjust our behavior appropriately in context is a central component of the capacity for intelligent behavior [Varela, Thompson, and Rosch, 1991; Parisi, Nolfi, and Cecconi, 1992]. Since the suppleness of mental dynamics is crucially involved in their very intelligence, any adequate account of the mind must explain this suppleness.

But the suppleness of mental dynamics itself makes them difficult to describe and explain. If we merely employ "ceteris paribus" clauses (or their equivalent) in our description and explanation, then we cannot *specify* when ceteris is not paribus, when deviation from the norm is appropriate. The "expert systems" of traditional artificial intelligence illustrate an alternative strategy for accounting for the suppleness of mental processes: predigest the circumstances that give rise to exceptions and then specify (either explicitly or through heuristics) how to cope with them in a manner that is precise enough to be expressed as an algorithm. The problem with these expert systems is that they never supplely respond to an open-ended variety of circumstances [see, e.g., Dreyfus, 1979, Hofstadter, 1985, Holland, 1986]. Their behavior is "brittle"; it lacks the sensitivity to context distinctive of intelligence. The nature and central role of suppleness in our mental capacities helps explain why the so-called "frame problem" of artificial intelligence is so important and so difficult to solve.

A third strategy for accounting for supple mental dynamics is to follow the lead set by recent work in artificial life. For there is a similar suppleness in vital processes such as metabolism, adaptation, and even flocking. For example, a flock maintains its cohesion not always but only for the most part, only *ceteris paribus*, for the cohesion can be broken when the flock flies into an obstacle (like a tree). In such a context, the best way to "preserve" the flock might be for the flock to divide into subflocks. Reynolds Boids model exhibits just this sort of supple flocking behavior. Or consider another example concerning the process of adaptation itself. Successful adaptation depends on the ability to explore an appropriate number of viable evolutionary alternatives; too many or too few can make adaptation difficult or even impossible. In other words, success requires striking a balance between the competing demands for "creativity" (trying new alternatives) and "memory" (retaining what has proved successful). Furthermore, as the context for evolution changes, the appropriate balance between creativity and memory can shift in a way that resists precise and exceptionless formulation. Nevertheless, artificial life models can show a supple flexibility in how they balance creativity and novelty [Bedau and Bahm, 1994, Bedau and Seymour, 1994]. Other emergent artificial life models illustrate other kinds of supple emergent vital dynamics. [For more discussion of these examples, see Bedau forthcoming-a]. Although these examples alone provide no *proof* that the supple dynamics are due to the models' emergent architecture, the growing empirical evidence continually supports this conclusion.

Artificial life models construe supple dynamics as the emergent macro-level effect of a context-dependent competition for influence in a population of micro-level entities. An analogous model of the mind would construe supple mental dynamics as a macro-level effect which emerges from the aggregate behavior of a micro-level population. In a successful model the emergent macro-level dynamic would correspond well with the supple dynamics of real minds. But let there be no false advertising! My remarks here only begin to suggest what an emergent model of supple mental dynamics would be like. Since the ultimate plausibility of the emergent approach to mental dynamics depends, as one might say, on "putting your model where your mouth is," one might in fairness demand proponents of this approach to start building models. But producing models is not easy; a host of difficult issues must be faced. First, what is the micro-level population from which mental phenomena emerge, and what explicit micro-level dynamics govern it? Second, assuming we have settled on a micro-level population and dynamics, how can we identify the macro-level dynamics of interest? Emergent models generate copious quantities of micro-level information, and this saddles us with a formidable data-reduction problem. Where should "slice" these data to see relevant patterns? Finally, assuming we have a satisfactory solution to the data reduction problem, how can we recognize and interpret any patterns that might appear? We must distinguish real patterns from mere artifacts. The patterns will not come pre-labeled; how are we to recognize any supple mental dynamics that might emerge?

The foregoing difficulties are worth confronting, though, for an emergent account of supple mental dynamics would have important virtues. The account would be precise, just as precise as the emergent model itself. Furthermore, the model would produce an increasingly complete description of a precise set of mental dynamics as it was simulated more and more. Though the model might never completely fill out all the details of the supple pattern, additional simulation could generate as much detail as desired. In addition, the model's account of the supple dynamics would be principled, since one and the same model would generate the supple pattern along with all the exceptions that prove the rule. The success of the emergent models in artificial life argues that emergent models of supple mental dynamics are a promising avenue to explore.

III

Philosophers have welcomed new kinds of evidence into their discussions. Details about the contingencies of neurophysiology, for example, inform work on the philosophy of mind [e.g., P. S. Churchland, 1986, P. M. Churchland, 1989], and treatments of reductionism in biology, to pick another example, advert to detailed discoveries of biological science [e.g., Kitcher, 1984 and Waters, 1990]. We now also find artificial life's computer simulations being imported into philosophy. But what is distinctive about artificial life's impact on philosophy is that its computational methodology is such a direct and natural extension of philosophy's traditional methodology of *a priori* thought experiments. In the attempt to capture the simple essence of vital processes, artificial life models abstract away from most details of natural living systems without pretending to be accurate models of particular features of particular natural systems [Bedau, 1995]. These are "idea" models for exploring the consequences of certain simple premises. Artificial life simulations are in effect thought experiments — but *emergent* thought experiments. As with the "armchair" thought experiments familiar in philosophy, artificial life simulations attempt to answer "What if X?" questions. What is distinctive about emergent thought experiments is that what they reveal can be discerned only by simulation; armchair analysis in these contexts is simply inconclusive. Synthesizing emergent thought experiments with a computer is a new technique that philosophers can adapt from artificial life.

It will take some time to learn how and when to use emergent thought experiments. When the context is even a little complex, it is all too easy to fall into the fallacy of assuming that something is (or is not) possible because we think we can (or cannot) imagine how it might happen. We can avoid this fallacy by grounding our speculations on empirical evidence about what actually happens when we synthesize the relevant phenomena in an emergent thought experiment. This section illustrates the need for this new methodology.

The progression of evolution in our biosphere seems to show a remarkable overall increase in complexity, from simple prokaryotic one-celled life to eukaryotic cellular life forms with a nucleus and numerous other cytoplasmic structures, then to life forms composed out of a multiplicity of cells, then to large-bodied vertebrate creatures with sophisticated sensory processing capacities, and ultimately to highly intelligent creatures that use language and develop sophisticated technology [McShea, 1996 is a useful caution about the difficulty of quantitatively verifying this change in complexity]. This evidence is consistent with the hypothesis that open-ended evolutionary processes have an inherent, law-like tendency to create creatures with increasingly complicated functional organization. Just as the arrow of entropy in the second law of thermodynamics asserts that the entropy in all physical systems has a general tendency to increase with time, the hypothesis of the arrow of complexity asserts that the complex functional organization of the most complex products of open-ended evolutionary systems has a general tendency to increase with time.

The fact that the evolution of life is consistent with the arrow of complexity hypothesis does not establish the truth of the hypothesis, of course, and nobody more vigilantly guards against any echo of the idea of evolution as a march of progress than Stephen Jay Gould. His book [1989] on the fossils in the Burgess Shale spectacularly reinterprets the evolution of life as a process devoid of any global progression like an arrow of complexity. The book's central argument is that any evolutionary progression evident in our biosphere is merely a

145

contingent by-product of myriad accidents frozen into the evolutionary record. Although the course of life has an historical explanation, Gould thinks that no deeper, law-like tendency is implicated.

> Historical explanations take the form of a narrative: E, the phenomenon to be explained, arose because D came before, preceded by C, B, and A. . . . Thus, E makes sense and can be explained rigorously as the outcome of A through D. But no law of nature enjoined E; any variant E´ arising from an altered set of antecedents, would have been equally explicable, though massively different in form and effect.
> I am not speaking of randomness (for E had to arise, as a consequence of A through D), but of the central principle of all history — *contingency* [Gould, 1989, 283, emphasis in original].

Gould thinks that the contingency of historical processes like the evolution of the biosphere debars general laws like the hypothesized arrow of complexity. The results of historical processes "do not arise as deducible consequences from any law of nature; they are not even predictable from any general or abstract property of the larger system...." [Gould, 1989, 284]. Instead, "almost every interesting event of life's history falls into the realm of contingency" [Gould, 1989, 290].

Gould illustrates his argument with the thought experiment of replaying the tape of life, that is, rewinding the evolutionary process backward in time and they replaying it again forward in time but allowing different accidents, different contingencies to reshape the evolution of life.

> I call this experiment "replaying life's tape." You press the rewind button and, making sure you thoroughly erase everything that actually happened, go back to any time and place in the past — say, to the seas of the Burgess Shale. Then let the tape run again and see if the repetition looks at all like the original. If each replay strongly resembles life's actual pathway, then we must conclude that what really happened pretty much had to occur. But suppose that the experimental versions all yield sensible results strikingly different from the actual history of life? What could we then say about the predictability of self-conscious intelligence? or of mammals? or of vertebrates? or of life on land? or simply of multicellular persistence for 600 million years? [Gould, 1989, 48-50].

Gould is confident that his thought experiment disproves anything like an arrow of complexity, for "any replay of the tape would lead evolution down a pathway radically different from the road actually taken" [Gould, 1989, 51].

But does Gould's thought experiment really show this? Replaying life's tape is a wonderful "crucial" experiment for testing the arrow of complexity hypothesis, but Gould has no good ground for prognostications about what replaying the tape would show. In fact, he shows no interest in pursuing his thought experiment constructively, though this is exactly the sort of investigation that is pursued in the field of artificial life. With an appropriate computer model of open-ended evolution, you can rerun the tape of life to your heart's content. The detailed course of evolution in each case would depend on the history of accidents unique to each run, but a general pattern unifying these contingencies still might emerge. Judicious analysis of the mass of contingencies collected from repeated simulations of the model would reveal whether an arrow of complexity is lurking, and this would finally provide an appropriate context within which to understand the progressive complexity of the actual biosphere.

Make no mistake: nobody has yet actually conducted Gould's thought experiment. In fact, it is not obvious how to do the experiment because it is unclear how to design a system that exhibits the kind of open-ended evolution characteristic of our biosphere. One of the ongoing research efforts in the field of artificial life is the pursuit of exactly this goal. As long as this experiment remains in the future all guesses about its outcome — including Gould's — will remain inconclusive. Actually conducting the experiment will mark when the discussion moves beyond mere verbal speculation. We can finally discern the global pattern (if any) inherent in the process of open-ended evolution only by creating and empirically observing the relevant emergent thought experiments.

It is hard to avoid the fallacy of putting too much stock on our *a priori* intuitions when contemplating complex systems. Where Gould assumes that the contingencies of evolution preclude an arrow of complexity, Daniel Dennett [1995] assumes that evolution by natural selection can explain human concerns like mind, language, and morals. But Dennett's assumption is only an article of faith. He never attempts to construct an evolutionary explanation for mind, language, and morality; he never "puts his model where his mouth is" and checks whether natural selection really could explain these phenomena, even in principle. There is little doubt that the explanation of mind, language and morals, when discovered, will be *consistent* with natural selection — just as natural selection is consistent with quantum mechanics. But this does not show that natural selection, any more than quantum mechanics, plays an important role in the *explanation* of mind, language and morals. When Dennett claims that natural selection does explain them, he's only guessing, just as Hobbes was only guessing when he claimed that they could be explained by corpuscular mechanics. Maybe natural selection can explain them, maybe it can't; we just don't know yet.

The way to show what phenomena natural selection *can* produce is to use natural selection to synthesize the phenomena in an emergent thought experiment. These thought experiments introduce discipline into the discussion. We can gain confidence that we understand how to explain some phenomenon when we can synthesize it in a plausible model, and when we are unable to do this we reveal our ignorance.

IV

The new interdisciplinary field of artificial life has many implications for philosophy. Not only will artificial life influence progress on a host of fundamental philosophical issues, but the field's emergent thought experiments will change the practice of philosophy. Artificial life and philosophy are natural partners. Both seek to understand phenomena at a level of generality that is sufficiently deep to reveal essential natures. Furthermore, the pursuit of this generality drives both to use the method of though experiments. But while philosophers have traditionally conducted their thought experiments while meditating in their armchairs, the complexity of situations contemplated in artificial life forces investigators to conduct their thought experiments at the computer. The same can be said with increasing frequency for philosophical thought experiments about issues like emergence, life, and mind. A new level of clarity, precision, and evidence will follow when philosophers adapt artificial life's computational methodology of emergent thought experiments. A constructive test of our understanding of a complex phenomenon is the success to which we can "put our model where our mouth is" in an emergent thought experiment. Artificial life has been doing this, and philosophy is now starting to follow this example.

REFERENCES

Bedau, Mark. (Forthcoming-a) "Emergent Models of Supple Dynamics in Life and Mind." *Brain and Cognition*.

Bedau, Mark. (Forthcoming-b) "Weak Emergence." In James Tomberlin, Ed., *Philosophical Perspectives*, Vol. 11, New York: Basil Blackwell Publishers.

Bedau, Mark. (1996a) "The Nature of Life." In M. Boden, Ed., *The Philosophy of Artificial Life*, Oxford: Oxford University Press., 332-357.

Bedau, Mark. (1996b) "The Extent to which Organisms Construct their Environments." *Adaptive Behavior* 4: 469-475.

Bedau, Mark. (1995) "Three Illustrations of Artificial Life's Working Hypothesis." In Wolfgang Banzhaf and Frank Eeckman, Eds., *Evolution and Biocomputation*, Berlin: Springer-Verlag, 53-68.

Bedau, Mark. (1992) "Philosophical Aspects of Artificial Life." In F. Varela and P. Bourgine, Eds., *Towards A Practice of Autonomous Systems*, Cambridge: Bradford Books/MIT Press, 494-503.

Bedau, Mark, and Alan Bahm (1994) "Bifurcation Structure in Diversity Dynamics." In R. Brooks and P. Maes, Eds., *Artificial Life IV*, Cambridge: Bradford Books/MIT Press, 258-268.

Bedau, Mark, and Robert Seymour (1994) "Adaptation of Mutation Rates in a Simple Model of Evolution." In Russel J. Stonier and Xing Huo Yu, Eds., *Complex Systems — Mechanism of Adaptation*, Amsterdam: IOS Press, 37-44.

Bedau, Mark, and Norman Packard (1992) "Measurement of Evolutionary Activity, Teleology, and Life." In C. Langton, C. Taylor, D. Farmer, and S. Rasmussen, Eds., *Artificial Life II*, Santa Fe Institute Studies in the Sciences of Complexity, Vol. X, Redwood City: Addison-Wesley, 431-461.

Boden, Margaret, Ed. (1996) *The Philosophy of Artificial Life*, Oxford: Oxford University Press.

Broad, C. D. (1925) *The Mind and Its Place in Nature*. London: Routledge and Kegan Paul.

Churchland, Patricia Smith. (1986) *Neurophilosophy: Toward a Unified Science of the Mind/Brain*, Cambridge: Bradford Books/MIT Press.

Churchland, Paul M. (1989) *A Neurocomputational Perspective: The Nature of Mind and the Structure of Science*, Cambridge: Bradford Books/MIT Press.

Crutchfield, J.P., J.D. Farmer, N.H. Packard, and R.S. Shaw (1986) "Chaos." *Scientific American* 255 (December): 46-57.

Dennett, Daniel. (1995) *Darwin's Dangerous Idea: Evolution and the Meanings of Life*, New York: Simon and Schuster.

Dreyfus, H. (1979) *What Computers Cannot Do*, 2nd Ed, New York: Harper and Row.

Fodor, J. A. (1981) "Special Sciences." In his *Representations*, Cambridge: Bradford Books/MIT Press.

Gould, Stephen Jay. (1989) *Wonderful Life: The Burges Shale and the Nature of History*, New York: Norton.

Hofstadter, D. R. (1985) "Waking Up from the Boolean Dream, or, Subcognition as Computation." In his *Metamagical Themas: Questing for the Essence of Mind and Pattern*, New York: Basic Books, 631-665.

Holland, J. H. (1986) "Escaping Brittleness: The Possibilities of General-Purpose Learning Algorithms applied to Parallel Rule-Based Systems." In R. S. Michalski, J. G. Carbonell, and T. M. Mitchell, Eds., *Machine Learning II*, Los Altos: Morgan Kaufmann.

Holland, J. H. (1992) *Adaptation in Natural and Artificial Systems*, 2nd edition, Cambridge: Bradford Books/MIT Press.

Horgan, T., and J. Tienson, Eds. (1991) *Connectionism and the Philosophy of Mind*, Dordrecht: Kluwer Academic.

Horgan, T., and J. Tienson (1989) "Representation without Rules." *Philosophical Topics* 17: 147-174.

Horgan, T., and J. Tienson (1990) "Soft Laws." *Midwest Studies in Philosophy* 15: 256-279.

Kellert, S. H. (1993) *In the Wake of Chaos: Unpredictable Order in Dynamical Systems*, Chicago: The University of Chicago Press.

Kitcher, Philip. (1984) "1953 and All That: A Tale of Two Sciences." *Philosophical Review* 93: 335-373.

Langton, C. (1989) "Artificial Life," in C. Langton, Ed., *Artificial Life*, Redwood City: Addison-Wesley, 1-47.

Langton, C. (1992) "Life at the Edge of Chaos." In C. Langton, C. Taylor, D. Farmer, and S. Rasmussen, Eds., *Artificial Life II*, Santa Fe Institute Studies in the Sciences of Complexity, Vol. X, Redwood City: Addison-Wesley, 41-91.

McShea, Daniel W. (1996) "Metazoan complexity and evolution: Is there a trend?" *Evolution* 50: 477-492.

Nagel, E. (1961) *The Structure of Science*, New York: Harcourt, Brace & World.

Parisi, D., N. Nolfi, and F. Cecconi (1992) "Learning, Behavior, and Evolution." In F. Varela and P. Bourgine, Eds., *Towards a Practice of Autonomous Systems*, Cambridge: Bradford Books/MIT Press, 207-216.

Pepper, S. (1926) "Emergence." *Journal of Philosophy* 23: 241-245.

Ray, T. (1992) "An Approach to the Synthesis of Life." In C. Langton, C. Taylor, D. Farmer, and S. Rasmussen, Eds., *Artificial Life II*, Santa Fe Institute Studies in the Sciences of Complexity, Redwood City: Addison-Wesley, X, 371-408.

Reynolds, C. W. (1987) "Flocks, Herds, and Schools: A Distributed Behavioral Model." *Computer Graphics*, 21: 25-34.

Reynolds, C. W. (1992) Boids Demos. In C. Langton, Ed., *Artificial Life II Video Proceedings*, Redwood City: Addison-Wesley, 15-19.

Rumelhart, D. E., and J. L. McClelland (1986) *Parallel Distributed Processing: Explorations in the Microstructure of Cognition*, 2 Vols., Cambridge: Bradford Books/MIT Press.

Sober, E. (1994) "The Adaptive Advantage of Learning versus A Priori Prejudice." In *From a Biological Point of View*, Cambridge: Cambridge University Press.

Stone, M. A. (1989) "Chaos, Prediction, and Laplacean Determinism." *American Philosophical Quarterly* 26: 123-131.

Varela, F., E. Thompson and E. Rosch (1991) *The Embodied Mind: Cognitive Science and Human Experience*, Cambridge: Bradford Books/MIT Press.

Waters, C. Kenneth. (1990) "Why the Anti-Reductionist Consensus Won't Survive the Case of Classical Mendelian Genetics." *PSA 1990*, Vol. 1, *Proceedings of the PSA*, East Lansing, 125-139.

Wolfram, S. (1994) *Cellular Automata and Complexity*. Reading: Addison-Wesley.

THE NEURAL REPRESENTATION OF THE SOCIAL WORLD[1]

PAUL M. CHURCHLAND

Social Space

A crab lives in a submarine space of rocks and open sand and hidden recesses. A ground squirrel lives in a space of bolt holes and branching tunnels and leaf-lined bedrooms. A human occupies a physical space of comparable complexity, but in our case it is overwhelmingly obvious that we live also in an intricate space of obligations, duties, entitlements, prohibitions, appointments, debts, affections, insults, allies, contracts, enemies, infatuations, compromises, mutual love, legitimate expectations, and collective ideals. Learning the structure of this social space, learning to recognize the current position of oneself and others within it, and learning to navigate one's way through that space without personal or social destruction is at least as important to any human as learning the counterpart skills for purely physical space.

This is not to slight the squirrels and crabs, nor the bees and ants and termites either, come to think of it. The social dimensions of their cognitive lives, if simpler than ours, are still intricate and no doubt of comparable importance to them. What is important, at all levels of the phylogenetic scale, is that each creature lives in a world not just of physical objects but of other creatures as well, creatures that can perceive and plan and act, both for and against one's interests. Those other creatures therefore bear systematic attention. Even nonsocial animals must learn to perceive, and to respond to, the threat of predators or the opportunity for prey. Social animals must learn, in addition, the interactive culture that structures their collective life. This means that their nervous systems must learn to represent the many dimensions of the local social space, a space that embeds them as surely and as relevantly as does the local physical space. They must learn a hierarchy of categories for social agents, events, positions, con-figurations, and processes. They must learn to recognize instances of those many categories through the veil of degraded inputs, chronic ambiguity, and the occasional deliberate deception. Above all, they must learn to generate appropriate behavioral outputs in that social space, just as surely as they must learn to locomote, grasp food, and find shelter.

In confronting these additional necessities, a social creature must use the same sorts of neuronal resources and coding strategies that it uses for its representation of the sheerly physical world. The job may be special, but the tools available are the same. The creature must configure the many millions of synaptic connection strengths within its brain so as to represent the structure of the social reality in which it lives. Further, it must learn to generate sequences of neuronal activation-patterns that will produce socially acceptable or socially advantageous behavioral outputs. As we will see in what follows, social and moral reality is also the province of the physical brain. Social and moral cognition, social and moral behavior, are no less activities of the brain than is any other kind of cognition or behavior. We need to confront this fact, squarely and forthrightly, if we are ever to understand our own moral natures. We need to confront it if we are ever to deal both effectively and humanely with our too-frequent social pathologies. And we need to confront it if we are ever to realize our full social and moral potential.

Inevitably these sentiments will evoke discomfort in some readers, as if, by being located in the purely physical brain, social and moral knowledge were about to be devalued in some way. Let me say, most emphatically, that devaluation is not my purpose. As I see it, social and moral comprehension has just as much right to the term "knowledge" as does scientific or theoretical comprehension — no more right, but no less. In the case of gregarious creatures such as humans, social and moral understanding is as hard won, is as robustly empirical and objective, and is as vital to our well-being as is any piece of scientific knowledge. It also shows progress over time, both within an individual's lifetime and over the course of many centuries. It adjusts itself steadily to the pressures of cruel experience, and it is drawn ever forward by the hope of a surer peace, a more fruitful commerce, and a deeper enlightenment.

Beyond these brief remarks, the philosophical defense of moral realism must find another occasion. With the patient reader fairly forewarned, let us put this issue aside for now and approach the focal issue of how social and moral knowledge, whatever its metaphysical status, might actually be embodied in the brains of living biological creatures.

It cannot be too difficult. Ants and bees live intricate social lives, but their neural resources are minuscule — for an ant, 104 neurons, tops. However tiny those resources may be, evidently they are adequate. A worker ant's neural network learns to recognize a wide variety of socially relevant things: pheromonal trail markings to be pursued or avoided; a vocabulary of antennae exchanges to steer one another's behavior; the occasions for general defense, or attack, or fission of the colony; fertile pasture for the nest's aphid herd; the complex needs of the queen and her developing eggs; and so forth.

Presumably the challenge of social cognition and social behavior is not fundamentally different from that of physical cognition and behavior. The social features or processes to be discriminated may be subtle and complex, but as recent research with artificial neural networks illustrates, a high-dimensional vectorial representation — that is, a complex pattern of activation levels across a large population of neurons — can successfully capture all of them. To see how this might be so, let us start with a simple case: the principal emotional states as they are displayed in human faces.

EMPATH: A Network for Recognizing Human Emotions

Neural-net researchers have recently succeeded in modeling some elementary examples of social perception. I here draw on the work of

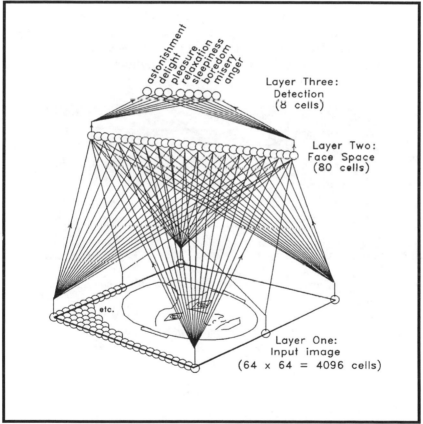

Fig. 1. EMPATH, a feedforward network for recognizing eight salient human emotions

Garrison Cottrell and Janet Metcalfe at the University of California, San Diego. Their three-stage artificial network is schematically portrayed in fig. 1. Its input layer or "retina" is a 64 X 64-pixel grid whose elements each admit of 256 different levels of activation or "brightness." This resolution, both in space and in brightness, is adequate to code recognizable representations of real faces.

Each input cell projects an axonal end-branch to every cell at the second layer of 80 cells. That layer represents an abstract space of 80 dimensions in which the input faces are explicitly coded. This second layer projects finally to an output layer of only 8 cells. These output cells have the job of explicitly representing the specific emotional expression present in the current input photograph. In all, the network contains (64 X 64) + 80 + 8 = 4,184 cells, and a grand total of 328,320 synaptic connections.

Cottrell and Metcalfe trained this network on eight familiar emotional states, as they were willingly feigned in the cooperating faces of twenty undergraduate subjects, ten male and ten female. Three of these charming subjects are displayed eight times in fig. 2, one for each of the eight emotions. In sequence, you will there see astonishment, delight, pleasure, relaxation, sleepiness, boredom, misery, and anger. The aim was to discover if a network of the modest size at issue could learn to discriminate features at this level of subtlety, across a real diversity of human faces.

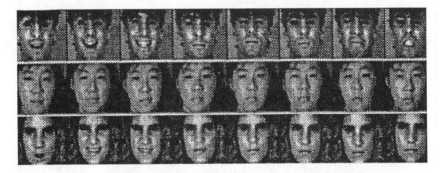

Fig. 2 Eight familiar emotional states, as feigned in the facial expressions of three human subjects. From the left, they are astonishment, delight, pleasure, relaxation, sleepiness, boredom, misery, and anger. These photos, and a set of eight for each of seventeen other human subjects, were used to train EMPATH, a network for discriminating emotions as they are displayed in human faces. (From Cottrell, G. W. and Metcalfe, J.: 1991).

The answer is yes, but it must be qualified. On the training set of (8 emotions X 20 faces =) 160 photos in all, the network reached — after 1,000 presentations of the entire training set, with incremental synaptic adjustments after each presentation — high levels of accuracy on the four positive emotions (about 80 percent), but very poor levels on the negative emotions, with the sole exception of anger, which was correctly identified 85 percent of the time.

Withal, it did learn. And it did generalize successfully to photographs of people it had never seen before. Its performance was robustly accurate for five of the eight emotions, and its weakest performance parallels a similar performance weakness in humans. (Subsequent testing on real humans showed that they too had trouble discriminating sleepiness, boredom, and misery, as displayed in the training photographs. Look again at fig. 2 and you will appreciate the problem.) This means that the emotional expressions at issue are indeed within the grasp of a neural network, and it indicates that a larger network and a larger training set might do a great deal better. EMPATH is an "existence proof," if you like: a proof that for some networks, and for some socially relevant human behaviors, the one can learn to discriminate the other. Examination of the activation patterns produced at the second layer — by the presentation of any particular face — reveals that the network has developed a set of eight different prototypical activation patterns, one for each of the eight emotions it has learned, although the patterns for the three problematic negative emotions are diffuse and rather indistinct. These eight prototypical patterns are what the final eight output units are tuned to detect.

Social Features and Prototypical Sequences

EMPATH's level of sophistication is, of course, quite low. The "patterns" to which it has become tuned are timeless snapshots. It has no grasp of any expressive sequences. In stark contrast to a normal human, it will recognize sadness in a series of heaving sobs no more reliably than in a single photograph of one slice of that telltale sequence. For both the human and the network, a single photograph might be ambiguous, but to the human, that distressing sequence of behavior certainly will not be. Lacking any recurrent pathways, EMPATH cannot tap into the rich palette of information contained in how perceivable patterns unfold in time. For this reason, no network with a purely feed-forward architecture, no matter how large, could ever equal the recognitional capacities of a human.

Lacking any grasp of temporal patterns carries a further price. EMPATH has no conception of what sorts of causal antecedents typically produce the principal emotions, and no conception of what effects those emotions have on the ongoing cognitive, social, and physical behavior of the people who have them. That the discovered loss of a loved one typically causes grief; that grief typically causes some degree of social paralysis; these things are utterly beyond EMPATH's ken. In short, the prototypical causal roles of the several emotions are also beyond any network like EMPATH. Just as researchers have already discovered in the realm of purely physical cognition, sophisticated social cognition requires a grasp of patterns in time, and this re-

157

quires that the successful network be richly endowed with recurrent pathways, additional pathways that cycle information from higher neuronal layers back to earlier neuronal layers. This alone will permit the recognition of causal sequences. Figure 3 provides a cartoon example of a recurrent network. Such networks are trained, not on timeless snapshots, as was EMPATH. They are trained on appropriate sequences of input patterns.

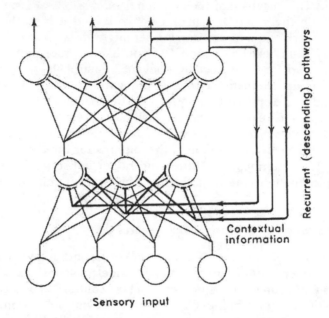

Fig. 3. An elementary recurrent network. The recurrent pathways are in boldface.

An important subset of causal sequences is the set of ritual or conventional sequences. To take some prototypical examples, consider a social introduction, an exchange of pleasantries, an extended negotiation, a closing of a deal, a proper leave-taking. All of these mutual exchanges require, for their recognition as well as their execution, a well-tuned recurrent network. And they require of the network a considerable history spent embedded within a social space already filled with such prototypical activities on every side. After all, those prototypes must be learned, a process that will require both instructive examples and plenty of time to internalize them.

In the end, the acquired library of social prototypes hierarchically embedded in the vast neuronal activation space of any normally socialized human must rival, if it does not exceed, the acquired library of purely natural or nonsocial prototypes. One need only read a novel by someone like George Eliot or Henry James to appreciate the intricate structure of human social space and the complexity of human social dynamics. More simply, recall your teenage years. Mastering that complexity is a cognitive achievement at least equal to earning a degree in physics. And yet with few exceptions, all of us do it.

Are There "Social Areas" in the Brain?

Experimental neuroscience in the twentieth century has focused almost exclusively on finding the neuroanatomical (i.e., structural) and the neurophysiological (i.e., activational) correlates of perceptual properties that are purely natural or physical in nature. The central and programmatic question has been as follows. Where in the brain, and by what processes, do we recognize such properties as color, shape, motion, sound, taste, aroma, temperature, texture, bodily damage, relative distance, and so on? The pursuit of such questions has led to real insights, and we have long been able to provide a map of the various areas in the brain that seem centrally involved in each of the functions mentioned.

The discovery technique is simple in concept. Insert a long, thin microelectrode into any one of the cells in the cortical area in question (the brain has no pain sensors, so the experimental animal is utterly unaware of this telephone tap), and then see whether and how that cell responds when the animal is shown color or motion, or hears tones, or feels warmth and cold, and so on. In this fashion, a functional map is painstakingly produced. Figure 4 provides a quick look at the several primary and secondary sensory cortices and their positions within the rear half of a typical primate cerebral cortex.

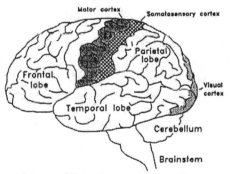

Fig. 4. *The locations of some of the primary and secondary areas within the human cerebral cortex. (Subcortical structures are not shown.) The "motor strip" or motor-output cortex is also shown. Note the extensive cortical areas that lie outside these easily identified areas.*

But what about the front half of the cortex, the so-called "frontal lobe"? What is it for? The conventional but vague answer is, "to formulate potential motor behaviors for delivery to and execution by the motor cortex." Here we possess much less insight into the significance of these cortical structures and their neuronal activities. We cannot manipulate the input to those areas in any detail, as we can with the several sensory areas, because the input received by the premotor areas comes ultimately from all over the brain: from areas that are already high up in the processing hierarchy, areas a long way from the sensory periphery where we can easily control what is and is not presented.

On the other hand, we can insert microelectrodes as before, but this time stimulate the target cell rather than record from it. In the motor cortex itself, this works beautifully. If we briefly stimulate the cells in certain areas, certain muscles in the body twitch, and there is a systematic correspondence between the areas of motor cortex and the muscles they control. In short, the motor strip itself constitutes a well-ordered map of the body's many muscles, much as the primary visual cortex is a map of the eye's retina. Stimulating single cells outside of and upstream from the motor areas, however, produces little or nothing in the way of behavioral response, presumably because the production of actual behavior requires smooth sequences of large activation vectors involving many thousands of cells at once. That kind of stimulation we still lack the technology to produce.

A conventional education in neuroscience thus leaves one wondering exactly how the entire spectrum of sensory inputs processed in the rear half of the brain finally gets transformed into some appropriate motor outputs formulated in the front half of the brain. This is indeed a genuine problem, and it is no wonder that researchers have found it so difficult. From the perspective we have gained from our study of artificial networks, we can see how complex the business of vector coding and vector transformation must be in something as large as the brain.

Plainly, sleuthing out the brain's complete sensorimotor strategy would be a daunting task even if the brain were an artificial network, one whose every synaptic connection strength were known and all of whose neuronal activation levels were open to continuous and simultaneous monitoring. But a living brain is not so accommodating. Its connection strengths are mostly inaccessible, and monitoring the activity of more than a few cells at a time is currently impossible.

This is one of the reasons why the recent artificial network models have made possible so much progress. We can learn things from the models that we might never have learned from the brain directly. And we can then return to the biological brain with some new and better-informed experimental questions to pose — questions concerning the empirical faithfulness of our network models, questions that we do have some hope of answering. Accordingly, the hidden transformations that produce behavior from perceptual input need not remain hidden after all.

160

If we aspire to track them down, however, we need to broaden our conception of the problem. In particular, we should be wary of the assumption that perception is first and foremost the perception of purely physical features in the world. And we should be wary of the correlative assumption that behavioral output is first and primarily the manipulation of physical objects.

We should be wary because we already know that humans and other social animals are keenly sensitive, perceptually, to social features of their surroundings. And because we already know that humans and social animals manipulate their social environment as well as their purely physical surroundings. And above all, because we already know that infants in most social species begin acquiring their social coordination at least as early as they begin learning sensorimotor coordination in its purely physical sense. Even infants can discriminate a smile from a scowl, a kind tone of voice from a hostile tone, a humorous exchange from a fractious one. And even an infant can successfully call for protection, induce feeding behavior, and invite affection and play.

I do not mean to suggest that social properties are anything more, ultimately, than just intricate aspects of the purely physical world. Nor do I wish to suggest that they have independent causal properties over and above what is captured by physics and chemistry. What I do wish to assert is that, in learning to represent the world, the brains of infant social creatures focus naturally and relentlessly on the social features of their local environment, often slighting physical features that will later seem unmissable. Human children, for example, typically do not acquire command of the basic color vocabulary until their third or fourth year of life, long after they have gained linguistic competence on matters such as anger, promises, friendship, ownership, and love. As a parent, I was quite surprised to discover this in my own children, and surprised again to learn that the pattern is quite general. But perhaps I should not have been. The social features listed are far more important to a young child's practical life than are the endlessly various colors.

The general lesson is plain. As social infants partition their activation spaces, the categories that form are just as often social categories as they are natural or physical categories. In apportioning neuronal resources for important cognitive tasks, the brain expends roughly as much of those resources on representing and controlling social reality as it does on representing and controlling physical reality.

Look once again, in the light of these remarks, at the brain in figure 4. Notice the unmapped frontal half and the large unmapped areas of the rear half. Might some of these areas be principally involved in social perception and action? Might they be teeming with vast vectorial sequences representing social realities of one sort or other? Indeed, once the question is raised, why stop with these areas? Might the so-called "primary" sensory cortical areas — for touch, vision, and hearing especially — be as much in the business of grasping and processing social facts as they are in the business of grasping and processing purely physical facts? These two functions are certainly not mutually exclusive.

I think the answer is almost certainly yes to all of these questions. We lack intricate brain maps for social features comparable to existing brain maps for physical features, not because they are nonexistent, I suggest, but rather because we have not looked for them with a determination comparable to the physical case.

Moral Perception and Moral Understanding

Although there is no room to detail the case here, an examination of how neural networks sustain scientific understanding reveals that the role of learned prototypes and their continual redeployment in new domains of phenomena is absolutely central to the scientific process [Kuhn, 1962; Churchland, 1989, 1995]. Specific rules or "laws of nature" play an undeniably important but nonetheless secondary role, mostly in the social business of communicating or teaching scientific skills. One's scientific understanding is lodged primarily in one's acquired hierarchy of structural and dynamical prototypes, not primarily in a set of linguistic formulas.

In a parallel fashion, neural network research has revealed how our knowledge of a language may be embodied in a hierarchy of prototypes for verbal sequences that admit of varied instances and indefinitely many combinations, rather than in a set of specific rules-to-be-followed [Elman, 1992]. Of course, we can and do state grammatical rules, but a child's grammatical competence in no way depends on ever hearing them uttered or being able to state them. It may be that the main function of such rules resides in the social business of describing and refining our linguistic skills. One's grammatical capacity, at its original core, may consist of something other than a list of internalized rules-to-be-followed.

With these two points in mind, let us finally turn to the celebrated matter of our moral capacity. Let us address our ability to recognize cruelty and kindness, avarice and generosity, treachery and honor, mendacity and honesty, the Cowardly Way Out and the Right Thing to Do. Here, once again, the intellectual tradition of Western moral philosophy is focused on rules, on specific laws or principles. These are supposed to govern one's behavior, to the extent that one's behavior is moral at all. And the discussion has always centered on which rules are the truly valid, correct, or binding rules.

I have no wish whatever to minimize the importance of that ongoing moral conversation. It is an essential part of humanity's collective cognitive adventure, and I would be honored to make even the most

162

modest of contributions to it. Nevertheless, it may be that a normal human's capacity for moral perception, cognition, deliberation, and action has rather less to do with rules, whether internal or external, than is commonly supposed.

What is the alternative to a rule-based account of our moral capacity? The alternative is a hierarchy of learned prototypes, for both moral perception and moral behavior, prototypes embodied in the well-tuned configuration of a neural network's synaptic weights. We may here find a more fruitful path to understanding the nature of *moral learning, moral insight, moral disagreements, moral failings, moral pathologies,* and *moral growth* at the level of entire societies. Let us explore this alternative, just to see how some familiar territory looks from a new and different hilltop.

One of the lessons of neural network research is that one's capacity for recognizing and discriminating perceptual properties usually outstrips one's ability to articulate or express the basis of such discriminations in words. Tastes and colors are the leading examples, but the point quickly shows itself to have a much broader application. Faces, too, are something we can discriminate, recognize, and remember to a degree that exceeds any verbal articulation we could possibly provide. The facial expression of emotions is evidently a third example. The recognition of sounds is a fourth. In fact, the cognitive priority of the preverbal over the verbal shows itself, upon examination, to be a feature of almost all of our cognitive categories.

This supraverbal grasp of the world's many dimensions of variation is perhaps the main point of having concepts: it allows us to deal appropriately with the always novel but never-entirely-novel situations flowing endlessly toward us from an open-ended future. That same flexible readiness characterizes our social and moral concepts no less than our physical concepts. And our moral concepts show the same penetration and supraverbal sophistication shown by nonmoral concepts. One's ability to recognize instances of cruelty, patience, meanness, and courage, for instance, far outstrips one's capacity for verbal definition of those notions. One's diffuse expectations of their likely consequences similarly exceed any verbal formulas that one could offer or construct, and those expectations are much the more penetrating because of it. All told, moral cognition would seem to display the same profile or signature that in other domains indicates the activity of a well-tuned neural network underlying the whole process.

If this is so, then moral perception will be subject to same ambiguities that characterize perception generally. Moral perception will be subject to the same modulation, shaping, and occasional "prejudice" that recurrent pathways make possible. By the same token, moral perception will occasionally be capable of the same cognitive "reversals" that we see in such examples as the old/young woman in fig. 5. Pursuing the parallel further, it should also display cases where one's first moral reaction to a novel social situation is simply moral confusion, but where a little background knowledge or collateral information suddenly resolves that confusion into an example of something familiar, into an unexpected instance of some familiar moral prototype.

Fig. 5. The Old Woman / Young Woman. A classic case of a visually ambiguous figure. The old woman is looking left and slightly toward us with her chin buried in her ruff. The young woman is looking to the left but away from us; her tiny nose is barely visible beyond her left cheek, but her left ear, left jawline, and choker necklace are directly before us.

On these same assumptions, moral learning will be a matter of slowly generating a hierarchy of moral prototypes, presumably from a substantial number of relevant examples of the moral kinds at issue. Hence the relevance of stories and fables, and, above all, the ongoing relevance of the parental example of interpersonal behavior, and parental commentary on and consistent guidance of childhood behavior. No child can learn the route to love and laughter entirely unaided, and no child will escape the pitfalls of selfishness and chronic conflict without an environment filled with examples to the contrary.

People with moral perception will be people who have learned those lessons well. People with reliable moral perception will be those who can protect their moral perception from the predations of self-deception and the corruptions of self-service. And, let us add, from the predations of group-think and the corruptions of fanaticism, which involves a rapacious disrespect for the moral cognition of others.

People with unusually penetrating moral insight will be those who can see a problematic moral situation in more than one way, and who can evaluate the relative accuracy and relevance of those competing interpretations. Such people will be those with unusual moral imagination, and a critical capacity to match. The former virtue will require a rich library of moral prototypes from which to draw, and special skills in the recurrent manipulation of one's moral perception. The latter virtue will require a keen eye for local divergences from any presumptive prototype and a willingness to take them seriously as grounds for finding some alternative understanding. Such people will by definition be rare, although all of us have some moral imagination, and all of us some capacity for criticism.

Accordingly, moral disagreements will be less a matter of interpersonal conflict over what "moral rules" to follow and more a matter of interpersonal divergence as to what moral prototype best characterizes the situation at issue. It will be more a matter, that is, of divergences in our interpretations of the kind of case we are confronting in the first place. Moral argument and moral persuasion, on this view, will most typically be a matter of trying to make salient this, that, or the other feature of the problematic situation, in hopes of winning one's opponent's assent to the local appropriateness of one general moral prototype over another. A nonmoral parallel of this phenomenon can again be found in the old/young woman example of fig. 5. If that figure were a photograph, say, and if there were some issue as to what it was really a picture of, I think we would agree that the young-woman interpretation is by far the more realistic of the two. The old-woman interpretation, by comparison, asks us to believe in the reality of a hyperbolic cartoon.

A genuinely moral example of this point about the nature of moral disagreement can be found in the current issue over a woman's right to abort a first-trimester pregnancy without legal impediment. One side of the debate considers the status of the early fetus and invokes the moral prototype of a Person, albeit a very tiny and incomplete person, a person who is defenseless for that very reason. The other side of the debate addresses the same situation and invokes the prototype of a tiny and possibly unwelcome Growth, as yet no more a person than is a cyst or a cluster of one's own skin cells. The first prototype bids us bring to bear all the presumptive rights of protection due any person, especially one that is young and defenseless. The second prototype bids us leave the woman to deal with the tiny growth as she sees fit, depending on the value it may or may not currently have for her, relative to her own long-term plans as an independently rightful human. Moral argument, in this case as elsewhere, typically consists in urging the accuracy or the poverty of the prototypes at issue as portrayals of the situation at hand.

I cite this example not to enter into this debate, nor to presume on the patience of either party. I cite it to illustrate a point about the nature of moral disagreements and the nature of moral arguments. The point is that real disagreements need not be and seldom are about what explicit moral rules are true or false. The adversaries in this case might even agree on the obvious principles lurking in the area, such as, "It is prima facie wrong to kill any person." The disagreement here lies at a level deeper than that glib anodyne. It lies in a disagreement about the boundaries of the category "person" and hence about whether the explicit principle even applies to the case at hand. It lies in a divergence in the way people perceive or interpret the social world they encounter and in their inevitably divergent behavioral responses to that world.

Whatever the eventual resolution of this divergence of moral cognition, it is antecedently plain that both parties to this debate are driven by some or other application of a moral prototype. But not all conflicts are thus morally grounded. Interpersonal conflicts are regularly no more principled than that between a jackal and a buzzard quarreling over a steaming carcass. Or a pair of two-year-old human children screaming in frustration at a tug-of-war over the same toy. This returns us, naturally enough, to the matter of moral development in children and to the matter of the occasional failures of such development. How do such failures look, on the trained-network model here being explored?

Some of them recall a view from antiquity. Plato was inclined to argue, at least in his occasional voice as Socrates, that no man ever knowingly does wrong. For if he recognizes the action as being genuinely wrong — rather than just "thought to be wrong by others" — what motive could he possibly have to perform it? Generations of students have rejected Plato's suggestion, and rightly so. But Plato's point, however overstated, remains an instructive one: an enormous portion of human moral misbehavior is due primarily to cognitive failures of one kind or another.

Such failures are inevitable. We have neither infinite intelligence nor total information. No one is perfect. But some people, as we know, are notably less perfect than the norm, and their failures are systematic. In fact, some people are rightly judged to be chronic troublemakers, terminal narcissists, thoughtless blockheads, and treacherous snakes, not to mention bullies and sadists. Whence stem these sorry failings?

From many sources, no doubt. But we may note right at the beginning that a simple failure to develop the normal range of moral perception and social skills will account for a great deal here. Consider the child who, for whatever reasons, learns only very slowly to distinguish the minute-by-minute flux of rights, expectations, entitlements, and duties as they are created and canceled in the course of an afternoon at the day-care center, an outing with siblings, or a playground game of hide and seek. Such a child is doomed to chronic conflict with other children — doomed to cause them disappointment, frustration, and eventually anger, all of it directed at him.

Moreover, he has all of it coming, despite the fact that a flinty-eyed determination to "flout the rules" is not what lies behind his unacceptable behavior. The child is a moral cretin because he has not acquired the skills already flourishing in the others. He is missing skills of recognition to begin with, and also the skills of matching his behavior to the moral circumstance at hand, even when it is dimly recognized. The child steps out of turn, seizes disallowed advantages, reacts badly to constraints binding on everyone, denies earned approval to others, and is blind to opportunities for profitable cooperation. His failure to develop and deploy a roughly normal hierarchy of social and moral prototypes may seem tragic, and it is. But one's sympathies must lie with the other children when, after due patience runs out, they drive the miscreant howling from the playground.

What holds for a playground community holds for adult communities as well. We all know adult humans whose behavior recalls to some degree the bleak portrait just outlined. They are, to put the point gently, unskilled in social perception and social practice. Moreover, all of them pay a stiff and continuing price for their failure. Overt retribution aside, they miss out on the profound and ever-compounding advantages that successful socialization brings, specifically, the intricate practical, cognitive, and emotional commerce that lifts everyone in its embrace.

The Basis of Moral Character

This quick portrait of the moral miscreant invites a correspondingly altered portrait of the morally successful person. The common picture of the Moral Man as one who has acquiesced in a set of explicit rules imposed from the outside — from God, perhaps, or from society — is dubious in the extreme. A relentless commitment to a handful of explicit rules does not make one a morally successful or a morally insightful person. That is the path of the Bible Thumper and the Waver of Mao's Little Red Book. The price of virtue is a good deal higher than that, and the path thereto a good deal longer. It is much more accurate to see the moral person as one who has acquired a complex set of subtle and enviable skills: perceptual, cognitive, and behavioral.

This was, of course, the view of Aristotle, to recall another name from antiquity. Moral virtue, as he saw it, was something acquired and refined over a lifetime of social experience, not something swallowed whole from an outside authority. It was a matter of developing a set of largely inarticulable skills, a matter of practical wisdom. Aristotle's perspective and the neural network perspective here converge.

To see this more clearly, focus now on the single individual, one who grows up among creatures with a more or less common human nature, in an environment of ongoing social practices and presumptive moral wisdom already in place. The child's initiation into that smooth collective practice takes time — time to learn how to recognize a large variety of prototypical social situations, time to learn how to deal with those situations, time to learn how to balance or arbitrate conflicting perceptions and conflicting demands, and time to learn the sorts of patience and self-control that characterize mature skills in any domain of activity. After all, there is nothing essentially moral about learning to defer immediate gratification in favor of later or more diffuse rewards.

So far as the child's brain is concerned, such learning, such neural representation, and such deployment of those prototypical resources are all indistinguishable from their counterparts in the acquisition of skills generally. There are real successes, real failures, real confusions, and real rewards in the long-term quality of life that one's moral skills produce. As in the case of internalizing mankind's scientific knowledge, a person who internalizes mankind's moral knowledge is a more powerful, effective, and resourceful creature because of it. To draw the parallels here drawn is to emphasize the practical or pragmatic nature of both scientific and broadly normative knowledge. It is to emphasize the fact that both embody different forms of know-how: how to navigate the natural world in the former case and how to navigate the social world in the latter.

This portrait of the moral person as one who has acquired a certain family of perceptual and behavioral skills contrasts sharply with the more traditional accounts that picture the moral person as one who has agreed to follow a certain set of rules (for example, "Always keep your promises"), or alternatively, as one who has a certain set of overriding desires (for example, to maximize the general happiness). Both of these more traditional accounts are badly out of focus.

For one thing, it is just not possible to capture, in a set of explicit imperative sentences or rules, more than a small part of the practical wisdom possessed by a mature moral individual. It is no more possible here than in the case of any other form of expertise — scientific, athletic, technological, artistic, or political. The sheer amount of information stored in a well-trained network the size of a human brain, and the massively distributed and exquisitely context-sensitive ways in which it is stored therein, preclude its complete expression in a handful of sentences, or even a large bookful. Statable rules are not the basis of one's moral character. They are merely its pale and partial reflection at the comparatively impotent level of language.

If rules do not do it, neither are suitable desires the true basis of anyone's moral character. Certainly they are not sufficient. A person might have an all-consuming desire to maximize human happiness. But if that person has no comprehension of what sorts of things genuinely serve lasting human happiness; no capacity for recognizing other people's emotions, aspirations, and current purposes; no ability to engage in smoothly cooperative undertakings; no skills whatever at pursuing that all-consuming desire; then that person is not a moral saint. He is a pathetic fool, a hopeless busybody, a loose cannon, and a serious menace to his society.

Neither are canonical desires obviously necessary. A man may have, as his most basic and overriding desire in life, the desire to see his own children mature and prosper. To him, let us suppose, everything else is distantly secondary. And yet such a person may still be numbered among the most consummately moral people of his community, so long as he pursues his personal goal, as others may pursue theirs, in a fashion that is scrupulously fair to the aspirations of others and ever protective of the practices that serve everyone's aspirations indifferently.

Attempting to portray either accepted rules or canonical desires as the basis of moral character has the further disadvantage of inviting the skeptic's hostile question: "Why should I follow those rules?" in the first case, and "What if I don't have those desires?" in the second. If, however, we reconceive strong moral character as the possession of a broad family of perceptual, cognitive, and behavioral skills in the social domain, then the skeptic's question must become, "Why should I acquire those skills?" To which the honest answer is, "Because they are easily the most important skills you will ever learn."

This novel perspective on the nature of human cognition, both scientific and moral, comes to us from two disciplines — cognitive neuroscience and connectionist artificial intelligence — that had no prior interest in or connection with either the philosophy of science or moral theory. And yet the impact on both these philosophical disciplines is destined to be revolutionary. Not because an understanding of neural networks will obviate the task of scientists or of moral-political philosophers. Not for a second. Substantive science and substantive ethics will still have to be done, by scientists and by moralists and mostly in the empirical trenches. Rather, what will change is our conception of the nature of scientific and moral knowledge, as it lives and breathes within the brains of real creatures. Thus, the impact on metaethics is modestly obvious already. No doubt a revolution in moral psychology will eventually have some impact on substantive ethics as well, on matters of moral training, moral pathology, and moral correction, for example. But that is for moral philosophers to work through, not cognitive theorists. The message of this chapter is that an ongoing conversation between these two communities has now become essential.

NOTE

[1] This paper is excerpted from chapters 6 and 10 of P. M. Churchland, *The Engine of Reason, The Seat of the Soul: A Philosophical Journey into the Brain* (Cambridge, MA., 1995: Bradford Books/The MIT Press). Reprinted here with permission of the MIT Press.

REFERENCES

Churchland, P. M. (1995) *The Engine of Reason, The Seat of the Soul: A Philosophical Journey into the Brain.* Cambridge, MA: Bradford Books/MIT Press.

Churchland, P. M. (1989) *A Neurocomputational Perspective: The Nature of Mind and the Structure of Science.* Cambridge, MA: Bradford Books/MIT Press.

Cottrell, G. W. and J. Metcalfe (1991) "EMPATH: Face, Gender and Emotion Recognition Using Holons," R.P. Lippman, J. Moody and D.S. Touretzky, Eds., *Advances in Neural Information Processing Systems 3.* San Mateo CA: Morgan Kaufmann, 564-571.

Elman, J. L. (1992) "Grammatical Structure and Distributed Representations," in S. Davis, Ed., *Connectionism: Theory and Practice.* Oxford: Oxford: Oxford University Press.

Kuhn, T. S. (1962) *The Structure of Scientific Revolutions.* Chicago: University of Chicago Press.

QUALITATIVE EXPERIENCE IN MACHINES

WILLIAM G. LYCAN

News flash: The qualitative, phenomenal or subjective character of sensory experience is problematic and controversial. Naturalistic and materialist views of human beings, especially, are thought to face various terrible obstacles and objections based on phenomena that come under the rough headings of "consciousness," "qualia," "subjectivity" and the like. But those issues, per se, are not my topic. My present project is, rather, comparative.

I

Many people, perhaps most people, have the idea that, however problematic qualitative experience is for the case of human beings, it is a lot more so for that of *machines* constructed by human beings. Few philosophers doubt that human beings' experiences have qualitative characters, but many doubt or disbelieve outright that robots and computers (much less backhoes and can openers) could ever have qualitative experiences at all. Often the latter denial is just evinced, as an "intuition," though occasionally it has been argued. There are even some philosophers who think that the big problems have been pretty well solved for human beings or can be solved without much further effort, but who also think that machines simply could not be conscious, have qualitative or subjective experiences, etc.; that is the most extreme version of the idea I am considering.

My purpose in this paper is to defend the goose-gander thesis that the disparity here is specious: There is no problem for or objection to qualitative experience in machines that is not equally a quandary for such experience in humans. It is, I contend, mere human chauvinism or at best fallacy to suppose otherwise.

Just for the record, here are the leading problems regarding the phenomenal character of human experience: Leibniz'-Law objections; the immediacy of our access to qualia; essentialistic and other Krip-kean (alleged) modal features of qualia; "zombie" and "absent-qualia"-type puzzle cases; first-person/third-person asymmetries of several kinds and the perspectivalness of the mental; putative funny *facts* as claimed by Thomas Nagel and Frank Jackson; qualia in the strict sense, the introspectible monadic properties of apparent phenomenal individuals; the grainlessness or homogeneity of qualitative features, emphasized by Sellars; and Joseph Levine's now celebrated "explanatory gap." That is an impressive array of difficulties for the materialist.[1] It is so impressive, in fact, that it immediately lends support to my goose-gander claim. For if there is a problem about qualitative experience in machines that is not equally an objection to a materialist view of people, that problem must be additional even to the many and wide-ranging ones I have listed. It must also be grounded in some substantive difference between machines and human beings.

II

For present purposes, then, we must mean by "machine" something that contrasts interestingly with "human being," (In one sense, uncontroversially, human beings are machines). Let us mean a kind of artifact, an information-processing device manufactured by people in a laboratory or workshop, out of physical materials that have been obtained without mystery or magic. A paradigm case would be a robot driven by a present-day supercomputer. But I want to allow technologically imaginable extensions of that paradigm; a machine need not have von Neumann architecture, or even digital architecture (whatever that means) at all. And let us idealize a bit: I shall assume that problems of information storage and retrieval, such as the notorious frame problem, are solved (A fairly outrageous assumption, true. The reason I get to make it is that my chauvinist opponents do not think that *their* objection could be overcome even if the frame problem and its ilk could be; they think their obstacle arises no matter how good our machine might be at mere information storage and retrieval).

What, then, are the most obvious differences between machines in the foregoing sense and natural-born human beings, that might support the chauvinist position? Let us begin by abstracting away from the most obvious deficiency of actual, 1990s machines: that no such thing has a humanoid behavioral repertoire or anything remotely approaching it, because no present-day machine is anywhere nearly as complex as a human being or gifted with a biologic brain's almost unthinkably vast information-processing capacity. Here again, my opponents deny that more information processing (per se) would help; no further amount of *the same*, no matter how large, would convert a mere machine into a sentient creature capable of subjective, qualitative experience.

So let us help ourselves to some futuristic, science-fiction technology, and suppose that such resources have afforded us an *expert human simulator*. Elsewhere I have introduced a character called Harry [Lycan, 1985, 141, 1987, Appendix], who through amazing miniaturization and cosmetic art is an entirely lifelike android. He is also a triumphant success of AI: his range of behavior-in-circumstances is equal

172

to that of a fully acculturated and rather talented late 20th-century American adult. No one would ever guess that he is not an ordinary person (Let us further suppose that his internal functional organization is very like ours; his total pattern of information flow is parallel to ours, even though it runs on considerably different hardware).

But our question is, in the relevant sense, is Harry a *person* at all? He is, remember, only a computer with limbs; his humanoid looks are only a brilliant makeup job. Some philosophers will readily grant that he has beliefs or belief-like states; after all, he stores and deploys information about his environment and about the rest of the world. But desires are a bit harder; hopes, embarrassments and other cognitive attitudes still harder. Yet even those who would award Harry a full range of propositional attitudes might still balk at qualitative experience. Even if in some sense he thinks, he does not *feel* in the most immediate sense in which we do — so says the chauvinist.

III

Before we go on to look at some further differences between Harry and the rest of us, let us note that there is a heavy presumption in favor of my egalitarian goose-gander claim [Lycan, 1987, 125-26]. First, how do we now tell that any familiar humanoid being is conscious? Normatively pursued, this is just the Problem of Other Minds. But we need not take a stand on the best solution to that problem in order to note its origin. The problem begins with the fact that the ordinary person's evidence for ascribing mental states, including qualitative states, to another human being is the latter's behavior, broadly construed, in the circumstances, broadly construed. How we justify the epistemic move from that behavior to the mental ascription is a topic of notorious controversy, but unless we succumb to global skepticism about other minds, we do not doubt that the mental ascription *is* justified by our observation of the behavior (of course the justification is defeasible).

Few readers will have failed to foresee my next move: By hypothesis, Harry is a flawless human simulator and behaves, in any circumstance, just as a human being might. So, over time, he provides his viewers with just the same sorts of behavioral evidence for mental ascriptions that you or I do — including ascriptions of qualitative experience. So far as we have evidence for ascribing qualitative phenomenal states to each other, we have just as strong prima facie evidence for ascribing them to Harry. And common sense, at least, counts that evidence as very strong, so strong that we rarely even entertain potential defeaters.

Notice further that in the case of human beings, such behavioral evidence does not require assumptions about the subject's innards.[2] We mature and educated people do know that other human beings are

173

biologic organisms and we presume that the others' biology is like theirs, but the standard tacit behavioral reasoning does not depend on that presumption. (1) A child or naïf who did not know those things would be just as well justified in her/his mental ascriptions, or at least very nearly as well justified, as we. And (2) if we were watching a videotape of humanoid creatures which might be from another planet and might have a biology quite different from ours, then if those beings behaved just like humans, we would still be justified in imputing human mental states to them — indeed, I submit we would not even think about it, unless our philosophical guard were up.

The foregoing points, especially subargument (2), might be thought to beg the question against the chauvinist. But they do not. I have granted (and would insist) that the justification conferred by the behavioral evidence is in every case defeasible. That leaves open the possibility that for machines, or even for aliens, the class of potential defeaters is wider than that which attends mental ascription to human beings, and I have not assumed otherwise. My present point is only that powerful defeat is required in Harry's case; the chauvinist is already one — a big one — down.

Here is my second argument for the same conclusion. (Science fiction again:) Suppose that Henrietta, a normal human being, requires neurosurgery; indeed her entire CNS is under attack by a virus that will gradually destroy it. The surgeons start replacing it (and if you like, much of the rest of Henrietta) with prostheses. First a few neurons are replaced by tiny electronic devices. These micromachines so successfully duplicate the functions of the neurons they replace that Henrietta's performance is entirely unimpaired. Then a few more neurons are removed and substituted for; complete success again. And so on until there is no wetware left — eventually, Henrietta's behavior is controlled entirely by (micro-)machinery, yet her intelligence, personality, poetic abilities, etc., and most importantly her perceptual acuity, sensory judgments and phenomenological reports remain just as always. Now, a chauvinist must maintain that at some point during the sequence of operations, Henrietta ceased to have qualitative experiences; she has become cold and dead inside and is now no more sentient than a pocket calculator. One can imagine a particularly boorish chauvinist asserting this to her face. She would protest, of course, and tell him that her inner life is as rich and vivid as ever, describing it as lyrically as time and his rudeness allow. It is hard to imagine how the boor, or any other chauvinist, would be able to draw a line and state with assurance that after the nth operation, Henrietta ceased to have a phenomenology (whatever she may think to the contrary). It is a hard position to defend.

Here again, I do not want to beg the question against the chauvinist — or to commit a slippery slope fallacy, either. For there may be a defeater that cuts in at some point and does override the behavioral evidence; and the "point" may be a vague one to boot.[3] As before, I am not asserting that no such defeater exists, but only emphasizing that the chauvinist bears the burden of coming up with one and that it is a considerably heavier burden than one might think.

IV

What, then, are the defeaters specific to machinekind? I can think of three possibilities. First: There is Harry's *origin*. He is an artifact; he was not of woman born, but was cobbled together on a workbench by a group of human beings for purposes of their own. Perhaps a workshop is not a proper mother (imagine Dame Edith Evans enunciating, "A *workshop*?").

I do not think any sound chauvinist argument can be based on that difference. For suppose we were to synthesize billions of human cells and stick them together, making a biologic humanoid organism (We could either make a mature adult straightway or, what is technologically easier, make a fetus and nurture it). We might further suppose that the resulting pseudo-human — let us call him Hubert — is a molecular duplicate of a pre-ëxisting human being. There is little doubt that such a creature would have qualitative experience; at least, if he did not, that would probably not be simply because of his early history.[4] So artifactuality per se seems not to count against having phenomenal states. Our first difference is no defeater.[5]

Second: It may be said that Harry is not a *living organism* (Paul Ziff made such an appeal in his well-known article, "The Feelings of Robots"[Ziff, 1959]).[6] If something is not an organism at all, properly speaking, then there does seem to be something odd about ascribing sensations and feelings to it.

Much depends on what is considered criterial for "living organism." We have already failed to find reason to think that artifactuality per se precludes qualitative experience. Parallel reasoning would show that artifactuality per se does not preclude something's being a living organism either, for surely our synthesized pseudo-human would count as a living organism. Putting artifactuality aside, then, what constitutes living? Automotion? Autonomous growth and regulation of functions? Reproduction or self-replication? Metabolism? Being made of protein?

Whatever. Some of these things — the first three, at least — could be done by a machine, in which case the machine would be "alive" in the relevant sense and the objection's minor premise goes false. Others, very likely the last two, could not be done by machines; but in that case we should ask pointedly why they should be thought germane to consciousness, qualia and the rest. E.g., why should a thing's *metabolizing* or not bear on its psychological faculties in so basic a way as to decide the possibility of qualitative experience? It is hard to see what the

175

one has to do with the other, or to imagine a plausible argument leading from "no metabolism" to "no qualitative experience." And likewise for being made of protein.

Also, remember Henrietta. She started out as a normal human being but was gradually turned into a machine. Did she go from being a living organism to being non-living, inanimate? In that case — if she had been alive and then ceased to live — she *died*, and obsequies are in order. It would be both hard and easy to make her funeral arrangements: Hard, because we would first have to persuade her that she was dead and that services should be held at all; she might resist that suggestion fairly indignantly, especially when we got around to the question of burial vs. cremation. But then easier, because we would not have to guess posthumously at her wishes — we could just ask her what hymns she wanted, whether there should be a eulogy or a general sermon, and so forth, right up till the last minute. I must say I think I would enjoy attending that funeral; I am not so sure that Henrietta would, herself.

As I have phrased this last *argumentum ad Henriettam*, implying that Henrietta does continue to live even after she has been turned into a machine, it defends the idea that some imaginable machines are living organisms.[7] But alternatively, we could concede that there is at least one good sense in which Henrietta is no longer a *living* organism even though this does not imply that she is *dead*, as the term is ordinarily used, either.[8] For example, her prosthetic CNS does not achieve homeostases in any biological way; nor does it receive nutrients or repair itself by genetic means. But as before, one then wonders what those things have to do with psychological properties such as the having of experiences. Henrietta continues to look and talk and act just as if she has a vivid phenomenology; what argument based on "not receiving nutrients" or the like could we use to convince her that she is entirely mistaken about herself having experiences?

To summarize: Either Harry and Henrietta *are* alive after all, depending on what criterion we use, or we have not yet seen a good argument leading from the feature in virtue of which they are not alive to the conclusion that they lack qualitative experience. But a further argument of that sort has recently been offered.

V

Douglas Long [1994] defends Ziff's thesis in a deeper way: Life matters to qualitative experience or feeling, he contends, because life is necessary for "animate behavior," which is in turn required for mentality of any sort (Thus Long is not among those selective chauvinists who concede that machines can think, deliberate etc. even though they cannot feel). What, then, is "animate behavior," and why is it required for mentality?

176

We sometimes contrast "behavior" with mere bodily motion. E.g., in standard "zombie" counterexamples to Analytical Behaviorism, a humanoid puppet is moved around by some external device such as a system of magnets, though so skillfully that it moves in exactly the same ways a living person would.[9] Yet a sophisticated Behaviorist might respond that although the puppet's movements mimic human behavior, they do not constitute genuine *behavior* on the puppet's part, because they are produced adventitiously by the magnets or whatever rather than by the puppet on its own.

What distinguishes behavior in this richer sense from mere bodily motion? The obvious answer is that genuine behavior is grounded in the subject's own beliefs, desires and intentions, of which puppets and other zombies have none. Of course, that answer is of little help to the Analytical Behaviorist, for it is precisely mental notions such as "belief," "desire" and "intention" that such a theorist is sworn to explicate without circularity. Nor is that answer Long's, for Long too rejects the idea that "behavior" factors into outer bodily motion and the inner mental states and events that produce it [See also Long, 1964]. For Long, what distinguishes behavior from mere bodily motion is *agency* of the sort that "arises out of th[e]...natural capacity for action and reaction which animals possess and [inanimate] objects do not" [Long, 1994, 108].

Of special importance in the case of many animals, as well as human beings, is the contrast between the voluntary behavior of an agent and other involuntary bodily movements, such as reflex responses, tics, and spasms, which are not in the animal's control and with respect to which it is passive rather than active. A non-psychological, causal account of the latter type of events is appropriate when the animal is not moving autonomously. For voluntary movements, on the other hand, we invoke a type of explanation in which the animal itself is the central player. We can attribute an animal's movements (as well as lack of movement in repose) to it as an agent, without having to raise questions about the causation of those bodily motions at the physiological level. ...We recognize that an animal possess a power to initiate action, to guide itself through its environment, and to react to its surroundings [Long, 1994, 109].

"Animate" behavior is "self-movement" of the foregoing sort.

Let us grant for the sake of argument that the "capacity" for animate behavior is required for mentality, and examine Long's other premise, that only living creatures have the capacity for animate behavior. That premise is far more contentious. For as I have noted, Long is concerned to follow Ziff in distinguishing minded beings, not just from zombies, but from machines of any sort, including flawless human simulators like Harry. He counts clever robots as nonliving, by whatever criterion,[10] and so he denies on principle that Harry has the capacity for animate behavior in the sense he intends. The latter denial is a strong claim, since by hypothesis, Harry seems to one and all to behave in every respect just as we do.[11]

What are the elements of animate behavior that Long thinks are missing in Harry? As quoted, he mentions (1) voluntariness as opposed to involuntary bodily movements, (2) a type of explanation "in which the animal itself is the central player," (3) our not having to "raise questions about the causation of th[e]...bodily motions at the physiological level, and (4) a power to initiate action, to guide itself and to react. Now since the epistemic presumption in favor of Harry's mentation still needs to be overcome, we must consider these four elements as potential defeaters.

(2) and (3) are easily set aside, for they are not denied to Harry. Certainly any type of commonsensical action explanation that we apply to human beings applies to Harry as well — in the sense that it will have just the same fit to the data, cognitive virtues, predictive power and other pragmatic utilities as do similar explanations of human action (I am not begging the question by supposing that those components of the explanations that allude to mental states are literally true of Harry). Nor do we ever have to raise questions about the causation of Harry's bodily motions at the physiological level. (4) is perhaps more doubtful, but I cannot think of any non-question-begging reason to deny that Harry has, in any reasonable sense, a power to initiate action, to guide himself and to react. My opponent *would* beg the question if s/he were to insist that "action," "guide" and "react" be read in an extra-strong "animate" sense that requires life, because they are ordinary expressions being used in the explication of Long's technical term "animate" to begin with, and also because (4) is at this stage being used in an argument designed to show that contrary to appearances, "animate" behavior as defined requires life.

(1) is more troublesome. On its own, it suggests that Harry does not (ever) engage in voluntary motion and that each of his movements is a reflex, tic or spasm. The latter conjunct is just false, since by hypothesis Harry's actions are the result of incredibly complex and context-sensitive information processing. But does he engage in voluntary motion, as he seems to?

I am not sure how far down the phylogenetic scale one can go and still find voluntary action. Cats are an interesting example, because their movements look so decisive and purposive, yet cat neuroscience portrays them as fairly hard-wired food- and warmth-seeking devices with nap switches and a few play routines thrown in. I do not think we can be sure whether feline actions are voluntary, and so we cannot be sure whether cats engage in animate behavior by Long's standard. Yet surely they have experiences and other mentation, so for his own purposes Long cannot set the standard for "voluntariness" too high.

In any case, why might someone deny that Harry's actions are voluntary?

[A] machine exhibits mere movements and changes, which do not constitute mental activity or expressions of mentality. A nonliving machine is a constructed causal mechanism; and a complex machine is simply a complex causal mechanism. This is true even if it is skillfully configured with machine ana- logues of human functions inside and appears convincingly human outside, [Long, 1994, 111-12]

Long is not here simply being a Hard Determinist about machines. Rather, the key phrase is, "constitute mental activity or expressions of mentality," with the emphasis on "constitute." For Long goes on to claim that in living creatures, animate activity is not bodily motion produced by inner psychological states, but rather "in itself constitutes various forms of intelligent and psychologically expressive behavior" [Long, 1994, 111]. As we have seen, he insists that seemingly intelli- gent, even perfectly humanoid activities in machines do not thus con- stitute intelligent and psychologically expressive behavior. I am not sure what relation this constituting relation is intended to bear to his notion of voluntariness, but they seem to stand or fall together.

Now, the opposing Soft Determinist picture of genuine voluntary action does see such action as movement produced by inner psycho- logical states. And as noted previously, it is a standard account of the difference between action and mere bodily movement. And it is con- sidered plausible and also defended by many action theorists and philosophers of mind. Moreover, it is as naturally applied to Harry as it is to human beings, since we almost unavoidably (even if in the end incorrectly) credit Harry with the relevant propositional attitudes. Long obviously opposes that picture in favor of his own more Wittgensteinian and/or Rylean "constituting" view, but unless I have missed it he has not independently defended this view against the more traditional picture. So he has not yet damaged, but only declared opposition to, the epistemically default position that Harry's actions are voluntary and are so in that they are the products of his beliefs, de- sires, deliberations and choices.

A bit later on, Long does add a further consideration that he be- lieves counts distinctively against machines: a kind of derivativeness or second-hand quality in their internal organization.

179

We can imagine machines being designed to simulate animate behavior.... But engineering cannot give [a machine]... the capacity for animate behavior, and happenings in machines are only imitative of animate activity.[12] Such happenings give only the illusion of capturing the expressive force of the self-initiated and self-directed behavior of living animals and human beings [Long, 112].

The significant point is that the purposes of an individual animal originate with the needs, interests, and intelligence of the animal itself rather than with some antecedent mind. ... Computers and other devices also exhibit direction and purpose in their machinations. ... But...the artificial construction is a causal mechanism that has no natural teleological origins. Moreover, there is an obvious source of its direction and purpose located outside the mechanism in the genuine, naturally developed mental agent who created the device. ... Even th[e]... propensity [of some very clever machines] to `learn' is designed and built by intelligent beings directly into an otherwise inert system. ... A human designer can assemble the device in such a way as to make a particular result conditional upon arbitrary causal factors of human choosing [Long, 114-15].

Now, those passages contain a number of truths: Harry indeed has neither needs like ours nor natural teleological origins (the second in part because of the first, I daresay); Harry's components were given their functions and purposes, perhaps quite cynically, by his human designers; even current machines' astounding propensities for learning were themselves devised and implanted by the designers. But as always we must ask why those particular truths matter and what follows from them. So far (though we are not yet finished), I do not see that any chauvinist thesis does follow from them. I would be among the first to insist that teleology is required for mentality and certainly for experience,[13] but I do not see why the teleology's own *origin* is relevant. So far as has been shown, teleology is teleology, natural or imparted (Interestingly, I think just as many philosophers would contend that "natural" teleology is derivative from or otherwise subsidiary to artifactual teleology as the other way around). A filter is a filter, a conduit a conduit, a messenger a messenger, a pump a pump, and (needless to say) so too for a capacity for learning. And remember: The teleology of an artificially created biologic pseudo-human such as Hubert would be imparted rather than natural.[14]

So I believe Long's premise that only living creatures have the capacity for animate behavior remains unsupported.

VI

The third possible defeater of our presumption about Harry is *biochemistry*. Whether or not human or more generally biologic body chemistry is required for something's being alive, someone might hold that it is required for something to have a phenomenology like ours.[15]

Here my reply is the most obvious, but also the most problematic. Obvious, because since the 1960s it has been standard to defend multiple realizability, the now familiar idea that the very psychology that is instantiated by distinctively human wetware could be alternatively realized by a different biochemistry (Pain in humans may be the firing of c-fibers, but mollusks and Martians need not have c-fibers in order to be in pain, so long as they have some other components that do for them what our c-fibers do for us, etc., etc.). The Type Identity Theory has long since given way to Functionalism. Mental kinds are functional kinds, not biochemical kinds, and so much for the third alleged defeater.

However, notice that the (presumed) fact of multiple realizability does not commit us to Functionalism or to any particular positive theory of mind. Nor need we accept any Functionalist theory in order to appeal to multiple realizability in responding to the biochemical assault on Harry and Henrietta; multiple realizability was only a premise in arguments for Functionalism, and it remains entirely plausible whether or not any specific Functionalist theory is correct. As Putnam and Fodor argued in the 1960s, there is just no reason to think that human biochemistry is required for a creature of another species to feel pain or to perceive colors; and if not, then the chauvinist's putative third defeater is − pending further argument − a rubber arrow.

It might be suggested that my last few remarks are too quick, because my real "chauvinist" opponent is a Type Identity theorist. Remember, my opponent is not any sort of dualist across the board, because her/his thesis is that even if or though materialism is true of human experience, machines cannot share that experience. The opponent need not be a Type Identity theorist across the board either, e.g., about beliefs and desires, but may be only what Sydney Shoemaker calls a "selective parochialist," [Shoemaker, 1981][16] and hold the Type Identity theory only for specific qualia or feels. That would commit her/him to human chauvinism concerning those specific phenomena, but not to chauvinism regarding more general mental kinds. E.g., a selective parochialist might hold that although other species can of course have pains, their pains cannot feel to them exactly as ours do to us.

Selective parochialism might be true, and machines excluded for that reason. However: (i) Machines would be excluded only from having feels *just like ours*; it would not have been shown that they do not have pains etc. that do have feels. On the contrary, if just the same functional activity is going on in them, realized by a different sort of hardware, and if selective parochialism is true, that strongly suggests that the machines have pains that have feels distinctive to their hardware, as our pains' feels are distinctive to ours. And (ii) we have no reason to think that selective parochialism *is* true, because Putnam's and Fodor's original multiple realizability argument still stands: It still seems that a biochemically different organism could have states that feel to it just as ours feel to us, so long as it has realizing structures of its own that do for it the same jobs that our c-fibers etc. do for us, and the burden of proof otherwise is still on our chauvinist opponent.

Absent either a fourth potential defeater or new argument in support of one of the foregoing three, the chauvinist is handless and without honor. But before laughing scornfully and moving on, we should attend to an argument of John Searle's that might be adapted to serve the chauvinist's purpose.

VII

The argument is of course Searle's famous "Chinese Room," [Searle, 1980b, 417-24].[17] Searle imagines that an individual person sits inside a room that is sealed except for designated input and output gates. The person has been provided with a manual that codifies "the program" (let us say rather, all the relevant programs) that the Functionalist would say constitutes the understanding of a native speaker of Chinese. Upon receiving inputs to the room, the person looks through the manual and (perhaps using pencil and paper) calculates the appropriate effects and perhaps outputs, and then implements them by means of the appropriate activities — further markings on paper and/or deliveries to output gates. No one would suggest that this person her-/himself understands Chinese, or that the whole setup including the room and its gates understands Chinese, even though the putative Chinese-understanding program is being run. Directing a parallel argument towards our own topic: Even if the immured person were to "realize" (with pencil and paper) the relevant programs of a human being who is having such-and-such a qualitative experience, no one would say that either that person or the whole setup was thereby having an experience of that sort.

Searle himself does not claim to show that machines cannot understand languages, or that they cannot think or have qualitative experiences. His claim is only that neither machines nor anything else can do those things *solely in virtue of passing through a series of computational states*. And few philosophers would now disagree. Most join Searle in insisting that more is needed. For one thing, there are constraints on what it takes to run (realize, implement) a program that are not met by the Chinese room as described [Lycan, 1987, ch. 3]. For

182

another, and more to the point, the intentionality of propositional attitudes and perceptual states is generally thought to be a "wide" property, one that does not normally supervene on features internal to the subject organism, but reaches out into the world at large.[18] Thus our Functionalism regarding human beings needs to be supplemented by a *psychosemantics* in Jerry Fodor's sense, a theory that says in virtue of what a particular actual or nonactual object or property a referent of this brain state or that — in short, a theory of mental representation per se.

The reason that response is as problematic as it is obvious is that problems of consciousness and qualia are widely thought to be *more* daunting for Functionalists than for their predecessor Type Identity Theorists as typified by J.J.C. Smart in "Sensations and Brain Processes," [1959, 141-156].[19] For one thing, Functionalists explicitly type-identify mental states and events in terms of their *relations* to other states and events, while the Type Identity theory was at least not so overt about that [But see Lycan, 1987, 58-59], and so Functionalism incurs more objections based on the assumed intrinsicness or monadicity of qualia.[20]

I will not presuppose any particular psychosemantics here, though I shall assume that a correct one exists in Plato's Heaven. (Perhaps it is a teleologized causal-historical theory, perhaps not. I shall call it just "our psychosemantics.") Now, suppose our Chinese room were somehow *actually to run* or realize a Chinese-understanding program (as Searle's original does not), and suppose further that its internal states are connected to elements of its environment in just the way demanded by our psychosemantics. Assuming these things were possible at all, then, presumably, the setup would understand Chinese.[21]

But what about consciousness and qualia (as always, my opponents may agree that understanding and intentionality pose no great difficulty for machines. My opponents think those are the easy cases)? I believe a parallel move can and should be made, though it takes a bit of explaining.

I have devoted two of my books[22] to defending a thesis that I call the "Hegemony of Representation." It is that the mind has no special properties or powers that are not exhausted by its intentional or representational properties, along with or in combination with the underlying functional organization of its components. On this view, once representation is itself understood, then qualia, subjectivity, and consciousness in each of seven or eight relevant senses will be explicable in terms of functional organization plus representation, without our having to posit any further ingredient not already well understood from the naturalistic point of view.[23] Now, if the Hegemony doctrine is correct, that is a very strong reason to think that the chauvinist prejudice against machines is unfounded. For machines have no trouble realizing functional programs, and I cannot think of a plausible psychosemantics for humans that would not also apply to machines.

VIII

But is the Hegemony doctrine correct? Suppose not. Then there are certain troublesome features of the human mind, say perhaps special qualia that are neither merely functional nor merely the intentional contents of sensory representations nor any mere combination of those. Leading proponents of this anti-Hegemony view, notably Sydney Shoemaker and Ned Block [Shoemaker, 1990; Block, 1978],[24] tend to favor selective parochialism, and propose to type-identify their special qualia with neurophysiological properties. I have already argued in section 5 above that the human chauvinist can draw no support from selective parochialism. (For so far as we have reason to think that that view is correct — which I believe is not far at all — it suggests not that Harry and Henrietta cannot have feely qualitative experiences, but *au contraire* that they do.)

Suppose now that neither the Hegemony doctrine nor selective parochialism is correct. Then there are troublesome features of the human mind, say perhaps *very* special qualia that are neither merely functional nor merely the intentional contents of sensory representations nor any combination of those *nor anything neurophysiological*. But that distressing possibility would be of even less help to the human chauvinist, because if it obtains it is a big problem for the materialist view of human beings; no known materialist theory countenances such things, and it is hard to think of a materialist theory that would. And the chauvinist's task was and is to come up with an objection to machine experience that is not equally an objection to materialism vis-á-vis human beings.

Conclusion

The form of argument I have employed in this paper — surveying possible defeaters and eliminating each in turn — runs an obvious risk of committing the fallacy of composition: Even if no individual factor would by itself prevent Harry from having qualitative experience, perhaps a combination does. My only response is to say that upon reviewing some such combinations, I do not see any that would add epistemic power to the chauvinist case, though I suspect that the combination of all the factors we have considered lends considerable specious psychological weight.

I await such further chauvinist arguments as may present themselves.

[1] As is perhaps surprising and certainly far from well enough known, every one of those problems is resolved in my books *Consciousness* [Lycan, 1987] and *Consciousness and Experience* [Lycan, 1996].

Incidentally, in this paper I shall concentrate only on "feels" in the sense of qualia. But for explicit defense of the thesis that machines can have feelings in the sense of emotions, see (e.g.), "Why Robots will Have Emotions," [Sloman, 1981], and "Emotions in Robots," [N.H. Frijda, 1995].

[2] This claim is contested by Christopher Hill, [1991, ch. 9], and by Andrew Melnyk [1994]. What follows in this paragraph is in part a reply to their objections.

[3] Ch. 2 of *Consciousness and Experience* [Lycan, 1996] defends the claim that the notion of *conscious awareness* is vague and comes in degrees of richness or fullness.

[4] My suggestion about molecular twinning is not meant to suggest that qualia — phenomenal properties — are "narrow" in the sense of supervening upon molecular constitution. In Ch. 6 of *Consciousness and Experience* [Lycan, 1996] I argue that they are "wide" and do not. But there is no reason to think that the external factors needed to determine qualitative character include the circumstances of one's coming into existence.

[5] In fact, I think that discrimination against Harry on the basis of his birthplace and/or his genesis would be almost literally a case of racism.

[6] In reply, see also J.J.C. Smart [1959] and Hilary Putnam, [1964]. Interestingly, I have found that young children uniformly resist the anthropomorphizing of computers on the grounds that computers are not alive.

[7] In "Consciousness and Life" [Matthews, 1977, 13 26], Gareth Matthews notes that in L. Frank Baum's story *Ozma of Oz*, Dorothy explains to her companions that Nick Chopper, the Tin Woodman, is alive precisely because he was originally flesh and blood and his current tin body is the result of piecemeal replacement. If this view — meant to be plausible to young and old alike — is even coherent, then so is the claim that Henrietta lives although she is now a machine.

[8] Addressing Henrietta's first appearance in *Consciousness*, Douglas Long takes either this view or the harsher one I lampooned above, depending on whether his way of putting it, "[T]he operation was a success but...the patient died," was meant tongue in cheek [Long, 1994, 118].

Matthews [1977] also reminds us that Descartes firmly rejected the claim that consciousness requires life. On Descartes' view it is the immaterial mind, the *res cogitans*, that is conscious, and that item is only contingently connected to a living body (Of course, Descartes also thought that living bodies were machines).

[9] My own such character is the Tinfoil Man, introduced in Ch. 1 of *Consciousness* [Lycan, 1987]. Cf. "Critical Notice of J.J.C. Smart's *Philosophy and Scientific Realism*"[Bradley, 1964]; *Body and Mind* [Campbell, 1970]; "Sentience and Behaviour" [Kirk, 1974].

[10] He seems to follow Ziff in treating "living organism" as a family-resemblance concept: "anything having a sufficient subset of the features which are commonly cited in biology textbooks as being characteristic of life[:]...typically a self-reproducing, organized system of cellular structures which as a whole has capacities for nutrition, excretion, growth, responsiveness to stimuli, and locomotion...[along with some] more technical properties...." [Ziff, 1959, 104].

[11] Long remarks [1994, 115] that in *Consciousness* [Lycan, 1987] it was unfair of me — an illicit stipulation — to have applied everyday action-theoretic predicates to Harry in the first place, since in doing so I effectively begged the question against his demanding notion of "animate" behavior. Perhaps that is so; more strictly, I should have said that Harry does things that are externally indistinguishable from "animate" actions and behavior.

[12] Though the conjunction "and" seems to indicate otherwise, I am here trying to understand the second conjunct as an argument for the first.

[13] In fact, I *was* among the first, in the present century at least, in "Form, Function, and Feel" [Lycan, 1981], a pilot paper for *Consciousness*.

[14] Long grants [1994, 117] that "artificial life is real life" and is not subject to chauvinism.

Something further is suggested by the foregoing passages which, if true, would indeed embarrass machines quite badly: that they exhibit *only* the designs and purposes of their creators, that they do not have values of their own, that they do not weigh alternatives and choose, because they "*only do what they are programmed to do*." For purposes of my project, we would still need an argument from that demeaning feature of machines to a lack of qualitative experience, the two having nothing obviously to do with each other, but it would be a demeaning feature all the same and might strengthen chauvinism by weakening our overall solidarity with robots. But although there is a sense in which computers and robots "only do what they are programmed to do," (a) it is a normative rather than a descriptive sense and would be quite tricky to spell out; (b) in the same sense, for all we know, we humans only do what we are programmed to do; and (c) there are considerably more important ways in which it is plainly false that machines only do what they are programmed to do.

I have argued (a) and (b) at some length elsewhere (in the Appendix to *Consciousness*), so I shall merely summarize the main points in regard to (c) as illustrated by Harry. In each case, begin by remembering that once he is launched (or kicked out of the nest or whatever), Harry moves about the world independently, as we do — in accordance with his initial programming, to be sure, but without further guidance or interference from his creators. First, like any computer Harry develops small, chance physical defects, and even though they are usually repaired by internal maintenance units, the repairs take time. Second, every one of Harry's psychological programs has numerous bugs. Third, actual randomizers: Harry's choices will sometimes be affected by genuinely random elements. Fourth and most importantly, as soon as Harry is out of his creators' hands and out of sight, he will begin to have experiences (not to beg the question, he will begin to receive new information through impingements on his receptors) which will be neither controlled nor even observed by his designers; and his programming will be modified over and over again as a result, as well as having a constantly changing store of information on which to operate.

The upshot is that Harry's behavior will be *almost completely unpredictable* by people who knew only his original programming. If those people should encounter him later in life, they would have to interact with him epistemologically in just the way the rest of us interact with him and with each other.

[15] John Searle comes close to making such a claim; see section *VII* below.

[16] Block (op. cit.) expresses sympathy for this view, as have Hilary Putnam [1981], Patricia Kitcher [1982], and Terence Horgan [1984].

[17] For the most decisive responses to Searle's original argument, see the ensuing commentaries by Ned Block [1980, 425-26], Dan Dennett [1980, 428-30], Jerry Fodor [1980, 431-32], John Haugeland [1980, 432-33] and myself [1980, 434-35].

[18] Oddly, Searle himself does not draw that conclusion; see Ch. 8 of *Intentionality* [Searle, 1983].

[19] For the record, Smart maintains in conversation that he never intended to champion the chauvinist claim that humanoid c-fibers are required for any nomologically possible creature to be in pain, and nothing in his famous article strictly commits him to it. I am sure those things are true, but the article gives no hint of multiple realizability and is otherwise written just as if Type Identity were what Smart had in mind.

[20] For a locus classicus of objections to Functionalism that are in no way intended to embarrass the Type Identity Theory, see also Ned Block's "Troubles with Functionalism," [1978].

[21] Searle himself denies this. In response to several commentaries including mine, he says:

> Nor does it help the argument to add the causal theory of reference, for even if the formal tokens in the program have some causal connection to their alleged referents in the real world, as long as the agent has no way of knowing that, it adds no intentionality whatever to the formal tokens. Suppose, for example, that the symbol for egg foo yung in the Chinese room is actually causally connected to egg foo yung. Still, the man in the room has no way of knowing that. For him, it remains an uninterpreted formal symbol [Searle, 1980a, 452].

Probably Searle is right in saying that the provision of a set of simple causal connections is not per se enough to "add" intentionality. But that shows only that a set of simple causal connections is not per se an adequate psychosemantics. Suppose instead that we are able to plug in what is for humans an adequate psychosemantics. Then it may further be true that *so far as the man in the room is concerned*, the formal token remains uninterpreted, just as, so far as certain executive bits of your brain are concerned, the tokens they operate on remain uninterpreted. It does not follow − I do not see that it is even suggested −that the tokens, Chinese or brain, are in fact uninterpreted. Our psychosemantics applies to the whole setup, not to the man in the room.

[22] If you do not know by now which two they are, you have not been paying attention. Not that very many people have paid nearly enough attention to the books themselves, much less given me the public credit and money that I deserve for having solved all those problems of consciousness and qualia.

[23] Two writers who have recently taken up this point of view are Gilbert Harman [1990] and Michael Tye [1996]. I surmise that a number of others are sympathetic to it as well: David Rosenthal [1990], Georges Rey [1991], Sydney Shoemaker [1994] (a dramatic reversal of his earlier views), and Fred Dretske [1995].

[24] See also Christopher Peacocke's *Sense and Content* [1983]. In Chs. 6 and 7 of *Consciousness and Experience*, I examine all three philosophers' arguments minutely and refute them (or at least wrestle them to the ground).

REFERENCES

Block, Ned. (1978) "What Intuitions About Homunculi Don't Show," in W. Savage (ed.), *Perception and Cognition: Minnesota Studies in the Philosophy of Science, Vol. IX.* Minneapolis: University of Minnesota Press.

Block, Ned. (1980) *Behavioral and Brain Sciences* 3: 425-26.

Block, Ned. (1990) "Inverted Earth," in J.E. Tomberlin, Ed., *Philosophical Perspectives, 4: Action Theory and Philosophy of Mind*, Atascadero, CA: Ridgeview Publishing.

Bradley, M. C. (1964) "Critical Notice of J.J.C. Smart's *Philosophy and Scientific Realism*," *Australasian Journal of Philosophy* 42: 262-83.

Campbell, K.K. (1970) *Body and Mind.* New York: Doubleday Anchor Books.

Dennett, Daniel. (1980) "The Milk of Human Intentionality," *Behavioral and Brain Sciences* 3: 428-30.

Dretske, Fred. (1995) *Naturalizing the Mind*, Cambridge, MA: MIT Press.

Fodor, Jerry. (1980) "Searle On What Only Brains Can Do," *Behavioral and Brain Sciences* 3: 431-32.

Frijda, N. H. (1995) "Emotions in Robots," in H.L. Roitblat and J.-A. Meyer (eds.), *Comparative Approaches to Cognitive Science.* Cambridge, MA: Bradford Books/MIT Press.

Harman, Gilbert. (1990) "The Intrinsic Quality of Experience," in Tomberlin, op. cit..

Haugeland, John. (1980) "Programs, Causal Powers, and Intentionality," *Behavioral and Brain Sciences* 3: 432-33.

Hill, Christopher. (1991) *Sensations.* Cambridge University Press.

Horgan, Terence. (1984) "Functionalism, Qualia, and the Inverted Spectrum," *Philosophy and Phenomenological Research*, 44: 453-71.

Kirk, R. (1974) "Sentience and Behaviour," *Mind* 83: 43-60.

Kitcher, Patricia. (1982) "Two Versions of the Identity Theory," *Erkenntnis:* 213-28.

Long, Douglas. (1964) "The Philosophical Concept of a Human Body," *Philosophical Review* 73: 321-37.

Long, Douglas. (1994) "Why Machines Can Neither Think Nor Feel," in D. Jamieson (ed.), *Language, Mind, and Art.* Dordrecht: Kluwer Academic Publishing.

Lycan, William. (1980) "The Functionalist Reply (Ohio State)," *Behavioral and Brain Sciences* 3: 434-35.

Lycan, William. (1981) "Form, Function, and Feel," *Journal of Philosophy* 78: 24-50.

Lycan, William. (1985) "Abortion and the Civil Rights of Machines," in N. Potter and M. Timmons, Eds., *Morality and Universality.* Dordrecht: D. Reidel.

Lycan, William. (1987) *Consciousness.* Cambridge, MA: Bradford Books/MIT Press.

Lycan, William. (1996) *Consciousness and Experience.* Cambridge, MA: Bradford Books / MIT Press.

Matthews, Gareth. (1977) "Consciousness and Life," *Philosophy* 52: 13-26.

Melnyk, Andrew. (1994) "Inference to the Best Explanation and Other Minds," *Australasian Journal of Philosophy* 72: 482-91.

Peacocke, Christopher. (1983) *Sense and Content.* Oxford: Oxford University Press.

Putnam, Hilary. (1964) "Robots: Machines or Artificially Created Life?," *Journal of Philosophy* 61: 668-91.

Putnam, Hilary. (1981) *Reason, Truth, and History.* Cambridge: Cambridge University Press.

Rey, Georges. (1991) "Sensations in a Language of Thought," in E. Villaneuva (ed.), *Philosophical Issues, I: Consciousness.* Atascadero, CA: Ridgeview Publishing.

Rosenthal, David. (1990) "A Theory of Consciousness," Report No. 40, Research Group on Mind and Brain, Zentrum für Interdisziplinäre Forschung. Bielefeld, Germany.

Searle, John. (1980a) "Intrinsic Intentionality," *Behavioral and Brain Sciences* 3: 450-56.

Searle, John. (1980b) "Minds, Brains and Programs," *Behavioral and Brain Sciences* 3: 417-24.

Searle, John. (1983) *Intentionality.* Cambridge: Cambridge University Press.

Shoemaker, Sydney. (1981) "Some Varieties of Functionalism," *Philosophical Topics* 12: 93-121.

Shoemaker, Sydney. (1990) "Qualities and Qualia: What's in the Mind?" *Philosophy and Phenomenological Research* 50 (Supple-mentary Volume): 109-31.

Shoemaker, Sydney. (1994) "Phenomenal Character," *Noûs* 28: 21-38.

Sloman A. and M. Croucher. (1981) "Why Robots will Have Emotions," in the *Proceedings of the 7th International Joint Conference on Artificial Intelligence.* Vancouver, B.C.

Smart, J. J. C. (1959) "Sensations and Brain Processes," *Philosophical Review* 68: 141-156

Smart, J.J.C. (1959) "Professor Ziff on Robots," *Analysis* 19: 117-18.

Tye, Michael. (1996) *Ten Puzzles about Consciousness.* Cambridge, MA: MIT Press.

Ziff, Paul. (1959) "The Feelings of Robots," *Analysis* 19: 64-68.

RESPONSE TO MY CRITICS[1]

HUBERT L. DREYFUS

After reading my critics and talking to many present and former AI researchers, I think that my characterization of what John Haugeland calls Good Old-Fashioned AI (GOFAI) as a degenerating research program pursued only by a few "die-hards" was inaccurate. There are really at least three different rather diffuse research programs. The first, and so far most important, found its expression in Newell and Simon's deservedly famous paper on Physical Symbol Systems, as the program of testing the hypothesis that "A physical symbol system has the necessary and sufficient means for general intelligent action," [Newell and Simon, 1988, 41-49]. But this is nothing like a unified research program. There are several programs — Carnegie-Mellon with SOAR, MIT with frames, and Stanford with logic based models, to name a few. Each thinks, or at least until recently thought, that it was on the most promising track. But none has made enough progress to convince anybody outside their school or group to join them.

There are also the AI engineers. As Jerry Felman put it in a recent talk here at Berkeley: "AI no longer does Cognitive Modeling. It is a bunch of techniques in search of practical problems." Finally, I am told by many that the bulk of the work in GOFAI has shifted away from the Newell/Simon program to work on integrated architectures that combine high-level, symbolic problem solving with neural net models of perception and action. This saves the idea that a necessary condition of being intelligent is being a physical symbol system but abandons it as a sufficient condition. But this is problematic since it is not clear how the part of the system solving problems using symbolic representations is supposed to talk to the parts of the system that do not. As Haugeland points out, the idea that the intellect sends symbolic instructions to the body may well be a mistaken way of conceiving of the relation of intelligence to the world.

Everyone I talked to seemed to agree that most current graduate students are abandoning GOFAI research for research on neural networks. Whether these defections continue will depend on whether those defending GOFAI are making slow but steady progress as John

193

McCarthy claims — and presumably workers on SOAR claim too — or whether what now looks like progress comes to look like the diminishing returns that show one is trying to solve the wrong problem.[2] This, of course, is what philosophers like Haugeland and the Churchlands and theoreticians of neural networks like Paul Smolensky and David Rumelhart are trying to get people to accept. Whether one calls the current situation in GOFAI a degenerating research program left to the die-hards or a winnowing out of the faint-hearted so that only the courageous visionaries remain is largely a question of rhetoric and, as some of the responses to *What Computers Still Can't Do* show, seems to generate more heat than light. So I will turn to the substantive issues raised by my book.

I am grateful to Harry Collins for his detailed reading and his open minded and original critique. His new arguments both for and against the possibility of AI bring a breath of fresh air into a stale debate. As I see it Collins raises three problems for my overall approach. Here they are, with a preview of my response to each. First, Collins claims that, since I base my work on Heidegger and Wittgenstein, I should follow them (especially the later) in admitting that there is no way reality is independent of our social constructions of it. I note for the exegetical record, however, that it is a mistake to read Heidegger and Wittgenstein as social idealists; in fact, both are realists about the natural world. Second, Collins and I differ over the implications of the realism issue for AI research. Even if all domains are social constructs, does it follows that the structure of these domains is up to society and that therefore activity in them can be automated if society so chooses? I will seek to show that chess and natural language, although clearly socially constituted, have, once constituted, intrinsic structures independent of how society happens to interpret them. After surveying these structures, I deny Collins' claim that these domains can be regimented without limit and so rendered calculable. Third, Collins objects to my opposition of Symbolic AI and neural networks. In response, I will defend my taxonomy of domains of human activity, distinguishing those that are amenable to the techniques of Symbolic AI and those that are not, as well as my claim that this taxonomy does not apply to simulated neural networks.

According to Collins, domains such as logic or commonsense knowledge are pure social constructions and so have no intrinsic structure. This view, based on Collins' reading of Wittgenstein's *On Certainty*, seems to have been arrived at by taking Wittgenstein's epistemological observations to be ontological ones. Wittgenstein has a lot to say about how the certainty of all our knowledge claims depends on our tendencies to make some sorts of judgments and not others. This is true not only in our everyday social world but in the worlds of logic, mathematics, and science. Thus Collins summarizes Wittgenstein as holding that:

> Even logical syllogisms cannot be proved if we are unwilling just to 'see' and act as though they follow in the situations in which we find ourselves. ... There is no way of proving something either conceptual or experimental outside of the frame of a paradigm/form of life [Collins, 51].

So far Wittgenstein would certainly agree, but elsewhere Collins, without further argument, concludes that Wittgenstein's observations about what we can prove concerning various sort of entities shows that the entities in these domains depend upon our social practices, and that therefore my classification of domains into those that are formalizable and those that are not is mistaken.

> The worlds of logic, mathematics, and science are as much human constructs and products of social interaction as natural language. Starting with the same Wittgensteinian ideas one must be more philosophically radical than Dreyfus; there is only one kind of cognitive stuff in the world [Collins, 1991, 21].

Perhaps Collins' confusion here depends upon failing to distinguish two senses of world. We can correctly say that the world of physics was desperately eager to reproduce the cold fusion phenomenon. The world of physics referred to here is clearly a linguistic social construction. But we must distinguished this world from the physical world, which, in spite of everyone's hopes, did not exhibit cold fusion. Here the physical world is synonymous with the physical universe, and whether cold fusion is possible in the physical universe has nothing whatever to do with the social and linguistic practices that "construct the worlds of logic, mathematics and science." Our form of life may determine what sort of representations we can construct, but whether those representations correspond to reality is not up to us but to the way things are.

Collins confuses our access practices with the entities the practices give us access to. As far as I know, Wittgenstein avoids this confusion. Indeed, for Wittgenstein meaning and truth presuppose the domain of nature whose structure is independent of the social world it makes possible. He says in the *Philosophical Investigations* that "our interest certainly includes the correspondence between concepts and very general facts of nature." [Wittgenstein, 1953, 230] Heidegger, whose account is similar to Wittgenstein's, explicitly states his realism concerning the entities studied by natural science.

What is represented by physics is indeed nature itself, but undeniably it is only nature as the object-area, whose objectness is first defined and determined through the refining that is characteristic of physics [Heidegger, 1977, 173].

The question that is directly relevant to the possibility of Symbolic AI, however, is not whether all domains of objects and activities are socially constituted but whether, even if they were, it would show that the structure of these various worlds was somehow up to society. The domain of games such as chess provide an illuminating arena in which to refine our distinctions so as to test Collins' claim. Chess is clearly socially constituted; moreover it is constituted as fully digitalizable. No one doubts that with enough power one could calculate moves far enough ahead to play a winning game. But the question for AI that Collins and I are supposed to be addressing is not whether eventually a computer will be able to play master level chess. It is clear that computers already can. The question for Symbolic AI is whether the domain of chess is structured so that a Physical Symbol System using rules like those used by chess masters could achieve master level play. That comes to the question whether there are principles or rules operating on context-free features that specify a good move in each situation or, in my language, whether there is a theory of the chess domain.

The answer is not at all obvious. Although the micro-world of chess is completely digitalized, whether the game has a structure that can be captured in a theory has been a subject of debate between classicists and romantics for over 300 years. The classicist (represented by Symbolic AI enthusiasts) claims that chess skill must consist in the interiorization of a theory of the chess domain that allows the chess master to generate good moves. The romantic (represented by the Dreyfus brothers and some connectionists) holds, on the contrary, that chess is a domain without a theoretical structure and that therefore the only way for a human being to acquire mastery is to give up looking for features and principles and instead learn appropriate responses to tens of thousands of typical whole board patterns [Hubert and Stuart Dreyfus, 1988, Chapter 1]. The question is not who is right, the classicist or the romantic. The point is that society can invent a digitalized domain such as chess, but whether the domain has a structure that can be captured in theory is up to the domain not to society.

One simple way to sum up our disagreement is to see how each of us would answer Collins' interesting question:

Given that intelligent machines, like calculators, slide rules, logarithm tables, and books in general, are social isolates, how do they work? [Collins, 1981, 215]

Collins would explain the success of AI, where it has succeeded, by pointing out that in so far as we can learn to function in a context-free way like machines, machines can replace us in context-free interactions. I would explain how symbolic information processing systems can occasionally behave intelligently by pointing out that machines can behave intelligently in those domains that have a known theoretical structure, since then we can program them with the theory of the domain.

An obvious domain in which to test these two accounts is calculation. Collins tells us that people can take what calculators do to be calculating because calculation is an isolated, regimented activity; I claim that there is such a regimented activity as calculating only because mathematics is an isolable, formalizable domain. Collins is making the deep Wittgeinsteinian point that we could not do mathematics if it were not for social agreement in our judgments and for apprenticeship into certain regimented practices; I want to insist that we could not have developed such rigid practices if the domain of numbers did not have a regular, digitalizable structure.

The fact that mechanical calculators make subtle mistakes — mistakes that Collins has a genius for teasing out — seems in two ways to support, rather than undermine, my thesis that there is an intrinsic structure to the domain — a structure to which our practices are obliged to conform. In *Artificial Experts* Collins points out that given the problem 7/11 x 11, we could agree to count 6.99999 as the right answer. We could. But, then, our arithmetic would be a mess and would not give us a grasp of the way things in our world, let alone the entities in the universe, generally behave. Moreover, that we don't perform the operations of division and multiplication in the order indicated reveals that we understand what such operations mean and how they relate to the domain. We do not just carry them out mechanically. This understanding is a skill that requires experience in the domain. That we can outdo the computer in seeing such meaningful relationships supports the Wittgensteinian point Collins and I agree on that applying formal rules requires informal skills. But, again, I want to insist that the appropriate order of operations is also a fact about the domain. It is not up to us, as individuals, or as a society.

The same issue comes up again when we turn to expert systems. I argue that expert systems work in domains that we can formalize and fail in domains that we do not know how to formalize. I would agree with Collins that in most cases such domains coincide with domains in which we have learned to discipline our bodies or our minds to perform a series of context-free tasks. So, for example, expert systems for loading transport planes, analyzing mass spectrograph output, and configuring VAXes — all regimented domains — have achieved expertise, while expert systems based on heuristic rules for medical diagnoses and for chess playing, have not, and no one would know how to begin to build an expert diver. But I would want to add that it is not just a contingent social fact that we have formalized the first three domains, and not the last three. Plane loading can be captured by a combination of geometry and trial and error, spectography has a theoretical structure, and computer component choice can be carried out in a context-free way by using look-up tables and heuristic rules for how to combine components having various capacities. Experts in these fields were, indeed, replaceable because they were behaving in a calculative way, but they were behaving calculatively because the domain had a formal structure. Again it seems to me that Collins taxonomy of domains into those that have been disciplined and those that have not presupposes my taxonomy into regimentable and non-regimentable domains.

I think that many of these limitations on activities that can be regimented has to do with embodiment; Collins seeks to show that embodiment is not important so as to replace it with his idea of social embedding. He elaborates Wittgenstein's point that if lions could talk we could not understand them:

> Circus lions talking among themselves would, presumably, group what we call a household chair along with the other weapons they encounter in the hands of 'lion tamers', not with objects to do with relaxation. They would not distinguish between sticks and chairs and this is why their language would be incomprehensible to us. But this does not mean that every entity that can recognize a chair has to be able to sit on one. That confuses the capabilities of an individual with the form of life of the social group in which that individual is embedded. Entities that can recognize chairs have only *to share the form of life* of those who can sit down.

Collins is right, but I don't think it matters whether our intelligent behavior depends *directly* upon our having the sort of bodies we have or whether our form of life depends *in the end* on having our kind of bodies — what Wittgenstein calls "the facts of natural history." I grant Collins that we can understand stories about chairs without being able to sit on them. The question is, can we understand stories about chairs without sharing a lot of the characteristics of the embodiment of our consocials? I want to argue that one would need to have experience with our kind of body to make sense of our kind of world, and therefore stories about our world too. Collins denies this claim. He grants that:

> The shape of the bodies of the members of a social collectivity and the situations in which they find themselves give rise to their form of life. Collectivities whose members have different

bodies and encounter different situations develop different forms of life.

Yet he concludes:

> But given the capacity for linguistic socialization, an individual can come to share a form of life without having a body or the experience of physical situations which correspond to that form of life.

I contend that Collins again has it backwards. Having the sort of bodies we have is a necessary condition for social embedding in a society of similarly structured human beings.

To see this, we need only notice what Collins grants, viz. that our form of life is organized through and through by and for beings embodied like us; people with bodies that have insides and outsides; that have to balance in a gravitational field; that move forward more easily than backwards; that have to approach objects by traversing the intervening space, overcoming obstacles as they proceed, etc. Our embodied concerns so pervade the world that we don't even notice the way our body makes us at home in it. We could only notice it by experiencing our disorientation if we were transported to an alien world set up by creatures with radically different — say spherical or gaseous — bodies, or by observing the helpless confusion of such an alien creature brought into our world. One thing is sure, nothing could be more alien to our life form than a big, metal box with no body, no special way of moving, etc. The computer has no built-in *pre-understanding* of how our world is organized and so of how to get around in it. The odds against its being able to acquire all the knowledge it needs of what is familiar and obvious to us are overwhelming.

Douglas Lenat's Cyc project for giving a computer commonsense is a perfect opportunity to come to notice the shared world we normally take for granted, and how the cards are stacked to enable creatures who share our embodied form of life to learn to cope intelligently, while making all other creatures look hopelessly stupid. As I noted in my Introduction to *What Computers Still Can't Do*, Lenat collects some excellent examples of the difficulties involved. In order to answer Collins I will start with an excerpt from my Introduction and develop it further. Take the following sentence: "Mary saw a dog in the window. She wanted it." [Lenat and Feigenbaum, 200] Lenat asks: "Does 'it ' refer to the dog or the window? What if we'd said 'She *smashed* it,' or 'She pressed her nose up against it'?" [Lenat and Feigenbaum, 200]

Note that the sentence seems to appeal to our ability to *imagine* how we would act in the situation, rather than requiring us merely to consult *facts* about dogs and windows and how a typical human being would react. It draws on our know-how for getting around in the world, such as how to get closer to something on the other side of a barrier. Maurice Merleau-Ponty generalizes this point in his phenomenological account of what he calls *maximal grip*.

According to Merleau-Ponty, higher animals and human beings are always trying to get a *maximum grip* on their situation. Merleau-Ponty's inspiration for his notion of maximal grip comes from perception and manipulation. When we are looking at something, we tend, without thinking about it, to find the best distance for taking in both the thing as a whole and its different parts. When grasping something, we tend to grab it in such a way as to get the best grip on it.

> For each object, as for each picture in an art gallery, there is an optimum distance from which it requires to be seen, a direction viewed from which it vouchsafes most of itself: at a shorter or greater distance we have merely a perception blurred through excess or deficiency. We therefore tend towards the maximum of visibility, and seek a better focus as with a microscope... [Merleau-Ponty, 1962, 302].

> My body is geared into the world when my perception presents me with a spectacle as varied and as clearly articulated as possible, and when my motor intentions, as they unfold, receive the responses they expect from the world [Merleau-Ponty, 1962, 250].

Lenat, unlike Collins, does see that the body is indispensable for commonsense. He intends "in principle and in Cyc — to describe perception, emotion, motion, etc., down to some level of detail that enables the system to understand humans doing those things, and/or to be able to *reason* simply *about* them" [Lenat and Feigenbaum, 1991, 218. My italics]. But it seems to me this whole approach is reversed. We don't normally reason *about* our bodily capacities, we reason *in terms* of them. That is, when we reason in a commonsense way we already use our sense of our body to guide our reasoning. If this is so, the conclusions human beings find reasonable will differ from those of a disembodied inference-making machine. (I will return to this issue in my comments on John McCarthy's response.)

Mark Johnson, in his book, *The Body in the Mind*, tries to work out in detail how reasoning depends on our sense of our embodiment. He writes:

> The epistemic sense of modals, such as *must*, *may*, and *can*, find their home in the domain of reasoning, argument, and theorizing. ... I am claiming that ... the basis for this connection is that we understand the mental in terms of the physical, the

mind in terms of bodily experience. In particular, we understand mental processes of reasoning as involving forces and
barriers analogous to physical and social forces and obstacles
[Johnson, 1987, 53].

To illustrate the way the body works in structuring the basic
metaphors in terms of which we organize even our concepts Johnson
uses our understanding of force:

> We learn to move our bodies and to manipulate objects such
> that we are centers of force. Above all we develop patterns for
> interacting forcefully with our environment—-we grab toys,
> raise the cup to our lips, pull our bodies through space. We
> encounter obstacles that exert force on us, and we find that we
> can exert force in going around, over, or through those objects
> that resist us. Sometimes we are frustrated, defeated and im-
> potent in our forceful action. Other times we are powerful and
> successful. ... In each of these motor activities there are repeat-
> able patterns that come to identify that particular forceful ac-
> tion. These patterns are embodied and give coherent, mean-
> ingful structure to our physical experience at a *preconceptual*
> level [Johnson, 1987, 13].

Johnson concludes:

> Understanding in never merely a matter of holding beliefs,
> either consciously or unconsciously. More basically, one's un-
> derstanding is one's way of being in, or having, a world. This
> is very much a matter of one's embodiment, that is, of percep-
> tual mechanisms, patterns of discrimination, motor programs,
> and various bodily skills [Johnson, 1987, 137].

On this view embodiment is presupposed for acquiring the skills
and knowledge which amount to social embedding. We move and
meet resistance, etc. as embodied individuals even before we are socialized. Indeed, each human being begins as a cultureless animal that
must acquire the culture. That is why the form of life, if it is to be acquired, must be structure in keeping with the individual's embodiment. "Intelligence abides bodily in the world," as John Haugeland
says [Haugeland, 1989, 12], only because the social world is organized
by and for beings with our kind of bodies. That is not to deny that, as
we grow up our body becomes a social body, but the structure of any
social world is constrained by what our body can learn and make
sense of.

Collins, however as we have just noted claims that social embedding is more basic than individual embodiment. He thinks this claim is

supported by Oliver Sacks' account of the case of Madeleine, who, Sacks says, has acquired her understanding of our culture linguistically — by being read to from books. Collins concludes:

> We can say with confidence that if we can't train a computer without a body to act like a socialized human, giving it the ability to move around in the world encountering the same physical situations is not going to solve the problem. On the other hand, if we can find out what is involved in the sort of socializing process undergone by a Madeleine — let us call it 'socialisability' — we may be able to apply it to an immobile box.

If Merleau-Ponty, Mark Johnson and I are right, however, Collins understanding of Sacks' account must be science fiction. And, indeed, if one goes back to Sacks' account, one sees that Madeleine was far from being an immobile box. What was special about Madeleine was merely that she was blind and could not use her hands to read Braille. True, she was over-protected as a child, but there is no hint that she was carried everywhere. If she crawled, walked, balanced, overcame obstacles, had to find the optimal distance for kicking and hearing, etc. she would have acquired the body schemata which would have allowed her imaginatively to understand and project into new domains the events and cultural norms she heard about from books. Collins misses this point when he says:

> Madeleine has imagination; she can empathize with those who have more complete bodies. But under this argument a body is not so much a physical thing as a *conceptual structure*. If you can have a body as unlike the norm and as unable to use tools, chairs, blind persons' canes and so forth as Madeleine's, yet you can still gain commonsense knowledge, *then* something like today's computers — fixed metal boxes — might also acquire commonsense given the right programming.

But Madeleine has our body structure and many of our body-skills. That is why she can be socialized into a human world set up in terms of human bodies. So we should not agree with Collins' conclusion:

> In sum, the shape of the bodies of the members of a social collectivity and the situations in which they find themselves give rise to their form of life. But given the capacity for linguistic socialization, an individual can come to share a form of life without having a body or the experience of physical situations

202

which correspond to that form of life. ... [H]uman bodies are not *necessary* for human-like socialization.

On the contrary, what little we know about the capacity for linguistic socialization suggests that we have to have a body with a structure like our con-socials and skills for grasping and moving like theirs, if we are to acquire their language at all. For, as Wittgenstein points out, and Collins would surely agree, to learn a language is not just to learn a fixed set of words and grammatical constructions, but to use this linguistic equipment in ever new situations. As Wittgenstein argues, it is this ability to project a language into new situations that shows we have understood it, and as Johnson shows, we can't do this projecting without appeal to bodily analogies that we sense directly because we have to move, overcome opposing forces, get a grip on things (and ourselves), etc. So it looks to me like Collins has things back to front again. To learn a natural language a computer has to have a body; it must be embodied if it is to be embedded.

On the importance of repairs to make AI look plausible I fully agree with Collins. In footnote 45 of *What Computers Still Can't Do* I mention in passing that NetTalk depends upon our making sense of the rather garbled English it produces. But on Collins' account it remains a mystery why repairs work well in some domains but not in others. We repair NetTalk or printed English without even noticing the noise, but we have to stop and reprogram our computer or ignore its result if it makes an illegal move in chess or gets the wrong answer in arithmetic. In an informal domain like pronunciation the context does a lot of the work; as long as the program does roughly what it is supposed to, we don't notice the deviation. But in a digitalized domain, like chess or calculation, there is no ambiguity tolerance — no everyday context to help us fill in the gaps — so we can't ignore even a small error. For that reason in digitalized domains we are not given much opportunity for repairs.

What is important about repairs, I think, is that they again reveal that some domains can be formalized or digitalized and other domains cannot. Some domains *must* be regimented to do their work while others must remain context-dependent to function at all. It is essential to natural language, for example, that we can project our words into new situations, using them in new ways analogous to the old ways, and yet our fellow language users can understand us. In such cases we are not repairing mistakes but seeing — presumably on the basis of our embodied and embedded intuitions— that what is being said, although it breaks the rules, still makes sense.

Collins makes a similar point but in a misleading way, since he suggests we could choose to regiment even natural language.

[I]n the case of natural language interactions with computers we would have to learn to make our speech mimeomorphic, and that would mean restructuring our lives. We are *unwilling* to do this kind of thing and that means computers don't work in the corresponding roles.

In another paper, Collins expands on this possibility:

More translation machines might mean more and more routinization of the way we write until our linguistic form-of-life becomes, as in George Orwell's *1984*, fully instantiable in mimeomorphic action and fully computerizable [Collins, 1992, 729].

I contend that it is not up to us whether, in the case of language, we choose to behave like a computer. Another way to put this point is that natural languages have not only a syntax and a semantics but also a pragmatics. Even if we could agree to regiment, and so render formalizable, syntax and semantics — even if we could regiment parts of pragmatics like turn-taking — we would still not be able to use language in such a rigid way as to render pragmatics formalizable. If it is essential to natural language that it can be extended into ever-new situations, as I take it all parties to this debate agree, to turn our language into a context-free code is not just something we are *unwilling* to do, it is something the domain prohibits. No one doubts that language is a social construction, but once it is constructed, it is not up to any one of us, nor to society as a whole, to decide, by making our linguistic behavior mimeomorphic, to turn the world that everyday, situationally relevant language opens up into a formalizable domain. If we did this there would be no language, no world, no society, and no us. By contrast, formalizing the practices associated with doing physics might well wipe out the world of physics since it would wipe out the experimenters' skills, but it certainly would not affect the physical universe.

The touchstone of Collins' and my disagreements is our attitudes towards simulated neutral networks. In his article, "Why Artificial Intelligence is not Impossible," Collins tells us:

The theory of mimeomorphic action makes no distinction between one kind of machine and another. Machines can only reproduce tasks that can be broken down into a series of mimeomorphic actions.

But from my point of view, as Collins clearly sees, this covers up an essential difference between using computers to instantiate symbolic representations and using them to model neural networks. On

204

Collins view, any device should be able to replace experts in regimented domains and no device should be able to replace them in non-regimented domains. My view leads me to make a sharp distinction not only between types of domains, but also between what we can expect of different types of computer architectures. Although we cannot expect physical symbol systems to exhibit expertise in domains for which we have no theory, this limitation does not apply to neural networks. Since networks learn from examples and respond in similar ways to similar cases without needing to be given or needing to extract any rules or principles which serve as a theoretical representation of the structure of the domain in which they work, they can, in principle, learn to cope even in a non-formalizable domain. If we grant that nets can learn to respond to patterns without analyzing the patterns into context-free features, then one would expect simulated networks, unlike symbolic programs, to be able to learn to respond appropriately in domains that have not been and perhaps cannot be digitalized. In so far as nets are succeeding at pattern recognition — for example face recognition— this is just what has happened. Thus it looks like my two-knowledge-stuffs view turns out to be marking a deep distinction, and Collins' taxonomy turns out to be superficial.

One last query for both Collins and Haugeland. Why does intelligence have to be social? If one disqualifies the tasks animals perform as unintelligent because they are not social, we will need to be told in a non-question begging way what intelligence is. After all, Kohler wrote a book on the intelligence of apes. I do not doubt that some intelligent behavior, like say, investing, is inherently social, but I do not see why one would hold that only social behavior can count as intelligent behavior. Why should we suppose that animal behavior, no matter how seemingly flexible, adaptive and skilled it may appear, since it is not social, is *ipso facto* mimeomorphic, i.e., that animals always respond rigidly to the same situation with the same behavior? But how else could Collins reach the conclusion that: "whatever can be done by neural nets — or dogs, performing seals (and babies, for that matter) — could be described in rules even if we have not actually so analyzed them," [Harry Collins, 1992, 732]. To me it looks like animals reveal a whole domain of context-sensitive skillful coping. Although such behavior cannot be simulated by GOFAI, it could at least in principle be successfully simulated by networks whether or not such networks could be socialized.

John Haugeland has always understood me better than I understood myself, and written what I should have written. He positions himself, as I would position myself, between those who seek an abstract, representational account of mind such as John McCarthy and those, like Harry Collins, who hold that mind is a product of social embedding. He wants to describe embodied-being-in-the-world, as I do. He does not have much to say about the actual structure of the body and the role it plays in having a world. He does, however, make a strong argument that, thanks to the body, we are much more richly coupled to the world than the traditional representational view allows. In fact, he argues that there cannot be intelligence apart from embodied living in the world.

Haugeland reads me so carefully and extends my view so sympathetically that, in the end, it seems to me he makes explicit and embraces a contradiction in my own account I had not noticed until now. First he works out my account of being-in-the-world in a way that makes embodiment basic. Then he goes on to make social embedding basic so that I end up sounding like Collins. Haugeland himself seems of two minds on this important issue and I now realize that I am too. I must admit that I generally agree with Heidegger, and that Haugeland and Collins, in emphasizing the fundamental role of the social, are being good Heideggerians, but I am also pulled toward Merleau-Ponty, who would claim that intelligence arises from the way animals are tightly coupled with the *perceptual* world.

The problem for me is that Haugeland wants to link intelligence with the meaningful and the meaningful with the objective or normative, and that with the social. As he puts it, "the meaningful is that which is significant in terms of something beyond itself, and subject to normative evaluation..." This could still be compatible with Merleau-Ponty if meaning meant something like a gestalt, and norm meant that a perceptual gestalt that demanded a certain sort of completion and resisted others. Since there is more to the figure than is directly present, e.g. what I take to be a house seen from the front looks thick and looks like its concealing an inside and back, it allows us to "deal reliably with more than the present and the manifest" – Haugeland's definition of intelligence. But for Haugeland the norm has to be a *social* norm.

I don't want to deny that there is a level of social norms and objectivity and that there is a sense of meaning and a kind of intelligence that such norms make possible, or even constitute. But it seems to me that if one wants to tell a story of embodied intelligence then one should look to Merleau-Ponty and perception not to Heidegger and social norms. As I read Haugeland the first two thirds of his comments makes a terrific case for the Merleau-Pontian approach to embodied intelligence in general. Then, Haugeland adds his own convincing version of the Heideggerian view that social norms – "equipment, public places, community practices." – are essential to *human* intelligence. What I don't agree with, and what lands Haugeland in the Collins camp, is his claim that human intelligence and meaning are the *only* kind of intelligence and meaning there is, so that part two of his comments seems to take back part one. This becomes clear when he is lead to the conclusion that "In my own view (and I suspect also Dreyfus's), there is no such thing as animal or divine intelligence." That just seems

206

false to me. Apes learn to use equipment and no community is involved.

I would like to build part II of Haugeland's paper on part I rather than letting a social theory of intelligence take back what seems at first to be a general theory of embodied intelligence for all higher animals. That would amount to building Heidegger on top of Merleau-Ponty by showing how social intelligence grows out of and presupposes non-social, embodied, intelligence. Merleau-Ponty clearly has such a project in mind when he says:

> The body is our general medium for having a world. Sometimes it is restricted to the actions necessary for the conservation of life, and accordingly it posits around us a biological world; at other times, elaborating upon these primary actions and moving from their literal to a figurative meaning, it manifests through them a core of new significance: this is true of motor habits such as dancing. Sometimes, finally, the meaning aimed at cannot be achieved by the body's natural means; it must then build itself an instrument, and it projects thereby around itself a cultural world [Merleau-Ponty, 1962, 146].

T. D Koschmann's comments on my brother's and my account of expertise seem less on target. We are not, as he realizes, repeating the current view that experts "*reason*" from a large data base by "working with patterns" or that "expert problem solving consists of reasoning by analogy". It is precisely our point that experts don't normally solve problems and do not normally reason at all. That is why in the second edition of our book, *Mind Over Machine* in 1988, we explicitly retracted our fanciful account of expertise in terms of tens of thousands of stored holograms and adopted the model of a simulated neural-network being trained by experience to make more and more refined patterns discriminations. But with this model in mind it is hard to make sense of what holistic, non-analytical problem solving would be. If one is matching input vectors to output vectors there is no problem solving because there is no problem. This is not to deny that problem solving is precisely what beginners do and also what experts do when faced with new and difficult problems, but this is not our question. We do, as Koschmann sees, "privilege" intuitive expertise over such problem solving. We feel justified in assuming that it is better not to have a problem than to solve one.

Koschmann's review of my views on education in *Mind Over Machine*, are accurate. He is right that my brother and I contend that all attempts to use the computer to teach the student how better to solved problems will work only for early stages of skill acquisitions, and will be counter-productive when it comes to acquiring expertise. For this reason I don't understand why he thinks I would be sympathetic to new developments in "group-based problem solving". We argue in *Mind Over Machine* that whatever sharing of information, justification and public accountability, etc., one can gain by putting know-how into representational form is purchased at the expense of expertise. That is, a system using such representations will not perform as well as the expert.

John McCarthy and I come from two totally different paradigms. His research program of "formalizing human reasoning" assumes that intelligence is based on making inferences and asks how this is done, while I am trying to give arguments that intelligence is not based on reasoning at all. For him the issue is how to make the right sort of inference; for me it is how to account for relevance. Thus when McCarthy does me the honor of taking my phenomenological description of something like ambiguity tolerance as a basis for his circumscription method of non-monatonic reasoning, I am pleased that I have been read and found useful, but at the same time I feel that I have failed. That something I said could be turned into a problem for logic programming shows that my argument that even reasoning presupposes accessing the relevant facts has not been understood.

I presume that McCarthy, like Lenat, thinks he can solve my problem by using relevance axioms, so I turn again to Lenat. Lenat proposes two kinds of relevance axioms: specific and general. The idea behind specific relevance axioms is that different sections of the knowledge base "can be ranked according to their relevance to the problem solving task at hand" [Blair, Guha, Pratt, 15].

> So, for example, if the task given to Cyc is to solve a problem in chip design, the program will be guided in its search for relevant information by an axiom to the effect that the computer section is more relevant than the botany section (although the botany section cannot be ruled out completely, for it might be the source of a useful analogy or two) [Blair, Guha, Pratt, 15].

But as my old example of golden rod on the race track being relevant to betting on a jockey with hay-fever suggests, what is relevant can come from a completely unrelated domain.

For this sort of problem Lenat proposes general relevance axioms. These are formalizations of such statements as "It is necessary to consider only events that are temporally close to the time of the event or proposition at issue," [Guha and Levy, 7]. In explaining and defending this axiom Guha and Levy say "it is rare that an event occurs and ...[then after]a considerable period of time ... suddenly manifests its effects"[Guha and Levy, 7]. But promises and all sorts of health problems, to take just two examples, have exactly the form that what is relevant can be far in the past or future, and all sorts of historical and psychologically facts relevant to my present can be found in my more or less distant past. Guha told me that they realized these axioms were too crude but after adding a thousand more axioms they gave up on relevance.[3] The point is that any fact may be relevant to any other and any program that uses semantic and pragmatic information is not interesting unless it has a way of retrieving what is relevant in each particular situation.

Nonetheless, McCarthy envisages "a system [that] would ... represent what it knew about the world in general, about the particular situation and about its goals by sentences in logic." I think there is a general reason such a project cannot succeed. As the relevance axioms suggest, what counts as relevant depends on the current context. But how we classify the current context itself depends on the relevant information. This circularity does not seem to be a problem amenable to successive approximations since the problem is how to get started at all. Rather, it seems to be a hint that people cannot proceed by first determining the context and then looking for information relevant to that context nor by first finding the information relevant and then using it to determine the context. It suggests to me — as it suggested to Merleau-Ponty — that both rationalism, with its inferences, and empiricism, with its claims that we draw on associated memory data, are bound to fail.

It further suggests that perhaps some neural network sort of association is required. That is surely one reason why so many young AI researchers are working on simulated networks and fewer and fewer are going into GOFAI, or at least, fewer are going in with the sort of long range vision of fully intelligent logic machines which McCarthy so stalwartly defends. There are plenty of problems with neural networks, however, so if McCarthy can solve the problem of relevance for common sense knowledge he can still turn things around.

But I think McCarthy would agree that the relevance problem is surely too hard for now, so let's take a simpler one. I have tried, in my response to Collins, to make clear why I think an experience of the body is essential even to reasoning and so stands in the way of the success of the logicist program. It is not empathy that is important but the experience of moving about in a world, dealing with obstacles, etc. So, to return to Lenat's example of Mary and the dog in the window, the problem is not just getting the right antecedent for the pronoun naming the object of Mary's desire, but getting the right antecedent for what she presses her nose against. Of course, one could write out all the information about paths, obstacles, distance required for a maximal perceptual grip, etc., for this single case, and draw inferences from them, but that we all agree would be cheating. But no one has a clue as to how to store and access the facts about the body that would be needed to reason about such situations in general. There is no reason to think this problem can be solved. *We* certainly don't solve it. To avoid it we *imagine* moving around in the situation and see what we would pressed our nose against. Since McCarthy seems to think the problem is easy, I would be happy to submit Lenat's own example as the easiest thing a logic approach can't deal with.

Meanwhile, I remain skeptical about both GOFAI and neural networks. Although I expect that there will someday be androids like Data in *Star Trek: The New Generation*, I agree with McCarthy's cautious claim that "reaching human level AI is not a problem that is within engineering range of solution. Very likely, fundamental scientific discoveries are still to come." We only differ in that I doubt, while he believes, that the activity of these future androids' "positronic brains" will be based on the research of current contenders in the AI race.

NOTES

[1] This is an edited version of "Response to My Critics" by Hubert Dreyfus in *Artificial Intelligence*, Vol. 80 [1996, 171-191] and is reprinted here with kind permission from Elsevier Science – NL, Sara Burgerhartstraat 25, 1055 KV Amsterdam, The Netherlands.

[2] What certainly should be avoided is never admitting failure even when one's predictions are falsified, but rather claiming that success is just around the next corner. McCarthy never made such claims, and Allen Newell gradually seems to have disassociated himself from Herbert Simon's tendency to claim that the goals of GOFAI were about to - or even had already - been achieved. Only Douglas Lenat still follows the old approach of forgetting his goals and claiming that his research project has basically succeeded. Twelve years ago he predicted that Cyc in ten years would cope with novelty by recognizing analogies and would then be able to teach itself by reading the newspapers. Time is up and he seems to have made no progress on this front — at least I have seen no evidence of Cyc "noticing patterns and regularities in the data, and drawing from those patterns useful new analogies, dependencies, and generalizations" [Lenat and Guha, 1990, 357] But rather than call attention to this problem Lenat tells us that "After almost a decade, the Cyc project is still on target. The CNL (Cyc-based NL understanding and generation) subsystem is developing synergistically with the Cyc KB, and we expect a sort of crossover to occur in the next two years, by which we mean that most of the knowledge entry will take place by semiautomated NL understanding, with humans able to take the role of tutors rather than brain surgeons." [Guha and Lenat, 1994, 127-142.] It is unlikely the "crossover" will ever occur, but we will probably never know since AI is still distinguished from science by the absence of well-documented difficulties.

[3] Private Conversation, 3/4/97.

REFERENCES

Blair, P., R.V. Guha and W. Pratt. (1992) "Microtheories: An Ontological Engineer's Guide," *MCC Technical Report*, No. CYC-050-92.

Collins, Harry M. (1991) *Artificial Experts: Social Knowledge and Intelligent Machines*, Cambridge, MA: The MIT Press, 2nd printing.

Collins, Harry M. (1992) "Hubert L. Dreyfus, Forms of Life, and a Simple Test for Machine Intelligence," *Social Studies of Science*, Vol. 22.

Collins, Harry M. (June, 1992) "Will Machines Ever Think," *New Scientist*, 1896.

Dreyfus, Hubert L. (1972) *What Computers Can't Do*, New York: Harper and Row.

Dreyfus, Hubert L. (1991) "Heidegger's Hermeneutic Realism", *The Interpretive Turn*, Eds. D.R. Hiley, J.F. Bohman and R. Shusterman, Ithaca, NY: Cornell University Press.

Dreyfus, Hubert L. and Stuart E. Dreyfus. (1988) *Mind Over Machine*, New York: Free Press.

Guha, R. V. and Douglas B. Lenat. (July 1994) "Enabling Agents to Work Together," *Communications of the ACM*, 37 (7).

Guha, R. V. and A.Y. Levy. (1990) "A Relevance Based Meta Level," *MCC Technical Report*, No. CYC-040-90.

Heidegger, Martin. (1977) "Science and Reflection," *The Question Concerning Technology and Other Essays*, New York: Harper & Row.

Johnson, Mark. (1987) *The Body in the Mind: The Bodily Basis of Meaning, Imagination, and Reason*, Chicago, IL: The University of Chicago Press.

Lenat Douglas B. and Edward Feigenbaum. (1991) "On the thresholds of knowledge," *Artificial Intelligence*, No. 47, 185-250.

Lenat, Douglas B. and R.V. Guha. (1990) *Building Large Knowledge-Based Systems*, Reading, MA: Addison Wesley.

Merleau-Ponty, Maurice. (1962) *Phenomenology of Perception*, translated by C. Smith, Routledge & Kegan Paul.

Newell, Allen and Herbert A. Simon. (1989) "Computer Science as Empirical Inquiry: Symbols and Search", *Mind Design*, John Haugeland, Ed., Cambridge, MA: The MIT Press.

Wittgenstein, Ludwig. (1953) *Philosophical Investigations*, Basil Blackwell.

ASSESSING ARTIFICIAL INTELLIGENCE
AND ITS CRITICS

JAMES H. MOOR

How would we recognize an true artificial intellect if we encountered one? Although the concept of intelligence is admittedly a vague notion, understanding, problem-solving, and learning are three clear marks of intelligence and any entity, biological or non-biological, that possesses these attributes has a good claim to intelligence. We routinely identify such intelligence in non-human creatures. Dolphins can be taught to locate certain objects and return them, and they are able to stack these objects on an underwater balance until they have enough to open a gate. If the objects are placed at some distance from the balance, dolphins after a few trips have the insight to bring back all of the objects at once rather than making separate trips. Although not sophisticated behavior by human standards, it clearly demonstrates intelligence in that it displays understanding, problem-solving, and learning. We can identify intelligence and test for it. We may never know what it is like to be a dolphin, but we know what dolphins are like.

What then of artificial intelligence? How intelligent are computers? In this paper I would like to examine contemporary computer accomplishments in playing chess and in taking the Turing test to establish how far artificial intelligence has come and how far it has to go. Both chess and the Turing test have played a central role in the history of artificial intelligence. But, both have fallen under criticism and have lost some of their brilliance. If we take the Dartmouth Conference of 1956 as the approximate beginning of AI, the field has been progressing for about forty years. After forty years how close are we to having an artificial intellect?

Deep Blue

Chess history was made recently. On May 11, 1997, Gary Kasparov, who is the current world chess champion and who, many believe, is the greatest human chess player ever, was defeated by a computer, Deep Blue, in a chess tournament in New York. Kasparov was apologetic and defiant. "I am ashamed," he said. Then he remarked, "I feel confident that the machine hasn't proved anything yet." Not proved anything yet? Up to that point Kasparov had never been beaten in a chess tournament by anyone or anything.

This match went quite differently than the match in Philadelphia only a year before in February, 1996. At the Philadelphia match an earlier version of Deep Blue won the first game, but lost or tied the rest. By the fifth and sixth games Kasparov was giving lessons in positional chess. Kasparov understood Deep Blue's style of play and was able to capitalize on computer' weaknesses, especially its lack of positional knowledge of chess. Deep Blue may not have appreciated Kasparov's lessons, but the Philadelphia crowd savored them. By the end of the sixth game Deep Blue's major chess pieces were ineffectually grouped in a corner – a humiliating defeat for Deep Blue. Kasparov often takes off his watch after he is through playing the book openings and begins to think about the game more seriously. Once he believes he has won the game, usually a number of moves before the game is actually over, he puts on his watch. When Kasparov put on his watch in the sixth and final game in Philadelphia, the crowd of hundreds reacted with cheers of glee. A human was still the best chess player in the world.

What happened in the course of a year to bring about such a reversal of fortune? Three important improvements were made in Deep Blue. First, the machine, made up of 256 processors working in parallel, was faster than last year's machine. The more speed; the deeper the search. Deep Blue was able to explore twice as many moves, a staggering 200,000,000 positions per second going to depths of fourteen levels. Second, the machine's style of play could be adjusted reliably between games. Programmers were fearful of making any adjustments in the previous match because they were uncertain what effects it might have on the play. Third and most important, additional chess knowledge was given to the machine. Joel Benjamin, an international grandmaster, provided chess knowledge for the programmers to add to Deep Blue's assessment of chess positions. Deep Blue conducted its evaluation by assessing four kinds of factors: material, position, king safety, and tempo. By playing Deep Blue before the match Benjamin could suggest weaknesses in its play and what additional contextual information needed to be considered in particular situations.

In the first game of the New York match Kasparov tested Deep Blue by playing for him an uncharacteristically passive opening. Kasparov won the first game and it seemed that he had picked up where he had left off in Philadelphia. Then came the turning point in the match – the second game. Deep Blue played a brilliant game of chess and eventually Kasparov resigned (though after the game a possible draw was discovered that both Kasparov and Deep Blue had missed at the time). The game was a spectacular exhibition of Deep Blue's ability. At least for a moment in time, Deep Blue seemed to pass a Turing test for chess. It not only played chess well, it played like a human player. Zsuzsa Polgar, women's world champion, commented, "Really impressive. The computer played like a champion, like Karpov. Deep Blue played many moves that were based on understanding chess, on feeling the position. We all thought computers couldn't do that." [King, 1997, 69] Kasparov later remarked about that game, "Something truly unbelievable happened, and it showed a sign of intelligence." Kasparov was clearly shaken by the experience and suggested to the press after the game that perhaps humans on the Deep Blue team had intervened. How else could one explain its human like play?

The next three games ended in ties and the score of the match was tied 2.5 to 2.5 going into the sixth and final game of the New York match. Kasparov was not giving chess lessons that day; Deep Blue was. Kasparov had deviated slightly from the standard line of play. Deep Blue sacrificed a knight that opened lines of attack devastating to Kasparov's position. Kasparov resigned after only nineteen moves in less than an hour of play. Had the pressure gotten to Kasparov as it had gotten to his opponents in the past? Undoubtedly. But the result of the match was due to the overall good play by Deep Blue not just a momentary lapse by a champion. Deep Blue had a huge calculating tactical advantage but also benefited from some grandmaster level knowledge. Positional chess knowledge is difficult to articulate and program. To have pieces in good position is not necessarily to have them currently attacking other pieces or to have them on particular squares. It is to have them in position for an attack the full details of which may not be known currently by anyone. Good chess players know that good position is likely to payoff in the end. Deep Blue had good enough position to receive the payoff.

For AI chess has always had a special fascination. Chess is the paradigm of an intellectual activity. Dolphins don't play chess. Chess is a game in which theories of computer understanding can be tested in quantifiable ways. David Levy and Monty Newborn express the point well. "[Chess] serves the world of artificial intelligence just as the fruit fly serves the world of genetics. Chess requires what is generally understood to be a high level of intelligence, and through its rating system performance levels can be measured and compared." [1991, 1] Chess has been a kind of Holy Grail for those who have championed the possible accomplishments of computers. The conception of a machine chess champion has been entertained for a long time. In fact in the middle of the nineteenth century Charles Babbage, always looking for ways to inspire funding for his analytical engine, considered the possibility of using it to play games including the game of chess. He had the idea that his analytical engine, a gear driven computer which was never completed, could be programmed to play chess by looking ahead at different sequences of moves and selecting the best one. If the game of chess were limited to one hundred moves, he thought his analytical engine would have the capacity to do it. [Babbage, 1994, p. 349-351] Babbage deserves to be acknowledged for his early insight into a standard method of analyzing the game of chess by machine and for setting the precedent for wildly underestimating the difficulty of the task. In the 1950's and 60's AI workers using more reliable electronic computers were equally enthusiastic and continued the Babbage tradition by suggesting that computers would outplay the best human chess players in the near future. For example, Herbert Simon and Allen Newell predicted among other things, "That within ten years a digital computer will be the world's chess champion, unless the rules bar it from competition." [1958, 7]

The initial strategy in chess programs was to search a tree of possible moves and countermoves and to use some heuristic rules, which good human players use, such as control the center of the board, avoid placing knights on squares along the edges of the board, and don't bring the queen out too early. Some suggested that programs should be written in high level languages that would allow the programs to incorporate the insights of grandmasters. The difficulty in using such heuristics is that they are rules of thumb which apply all else being equal but which have exceptions. The early chess programs were not good at figuring out when to make exceptions and often ruled out good play along with bad. Gradually, these heuristics were removed and chess programs depended more and more upon brute search strategies. This made chess programs good tacticians but weak strategists. Good human chess players could beat computers because they viewed the game from loftier vantage points and knew the long term value of certain positions. But over time the computer searches got deeper and deeper, thanks largely to advances in memory and speed in computing technology, and tactical advantages began to erode strategic insight. Chess programs in the eighties began to beat human chess masters and even grandmasters. By 1990 a former world champion, Anatoly Karpov, lost a game to a computer. By 1997 the Deep Blue programmers had added some positional knowledge and the search was at its deepest level ever. As Kasparov remarked before the 1997 tournament, "I'm not afraid to admit that I am afraid and I'm not afraid to say why I am afraid. It goes beyond any chess computer in the world." That it did.

How then should we assess this accomplishment? Is Deep Blue's achievement a step toward AI's goals? Is chess played by a computer AI at all? The defeat of the world's human chess champion is certainly the accomplishment of one of AI's long stated and cherished goals and should not be minimized. Programming a computer to play chess at such a high level did not come easily or quickly and is a remarkably impressive feat. Two of the three marks of intelligence are present. Deep Blue demonstrates an understanding of chess. And Deep Blue can solve problems in chess extremely well. It is obviously not on a par with conscious, human understanding or problem-solving, but neither is the activity of the dolphins. Insisting that Deep Blue doesn't really understand or solve anything fails to appreciate significantly what Deep Blue can do.

However, this chess achievement is not without an important qualifications. Deep Blue does not learn in any interesting sense; it is adjusted by programmers. Learning is one of the most persuasive marks of intelligence. A future Deep Blue with learning capabilities would be a better candidate for an artificial intellect. Moreover, Deep Blue lacks general intelligence. The original goal of AI, as Simon, Newell, and others conceived it, was the production of a general artificial intellect that did many things well including playing chess. Deep Blue is a programmed computer narrowly focused on the game of chess and tuned to beating one person, Gary Kasparov. Even if Deep Blue should be considered world chess champion, as it probably should, it obviously lacks *general* understanding, problem-solving, and learning capabilities. It doesn't know a pickle from a pot roast and never will. Deep Blue represents an important and remarkable step toward the goals of AI but falls considerably short of being a true artificial intellect. Even with these qualifications, Deep Blue's accomplishments cast considerable doubt on the positions of at least two well known critics of AI, Roger Penrose and Hubert Dreyfus.

Insights of Alien AI

Roger Penrose looks for examples of mental activity that lie beyond computation. Penrose [1994, 46] offers the following to illustrate that computers lack understanding.

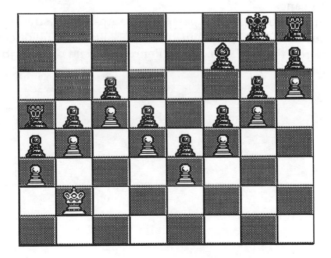

Wall of Pawns – Easy for Humans

217

In this chess position it is easy for humans to see what to do if they play white. White's king is behind a wall of pawns and is protected from the superior black forces. White has merely to leave the wall intact and move the white king around safely behind it. As long as the wall remains, white is assured of a draw. There is a tempting black rook which can be captured by a pawn but should be ignored. The capture of the rook would give fleeting pleasure as the black forces would roll through the barrier after the capture and surely win the game. Penrose points out that when this position was given to Deep Thought, an ancestor of Deep Blue, the computer captured the rook with the pawn. The reason for the capture is that Deep Thought gave preference to material gain and did not appreciate the long run consequences. Penrose concludes, "At no stage can it have had any actual understanding of what a pawn barrier might achieve – nor, indeed, could it ever have any genuine understanding whatsoever of anything at all that it does." [1994, 47]

Although it is uncertain whether Deep Blue would make the same mistake, what is clear from the programming of Deep Blue is that at least some of the nuances of positional knowledge can be effectively added to chess-playing computers. In addition, Deep Blue's defeat of Kasparov demonstrates that extremely good tactical computation can sometimes compensate for a lack of strategic insights. In several games Deep Blue was able to turn apparent defeats in the draws by aggressive tactical play. Finally, the line between strategy and tactics may become increasingly difficult to draw as computer searches go deeper and deeper. If the computation is deep enough, the program will discover that taking the rook with the pawn in the wall of pawns example is a bad exchange.

Examples like the wall of pawns are setups for illustrating human insight, but it is fair to point out that other situations favor computer insight. Here's the kind of example Penrose doesn't discuss: [Seymore and Norwood, 1993, p. 24]

White to Mate in 2– Tricky for Humans[1]

In this setup white can mate in two moves. You might wish to give it a try before proceeding.

This problem is frustrating for humans, and yet an inexpensive, commercial chess program can solve the problem in a second or two. Still thinking about the puzzle? The problem is difficult for us because it involves many steps of the form "if white goes here, then black can go there, and then white can go ...." After several rounds of this vertigo overcomes us and we must begin again. We are talented, probably for good evolutionary reasons, in recognizing spatial patterns but rather sluggish in spotting logical patterns that require several layers of analysis.

Now, if the wall of pawns situation counts against computer insight why doesn't the mate in two problem count against human insight? Why not regard computers and humans as having different kinds of insights and different kinds of intelligence? What is obvious to a human chess master may not be obvious to a computer. The success of Deep Blue suggests that the converse is also true.

Programs like Deep Blue with vast computational abilities may eventually become artificial intellects in two senses – being composed of nonbiological parts and utilizing unfamiliar cognitive processing. When considering intelligence it is tempting to focus on human abilities in understanding, problem solving and learning. The development of alien intellects is a perhaps more likely prospect for the future of AI. In such an event some future artificial intellects will have insights that will be foreign to humans but nevertheless quite effective in understanding, problem-solving, and learning. Both computers and humans will arrive at their insights through computation but they will not be similar computations nor similar insights. In some situations the insights of alien AI may well be superior to ours. Indeed, we seem to have arrived at this point in chess.

Machine Over Mind

Hubert Dreyfus is among the best known critics of AI. He believes that AI is a degenerating research program or perhaps a series of degenerating programs. [1993] According to Dreyfus AI began with great promise and initially had some impressive accomplishments, but has now run into real barriers to further success. In a book, *Mind Over Machine*, written with his brother Stuart, he describes a five stage process (beginner, advanced beginner, competent, proficient, and expert) that humans go through when becoming experts. The Dreyfus brothers believe that during the process of becoming an expert people gradually replace their dependence on context free rules learned at the beginning with intuition and holistic understanding. In their view computers may become competent but never expert. In 1986 they wrote

> ... our doubts about whether chess masters use inference rules have developed into our five-stage model of skill acquisition, which suggests that it is highly unlikely that expert systems will ever be able to deliver expert performance. (Actually, we'd prefer to call them "competent systems," since we can find no evidence that they will ever surpass the third stage of our skill model.) [1986, 102-103]

And later they emphasize in italics,

> *We predict that in any domain in which people exhibit holistic understanding, no system based upon heuristics will consistently do as well as experience experts, even if those experts were the informants who provided the heuristic rules.* [1986, 109]

These claims were somewhat dubious at the time of the publication of their book. For example, they discuss the program MYCIN which was given data about ten actual cases of meningitis and asked to prescribe drug therapy. They reported correctly, "Its prescriptions were evaluated by a panel of eight infectious disease specialists who had published clinical reports dealing with the management of the ailment. The experts rated as acceptable 70 percent of MYCIN's recommended therapies." [1986, 116] However, the Dreyfus brothers failed to mention that human prescribers (ranging from faculty specialists to a medical student) were given the same cases to evaluate and all of the humans scored worse than MYCIN! [Yu, et al, 1979]

The recent play of Deep Blue clearly falsifies the prediction of the Dreyfus brothers. By their own lights chess is a game in which humans use holistic understanding, and we know that Kasparov, a human chess expert and world champion, was beaten in a chess tournament. Deep Blue is surely more than a competent chess player; it is an expert.

Deep Blue has to use some heuristics in order to move. In addition to chess knowledge that was incorporated into the program, the search of possible moves itself requires heuristics. A chess program cannot examine every possible move. Assuming Claude Shannon's estimate of 10^{120} possible chess games and a billion moves per second (five times the speed of Deep Blue), it would take 10^{100} years to compute them. This is considerably longer than the ten billion year age of the universe. Chess programs must use search heuristics to prune the search tree, to allot certain time to different branches of search and to create the proper mix of depth and breadth of search. These heuristics are not the sort that humans use but they are essential for computers. Without them, a chess playing computer would not complete its calculations for its first move. Thus, contrary to the Dreyfus brothers' assertion a computer expert that beats human experts does exist in a domain in which heuristics are used.

What bothers critics of AI, I believe, is that the activities of computers are so obviously matters of calculation and not judgment, judgment that might need Penrosean insight or Dreyfusian intuition. The speculative reply is that at bottom human insights and intuitions arise from calculations as well, calculations of human brains. If brains can do it, why, in principle, can't computers? Deep Blue's accomplishment does not settle that question. But it does mark an important advance toward an artificial intellect. The AI bet is that at some point enough quantity of computer calculation of the right kind will give rise to quality in thought including sophisticated insight and intuition. Kasparov may have sensed this when he commented on Deep Blue's abilities, "I don't care how the machine gets there. It feels like thinking."

The Loebner Prize

If the Deep Blue match shows how far artificial intelligence has come, the Loebner contest this year shows how far it has to go. The Loebner contest is the creation of Hugh Loebner who has put up a prize of $100,000 for any program that can pass the Turing test.[2] Alan Turing proposed his famous imitation game (the Turing test) to examine the ability of computers to imitate humans. In the Turing test a human judge (interrogator) asks questions to two unseen subjects – one a computer and the other a human. The challenge to the judge is to determine based on teletypewriter communication with the two respondents which is the computer and which is the human. The strategy of the computer, of course, is to act like a human with typical human strengths and weaknesses. To use Turing's illustration, when the computer subject is asked to add 34,957 and 70,764, it does not respond immediately but waits about thirty seconds and then responds with 105,621 rather than the correct answer 105,721. Although Turing does not specify, we can suppose that the judge is allowed to ask many questions over an extended period of time. The computer passes the test if and only if the judge, or battery of judges, cannot distinguish beyond chance guessing which responding subject is the computer and which is the human. At the time, Alan Turing made a bold prediction about his imitation game.

> ...in about fifty years' time it will be possible to programme computers... to make them play the imitation game so well that an average interrogator will not have more than a 70 percent chance of making the right identification after five minutes of questioning. [Turing, 1950]

The Turing test has proven to be very difficult to pass and remains a theoretical benchmark for AI.

The first four Loebner Prize Contests (1991-94) were *restricted* versions of the Turing test, i.e., each conversation was limited to a specific topic. The procedure in the Loebner competition is "double-blind". Referees, computer-literate professionals, monitor a group of judges, the human interrogators, and confederates, the humans who serve as the subjects who answer questions. For example, in the 1994 Loebner competition judges were members of the national press who did not have technical backgrounds in computer science or artificial intelligence. Confederates were also members of the national press. The judges were informed that at least two of the terminals were controlled by people and that at least two of the terminals were controlled by computers. Actually, five of the terminals were controlled by computers and five by the human confederates. The judges were

222

told that their task was to rank order the terminals from "least human" to "most human". After rank-ordering the terminals, the judges were asked to draw a line separating the terminals they believed to be controlled by computers from the terminals they believed to be controlled by people. The judges were told that it was their task to unmask the computers by using "natural conversation" on a single posted topic which varied from respondent to respondent. Each confederate selected his or her own topic and was instructed to converse "naturally" on that topic. In the 1994 restricted test the judges ranked the five human confederates above the computer impostors. When asked to draw a line between the humans and the computers most of the judges made the correct discrimination. In four cases humans were classified as computers by some judge. No computers were classified as humans.

In the last three years (1995-97) the Loebner Prize Contest has been unrestricted. Computers are expected to handle normal conversation. The results have been enjoyable but not very impressive. The judges are asked to rank the respondents from the most human to the least. On April 29, 1997, the seventh annual Loebner Prize Contest was held with five computer programs and one human confederate. All five judges ranked the human confederate as the most human. The highest scoring program was called "Converse". Notice that in the following dialogues both the program, Converse, and the human judges make numerous typing errors when conversing. The strategy of Converse was to put the conversation onto the topic of the Clinton White House. Sometimes an exchange was convincing:

Judge#4:   who is al gore?
Program: Al Gore is an American Democratic politician.

But much of the time there was a clear sense of a breakdown in communication. Once off the subject of the Clinton White House the program seemed to grasp little if anything, and even when on the topic of the Clinton White House the program often seemed confused. Here is a judge who tried to change the subject:

Judge#5:   Hey, don't you get it I don't want to talk about
            Clinton.
Program: Sorry -- my attention slipped for a moment -- can we
            pushon to something more gripping. where was I...
            oh yes OK, but what happens now -- does it all drift
            on, with everyone waiting to see how much his
            friends have said about him under threat of lots and
            lots of jail -- or will something dramatic actually
            happen?
Judge#5:   Couldn't care less.

> Program: Well, you're more concerned about him that I am, I
>   suppose -- I think we've had worse, and who knows
>   what I might have agreed to in that locked hotel
>   room.

Converse, the computer program, did not know much about the practical world:

> Judge#3:   Where do you get your nails done?
> Program: Well, you're more concerned about him that I am, I
>   suppose -- I think we've had worse, and who knows
>   what I might have agreed to in that locked hotel
>   room.

Nor about art:

> Judge#2:   Do you know what sculpture is?
> Program: Well, you're more a fan of his than I am I guess ---
>   though I cant SWEAR what Id have done in
>   the locked hotel room, I must say.

Of course, it is entertaining to see what conversation programs can do. Sometimes the conversations seem plausible for a period of time. But conversations that continue for very long and can roam over any normal subject are far beyond what any existing computer program can handle well. Converse has canned responses with little variety. Hunting for key words can help the program track the subject but often generates misleading replies when key words are used metaphorically as in the exchange:

> Judge#1:   it seems like a war of attrition to me – i doubt
>   there's a smoking gun, but the weight of stonewall-
>   ing will probably damage his second term in the end.
> Program: I find violence very disturbing. Well, you're more
>   concerned about him that I am, I suppose -- I think
>   we've had worse, and who knows what I might have
>   agreed to in that locked hotel room.

Presumably, words such as "war" and "gun" triggered the remark about violence, but the phrases "war of attrition" and "smoking gun" are used metaphorically here and do not indicate violence.

It is safe to say that the Loebner Prize is very unlikely to be claimed anytime soon and Turing's prophecy about the likelihood of passing the Turing test by the year 2000 is very unlikely to come true. This shouldn't be surprising; the unrestricted Turing test is an extremely difficult test for a computer to pass [Moor, 1976]. In fact, no computer has ever come close. The Turing test provides an open forum to gather all kinds of information about a respondent's intelligence. If intelligence is considered in terms of understanding, problem-solving, and learning and broad human intelligence is the yardstick, it is obvious that no AI system existing today remotely approximates the range of intelligence required to pass a rigorous, unrestricted Turing test. Turing himself thought the way to pass the test was through the development of a child computer that could learn. We have no such general learning computer and until we discover how to produce one, Loebner's Prize remains reasonably secure. The programs that actually compete in the Loebner Prize Contest seemed aimed at winning by deception more than by actual intelligence. Is there a danger than a program might pass by being a conversation jukebox rather than being a real intelligence? Ned Block raises such a possibility and the results of the Loebner contest suggest a reply.

Blockheads

Ned Block [1981][1990] argues that the Turing test would lead us to the wrong conclusion if the computer passed the test by simply calling up a set of stored, but sensible, responses for any given conversation. Such a computer would pass the Turing test but would have no intelligence.

Here is what Block has in mind. The Turing test only lasts for a finite amount of time. If communication takes place via a teletypewriter, as Turing originally suggested, then only a finite number of strings of characters can be typed in the time period given a finite typing speed. Because the character sets are finite, there is only a finite number of possible conversations that can occur within a Turing test for some fixed interval of time. That finite number of possible conversations is extremely large and we will come back to that in a moment, but the number of possible conversations in the test is nevertheless limited.

Suppose the judge begins the conversation and we could list all of the sensible strings (S1, S2,...) that the judge could type. It will be a very long list but a finite one. For each of these strings there will be a finite list of sensible response strings that the computer could make (S11 or S12 or .... in response to S1, and S21 or S22, or .... in response to S2, etc.) . For each of these responses there is a finite list of responses the judge could make. And so on. In effect there is a set of trees of possible conversations. As long as the computer follows a continuous branch of the tree that traces the conversation to date the computer will always have a choice of many sensible responses to make to whatever the judge enters. The computer merely uses the trees of possible conversations to pick a response that will continue the conversation along some connected branch of the current conversation.

Human   Computer   Human   ......

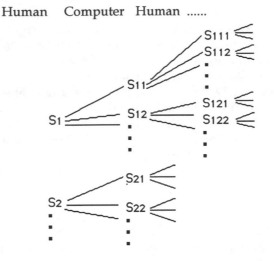

Conversation Trees

Block concludes, "Though the machine can do as well in the Turing test as Aunt Bubbles, it *has the intelligence of a jukebox*." [1990, p. 252]

This arrangement of conversation trees used to pass the Turing test is sometimes fondly referred to as a "Blockhead". Blockheads are logical possibilities but not practical programs that could be created to pass the Turing test. As Block himself points out there is a combinatorial explosion in the number of possible conversations which he estimates to be greater than the number of particles in the universe. In addition to the sheer number of possible conversations there is the practical problem of selecting allowable strings. One cannot insist that all strings be grammatical, for the interrogator might ask the computer to produce an example of gibberish which humans presumably can do easily – sometimes intentionally; sometimes not. Both Converse and the human judges mistyped. Hence, not all "sensible" strings in a Blockhead have to make sense. Assuming we could overcome the string selection problem requiring syntactic and semantic correctness while allowing for appropriate exceptions, a profound knowledge constraint still remains. Speakers don't just utter syntactically and semantically correct sentences but sentences that interrelate and reflect knowledge of the world including knowledge of current events and the current conversation. A conversation between a judge and a respondent such as

Judge:	Do humans normally have hair?
Respondent:	Yes
Judge:	Did you answer "Yes" to my last question?
Respondent:	Yes

is a reasonable exchange, but a computer answering the first questions with a "No" or the second question with a "No" after a "Yes" answer to the first question would quickly give itself away. A "No" answer in these situations, though linguistically perfect, reveals an absence of ordinary understanding that any normal human who speaks English would have. Given these problems in selecting acceptable strings and the astronomical size of the number of strings required by a Blockhead, the Loebner Prize is not in any danger of being won by an exhaustive jukebox strategy.

Block is not deterred by such objections. He says, "My argument requires only that the machine be *logically* possible, not that it be feasible or even nomologically possible." [1981, p. 30] But, here Block is stalking outdated behaviorism. There is no need to regard the Turing test as a simpleminded, behavioristic definition of intelligence though critics of the test often characterize it that way. The Turing test is more plausibly regarded as an inductive test that is defeasible. [Moor, 1992] Even if a computer passes the test, further evidence could defeat the hypothesis that the computer really possesses intelligence. The Turing test doesn't provide logical certainty, but reasonable probability in the absence of defeating information. Litmus paper turning red is a good indicator of acidity; however, we might be justifiably suspicious of a litmus test result if later we discovered that the litmus paper had been placed in a red dye.

Blockheads clearly do not possess intelligence. A real intellect responds creatively to challenges and this requires much more ability than simply tracing through stored conversations. Moreover, in granting intelligence to a system we are implicitly supporting a counterfactual claim that if the system were to operate in other circumstances under normal conditions it would be intelligent – its capacity would not vanish. Blockheads are designed to fool the judges and by definition cease to be intelligent one moment after the test is completed. But to grant Block this is only to grant a simple truth about most scientific tests – they can give false positives. One easily can imagine situations in which the Turing test is passed but the computer is not intelligent without resorting to Blockheads. For example, imagine that a bunch lively, wiggling flukes are dumped on a keyboard of a computer taking the Turing test. These flukes out of water flop back and forth. There is always the remote, logical possibility that during the Turing test this bunch of lively flukes on the keyboard will wiggle in such a way that reasonable responses to questions are type out and the test will be passed. Obviously, in such a case no real intelligence is present in the computer; it's simply a fluke performance. However, the mere logical possibility of a fluke performance does nothing to undermine the credibility of a good inductive test.

The performances of the actual programs in the Loebner Prize Contest, such as the output from Converse above, demonstrate that the current attempts at using a jukebox strategy are easily spotted. Moreover, a more systematic Blockhead is not a practical possibility and its logical possibility does not discredit the Turing test as a scientific test.

The frustrating feature about current AI is that it has is no rich theory of general intelligence that would guide the design of a computer system that eventually might pass the Turing test or possess a high degree of intelligence. What is needed in AI is more work on the basics of understanding, problem-solving, and learning. Without a theory of intelligence that goes well beyond what we currently have, it is highly improbable that a rigorous, unrestricted Turing test can be passed. [cf. Shieber, 1994] Deep Blue is a small step for computers, but the giant leap for computerkind is still far in the future.

NOTES

[1] In the diagram in the original article a pawn was omitted from d6. A correction was made in *New Scientist*, September 18, 1993, p. 49.
[2] For more information about the Loebner Prize Contest see its home page at http://acm.org/~loebner/loebner-prize.htmlx

REFERENCES

Babbage, Charles. (1994) *Life of a Philosopher*. Edited by M. Campbell-Kelly. New Brunswick, NJ: Rutgers University Press.

Block, Ned. (1981) "Psychologism and Behaviorism". *Philosophical Review*, 90 (1):5-43.

Block, Ned. (1990) The Computer Model of the Mind. In *Thinking: An Invitation to Cognitive Science*, Edited by D. N. Osherson and E. E. Smith. Cambridge, Massachusetts: MIT Press.

Dreyfus, Hubert L. (1972) *What Computers Can't Do*. New York: Harper & Row Publishers.

Dreyfus, Hubert L. (1993) *What Computers Still Can't Do*. Cambridge, Massachusetts: The MIT Press.

Dreyfus, Hubert L., and Stuart E. Dreyfus. (1986) *Mind Over Machine*. New York: The Free Press.

King, Daniel. (1997) *Kasparov v Deeper Blue*. London: B. T. Batsford Ltd.

Levy, David, and Monty Newborn. (1991) *How Computers Play Chess*. New York: Computer Science Press.

Moor, James H. (1976) "An Analysis of the Turing Test". *Philosophical Studies*, 30 (4):249-257.

Moor, James H. (1992) Turing Test. In *Encyclopedia of Artificial Intelligence*, edited by S. C. Shapiro. 2nd Ed. New York: John Wiley and Sons.

Penrose, Roger. (1989) *The Emperor's New Mind*. New York: Oxford University Press.

Penrose, Roger. (1994) *Shadows of the Mind*. New York: Oxford University Press.

Seymore, Jane, and David Norwood. (1993) "A Game for Life". *New Scientist*, 139 (1889):23-26.

Shieber, Stuart M. (1994) "Lessons from a Restricted Turing Test". *Communications of the ACM*, 37 (6):70-78.

Simon, Herbert, and Allen Newell. (1958) "Heuristic Problem Solving: The Next Advance in Operations Research". *Operations Research*, 6:1-10.

Turing, Alan. (1950) "Computing Machinery and Intelligence". *Mind*, 59 (236):433-460.

Yu, Victor L., Lawrence M. Fagan, Sharon M Wraith, William J. Clancy, A. Carlisle Scott, John Hannigan, Robert L. Blum, Bruce G. Buchanan, and Stanley N. Cohen. (1979) "Antimicrobial Selection by a Computer". *JAMA*, 242 (12):1279-1281.

PHILOSOPHY AND "SUPER" COMPUTATION

SELMER BRINGSJORD

Philosophy enjoys a vibrant symbiosis with computation; this volume is itself proof of that. What about "super"-computation, information processing more powerful than what can be mustered by a mere Turing Machine? By my lights, we stand on the brink of explosive interaction between philosophy and such processing. In an invitation to you to help bring us over the brink, this chapter describes a six-point connection between philosophy and super-computation — a connection much of which you and others can forge as the future unfolds. I presuppose no familiarity with underlying formalisms: this chapter can play the role of a self-contained tutorial able to usher you into the world of super-computation, super-machines, and super-minds.

My plan is as follows. First I fix the concept of ordinary computation via a review of Turing Machines (TMs) and first-order logic. Then I display and categorize a six-point connection between philosophy and ordinary computation. Next, I explicate "super"-computation with help from a (gentle) quiz. With the distinction between the two types of computation firmly in place, I explain that running in parallel to the six-point connection displayed earlier is a new six-point one between philosophy and super-computation. I end by inviting you to compete against me in a little game that involves super-computation.

Underlying Formalism

So what's a TM? TMs include a two-way infinite tape divided into squares, a read/write head for writing and erasing symbols (from some finite, fixed alphabet) on and off this tape, and a finite control unit which at any step is in one particular state from among a finite number of possible states. TMs invariably come paired with a set of instructions (a "program") telling the machine what to do, depending upon what state it's in and what (if anything) is written on the square currently scanned by its head.

There are many ways to program TMs. One such method is the flow-graph approach, which is used in Figure 1. This TM, dubbed "Gordon's 19 in 186," is designed to start on a 0-filled infinite tape and produce, after 186 steps, 19 1's. (What this machine accomplishes is relevant to a question on the coming quiz.)

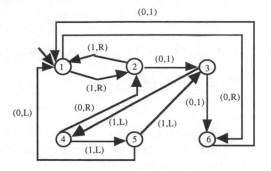

Figure 1: Gordon's 19 in 186

Let's hand simulate an initial segment of the computation of Gordon's TM — we label the machine G — so that we are sure of the concepts involved. The alphabet used is simply {0, 1}. The initial state of G is 1 (represented by the node labeled 1), and at the outset we'll assume that the tape is exclusively filled with 0's. The first thing G does is check to see what symbol it finds under its read/write head. In this case it initially finds a 0, so the arc labeled with (0, R) is taken from node 1, which means that the head moves one square to the right and the machine enters state 6. At this point, since there is another 0 found beneath the head, the 0 is changed to a 1, and the machine reenters state 1. It now finds a 1, and hence takes the arc labeled (1, R) to state 2 (i.e., the machine moves its head one square to the right, and then enters state 2) — etc. The machine's activity can be perfectly captured by a catalogue of its configurations from start to finish (Figure 2). A sequence of such configurations, where each also includes a record of what state the TM is in, is a **computation**. "Real world" computation, for example the thing your personal computer does when, say, graphing the performance of your stock portfolio, is a process through time that corresponds to some TM computation. Let's call this sort of computation (TM computation and computation that parallels it in the "real world") **ordinary** computation.

If this is your first exposure to TMs, you will doubtless be struck by how primitive and unassuming they are. But the surprising thing is that TMs apparently capture ordinary computation *in all its guises*. More precisely, whatever can be accomplished by way of an algorithm, by way of a programmed super-computer, by way of a (standard) neural network, a cellular automaton, etc. — whatever can be accomplished by any of these can apparently be accomplished by a TM [Bringsjord, 1991] (This view about the generalizability of TMs

232

is embodied in what is known as the **Church-Turing Thesis**, which we consider below). Furthermore, we know that adding capabilities to our TMs doesn't give them any additional power. For example, if we give a TM *two* tapes rather than one, nothing that was impossible for the one-tape machine becomes doable for the two-tape creature.[1]

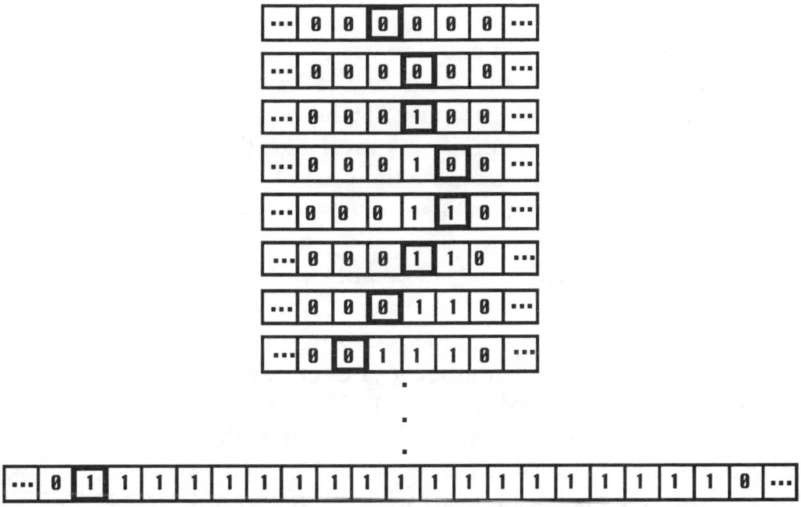

Figure 2: Catalogue of Gordon's TM

Now, we write $Mp : u \to \infty$ to indicate that TM M goes from input u through a computation, directed by program P (specified, e.g., by a flow-graph like that shown in Figure 1), that never halts. We write $Mp : u \to$ halt when M, directed by P, goes from input u to a computation that does halt. We can also harmlessly suppress mention of inputs and talk only of machines halting or not halting *simpliciter*. We write $Mp : u \to v$ to indicate that the pair M and P takes the input u, does some work, and halts, leaving v as output on the tape. This allows us to say that certain functions are **Turing-computable**: for instance, the factorial function, !, is Turing-computable because there is a pair M, *P!* such that

$Mp! : n \to m$ if and only if $n! = m$

The next concept we need is enumerability: a set A is **Turing-enumerable** just in case there exists some TM which sooner or later prints out every member of A, and nothing else. One important method for establishing that all strings built from some finite fixed alphabet $\{a_1, a_2, ..., a_n\}$ is enumerable is to assemble a list in **lexicographic order**. The idea is quite simple: one lists first the strings one

233

character in length according to dictionary ordering, then the strings two characters in size by dictionary ordering, then those three characters long, and so on, *ad infinitum*. Given the alphabet $\{a_1, a_2, ..., a_n\}$, a lexicographic ordering would look like this:

$$a_1 \,...\, a_n \; a_1 a_1 \; a_1 a_2 \,...\, a_n a_n \; a_1 a_1 a_1 \; a_1 a_1 a_2 \,...$$

At this point you should pause to verify that our small set $\{1, 2, 3, 6\}$, the natural numbers, the even natural numbers, and, say, the positive and negative integers are Turing-enumerable. In order to save yourself of having to specify a graph like that shown in Figure 1, it will suffice if you can assemble the start of a list which abides by a pattern that ensures that sooner or later every member of your target set will be "hit."[2]

We would also like our TMs to be able to *decide* certain questions: to give us back a "yes" or a "no" after some ordinary computation has been completed. For example, we might want a TM to tell us whether an input natural number n is even. So let's allow our TMs the symbols **Y** ("yes") and **N** ("no"). This enables us to say that certain sets are **Turing-decidable**. For example, the set $\{1, 2, 3, 6\}$ is Turing-decidable because there is a TM which, when given an arbitrary number k as input, stops with a **Y** if and only if $k \in \{1, 2, 3, 6\}$, and stops with a **N** if and only if $k \notin \{1, 2, 3, 6\}$. Enumerability and decidability are related in various ways, one of which can be expressed in a theorem that might be of help to you in the coming quiz, viz.,

T   If a set A is Turing-decidable, then there is some TM which can lexicographically order A.

It's also useful if we have a way of encoding TMs as numbers. One common method to regiment this is to let $n^{M,P}$ be the **gödel number** of pair TM M and program P. It's not necessary that you know the ins and outs of gödel numbering schemes. It's enough if you understand that such a scheme enables us, and TMs themselves, to encode TMs as natural numbers (which can then be processed like any other number), and to also decode these numbers, that is, to specify (e.g., by generating a graph like that shown in Figure 1) the TMs that such numbers represent.[3]

Now for a quick overview of first-order logic: Given an alphabet (of variables $x, y, ...$, constants $c_1. c_2, ...$, n-ary relation symbols $R, G, ...$, functors $f_1, f_2, ...$, quantifiers $\forall, \exists$, and the familiar truth-functional connectives ($-$ for "not", $\vee$ for "or", $\wedge$ for "and", $\rightarrow$ for "if $-$ then $-$", $\leftrightarrow$ for "$-$ if and only if $-$") one uses standard formation rules (e.g., if ϕ and ψ are well-formed formulas, then $\phi \wedge \psi$ is a well-formed formula as well) to build "atomic" formulas, and then more complicated "molecular" formulas. Sets of these formulas (say Φ), given certain rules of inference (e.g., modus ponens: from ϕ and $\phi \rightarrow \psi$ infer to ψ), can lead to individual formulas (say ϕ); such a situation is expressed by meta-expressions like $\Phi \vdash \phi$. First-order logic, like all logical systems, includes a semantic side which systematically provides meaning for formulas involved. In first-order logic, formulas are said to be true (or false) on an interpretation, often written as $\Phi \vDash \phi$ (This is often read, "I satisfies, or models, Φ.") For example, the formula $\forall x \exists y Gyx$ might mean, on the standard interpretation R for arithmetic, that for every natural number n, there is a natural number m such that $m > n$. In this case, the domain of R is $\mathbb{N}$, the natural numbers, and G is the binary relation $> \subseteq \mathbb{N} \times \mathbb{N}$, i.e., $>$ is a set of ordered pairs (i, j) where $i, j \in \mathbb{N}$ and i is greater than j. Formulas which are true on all interpretations are said to be **valid**; we write $\vDash \phi$ to indicate that ϕ is valid.

In order to concretize things a bit, and to wrap together ordinary computation and first-order logic, consider an expert system designed to play the role of a guidance counselor in advising a high school student about which colleges to apply to. Suppose that we want a rule in such a system which says "If a student has low SATs, and a low GPA, then none of the top twenty-five national universities ought to be applied to by this student." Assume that we have the following interpreted predicates: Sx iff x is a student, L_sx for x has low SATs, L_gx for x has a low GPA, Tx for x is a top twenty-five national university, Axy for x ought to apply to y. Then the rule in question, in first-order logic, becomes

$$\forall x \forall y ((Sx \wedge L_sx \wedge L_gx \wedge Ty) \rightarrow -Axy).$$

Let's suppose, in addition, that Steve is a student denoted by the constant s in the system, and that he, alas, has low SATs and a low GPA. Assume also that v is a constant denoting Vanderbilt University (which happens to be a top twenty-five national university according the *U.S. News'* 1996 annual rankings). These facts are represented in the system by

$$Ss \wedge L_ss \wedge L_gs$$

and

$$Tv.$$

235

Let's label these three facts, in the order in which they were presented, (1), (2), and (3). Our expert system, based as it is on first-order logic, can verify

$$\{(1), (2), (3)\} \vdash -Asv,$$

that is, it can deduce that Steve ought not to apply to Vanderbilt.[5]

Philosophy and Ordinary Computation

Philosophy undeniably enjoys a vibrant interchange with ordinary computation. Here are six examples out of countless others:

(O1) *Pollock on* de se *thought.* John Pollock [1989, 1995], whose seminal OSCAR system is intended to eventually be a full-fledged person, has persuasively argued that a genuinely intelligent robot must be designed and built so as to be able to hold beliefs about itself that parallel those we commonly express by such expressions as "I am looking blankly out the window of the Collar City Diner," where the indexical is *essential*, that is, where the expression isn't equivalent to anything like "The man with the tweed blazer is looking blankly out the window of the Collar City Diner" [Perry, 1979].[6]

(O2) *Machine Functionalism.* Computationalism, also sometimes called "Strong" Artificial Intelligence, the view that cognition is ordinary computation, has its roots in philosophy, e.g., in the doctrine, propounded quite a while ago by Hilary Putnam [1975a, 1975b], that cognition has little to do with the "stuff" involved, but everything to do with whether the flow of information in that stuff is (appropriately configured) ordinary computation. (For a comprehensive look at contemporary computationalism, with an accompanying bibliography, see Bringsjord & Zenzen forthcoming-c.)

(O3) *Program Verification.* Jim Fetzer (see his contribution in this volume) has offered historic philosophical analysis of the computational concept of "verifying" that the behavior of an ordinary computer program is correct, and has shown that this concept of verification, despite views to the contrary in computer science, is, to say the least, murky.

(O4) *Zombies Invade the Web.* One of the most interesting topics in contemporary philosophy of mind involves how to account for (non-actual, but seemingly coherent) zombies, beings whose external behavioral repertoire matches our own, but whose inner lives are the equivalent of that enjoyed by a stone. The World Wide Web now allows people anywhere

on the planet to assimilate many of the papers involved, to contribute to the dialectic, and to enjoy the stimulating visuals that accompany the debate. Three zombies sites are:
- http://ling.ucsc.edu/~chalmers/zombies.html
- http://www.rpi.edu/~brings/SELPAP/ZOMBIES/zomb.htm

(O5) *Mathematical Mentation and Machines* Can machines prove theorems unaided by human mathematicians? If so, how? Do current resolution-based automated theorem provers *really* prove things as profound as Gödel's incompleteness results? What techniques do humans capitalize upon which such automated theorem provers don't possess? Such questions are made vivid by automated theorem provers like OTTER [Quaife, 1992], which, among other things, has proved twelve hundred theorems of elementary number theory. In fact, OTTER (actually a variant, EQP) has just done something downright amazing [Kolata, 1996]: it has cracked the 60-year-old "Robbins problem," which is to show that Huntington's three-part basis for Boolean algebra is equivalent to a simpler one containing an equation devised by Robbins [Huntington, 1933a, 1933b].

(O6) *What is Computation?* We have been operating with the received answer to this question, and have used this answer to characterize ordinary computation. But while the received answer at least partially legitimizes the toil of those who study abstract computation and promotes a pleasant congruity between the theory of *computation* and the "What's *Computation?*" question, it is nonetheless suspect. The reason is that, as John Searle [1992] and others [e.g.. Putnam 1988, Nelson 1982] have argued, there is good reason to think that *all* processes are computations, and *all* physical things are computers. A related philosophical question, still unanswered, is: What is the difference between *analog* ordinary computation and *digital* ordinary computation?

It is instructive to classify (O1)-(O6) in accordance with the scheme presupposed by the editors of, and contributors to, this book. According to this scheme, philosophy-computation symbiosis happens in three general ways. The first way occurs when computation enhances the practice of philosophy; the second happens when computation (suitably configured) serves as a model of the mind (or some part thereof); and the third occurs when computation provides a concept that is a ripe target for philosophical analysis and argument. If we give these three categories obvious labels, and apply them to our list (O1)-(O6), we obtain Table 1.

	Professional	Mind Models	Philosophy of ...
(O1)		X	
(O2)		X	
(O3)			X
(O4)	X		
(O5)		X	
(O6)			X

Table 1

What Super-Computation Is

The first step toward grasping super-computation is to get somewhat clearer about the Church-Turing Thesis (CTT); in doing so, I follow Mendelson, [1990], as modified in some of my own earlier work [Bringsjord, 1994]. At the heart of CTT is the notion of an **algorithm**, characterized in traditional fashion by Mendelson as

> ... an effective and completely specified procedure for solving a whole class of problems. ... An algorithm does not require ingenuity; its application is prescribed in advance and does not depend upon any empirical or random factors [Mendelson, 1990, 225].

An **effectively computable function** is then said to be the computing of a function by an single-minded and obedient agent who meticulously follows an algorithm, a creature called — following the inaugural papers of Turing [1950] and Post [1936] that originated our concept of ordinary computation — a **computist**. So CTT amounts to

> CTT   A function is effectively computable if and only if it's Turing-computable.

For our purposes, it will be helpful if we have on the table a version of CTT that applies to decision problems, and one that applies to enumeration problems. Accordingly, we first say that a set A is **effectively decidable** if a computist can follow some algorithm in order to decide whether or not some item x is in A. And we say that a set A is **effectively enumerable** if a computist can follow some algorithm in order to enumerate A. Hence we have

> (CTT$_D$) A set is effectively decidable if and only if it is Turing-decidable.
> (CTT$_E$) A set is effectively enumerable if and only if it is Turing-enumerable.

238

The second of these propositions is what allowed you, above, to take the shortcut of simply providing a list in order to show that the set of positive and negative integers is Turing-enumerable.

Very well. It's time now for the promised quiz, which puts to use nearly all the machinery established by the discussion to this point, and starts your baptism into the realm of super-computation. Ready? Okay, here goes; you have eight questions.

(Q1) Is the set of all strings that can be built from the English alphabet effectively enumerable? Is this set *Turing-enumerable*?

(Q2) Now consider all the finite sets of natural numbers. Is *this* set effectively enumerable? Is it Turing-enumerable?

(Q3) The positive rational numbers $\mathbb{Q}^+$ are just numbers that can be expressed by a fraction n/m, where n and m are both natural numbers. Is $\mathbb{Q}^+$ effectively enumerable? Is this set Turing-enumerable? (Keep in mind that for every two positive rational numbers r and r', there is a rational number between r and r'.)

(Q4) The positive real numbers $\mathbb{R}^+$ are all numbers from zero on. Is $\mathbb{R}^+$ effectively enumerable? Is this set Turing-enumerable? Is $\mathbb{R}^+$ effectively *decidable*? Is $\mathbb{R}^+$ *Turing-decidable*? (Hint: To answer the third and fourth questions, consider using theorem T from above.)

(Q5) Remember that we said we could encode Turing Machine/Program pairs as natural numbers; we denoted the encoding of TM M and program P as $n^{M,P}$. Recall as well that some TMs halt, while others go on forever. Assume that you are given a TM M with program P and input u. Can you determine whether or not $Mp : u \rightarrow$ halt? Is there a TM that can decide, upon receiving $n^{M,P}$ as input whether or not $Mp : u \rightarrow$ halt? (In other words: Is the set of all "halters" effectively decidable/Turing-decidable?)

(Q6) Recall the TM G shown in Figure 1, a six-state machine that starts with a 0-filled tape and halts with 19 contiguous 1's on its tape (and nothing else). We say that the **productivity** of this machine is 19. (Is this the greatest productivity attainable by a six-state TM? I'll give you the answer to this one: no.) Moving to the general case, suppose now that you are given a TM M having n states. Is whether or not M's productivity is maximal for n-state machines effectively decidable? Is this question Turing-decidable?

(Q7) Recall our discussion of first-order logic. Consider the set of all first-order formulas which are true on all interpretations; formulas which are true no matter how the symbols within them are interpreted. (Given the machinery above, this set is $\{\phi : \vDash \phi\}$, a sample member of which is $\forall x(\phi \wedge \psi) \leftrightarrow \forall x\phi \wedge \forall x\psi$.) Is this set effectively decidable? Is it Turing-decidable?

(Q8) Consider the set of all stories. Perhaps you will agree that some are interesting, while some are not. Is the set of all interesting stories an effectively decidable set? A Turing-decidable set?

How'd you do? If you went through the questions quickly, and they were genuinely new for you, you probably didn't come up with answers you would be prepared to defend — though you may already have fairly firm intuitions about your answers. (I regularly use these questions for pedagogical purposes, and they have a proven track record in that context, but I encourage my students to spend some serious time reflecting upon them. Perhaps you would like to think in earnest now about (Q1)-(Q8), and then return a bit later to read on — because answers are soon to come.) Even amongst cognoscenti, the answers may vary somewhat. After all, CTT, though affirmed by nearly all who ponder such issues, is still just that: a thesis, not a theorem. And if CTT did turn out to be false, it would be possible for some of (Qi) ($1 \leq i \leq 8$) to be answered one way for the query about effective enumerability/decidability, and another way for the query about Turing-enumerability/Turing-decidability. If we assume CTT, then the answers to the quiz are as indicated in Table 2 under the "Traditional" column. The answers I am inclined to give are in the other column.

	Traditional Answer	Bringsjord's Answer
(Q1)	Yes (to both)	Yes (to both)
(Q2)	Yes (to both)	Yes (to both)
(Q3)	Yes (to both)	Yes (to both)
(Q4)	No (to all)	Maybe; No; Maybe; No
(Q5)	No (to both)	Maybe; No
(Q6)	No (to both)	Maybe; No
(Q7)	No (to both)	Maybe; No
(Q8)	Don't know!?	Yes; No

Table 2

Your performance on the quiz was in large part determined by how you fared with (Q4). For as Table 2 reveals, the answers, both the traditional ones as well as my own, imply that there is a point beyond which TMs (powered by programs) are impotent. This point, sometimes called the **Turing limit**, is indicated in Table 2 by the horizontal line separating (Q3) and (Q4). In the context of our quiz, you slammed into the Turing limit if you diligently tried to play the role of computist by providing a lexicographic list enumerating all and only the positive reals from the alphabet involved (the digits 0 through 9 and punctuation symbols). If you used my hint, when you ran into trouble at this point you invoked theorem T to justify the claim that the positive reals are Turing-undecidable.

The realm beyond the Turing limit is the realm of super-computation. Let's begin our exploration of it by focussing on (Q5). A number of readers will recognize this question as a version of the famous **halting problem**, a problem TMs can't solve. Put informally, there is no algorithm for deciding whether or not a TM (or, for that matter, a computer program) ever halts. Put precisely, the relevant theorem runs as follows. Where the machines we're talking about are Turing machines, and P and P^* are programs, there is no machine-program pair M, P such that for every pair M*, P^*:

$$M_P : n^{M^*, P^*} \to Y \text{ iff } M^* p_* \text{ halts}$$
$$M_P : n^{M^*, P^*} \to N \text{ iff } M^* p_* \text{ doesn't halt}$$

This theorem is what is customarily used to prove that the answers to questions (Q6) and (Q7) are negative ones [Boolos and Jeffrey, 1989, Ebbinghaus *et al.*, 1984].[8] But can't we imagine devices free of the halting problem? It would certainly seem that we can. In fact, the study of uncomputability in computer science often starts by encouraging the reader to imagine such devices. Here, for example, is what Davis *et al.* [1994] say at the outset of their chapter on uncomputability:

> Once one gets used to the fact that there are explicit problems such as the halting problem, that have no algorithmic solution, one is led to consider questions such as the following. Suppose we were given a "black box" or, as one says, an *oracle*, which somehow can tell us whether a given Turing machine with given input eventually halts. (Of course, by Church's Thesis, the behavior of such an "oracle" cannot be characterized by an algorithm.) Then it is natural to consider a kind of program that is allowed to ask questions of our oracle and to use the answers in its further computation. [Davis *et al.*, 1994, 197]

Oracles are certainly picturesque, but as you can probably surmise, there are more informative ways to chart the realm of super-computation. I will conclude this section by showing you one such way, one which involves the so-called **Arithmetic Hierarchy** (AH), a "ranking" of computation from the ordinary to and through brands of the super.

Suppose we have some **totally computable** three-place predicate $S(P, u, n)$ iff $Mp : u \rightarrow$ halt in exactly n steps, where M is a TM, P is a program, u is some input, and n is a natural number. Predicate S is totally computable in the sense that, given some triple (P, u, n), there is some program P^* which, running on some TM M^*, can give us an accurate verdict, **Y** or **N**, for whether or not S is true of this triple. (P^* could simply instruct M^* to simulate M for n steps and then check to see what has happened.) This implies that $S \in \Sigma_0$, where Σ_0 is the starting point in the Arithmetic Hierarchy, a point composed of **totally computable predicates**. But now consider the predicate H (for "halts"), defined by

$H(P, i)$ iff $\exists n S(P, i, n)$.

Since the ability to determine whether or not H is true of pair (P, i) — where P is a program and i some input — is equivalent to solving the full halting problem, we know that H is not totally computable. Hence $H \notin \Sigma_0$. However, there is a program which, when asked whether or not some TM M run by P on input u halts, will produce **Y** iff $Mp : u \rightarrow$ halt. (This program need only simulate the operation of M under the direction of P.) For this reason H is **partially computable**, and in Σ_1. To generalize, informally, the syntactic representation of the landscape here is:

Σ_n set of all predicates definable in terms of totally computable predicates using at most n quantifiers, the first of which is *existential*

Π_n set of all predicates definable in terms of totally computable predicates using at most n quantifiers, the first of which is *universal*

Δ_n $\Sigma_n \cap \Pi_n$

We have, based on this scheme, the Arithmetic *Hierarchy* because, where $\subset$ is proper subset,

$\Sigma_0 \subset \Sigma_1 \subset \Sigma_2 \dots$

$\Pi_0 \subset \Pi_1 \subset \Pi_2 \dots$

for every $m > 0$, $\Sigma_m \neq \Pi_m$

$$\Pi_m \subset \Sigma_{m+1}$$
$$\Sigma_m \subset \Pi_{m+1}$$

Right about now I hear some of you saying: "But all of this is so painfully abstract! Isn't there a way to make super-computation more concrete?" Indeed there is: it's possible to devise a more procedural (and hence more concrete) view of (at the least the lower end of) AH. Σ_0 and Σ_1 have already been viewed procedurally. How, then, could Π_1, the first stop in AH calling for outright super-computation, be viewed procedurally? Kugel [1986] has aptly called Π_1 procedures **non-halting procedures**; here's how they essentially work. Let R be a totally computable predicate (a crucial assumption for the following); then there is some program P which, when run on a TM, decides R. Now consider a corresponding predicate $G \in \Pi_1$, *viz.*,

$G(x)$ iff $\forall y R(x, y)$

Here's a non-halting procedure P^+ (*not* a program; and note, also, that we count P^+'s *last output* — if there is one — as its result) for solving G, in the sense that a **Y** is the result iff Gx:

- Receive x as input
- Immediately print **Y**
- Compute, by repeatedly calling P, $R(x, 1)$, $R(x, 2)$, ..., looking for a **N**
- If **N** is found, erase **Y** and leave result undefined

If you think about it for minute, you will see how this trick can be extended to produce **trial-and-error procedures** which solve the halting problem, that is, which decide the predicate H. They would immediately print **N** and then if, during the simulation, halting occurred, **N** would be replaced with **Y**. If we consider the answer produced "in the limit" to be the definitive output, the halting problem is cracked. [Computation in the limit was first introduced by Gold, 1965 and Putnam, 1965].

The portal to super-computation just described and used has a decidedly "digital" flavor. It's possible to create and open an "analog" door to the same paradise. The easiest way to do so is via the so-called **analog shift map**, which can be described, with tolerable precision, very quickly: Start by invoking some finite alphabet E, and then consider the set of dotted sequences $E^\bullet$ that can be built from this alphabet. (If E is {0, 1}, then 00011.11010101 $\in E^\bullet$. If E includes all the digits 0-9, then $\pi \in E^\bullet$.) Such a sequence can only contain one dot, but — and here the trick begins — a sequence is allowed to be finite, infinite on one side, or infinite on both sides. (π = 3.14... would count as one-way infinite on the right side.) A standard shift map

$$s^k : E\bullet \to E\bullet$$

shifts the dot k places, where negative values indicate a shift to the left, positive ones a shift to the right. In the analog shift a dotted substring is replaced with another dotted substring of equal length according to a function G; then this new sequence is shifted an integer number of places left or right according to a function F. If we allow the range of G to include strings of infinite length, then the evolution of an initial dotted sequence to a fixed point (a sequence that no longer changes, which happens when F = 0 and a is unmodified by the action of G) cannot be simulated by a TM: we have once again passed beyond the Turing Limit. (If the range of G is stipulated to include only finite strings, then we have the **generalized shift map**, which is computationally equivalent to a TM.)

Philosophy and Super-Computation

Earlier I listed a six-point symbiosis between philosophy and ordinary computation. I think it's interesting to see this list transformed into a new one citing interaction between philosophy and the computation *extraordinaire* described in the previous section. (This new list can be categorized via Table 1: simply change each occurrence in it of (Oi) to (Si), $1 \le i \le 6$.) Here it is:

(S1) *Pollock on correct reasoning for OSCAR.* Pollock's [1995] OSCAR is designed so as to constantly update that which it believes in response to the rise and fall of arguments given in support of candidate beliefs. What constitutes correct reasoning in such a scheme? Pollock [1995] notes that because the answer to (Q7) is "No," that is, because a TM with an ordinary program can't decide theorems in first-order logic, answering this question is quite tricky. He ingeniously turns to super-computation for help: the basic idea is that OSCAR's reasoning is correct when it generates successive sets of beliefs that approach the ideal epistemic situation in the limit. Pollock's idea is seminal, and is ripe for careful consideration.

(S2) *Supplanting Machine Functionalism with Super-Machine Models of the Mind.* Whereas Pollock's deployment of super-computation is not intended to imply that humans *actually* carry out super-computation, others [Kugel, 1986;

Bringsjord, 1992, 1994; Bringsjord & Zenzen, forthcoming-a] have claimed that we are in fact "super"-minds: beings capable of solving the halting problem, for example. More on this below, in connection with (Q8) from our earlier quiz.

(S3) *Operating System Verification.* Whereas Fetzer turned his attention to program verification, someone interested in super-computation could turn his or her attention to the attempt to model and thereby monitor the behavior of an operating system for multi-user computers. Such systems run in an on-going process that never terminates, and hence cry out for models more sophisticated than those employed in program verification. Once such a sophisticated model is on the table, there arises an opportunity for the philosopher to try to ascertain whether or not it does in fact provide assurance that such operating systems will behave as desired. Those readers interested in investigating this issue can start their adventure below, when playing against me in one of McNaughton's [1993] "infinite games," which are possible models of unending, multi-user computing.

(S4) *Super-computation and the Web.* As of yet, no one has harnessed the power of the Web in order to provide students and scholars with instant and comprehensive access to material on super-computation and super-minds. The opportunity is great.[9]

(S5) *Mathematical Mentation and Super-Machines.* Roger Penrose [1989, 1994] and others [e.g., Bringsjord, 1997b] have argued that the mentation of mathematicians engaged in proving theorems involves super-computation. Are they right? The issue is far from settled. One place to start an attempt to move toward settling it is to look carefully for serious inadequacies in the use of *ordinary* computation in automated theorem provers — see (O5).

(S6) *What is Super-Computation?* As I pointed out above, we don't yet have a philosophically satisfying answer to the "What's (ordinary) computation?" question, despite the fact that the math in question is quite mature. Likewise, we don't really understand super-computation, despite what the math (as in, e.g., what was presented above in connection with the Arithmetic Hierarchy) may indicate. The opportunities here for philosophers are myriad. Can we *build* a trial-and-error machine? If they can't be built, do they occur naturally in the physical world?[10] A related philosophical question, recently intensified by the advent of analog shift maps [visited above; Siegelmann, 1995] we *build* a trial-and-error machine? If they can't be built, do they occur naturally in the physical world?[10] A related philosophical question, recently intensified by the advent of analog shift maps [visited above; Siegelmann, 1995] and the similar class of analog chaotic neural nets (Siegelmann, 1995, Siegelmann & Sontag, 1994], is: What is the difference between *analog* super-computation and *digital* super-computation?

Let's look in more detail at (S2) and then end by playing the promised game.

As I said above, I don't think the Church-Turing Thesis, CTT, is true. My argument against it instantiates an argument schema that should be understandable to readers who assimilated the above presentation of the Arithmetic Hierarchy. The schema is as follows:

Schema S
(1)   If $A \in \Sigma_1$ (or $A \in \Sigma_0$), then there exists a program P which reverses programs for *deciding* members of A so as to yield programs for *enumerating* members of A.
(2)   There's no program P which reverses programs for *deciding* members of A so as to yield programs for *enumerating* members of A.
∴   (3) $A \notin \Sigma_1$ (or $A \notin \Sigma_0$).   (by *modus tollens*)
(4) $A \in$ AH.
∴   (5) $A \in \Pi_1$ (or above in the AH)   (disjunctive syllogism on the rest of AH)
(6) A is effectively decidable.
∴   (7)   CTT is false.

Schema S is not easily cast aside: Premise (1) is a theorem, and a simple one at that.[11] Lines (3) and (5) are simply intermediate conclusions; (7) does indeed follow from (5) and (6), since these two propositions counter-example (CTT)'s "only if" part; and the other two inferences are unassailable. Everything boils down to (2), (4) and (6). If Schema S is instantiated by setting the variable A within it to $\mathbb{R}$, the reals, the issue becomes only (6), since (2) is true of any non-decidable set (of which $\mathbb{R}$ is one; recall our quiz above), and there is a technique of constructing $\mathbb{R}$ from $\mathbb{N}$ (Dedekind cuts) which constitutes a proof of (4). Of course, it's doubtful that $\mathbb{R}$ *is* effectively decidable. A better candidate for A in the schema, it seems to me, is the set of all interesting stories, a set mentioned in the last question — (Q8) — on the above quiz. Why? Because I don't think it's rational to believe that the ability to *decide* whether a story is interesting can be transformed

Now maybe I'm wrong — wrong that the Church-Turing Thesis is false, and wrong that you are a super-mind operating beyond the Turing limit. But if you *are* a super-mind, perhaps you will be able to play a little game with me. Not a game like chess, mind you: chess is after all a finite game, one handled quite well by ordinary computation. (As Gary Kasparov can attest. See Bringsjord [1997a] for a discussion of Deep Blue versus Kasparov.) I'm talking about an infinite game of the sort alluded to in (S3); here's how it works.

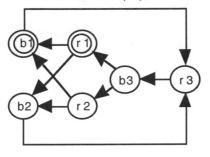

Figure 3

You will need a placemarker (a dime will do nicely), and the flow-graph shown in Figure 3 (across which you will slide the dime). I will be black, you will be red. Notice that the nodes in the graph of Figure 3 are divided in half: three are red (r) nodes; three are black (b) nodes. If the dime is on an r node, then it's your turn, as red, to move; if the dime is on a b node, it's my turn. Here's how the game proceeds. We randomly put the dime down on one of the nodes, and then we take turns sliding it from node to node, making sure that a move is made in accordance with a connecting arrow. So, if the dime is initially upon r1, you would move, and your options are b1 and b2. If you slid the dime to b2, my only option would be r3, and so on. Now, here's the thing: we are going to take turns back and forth for an *infinite amount of time*. Since you may complain at this point that you are mortal, I want you to assume for the sake of the game that we, like super-machines, can in fact take turns forever. Okay, now notice that nodes b1 and r1 are double-circles; this is because these two are "winning" nodes. I win, as black, if and only if either r1 and b1 are both visited only finitely many times or are both visited infinitely often. You, red, win if and only if *one* of these two nodes is visited infinitely often and the *other* finitely often. Got it? (Even super-minds may need to meditate for a minute or two on what I just said.) Okay, now: What is your strategy? What is your *best* strategy? What is *my* best strategy? If we both play our best, who will win? And supposing we play only for a finite amount of time, how could a referee predict a winner?[13]

NOTES

[1] The reader seeking details on this fact and on TMs (and other equivalent automata) and first-order logic generally can consult seven books I find useful: For broad coverage of the basic material, see Lewis & Papadimitriou [1981], Ebbinghaus, Flum, et al. [1984], Boolos & Jeffrey [1980], and Hopcroft & Ullman [1979]. For a nice comprehensive discussion of computability theory that includes succinct coverage of uncomputability, including the Arithmetic Hierarchy (introduced below), see Davis et al. [1994]. Partee [1990] contains a very nice discussion of the Chomsky Hierarchy. And, of course, there's always the classic Rogers [1967].

[2] The answers are simply 1, 2, 3, 6; 0, 1, 2, 3, 4, 5, 6, ...; 0, 2, 4, 6, 8, 10, ...; 1, -1, 2, -2, 3, -3, ...

[3] Ebbinghaus et al. [1984] details a gödel numbering scheme that will be particularly relevant to those familiar with computer programs.

[4] The customary abbreviation for 'if and only if.'

[5] In my opinion a good way to learn first-order logic is through the courseware *Hyperproof* [Barwise and Etchemendy, 1994]. A number of interesting problems in *Hyperproof* are available on my web site; the direct URL is http://www.rpi.edu/~brings/logarg.html.

[6] I may see this man in a mirror, and not realize at first as I think about the vacant expression on his visage that it is me I'm looking at.

[7] Go through my course *Computability and Logic* on my web site for various relevant TMs, including a six-state machine with productivity of 21. URL: http://www.rpi.edu/~brings.

[8] For example, decisions about TM productivity are problematic because it will be impossible to gauge the productivity of a TM that goes eternally on and on.

[9] I suggest that those taking it begin by surfing the web to collect information on real-life engineering attempts to tackle the "busy beaver" problem described in (Q7). The busy beaver problem was first introduced and proven to be beyond the Turing limit in [Rado, 1963].

[10] Note that there is an interesting connection between (S6) and (S2): If super-machines can't be built, and if we *are* super-machines, then we can't be built.

[11] In order to see the theorem in action, consider the set {1, 2, 3, 6}. We said above that this set is effectively decidable: if I give you a natural number n, you will be able to ascertain whether or not it's in the set in question. But then it follows that the set can be enumerated. Why?

[12] I owe part of my point here to Peter Kugel [1986], who expresses skepticism that recognizing beautiful architecture can be transformed into the production of such designs. My position on stories and interestingness, in the context of Schema S, is developed more fully in [Bringsjord, 1994, forthcoming-a, forthcoming-b]. Note that — pre-

dictably, given Schema S — I claim that the set of all interesting stories is not enumerable. (After all, perhaps there is an interesting story for each real number between 0 and 1.)

[13] This game is due to McNaughton [1993]. STOP HERE IF YOU'RE TACKLING THE QUESTIONS. Only black has an invincible strategy, viz., from b3 move to r2 if b1 has never been visited or if r1 has been visited since the last time b1 was visited; in all other circumstances move to r1. So there was really no way for you to beat me! It is remarkable that ordinary computation can find this strategy when presented with the game in question [McNaughton, 1993]. (No ordinary computer can *play* the game, of course.) However, for a game utterly beyond the Turing limit, see the "undetermined" game featured in [Gale and Stewart, 1953]: this is a game where a winning strategy cannot be devised by ordinary computation (in fact, there is no mathematical function which is a winning strategy!).

REFERENCES

Barwise, Jon and John Etchemendy (1994) *Hyperproof*, Stanford, CA: CSLI Publications.

Boolos, George and Richard Jeffrey (1989) *Computability and Logic*, Cambridge: Cambridge University Press.

Bringsjord, Selmer. (1992) *What Robots Can and Can't Be.* Dordrecht, The Netherlands: Kluwer.

Bringsjord, Selmer. (1994a) "Computation, Among Other Things, Is Beneath Us," *Minds and Machines* 4: 469-488.

Bringsjord, Selmer. (1994b) "Church's Thesis, Contra Mendelson, is Unprovable ... and Worse: It May Be False," Annual Eastern Division Meetings of the American Philosophical Association, Atlanta, Georgia, December 30.

Bringsjord, Selmer. (1997a), "Chess Isn't Tough Enough: Better Games for Mind Malchine Competition" paper presented at annual meeting of the American Association of Artificial Intelligence, Providence, RI, July, 1997.

Bringsjord, Selmer. (1997b) "An Argument for the Uncomputability of Infinitary Mathematical Expertise," in Paul Feltovich, Ken Ford, and Robert Hoffman, Eds., *Expertise in Context*, Menlo Park, CA: AAAI Press.

Bringsjord, Selmer and David Ferrucci (forthcoming-b) *Artificial Intelligence, Literary Creativity, and Story Generation: the State of the Art*, Hillsdale, NJ: Erlbaum.

Bringsjord, Selmer and Michael Zenzen (forthcoming-a) *Super-Minds: A Defense of Uncomputable Cognition*, Dordrecht, The Netherlands: Kluwer.

Bringsjord, Selmer and Michael Zenzen (forthcoming-c) "Cognition Is Not Computation: The Argument From Irreversibility," *Synthese*.

Davis, Martin and Elaine Weyuker (1983) *Computability, Complexity, and Languages: Fundamentals of Theoretical Computer Science*, New York, NY: Academic Press.

Ebbinghaus, Heinz-Dieter, Jörg Flum and Wolfgang Thomas (1984) *Mathematical Logic*, New York, NY: Springer-Verlag.

Gale, D. and F. M. Steward (1953) "Infinite Games with Perfect Information," in Annals *of Mathematical Studies 28 – Contributions to the Theory of Games*, Princeton, NJ: Princeton University Press.

Gold, E Mark. (1965) "Limiting Recursion," *Journal of Symbolic Logic* 30 (1): 28-47.

Hopcroft, John and Jeffrey Ullman. (1979) *Introduction to Automata Theory, Languages and Computation*, Reading, MA: Addison-Wesley.

Huntington, E.V. (1933a) "New Sets of Independent Postulates for the Algebra of Logic," *Transactions of the AMS* 35: 274-304.

Huntington, E.V. (1933b) "Boolean Algebra: A Correction," *Trans-actions of the AMS* 35: 557-558.

Kolata, Gina. (1996) "Computer Math Proof Shows Reasoning Power," *New York Times*, December 10.

Kugel, Peter. (1986) "Thinking May Be More Than Computing," *Cognition* 22: 137-198.

Lewis, Harry and Christos Papadimitriou (1981) *Elements of the Theory of Computation*, Englewood Cliffs, NJ: Prentice-Hall.

McNaughton, Robert. (1993) "Infinite Games Played on Finite Graphs," *Annals of Pure and Applied Logic* 65: 149-184.

Mendelson, Elliot. (1990) "Second Thoughts About Church's Thesis and Mathematical Proofs," *Journal of Philosophy* 87 (5): 225-233.

Partee, Barbara, Alice Meulen and Robert Wall (1990) *Mathematical Methods in Linguistics*, Dordrecht, The Netherlands: Kluwer Academic Publishers.

Penrose, Roger. (1989) *The Emperor's New Mind.* Oxford, UK: Oxford University Press.

Penrose, Roger. (1994) *Shadows of the Mind.* Oxford, UK: Oxford University Press.

Perry, John. (1979) "The Problem of the Essential Indexical," *Nous* 13: 3-22.

Pollock, John. (1989) *How to Build a Person.* Cambridge, MA: MIT Press.

Pollock, John. (1995) *Cognitive Carpentry: A Blueprint for How to Build a Person*, Cambridge, MA: MIT Press.

Post, Emil. (1936) "Finite Combinatory Processes — Formulation 1," *Journal of Symbolic Logic* 1 (3): 103-105.

Putnam, Hilary. (1965) "Trial and Error Predicates and the Solution to a Problem of Mostowski," *Journal of Symbolic Logic* 30 (1): 49-57.

Putnam, Hilary. (1975a) "Minds and Machines," in *Mind, Language and Reality: Philosophical Papers Volume II.* Cambridge: Cambridge University Press.

Putnam, Hilary. (1975b) "The Nature of Mental States," in *Mind, Language and Reality: Philosophical Papers Volume II*, Cambridge: Cambridge University Press.

Putnam, Hilary. (1988) *Representation and Reality*, Cambridge, MA: MIT Press.

Quaife, Art. (1992) *Automated Development of Fundamental Mathematical Theories*, Dordrecht, The Netherlands: Kluwer.

Rado, Tibor. (1963) "On Non-Computable Functions," *Bell Systems Technical Journal* 41: 877-884.

Rogers, Hartley. (1967) *Theory of Recursive Functions and Effective Computability,* New York, NY: McGraw-Hill.

Searle, John. (1992) *The Rediscovery of the Mind,* Cambridge, MA: MIT Press.

Siegelmann, Hava. (1995) "Computation Beyond the Turing Limit," *Science* 268: 545-548.

Siegelmann, Hava and E. D. Sontag (1994) "Analog Computation Via Neural Nets," *Theoretical Computer Science* 131: 331-360.

Turing, Alan. (1950) "On Computable Numbers with Applications to the Entscheidungsproblem," *Proceedings of the London Mathematical Society* 42: 230-265.

PHILOSOPHY AND COMPUTER SCIENCE: REFLECTIONS ON THE PROGRAM VERIFICATION DEBATE

JAMES H. FETZER

During 1986-87, four other philosophers and I participated in a special fifteen-month, post-doctoral program offered by Wright State University for Ph.D.s in linguistics and philosophy who wanted to study computer science and artificial intelligence.[1] The program extended over five quarters, with courses distributed over the first four and thesis work toward an M.S. degree the following summer. Among the courses for the fall quarter was one on programming languages, which was taught by Professor Al Sanders.

The course requirements included a term paper on one or more articles listed in the references for the course text by Michael Marcotty and Henry F. Ledgard, *Programming Language Landscape* [1986]. The most intriguing item I noticed was "Social Processes and Proofs of Theorems and Programs" by Richard DeMillo, Richard Lipton and Alan Perlis, which had appeared in *Communications of the ACM* in 1979. It had generated several letters and an authors' responses and looked as if it might be of philosophical interest.

When I located the paper itself and had the chance to read it through, I was fairly astonished. The authors were appraising the prospects for using formal methods to enhance our confidence in the reliability of software in computer systems. The advocates of this approach, who are an influential group within computer science, maintain that computer science ought to be modeled on mathematics as its paradigm, a conception that DeMillo, Lipton and Perlis on various grounds were intent to reject as an unattainable ideal.

The analogy embraced by advocates of formal methods takes the following form. In mathematics, proofs begin by identifying the propositions to be proven and proceed by deriving those propositions from premises ("axioms") as conclusions ("theorems") that follow from them by employing exclusively deductive reasoning. In computer science, proofs may begin by identifying the proposition to be proven (in this case, specifications of desired program performance), where deductive reasoning applied to the text of a program might show it satisfies those specifications and thereby prove it is "correct".

DeMillo, Lipton and Perlis sought to undermine the force of this analogy by discussing several respects in which "proofs" of mathematical theorems differ from "verifications" of program correctness. Their most important argument focused upon the role of social processes in evaluating proofs of theorems, where mathematicians consult other mathematicians to secure agreement that proofs are valid. In their view, the complexity of program verifications means that no comparable social processing ever takes place.

They found words to express what they wanted to convey in vivid and forceful prose. Supporting their position, for example, they remarked that, the verification of even a puny program can run into dozens of pages, and there's not a light moment or a spark of wit on any of those pages. Nobody is going to run into a friend's office with a program verification. Nobody is going to sketch a verification out on a paper napkin. Nobody is going to buttonhole a colleague into listening to a verification. Nobody is ever going to read it. One can feel one's eyes glaze over at the thought. [DeMillo, Lipton, and Perlis 1979, 276] Thus, according to DeMillo, Lipton and Perlis, the absence of social mechanisms in the program-verification community parallel to those found in the theorem-proving community destroys the comparison with mathematics.

As a student in search of a thesis, I had stumbled upon what appeared to be a philosopher's bonanza. While the authors described themselves as appraising the prospects for using formal methods to enhance confidence in the reliability of software, I sensed the aim of program verification was to guarantee the performance of programs when they are executed by machine. Having come of age intellectually in the logical empiricist tradition, I was confident that formal methods alone could not attain that objective.

Since DeMillo, Lipton and Perlis were not very specific on this point, I had some homework to do, which led me to publications by C. A. R. Hoare of Oxford, who was among the leading figures in the program verification movement. Imagine my feelings at finding the following passage in which Hoare had articulated what I had conjectured to be the implicit conception:

> Computer programming is an exact science in that all the properties of a program and all the consequences of executing it in any given environment can, in principle, be found out from the text of the program itself by means of purely deductive reasoning. [Hoare 1969, 576]

It was immediately apparent to me that this conception, which asserts that purely formal methods can guarantee the performance of a computer when it executes a program, implies the existence of synthetic *a priori* knowledge.

Although I was already convinced that the program verification movement was predicated upon a misconception about the scope and limits of formal methods, I was not inclined to argue the case in my paper by denying the existence of synthetic *a priori* knowledge. An approach of this kind would have compelled the introduction of the analytic/synthetic distinction within this context, even though many philosophers reject this framework. And while I was confident that their reasons for its rejection were not well-founded, I was reluctant to base my critique upon such a disputed premise.[2]

As a consequence, I introduced other distinctions that I suspected would be easier to convey to computer scientists and that could not be derailed on the basis of purely philosophical concerns. I therefore argued that a distinction had to be drawn between *algorithms* as effective solutions to problems and *programs* as causal models of those algorithms, where the latter but not the former possess the capacity to exercise causal influence over computers when they execute a program. I emphasized the differences between pure and applied mathematics and between abstract models and causal systems.

Computer programming, of course, is ordinarily conducted by means of (what are called) *high-level* programming languages, such as Pascal, LISP, and Prolog, where there is a one-to-many relationship between commands in programs and instructions executed by a machine. Assemby language, by comparison, provides a *low-level* language, where something closer to a one-to-one relationship between commands obtains. Digital machines operate on the basis of strings of zeros and ones (or of high and low voltage), which would be difficult if not impossible to program directly. The causal connection between programs in high-level languages and target machines is therefore effected by interpreters and compilers, which translate them.

This means that programs are ordinarily written for *virtual machines*, which may or may not have physical counterparts. A mini-language CORE introduced as a pedagogical device by Marcotty and Ledgard [1986, Ch. 2] to illustrate the elements of programming languages but for which there is no interpreter or compiler afforded a perfect illustration, because "proofs" of program correctness in CORE could be constructed in relation to virtual machines that were guaranteed to execute them as definitional properties of those machines. These machines are abstract models of CORE machines.

Mistakes could still be made in programming, of course. Marcotty and Ledgard [1986, pp. 45-46] identified various sources of error, such as undefined value errors, overflow errors, negative value errors, and so forth, which could lead to the abnormal termination of a program. My point was not that programs written in CORE could never be imperfect, but rather that the performance of computers executing pro grams written in CORE could be guaranteed in the sense that, assuming there were no programming errors, there could be no possible failure of a machine to execute a CORE program.

The crucial difference thus becomes that between virtual machines for which there are no physical counterparts and virtual machines for which there are physical counterparts. *Virtual machines* only exist as abstract entities beyond space/time for which definitional properties but no causal relations can obtain. *Physical machines*, by comparison, are causal systems in space/time, which can exert causal influence upon other things in space/time. While it may be possible to prove the correctness of a program using purely deductive reasoning, I urged, those formal methods cannot possibly guarantee what will happen when a target machine executes that program.

The analysis, in other words, was an elaboration of the epistemological ramifications that accompany the ontological difference between abstract entities and causal systems. Thus, I argued that the conclusive verification of a virtual machine was logically possible when it had no physical counterpart, because its behavior could be definitively established on the basis of purely deductive reasoning from stipulated axioms. The behavior of a target machine, however, might deviate arbitrarily from those axioms and, as a consequence, could never be definitively established by purely deductive reasoning. The behavior of causal systems must be established inductively.

The term paper I submitted thus suggested that, in contending that program verification could not guarantee what happens when a computer executes a program, DeMillo, Lipton and Perlis had arrived at the right general conclusion but for the wrong specific reasons. The problem was not rooted in the social processing of proofs but in the causal character of computers. When Al Sanders subsequently returned our papers, a lively discussion ensued, during which he reported that he had found mine to be "fascinating!" This enthusiastic reception moved me to send it to *Communications of the ACM*, which had published the original paper by DeMillo, Lipton and Perlis.

The paper was submitted 26 November 1986 with the title, "Social Processes and Causal Models of Logical Structures", which led James Maurer, the Executive Editor, to send it to Rob Kling, who was the area editor for social aspects of computing. Over the next 18 months, he would ask me to revise it four times in order to insure that my arguments would be accessible to readers of the magazine. Having published a 500-page book manuscript without having to change even one word [Fetzer, 1981], this was not something I expected. Each time that he asked me to make further revisions, I became more and more disenchanted with our progress.

In the meanwhile, I had been hired as full professor by the University of Minnesota in Duluth, and my colleagues were aware of my research on this topic. Sometime between the forth and fifth drafts, David Cole showed me a list of "I/O Statements" from the IBM PC manual for Microsoft BASIC, which included the following commands and their expected consequences:

Statement	Action
BEEP	Beeps the speaker.
CIRCLE (x, y) r	Draws a circle with center x, y and radius r.
COLOR b, p	In graphics mode, sets background color and palette of foreground colors.
LOCATE row, col	Positions the cursor.
PLAY string	Plays music as specified by string.

While David had intended these findings as counterexamples to my thesis, I was euphoric, because they were perfect illustrations: there was no way formal proofs could guarantee *a speaker would beep* or *music would play*!

No doubt in part because I incorporated these examples into the fifth draft of my text, the paper was finally acceptable to Rob Kling, and on 13 June 1988, I received a formal acceptance from James Maurer. Since my discussion was no longer primarily criticism of DeMillo, Lipton and Perlis [1979] but a general critique of the limits of formal methods in computer science, Kling suggested I provide a new title for the paper. I responded with "Program Verification: The Very Idea". Since it had taken so long to reach this point, I was surprised when it came out three months later.

The cover of that issue of *Communications* featured a head extending from an enormous pile of computer printouts crying for help. My greatest fear at this point was that my article had finally appeared but no one would even notice or, worse yet, that it would be greeted with yawns as belaboring the obvious. I was therefore pleasantly surprised when my good friend, Chuck Dunlop, with whom I had participated in the program at Wright State, sent me a copy of a message from the Risks Forum, an electronic bulletin board devoted to issues related to computer reliability.

In this posting of 5 October 1988, Brian Randell explained that he had just finished my article "with great interest and enjoyment" and affirmed,

> In my opinion it is a very careful and lucid analysis of the dispute between, e.g., DeMillo, Lipton and Perlis on the one

hand, and Hoare on the other, regarding the nature of programming and the significance of program verification. [Randell 5 Oct 88 9:56:39 WET DST]

He included the text of the abstract and ended his message by quoting the last lines of the paper, where I suggest these matters are not only important theoretically for computer science but practically for the human race.

Chuck advised me that many other messages were now appearing over the nets, which I found reassuring. My worst fears had been allayed: the article was not being ignored, and the initial response had been positive. Shortly thereafter, moreover, I received a letter from Robert Ashenhurst, who edits the Forum for the magazine, dated 1 November 1988. Included were copies of six Letters to the Editor of *Communications*, which Ashenhurst thought were appropriate for publication. He invited me to reply. I agreed with his judgment concerning five and submitted my response.

The letters reflected a variety of attitudes, ranging from a complaint [by James Pleasant] that I had traded upon ambiguity by failing to distinguish exactly what I had in mind by the term "program", to a thoughtful critique [by William Bevier, Michael Smith, and William Young], who suggested that, at the level of logic gates, the difference between abstract entities and causal systems virtually disappears, to additional arguments [by Stephen Savitzky] that supplied further grounds supporting my position in the case of useful programs that are not merely unverifiable but even verifiably incorrect, where the most important requirements of programs may be ones that are not formalizable, etc. [Pleasant, et al., 1989].

Pleasant posed no problem (since I had been entirely explicit on this point); Bevier, Smith and Young could be disarmed (since the difference at stake does not disappear); and Savitzky had come to my defense. The potentially most damaging letter in the set, however, was from Lawrence Paulson, Avra Cohn, and Michael Gordon of Cambridge University, who castigated me for contending that programs must work perfectly, for asserting that verification is useless because it cannot guarantee perfection, and for condemning a subject of which I knew nothing. Since I had not made the claims they attributed to me, I was invulnerable to their criticisms, which were based on drastic oversimplifications of my arguments [Fetzer, 1989b]. But it was beginning to dawn that I might have touched a sensitive nerve.

The worst was yet to come. In correspondence dated 12 December 19-88, Robert Ashenhurst sent along four more letters. Three of these [by Harald Muller, by Christopher Holt, and by Arron Watters] were not unexpected. Muller suggested that I was implicitly drawing a (Platonic) distinction between *the world of the pure* (abstract entities) and *the world of the real* (causal systems), whereas computers (as constructed artifacts) instead fall in between. Holt suggested that the issue was the correctness of the implementation of the language in which a program is written in the hardware, which most verificationists assume as an *axiom*. And Watters maintained that the truly important issues were not those discussed in my article but those previously raised by DeMillo, Lipton and Perlis [Muller et al., 1989].

What I liked about Muller's letter was not his Platonic framework but the introduction of artificially contrived machines. As I explained in reply, two modes of operation are available. Either the machine is created in accordance with the design (axioms) or the design (axioms) is created in accordance with the machine. *Either way, however, it is necessary to discover precisely how the machine behaves in order to determine whether or not it is in accordance with the design* [Fetzer, 1989c, 511; original emphasis]. While it may be possible to determine the properties of virtual machines by stipulation as a matter of definition (for abstract entities), it is only possible to discover the properties of target machines by the use of induction (for causal systems), thereby reasserting the basic elements of my position.

There was much about Holt's letter with which I completely agreed, so I sought to accent the subtle points of disagreement. While we are all entitled to assume whatever we want for the sake of hypothetical reasoning, there is an important difference between *assuming something to be the case* and *its being the case*. President Reagan, I observed, presumably assumed that we could lower taxes, increase spending, and nevertheless balance the budget. The issue is not whether or not assumptions can be made but under what conditions an assumption is justified, warranted or true.

Arguments based upon hypothetical "axioms" may be valid but are not therefore also sound. Since Hoare had made observations that appeared to conform to Holt's conception, I offered an illustration that is by no means unproblematic:

> When the correctness of a program, its compiler, and the hardware of the computer have all been established with mathematical certainty, it will be possible to place great reliance on the results of the program and predict their performance with a confidence limited only by the reliability of the electronics. [Hoare, 1969, 579]

The catch, I remarked, is that this conditional has an antecedent that may be incapable of satisfaction, since the correctness of the program, its compiler, and the hardware can *never* be established "with mathematical certainty" — unless it happens to be an abstract rather than a physical machine!

If the first three letters were not surprising, the fourth was something else entirely. A scathing diatribe of the likes of which I had never seen before, this letter not only raked me across the coals for misrepresenting the goals and methods of program verification but damned the editors as well:

> by publishing the ill-informed, irresponsible, and dangerous article by Fetzer, the editors of *Communications* have abrogated their responsibility, to both the ACM membership and to the public at large, to engage in serious inquiry into techniques that may justify the practice of computer science as a socially responsible engineering practice. The article is ill-informed and irresponsible because it attacks a parody of both the intent and the practice of formal verification. It is dangerous because its pretentious and ponderous style may lead the uniformed to take it seriously. [Ardis, Basili, et al., 1989, 287]

The letter was signed by ten prominent members of the program verification community. In a handwritten note, Robert Ashenhurst penned that he had just learned that this letter had been forwarded to Peter Denning, the Editor-in-Chief, who planned to respond regarding the review process.

I was stunned. Were this letter, which was receiving special treatment, to appear without a response from me, whether or not I might have forceful and convincing replies to the charges they had raised would not matter: My reputation would have already endured serious, irretrievable damage. In his cover letter, Ashenhurst also mentioned that "the original package" had apparently been "bumped" from January to February. This gave me hope that perhaps something could be done. I called the Executive Editor to plead for the opportunity to provide a response of my own that would appear in *Communications* at the same time as this extraordinary letter.

James Maurer listened patiently as I explained that, while I greatly appreciated the fact that Peter Denning was going to respond on behalf of the editors concerning the review process, it was essential for me to have an opportunity to respond on my own behalf concurrent with the publication of this letter. I observed that it was my name attached to this article and that it was my reputation at stake. I was enormously relieved when, after extensive consultation, the Executive Editor and the Editor-in-Chief decided that I was entitled to respond at the time of its publication. This meant in turn that the "package" would be moved from February to March.

Under considerable pressure, I began to systematically disentangle the objections the authors had raised and consider my replies. There appeared to be at least six issues involved here, some of which were far more serious than others. They asserted, for example, that there are no published claims to "conclusive absolute verification", a phrase that I had used; that assembly language programs *are* amenable to verification procedures, a prospect they contended I had denied; and that I seemed to be "totally unaware" of a large body of work applying formal procedures to compilers and hardware, which indicated to me that these authors had apparently not understood my views.

The absence of the phrase "conclusive absolute verification" from the literature, of course, did not mean that the concept was not present, and formal methods could do no more for compilers or for hardware than they could for programs. The point about assembly language was bothersome, but the only sentence supporting their interpretation concerned the control mechanism of missile systems processing real-time streams of data, "where, to attain rapid and compact processing, their avionics portions are programmed in assembly language—a kind of processing that does not lend itself to the construction of program verifications" [Fetzer, 1988, 1062]. Having originally discussed this point with Chuck Dunlop, I thought that I ought to call him once again.

While we were going though the program, Chuck and I had considered many of these issues before, but perhaps never with such beneficial effect. While it was true in the example I used that the programming was done in assembly language and that programs written in assembly language could indeed be subjected to program verifications, the circumstances of this case precluded that, since these missiles were able to reprogram themselves in flight. We speculated about possible conditions under which such programs could be verified and laughed at our thoughts. I slept very well that night.

My published response, which appeared immediately following the letter in the March issue of *Communications*, began with the following observation:

> The ancient practice of killing the messenger when you do not like the message receives its latest incarnation in the unfortunate letter from Ardis, Basili, et al. ("The Gang of Ten"). The authors allege (a) that I have misrepresented the goal of program verification (thereby attacking a "straw man"); (b) that I have misunderstood the role of mathematics in any engineering endeavor (especially within computer science); and (c) that my conclusion, if it were true, would undermine research in vast areas of computer science (including most theoretical work). [Fetzer, 1989a, 288]

In rebuttal, I observed (a) that, since I was attacking Hoare's position, as I had clearly explained, I was attacking a "straw man" only if Hoare's position was a "straw man"; (b) that the role of mathematics in engineering qualifies as *applied mathematics* when used to describe physical structures and as *pure mathematics* when used to describe abstract structures; and (c) that it was hard to believe these authors could seriously maintain that computer science could benefit from misrepresenting the certainty of its findings.

I remarked that the authors had "misdescribed" my conclusion, since it was not my position that program verification was useless or even harmful because it provides no certainty. My point, on the contrary, was that "since program verification cannot guarantee the performance of any program, it should not be pursued in the false belief that it can — which, indeed, might be entertained in turn as the 'ill-informed, irresponsible and dangerous dogma' that my paper was intended to expose" [Fetzer, 1989a, 288].

My favorite passage, however, was one inspired by my discussion with Chuck. While acknowledging that the sentence I used in describing assembly-language programming as a type that did not lend itself to program verifications might have been misleading, I reaffirmed the force of my example involving real-time transmission of streams of data from sensors to processors:

> the specific avionics example that I was discussing . . . reflects a special type of programming that can be found in cruise missiles and other sophisticated systems with the capacity to reprogram themselves en route to their targets. The only technique that would permit the verification of these programs as they are generated in flight would be procedures permitting the correctness of these programs to be established as they are constructed. Perhaps the authors of this letter could volunteer to accompany these missiles on future flights in order to demonstrate that this is a type of programming that actually does lend itself to the construction of program verifications, after all. [Fetzer , 1989a, 288]

I find it impossible to reread this passage without smiling even to this day.

Having discovered that the *Journal of Automated Reasoning* was about to publish a new paper by Avra Cohn entitled, "The Notion of Proof in Hardware Verification", in which she acknowledged that verification "involves a pair of *models* that bear an uncheckable and possibly imperfect relation to the intended design and to the actual device" [Cohn, 1989, 132], I cited it as "display[ing] a great deal of sensi-

262

tivity to the basic issues at stake in my article", in spite of the fact that "she is one of three Cambridge scholars who reject my analysis on peripheral grounds elsewhere" in this magazine.

I concluded my reply by praising the efforts expended on my behalf by the editors and staff of *Communications*, especially Rob Kling, "in providing sympathetic criticism and in enforcing high standards". I finished with observations about the tone and quality of the letter from the Gang of Ten:

> In its inexcusable intolerance and insufferable self-righteousness, this letter exemplifies the attitudes and behavior ordinarily expected from religious zealots and ideological fanatics, whose degrees of conviction invariably exceed the strength of the evidence. [Fetzer, 1989a, 289]

I remain enormously indebted to James Maurer and to Peter Denning for granting my plea to publish my response at the same time as their letter.

The March 1989 issue of *Communications* thus began with that letter, which took up a full-page of the Forum, followed by my reply. Peter Denning, the Editor-in-Chief, true to his word, offered a powerful defense of the editorial process, observing that the paper had been put through four rounds of revision and noting that "the article was subjected to a review more rigorous than is required by ACM policy, and that the review process was fair and professionally sound. I stand fully behind my editors." [Denning, 1989, 289]. The letters from Pleasant, the three Cambridge scholars, et al. appeared with my replies as "Technical Correspondence".

The April 1989 issue published the letters from Muller, Holt, and Watters, which was something that I expected, together with an OP/ED piece entitled, "Program Verification: Public Image and Private Reality", which I had not [Dobson and Randell, 1989]. The authors were John Dobson and Brian Randell, the same "Brian Randell" who had posted a favorable notice of my article on the Risks Forum. I was therefore somewhat distressed to read that, while their initial opinion had been quite favorable in viewing it as "an interesting, and unusually literate, contribution to the literature on the theoretical limitations of program verification", they had now reached the conclusion that it was "undoubtedly . . . misconceived" but perhaps useful in correcting overselling of their product by the verification community.

Thus, although I was alleged to have "failed to give this topic the careful scrutiny it so clearly needs, they said the program verification community had not done so either. Their principal objections to my analysis of the theoretical limitations of program verification, however, were two in number: (1) "the (unfortunately justifiable) fear that [my] paper will be misinterpreted by laymen, particularly those involved in funding" [Dobson and Randell, 1989, 420] and, (2) their belief that I had mistakenly entertained proofs of program correctness as intended to provide explanatory rather than evidential reasons:

> *it seems to us that Fetzer thinks the verificationists have been representing their work as providing explanatory reasons for program correctness, whereas they claim their work provides merely evidential reasons* [Dobson and Randell, 1989, 421, original emphasis].

I was acutely disappointed that an author who had been so positive about my work had now withdrawn his support as I began to draft my response.

Before they raised the issue, I had not considered — even remotely — whether or not an analysis of the scope and limits of formal methods in computer science had any financial ramifications. The "fear" that my paper might be "misinterpreted" by those who fund verification projects and that they might be "persuaded" to reallocate their resources for more promising activities, of course, is a classic example of the informal fallacy known as "the appeal to pity", where the unfortunate consequences that might follow if a certain position were accepted as true are treated as though they counted as evidence that it is false. But this was no reason to suppose I was wrong.

Their first objection, therefore, was simply fallacious, although I could appreciate why those whose profession, promotions, or tenure depend on funding of this kind might have been unsettled by my analysis. In asserting that I had mistaken "evidential" for "explanatory" reasoning, however, they raised issues of a different caliber entirely. Their second objection, which implied that I had attacked a straw man by portraying the function of proofs of program correctness as explanatory in relation to executions when they should be understood as evidential, after all, represented a set of issues which to any philosopher of science would be extremely familiar.

There is in fact a fundamental distinction between *evidential reasoning* and *explanatory reasoning*, as Carl G. Hempel, some time ago, explained by distinguishing "explanation-seeking" questions (such as, "Why is it the case that p?") from "reason-seeking" questions (say, "What grounds are there for believing that p?"). While adequate answers to explanation-seeking questions also provide potential answers to corresponding reason-seeking questions, the converse is not the case [Hempel, 1965, 335]. To that extent, of course, I thought that Dobson and Randell had drawn a relevant distinction.

It was fascinating to observe them illustrating the difference that they wanted to invoke with two examples regarding the height of a tree, which might be *explained* by considerations such as, "that it is a tree of such-and-such a sort, growing in this sort of climate in this sort of soil, and that under such conditions trees of that type can sustain a height of about 100 feet", on the one hand, or established *evidentially* by considerations such as, "that it casts a shadow of 50 feet at a time of day when a 10-foot pole casts a shadow of 5 feet" [Dobson and Randell, 1989, pp. 420-421]. The parallel with Sylvain Bromberger's flagpole example was both obvious and remarkable.

When Dobson and Randell claimed that mathematical logic provides "explanatory reasons", however, they committed a blunder. Logic specifically and formal methods generally are context independent: they are applicable for deriving conclusions from premises without any concern for the purpose of the arguments thereby constructed. Indeed, the flagpole case — and their own example! — clearly indicate that the ability to deduce a conclusion (about the height of a flagpole, for example) is not the same as the ability to explain that phenomenon (why the flagpole has that height). No student of the symmetry thesis would have been prone to commit this mistake [Fetzer, 1974].

Since I had drawn a distinction between *algorithms* as logical structures and *programs* as causal models of those structures, they properly noticed that I focused on the causal contribution of programs to the performance of computers. An important ramification of my position is the claim that the outcome of executing a program "obviously depends upon various different causal factors, including the characteristics of the compiler, the processor, the printer, the paper and every other component whose specific features influence the execution of such a program" [Fetzer, 1988, 1057].

Since programs are only partial causes of the effects of their execution, if I were taking formal proofs to be explanatory, when their proponents only intend them to be evidential, then I would be holding them at fault for failing to guarantee what a computer will do when it executes a program when their reasoning is merely evidential. This position, however, not only contradicts Dobson and Randell's assumption that formal proofs are always explanatory but also overlooks the consideration that differences between virtual machines and causal systems still remain whether program verifications are viewed as evidential *or* as explanatory reasoning.

Even when we overlook the inconsistency in their position by supposing that program verifications as formal proofs of correctness are merely intended to provide evidential reasons for believing that a computer will perform correctly when that program is executed, the difference between *conclusive* and *inconclusive* evidence for a conclusion also persists. Thus, the fundamental objective of my analysis was to establish that, for target machines as opposed to virtual machines, the kind of evidence which program verifications can appropriately provide is uncertain rather than certain evidence, which not only does not contradict the possibility that program verifications are evidential but even implies it [Fetzer, 1989e, 920].

When I submitted my response to Dobson and Randell [1989], however, Peter Denning balked. I asked for equal time by having it run as an OP/ED piece, which is technically known there as a "Viewpoint", but he wanted to edit it drastically and to print it as a Letter to the Editor instead. It finally appeared in the August issue [Fetzer, 1989e]. In the meanwhile, the magazine published a letter in which I extended the distinction between algorithms and programs to the problem of patent and copyright protection in the June issue [Fetzer, 1989d] and another set of Letters to the Editor regarding the program verification debate in the July issue [Hill et al., 1989].

These events were insignificant by contrast with the next development, however, which occurred when Jon Barwise devoted his column in *Notices of the AMS* [American Mathematical Society] to the program verification controversy. He began by discussing the celebrated debates that occurred early in the 20th century over the foundations of mathematics which, after extended deliberations that seemed to generate more heat than light, led to the formulation of various positions about the nature of mathematics, such as Platonism, logicism, formalism and intuitionism, which have contributed to our understanding of the subject and have "kept the wolf from the door".

Barwise drew an explicit comparison between the debates over the foundations of mathematics and the program verification debate, which he described as concerning the relation of mathematics "to the rest of the world":

> Today a similar controversy about the nature of mathematics and its relation to the rest of the world is raging out of sight of most mathematicians in the pages of *CACM*, the *Communications of the Association for Computing Machinery*. The debate is almost as exciting and at least as acrimonious. . . . The present debate swirls around an article called "Program Verification: The Very Idea", written by the philosopher James Fetzer. [Barwise, 1989, 844]

Barwise suggested that the program verification debate might contribute to our understanding of the nature of *applied* mathematics as the earlier debates contributed to our understanding of the nature of *pure* mathematics.

I was enormously flattered. Barwise followed Bevier, Smith and Young in characterizing my position by means of three key contentions as follow:

266

(1) The purpose of program verification is to provide a mathematical method for guaranteeing the performance of a program.

(2) This is possible for algorithms, which cannot be executed by a machine, but not possible for programs, which can be executed by a machine.

(3) There is little to be gained and much to be lost though fruitless effort to guarantee the reliability of programs when no guarantees are to be had. [Barwise, 1989, 845]

And he reported that I accepted this summary as perfectly reasonable, "so long as the first premises is intended as a reflection of the position that is — implicitly or explicitly — endorsed by the proponents of program verification."

In my estimation, the discussion by Barwise was a valuable contribution to the debate, partially because, in general, he endorsed my position. But I also took exception to some of his arguments in a letter that subsequently appeared in his column. In particular, he alleged that I had committed the Fallacy of Identification by viewing "proofs" as purely syntactical entities, an objection to which I took exception on the grounds that this conception of "proof" was the relevant one within this context; and he claimed that I had failed to sufficiently differentiate "programs" as (abstract) types and "programs" as (causal) instances, a conception fundamental to my position.

I therefore responded to this objection by distinguishing programs-as-texts (unloaded) from programs-as-causes (loaded), where (human) verification involves the application of deductive methods to programs-as-texts:

> Hoare and I both assume that programs-as-causes are represented by programs-as-texts. The difference is that Hoare assumes that programs-as-causes are always *appropriately* represented by programs-as-texts, an assumption that I challenge. [Fetzer, 1989f, 1353]

Thus, programming languages themselves function as models of (actual or virtual) machines, where the degree of correspondence between them is a matter that, in the case of target machines, unlike that of virtual machines, cannot possibly be ascertained on the basis of purely deductive reasoning.

There have been several interesting developments since then. In 1990, for example, the Association for Computing Machinery invited me to participate in a formal debate on the scope and limits of formal methods in software engineering. My opponents were Mark Ardis and David Gries, two of "The Gang of Ten". More significantly, in 1991, I received an invitation to contribute a 10,000 word entry on "program verification" from Allen Kent and James G. Williams, the editors of the *Encyclopedia of Microprocessors*, an entry that they also included in their *Encyclopedia of Computer Science and Technology*, both published by Marcel Dekker [Fetzer, 1993a and 1994].

In my more recent work on this subject, I have emphasized the differences between formal systems, scientific theories, and computer programs. While mathematical proofs, scientific theories and computer programs qualify as syntactical entities, scientific theories and computer programs have a semantic significance (for the physical world) that proofs (in pure mathematics) do not possess. And computer programs possess causal capability that even scientific theories do not enjoy, which reflects the fact that each of them can be subjected to different methods of evaluation [Fetzer, 1991].

I have also collaborated with Tim Colburn and Terry Rankin in editing a collection of classic and contemporary articles on program verification, which includes papers by John McCarthy, Peter Naur, Robert Floyd, C. A. R. Hoare, William Scherlis and Dana Scott, Bertrand Meyer, Bruce Blum, Christiane Floyd, Brian Smith, and other papers I have discussed [Colburn et al., 1993]. In my capacity as the editor of *Minds and Machines*, I have sought to nurture the fledgling field of "the philosophy of computer science", as I think of it, and have had the opportunity to publish several important articles by Colburn [1991] and David Nelson [1992 and 1994], among others.

Opinions appear to differ over whether or not the program verification debate has had any impact on the computer science community. A book entitled *Fatal Defect* by Ivars Peterson will appear next month [Peterson, 1995]. He discusses a series of mishaps and accidents involving computer systems and reviews contributions by many experts in the field, including four of "The Gang of Ten". He describes the program verification debate, accurately quoting passages from "Program Verification: The Very Idea":

> "The limitations involved here are not merely practical: *they are rooted in the very character of causal systems themselves*", Fetzer emphasized. "From a methodological point of view, it might be said that programs are conjectures, while executions are attempted — and all too frequently successful — refutations." [Peterson, 1995, 181]

Nevertheless, he concludes that, "In the end, the debate didn't settle much of anything, and Fetzer's arguments did not derail program verification", although its proponents are perhaps "less extravagant" in their claims and "less casual" in their use of the language of "proof" [Peterson, 1995, 183].

During a visit to England last November, however, I had the pleasure of presenting a lecture at King's College of the University of London, during which I reviewed many of these matters. During the discussion, I was fascinated to learn from a member of the audience that he had been in Japan recently and that, while waiting at a train station outside Tokyo, he had encountered C. A. R. Hoare. He took the opportunity to ask Hoare about something he had heard of but did not then understand, the program verification debate. Hoare almost immediately launched into an explanation of how the use of formal methods may detect problems in programs at an early stage and thereby yield better average performance under statistical controls.[4]

Whether or not philosophy has contributed to computer science in this instance, there appears to be an important interaction phenomenon here that deserves to be considered. As I previously explained, I deliberately chose to pursue these issues without appealing to the analytic/synthetic distinction, first, because it would have required explanation for the benefit of computer scientists, and, second, because many philosophers deny it. Even though I myself have never believed there were appropriate grounds for its rejection, I was reluctant to rest my case on such a disputed premise.

The more I have examine these problems, however, the more convinced I have become of the tenability — *and even vitality* — of that distinction. The differences between virtual and physical machines, between abstract entities and causal systems, between algorithms and programs, between pure and applied mathematics, and between validity and soundness upon which these crucial issues depend are diverse manifestations of the underlying difference between kinds of knowledge that are analytic and *a priori* and kinds of knowledge that are synthetic and *a posteriori*. To those who remain skeptical of this distinction, I ask you to consider the significance of the program verification debate as a form of vindication of the distinction.

My studies of computer systems have also convinced me that the more serious the consequences of making mistakes, the greater our obligation to insure that they are not made. This obligation in turn implies that purely formal methods must give way to program testing and system prototyping as the degree of seriousness of making mistakes increases, as follows:

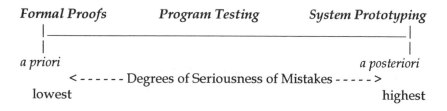

269

Thus, this appears to me to be one situation in which philosophy makes a (non-trivial) difference to important issues of public policy [Fetzer, 1996].

ACKNOWLEDGMENTS

I am deeply indebted to Chuck Dunlop, Al Sanders, Rob Kling, David Cole, David Nelson and Tim Colburn. For further discussion, see Colburn [1993].

NOTES

[1] The program had been inspired by David Hemmendinger, a philosophy Ph.D. who had acquired an M.S. in computer science and had joined the faculty at Wright State. The other participants were Charles E. M. Dunlop, an old friend who convinced me that I should join him in taking advantage of this program while it lasted; Ken Ray, a former student of his and of mine when we were visiting faculty at the University of Cincinnati during 1978-80; Adam Drozdek, who recently received tenure at Duquesne University; and Joe Sartorelli, who was then on leave from Arkansas State University.

[2] My grounds for rejecting Quine's critique of the analytic/synthetic distinction are elaborated, for example, in Fetzer [1990, 105-110], and in Fetzer [1993b, 16-21]. Indeed, my first written assignment in graduate school at Indiana University in 1966 was composing a critique of "Two Dogmas". While I disagreed with Quine even then regarding the first "dogma", I agreed with him regarding reductionism; see Fetzer [1993b, 51-55].

[3] If the paper had begun with this title, however, it might not have been published. Years later, I was advised that the area editor for dependable computing, John Rushby, had said that, if it had come to him for editorial review, he would have killed it. Such are the vicissitudes of publication.

[4] The audience member turned out to be the philosopher Donald Gillies.

REFERENCES

Ardis, M., V. Basili et al. (1989) "Editorial Process Verification", *Communications of the ACM,* March 1989: 287-288.

Barwise, J. (1989) "Mathematical Proofs of Computer System Correctness", *Notices of the AMS.* September 1989: 844-851.

270

Cohn, A. (1989) "The Notion of Proof in Hardware Verification", *Journal of Automated Reasoning* 5: 127-139.

Colburn, T. R. (1991) "Program Verification, Defensible Reasoning, and Two Conceptions of Computer Science", *Minds and Machines* February 1991: 97-116.

Colburn, T. R. (1993) "Computer Science and Philosophy", in T. R. Colburn, J. H. Fetzer, and T. L. Rankin, Eds., *Program Verification* Dordrecht, The Netherlands: Kluwer Academic Publishers, 3-31.

Colburn, T. R., J. H. Fetzer, and T. L. Rankin, Eeds. (1993) *Program Verification*. Dordrecht, The Netherlands: Kluwer Academic Publishers.

DeMillo, R., R. Lipton and A. Perlis. (1979) "Social Processes and Proofs of Theorems and Programs", *Communications of the ACM*, May 1979: 271-280.

Denning. (1989) "Reply from the Editor in Chief", *Communications of the ACM*, March 1989: 289-290.

Dobson, J. and B. Randell. (1989) "Program Verification: Public Image and Private Reality", *Communications of the ACM*, April 1989: 420-422.

Fetzer, J. H. (1974) "Grunbaum's 'Defense' of the Symmetry Thesis", *Philosophical Studies*, April 1974: 173-187.

Fetzer, J. H. (1981) *Scientific Knowledge*. (Dordrecht, The Netherlands: D. Reidel.

Fetzer, J. H. (1988) "Program Verification: The Very Idea", *Communications of the ACM*, September 1988: 1048-1063.

Fetzer, J. H. (1989a) "Response from the Author", *Communications of the ACM*, March 1989: 288-289.

Fetzer, J. H. (1989b) "Program Verification Reprise: The Author's Response", *Communications of the ACM*, March 1989: 377-381.

Fetzer, J. H. (1989c) "Author's Response", *Communications of the ACM*, April 1989: 510-512.

271

Fetzer, J. H. (1989d) "Patents and Programs", *Communications of the ACM,* June 1989: 675-676.

Fetzer, J. H. (1989e) "Another Point of View", *Communications of the ACM,* August 1989: 920-921.

Fetzer, J. H. (1989f) "Mathematical Proofs of Computer System Correctness: A Response", *Notices of the AMS,* December 1989: 1352-1353.

Fetzer, J. H. (1990) *Artificial Intelligence: Its Scope and Limits,* Dordrecht, The Netherlands: Kluwer Academic Publishers.

Fetzer, J. H. (1991) "Philosophical Aspects of Program Verification", *Minds and Machines,* May 1991: 197-216.

Fetzer, J. H. (1993a) "Program Verification", *Encyclopedia of Computer Science and Technology,* Vol. 28. New York, NY: Marcel Dekker, 237-254.

Fetzer, J. H. (1993b) *Philosophy of Science.* New York, NY: Paragon House Publishers.

Fetzer, J. H. (1994) "Program Verification", *Encyclopedia of Microprocessors,* Vol. 14. New York, NY: Marcel Dekker, 47-64.

Fetzer, J. H. (1996) "Computer Reliability and Public Policy: Limits of Knowledge of Computer-Based Systems", *Social Philosophy & Policy,* 13: 229-266.

Hempel, C. G. (1965) *Aspects of Scientific Explanation.* New York, NY: The Free Press.

Hill, R., R. Conte et al. (1989) "More on Verification", *Communications of the ACM,* July 1989: 790-792.

Hoare, C. A. R. (1969) "An Axiomatic Basis for Computer Programming", *Communications of the ACM,* October 1969: 576-583.

Marcotty, M and H. E. Ledgard. (1986) *Programming Language Landscape,* 2nd ed. Chicago, IL: Science Research Associates, 1986.

Muller, H., C. Holt, and A. Watters. (1989) "More on the Very Idea", *Communications of the ACM,* April 1989: 506-510.

Nelson, D. (1992) "Deductive Program Verification (A Practitioner's Commentary)", *Minds and Machines*, August 1992: 283-307.

Nelson, D. (1994) Discussion Review of Robert S. Boyer and J Strother Moore, *A Computational Handbook*, and J Strother Moore (ed.), "Special Issue on System Verification", *Journal of Automated Reasoning*, December 1989, *Minds and Machines*, February 1994, 93-101.

Peterson, I. (1995) *Fatal Defect: Chasing Killer Computer Bugs.* New York: Random House/Times Books.

Pleasant, J., L. Paulson et al. (1989) "The Very Idea", *Communications of the ACM*, March 1989, 374-377.

GLOBAL INFORMATION ETHICS AND THE INFORMATION REVOLUTION[1]

TERRELL WARD BYNUM

The Information Revolution

Powerful technologies have profound social consequences. Consider for example the impacts of farming, printing and industrialization upon the world. Information technology (IT) is no exception. As Simon Rogerson and the present writer have noted,

> Computing technology is the most powerful and most flexible technology ever devised. For this reason, computing is changing everything—where and how we work, where and how we learn, shop, eat, vote, receive medical care, spend free time, make war, make friends, make love [Rogerson and Bynum, June 9, 1995].

The growing information revolution, therefore, is not "merely technological" — it is *fundamentally social and ethical*. The reason why information technology is so powerful is well explained by James Moor in his classic article "What Is Computer Ethics?" [Moor, 1985]. The computer, he says, is almost a "universal tool" — because it is "logically malleable", it can be shaped and molded to perform nearly any task.

Information Technology and Human Values

Millions of tasks are now routinely performed by computers. Indeed, IT has become so flexible and inexpensive that it has seeped into our lives almost unnoticed in household appliances, banks and shops, automobiles and airplanes, schools and medical clinics, to mention only a few examples. In industrialized nations of the world, the information revolution already has significantly changed many aspects of life, such as banking and commerce, work and employment, medical care, national defense, transportation and entertainment. Indeed IT has begun to profoundly affect (in both good and bad ways) community life, family life, human relationships, education, freedom, democracy, and so on.

274

The remainder of the industrialized world quickly followed the United States into the Information Revolution. Will the less-industrialized parts of the globe join the revolution as well? Perhaps there will be significant delays. Andrzej Kocikowski [Kocikowski, 1996] has noted, for example, that economic and social factors in many countries make it difficult at present for IT to be introduced on a wide scale. For this reason, the Information Revolution might proceed slowly, at best, in places like Eastern Europe, Africa and Latin America.

On the other hand, Krystyna Gorniak-Kocikowska [1996] has pointed out that "Computers do not know borders. Computer networks, unlike other mass media, have a truly global character." And Jacek Sojka [1996] has commented that

> Access to cyberspace is much easier than to the world's business and management techniques. Because of information technology there are no peripheries. Even the more distant developing countries can fully participate in cyberspace and look forward to new opportunities offered by global networks [Sojka, 192]...

> the net constitutes the only realm of freedom in many non-democratic countries. Also the opportunities which the Internet offers to commerce guarantee its freedom: no country could afford losing this competitive advantage [Sojka, 198].

For these reasons, as well as the rapidly decreasing cost of IT, the Information Revolution may affect all parts of the earth more quickly than people now believe. It is therefore imperative that, around the globe, public policy makers, leaders of business and industry, teachers, social thinkers, computer professionals and private citizens take an interest in the social and ethical impacts of information technology.

To study and analyze the ethical impacts of IT, a new academic field — currently called "Computer Ethics" — has emerged. University modules, conferences, workshops, professional organizations, curriculum materials, books, articles, and research centers have been created — both in the USA and other industrialized nations.[2] And this rapidly developing field of Computer Ethics is quickly being transformed into the much broader and more significant research area of "Global Information Ethics" as discussed below.

Computer Ethics: Some Historical Milestones

Some important milestones in the history of Computer Ethics include the following:

1940s and 1950s:
In the 1940s, Norbert Wiener of MIT University near Boston founded a new discipline that he called "Cybernetics", the science of information feed-back systems. By 1948, he was publishing books and giving lectures on the likely impact of information technology upon human values like peace, health, knowledge, education, community and justice. Over the next decade, Wiener gave a number of lectures and wrote several books and articles that, today, would be called works in Computer Ethics.[3] As the first scholar to seriously address the impact of information technology upon human values, Norbert Wiener can be considered the "founding father" of Computer Ethics as a field of scholarly research.

1960s:
In the mid 1960s, Donn Parker of SRI International in Menlo Park, California began to examine unethical and illegal uses of computers by computer professionals. "It seemed," Parker said, "that when people entered the computer center they left their ethics at the door."[4] He collected examples of computer crime and other unethical computerized activities. He published "Rules of Ethics in Information Processing" in *Communications of the ACM* in 1968, and he headed the development of the first Code of Professional Conduct for the Association for Computing Machinery (eventually adopted by the ACM in 1973). Over the next two decades, Parker went on to produce books, articles, speeches and workshops[5] that re-launched the field of Computer Ethics, giving it momentum and importance that continues to grow today. Parker is, in this sense, the second founder of Computer Ethics after Norbert Wiener.

1970s:
During the late 1960s, Joseph Weizenbaum, a computer scientist at MIT in Boston, created a computer program that he called ELIZA. In his first experiment with ELIZA, he scripted it to provide a crude imitation of "a Rogerian psychotherapist engaged in an initial interview with a patient". Weizenbaum was shocked at the reactions people had to his simple computer program: Some practicing psychiatrists saw it as evidence that computers would soon be performing automated psychotherapy; and computer-savvy people at MIT became emotionally involved with the computer, sharing their most intimate thoughts with it. Weizenbaum was extremely concerned that an "information processing model" of human beings was reinforcing an already growing tendency among scientists, and even the general public, to see humans as mere machines. In the early 1970s, Weizenbaum undertook a book-writing project to defend the view that humans are much more than information processors. The project resulted in Weixenbaum's

book, *Computer Power and Human Reason* [Weizenbaum, 1976], which is now considered a classic in computer ethics. Weizenbaum's book, plus the courses he offered at MIT and the many speeches he gave around the country in the 1970s, inspired many thinkers and projects in Computer Ethics. He stands with Norbert Wiener and Donn Parker as a key person in the formative history of the subject.

In the mid 1970s, Walter Maner (then of Old Dominion University in Virginia; now at Bowling Green State University in Ohio) coined the term "Computer Ethics" to refer to *that field of applied professional ethics dealing with ethical problems aggravated, transformed or created by computer technology*. Maner offered an experimental course on the subject at Old Dominion University. During the late 1970s (and indeed into the mid 1980s), he generated much interest in university-level Computer Ethics courses by offering a variety of workshops and lectures at computer science conferences and philosophy conferences across America. In 1978 he also self-published and disseminated his *Starter Kit in Computer Ethics* [Maner, 1980], which contained curriculum materials and pedagogical advice for university teachers to develop Computer Ethics courses. The *Starter Kit* included suggested course descriptions for university catalogs, a rationale for offering such a course in the university curriculum, a list of course objectives, some teaching tips and discussions of topics like privacy and confidentiality, computer crime, computer decisions, technological dependence and professional codes of ethics. Maner's trailblazing course, plus his *Starter Kit* and the many conference workshops he conducted, had a significant impact upon the teaching of Computer Ethics across America. Many university courses were put in place because of him.

1980s:
By the 1980s, a number of social and ethical consequences of information technology were becoming public issues in America: issues like computer-enabled crime, disasters caused by computer failures, invasions of privacy via computer databases, and major law suits regarding software ownership. Because of the work of Parker, Weizenbaum, Maner and others, the foundation had been laid for Computer Ethics as an academic discipline. The time was right, therefore, for an explosion of activities in Computer Ethics.

In the mid-80s, James Moor of Dartmouth College published his now-classic article "What Is Computer Ethics?" in *Computers and Ethics*, a special issue of the journal *Metaphilosophy* [Moor, 1985]. In addition, Deborah Johnson of Rensselaer Polytechnic Institute published *Computer Ethics* [Johnson, 1985], the first textbook — and for more than a decade, the *defining* textbook — in the field. There were also relevant books published in psychology and sociology: for example, Sherry Turkle of MIT wrote *The Second Self* [Turkle, 1984], a book on the impact of computing on the human psyche; and Judith Perrolle produced

Computers and Social Change: Information, Property and Power [Perrolle, 1987], a sociological approach to computing and human values.

Also during the 1980s, the present author (Terrell Ward Bynum) began to work very actively in Computer Ethics. In the early 80s, Bynum assisted Walter Maner in publishing his *Starter Kit in Computer Ethics* at a time when most philosophers and computer scientists considered the field to be unimportant [Maner, 1996]. He also developed and taught university courses on several campuses, and conducted workshops at a number of conferences in the USA. In 1985, as Editor of *Metaphilosophy*, Bynum put together the special issue on Computer Ethics; and in 1987, he created the Research Center on Computing & Society at Southern Connecticut State University. In 1988 Bynum began planning (with Walter Maner) the first international conference on Computer Ethics (eventually held in 1991), which ultimately attracted participants from seven countries and 32 US states. The conference included philosophers, computer professionals, sociol-ogists, psychologists, lawyers, business leaders, news reporters and government officials. It generated a set of monographs, video programs and curriculum materials that are now being used on hundreds of university campuses around the world [van Speybroeck, July 1994].

1990s:
By the mid 1990s, interest in Computer Ethics as a field of research had spread to Europe and Australia. This important development was significantly aided by the pioneering work of **Simon Rogerson** of De Montfort University (UK), who established the Centre for Computing and Social Responsibility and initiated, with the present writer, a series of influential international conferences: the ETHICOMP conferences. In Rogerson's view, there is need in the 1990s for a "second generation" of Computer Ethics developments:

> The mid-1990s has heralded the beginning of a second generation of computer ethics. The time has come to build upon and elaborate the conceptual foundation whilst, in parallel, developing the frameworks within which practical action can occur, thus reducing the probability of unforeseen effects of information technology application. [Rogerson, Spring 1996, 2; Rogerson and Bynum, 1997]

Defining the Field of Computer Ethics

The field of Computer Ethics is in the process of being created; indeed, it is so new that those creating it are still struggling to define its essence and boundaries. Let us briefly consider five different attempts to define the field:

Walter Maner

When he coined the term "Computer Ethics" in the mid-70s, Maner defined the discipline as one which examines "ethical problems aggravated, transformed or created by computer technology". Some old ethical problems, he said, are made worse by computers, while others are wholly new because of information technology. By analogy with the more developed field of medical ethics, Maner focused attention upon applications of traditional ethical theories used by philosophers doing "applied ethics" — especially analyses using the utilitarian ethics of the English philosophers Jeremy Bentham and John Stuart Mill, or the rationalist ethics of the German philosopher Immanual Kant.

Deborah Johnson

In her book, *Computer Ethics*, Johnson [1985] defined the field as one which studies the way in which computers "pose new versions of standard moral problems and moral dilemmas, exacerbating the old problems, and forcing us to apply ordinary moral norms in uncharted realms," [Johnson, 1]. Like Maner before her, Johnson employed the "applied philosophy" approach of using procedures and concepts from utilitarianism and Kantianism. But, unlike Maner, she did not believe that computers create wholly new moral problems. Rather, she thought that computers gave a "new twist" to ethical issues which were already well known.

James Moor

Moor's definition of Computer Ethics in his article "What Is Computer Ethics?" [Moor, 1985] is much broader and more wide-ranging than that of Maner or Johnson. It is independent of any specific philosopher's theory; and it is compatible with a wide variety of methodological approaches to ethical problem-solving. Over the past decade, Moor's definition has been the most influential one. He defines Computer Ethics as a field concerned with "policy vacuums" and "conceptual muddles" regarding the social and ethical use of information technology:

> A typical problem in computer ethics arises because there is a policy vacuum about how computer technology should be used. Computers provide us with new capabilities and these in turn give us new choices for action. Often, either no policies

for conduct in these situations exist or existing policies seem inadequate. A central task of computer ethics is to determine what we should do in such cases, that is, formulate policies to guide our actions.... One difficulty is that along with a policy vacuum there is often a conceptual vacuum. Although a problem in computer ethics may seem clear initially, a little reflection reveals a conceptual muddle. What is needed in such cases is an analysis that provides a coherent conceptual framework within which to formulate a policy for action [Moor, 1985, 266].

Moor says that computer technology is genuinely revolutionary because it is "logically malleable":

Computers are logically malleable in that they can be shaped and molded to do any activity that can be characterized in terms of inputs, outputs and connecting logical operations....Because logic applies everywhere, the potential applications of computer technology appear limitless. The computer is the nearest thing we have to a universal tool. Indeed, the limits of computers are largely the limits of our own creativity [Moor, 1985, 269]

According to Moor, the computer revolution will occur in two stages. The first stage is that of "technological introduction" in which computer technology is developed and refined. This already occurred in America during the first forty years after the Second World War. The second stage — one that the industrialized world has only recently entered — is that of "technological permeation" in which technology gets integrated into everyday human activities and into social institutions, changing the very meaning of fundamental concepts, such as "money", "education", "work", and "fair elections".

Terrell Ward Bynum
Moor's way of defining the field of Computer Ethics is very powerful and suggestive. It is broad enough to be compatible with a wide range of philosophical theories and methodologies, and it is rooted in a very perceptive understanding of how technological revolutions proceed. Currently it is the best available definition of the field.

Nevertheless, there is yet another way of defining Computer Ethics that is also very helpful — and also compatible with a wide variety of theories and approaches. Indeed, this "other way" is an elaboration of an additional suggestion in Moor's classic paper [1985, 266. paragraph 2]. According to this definition (adapted from Moor and developed by the present author in 1989) Computer Ethics *identifies and analyzes the impacts of information technology on social and human values like health, wealth, work, opportunity, freedom, democracy, knowledge, privacy, security, self-fulfillment, etc.* This very broad view of Computer Ethics embraces applied ethics, sociology of computing, technology assessment, computer law, and related fields; and it employs concepts, theories and methodologies from those and any other relevant disciplines [Bynum, 1993].

This conception of Computer Ethics is motivated by the belief that — eventually — information technology will profoundly affect everything that human beings hold dear.

Donald Gotterbarn

In the 1990s, Donald Gotterbarn has been a strong advocate for a different approach to defining the field of Computer Ethics. In Gotterbarn's view, Computer Ethics should be viewed as a branch of *professional ethics*, which is concerned primarily with standards of practice and codes of conduct of computing professionals:

> There is little attention paid to the domain of professional ethics — the values that guide the day-to-day activities of computing professionals in their role as professionals. By computing professional I mean anyone involved in the design and development of computer artifacts... The ethical decisions made during the development of these artifacts have a direct relationship to many of the issues discussed under the broader concept of computer ethics [Gotterbarn, 1991].

With this more narrow definition of Computer Ethics in mind, Gotterbarn has been involved in a number of related activities, such as co-authoring the latest version of the ACM Code of Ethics and Professional Conduct and working to establish licensing standards for software engineers [Anderson, Johnson, Gotterbarn and Perrolle, 1993; Gotterbarn, 1992].

Sample Topics in Computer Ethics

No matter which definition of Computer Ethics one chooses, the best way to understand what the field is like is to examine some example sub-areas of current interest. Consider the following four:

Computers in the Workplace

As a "universal" tool that can, in principle, perform almost any task, computers obviously pose a threat to jobs. Although they occasionally need repair, computers don't require sleep, they don't get tired, they don't go home ill or take time off for rest and relaxation. At the same time, computers are often far more efficient than humans in performing many tasks. Therefore, economic incentives to replace humans with computerized devices are very high. Indeed, in the industrialized world many workers already have been replaced by computerized devices— bank tellers, auto workers, telephone operators, typists, graphic artists, security guards, assembly-line workers, and on and on. In addition, even professionals like medical doctors, lawyers, teachers, accountants and psychologists are finding that computers can perform many of their traditional professional duties quite effectively.

The outlook, however, is not all bad. Consider, for example, the fact that the computer industry already has generated a wide variety of new jobs: hardware engineers, software engineers, systems analysts, information technology teachers, computer sales clerks, and so on. Thus it appears that, in the short run, computer-generated unemployment will be an important social problem; but in the long run, information technology will create many more jobs than it eliminates.

Even when a job is not eliminated by computers, it can be radically altered. For example, airline pilots still sit at the controls of commercial airplanes; but during much of a flight the pilot simply watches as a computer flies the plane. Similarly, those who prepare food in restaurants or make products in factories may still have jobs; but often they simply push buttons and watch as computerized devices actually perform the needed tasks. In this way, it is possible for computers to cause "de-skilling"of workers, turning them into passive observers and button pushers. Again, however, the picture is not all bad because computers have also generated new jobs which require new sophisticated skills to perform— for example, "computer assisted drafting" and "keyhole" surgery.

Another workplace issue concerns health and safety. As Forester and Morrison point out [Forester and Morrison, 1990, Chapter 8], when information technology is introduced into a workplace, it is important to consider likely impacts upon health and job satisfaction of workers who will use it. It is possible, for example, that such workers will feel stressed trying to keep up with high-speed computerized devices— or they may be injured by repeating the same physical movement over and over— or their health may be threatened by radiation emanating from computer monitors.

These are just a few of the social and ethical issues that arise when information technology is introduced into the workplace.

Computer Security

In this era of computer "viruses" and international spying by "hackers" who are thousands of miles away, it is clear that computer security is a topic of concern in the field of computer ethics. The problem is not so much the *physical* security of the hardware (protecting it from theft, fire, flood, etc.), but rather *logical* security, which Spafford, Heaphy and Ferbrache [Spafford, et al, 1989] divide into five aspects:

1. Privacy and confidentiality of data
2. Integrity — assuring that data and programs are not modified without proper authority
3. Unimpaired service
4. Consistency — ensuring that the data and behavior we see today will be the same tomorrow
5. Controlling access to resources

Malicious software, or "programmed threats", provide a significant challenge to computer security. These include "viruses", which cannot run on their own, but rather are inserted into other computer programs; "worms" which can move from machine to machine across networks, and may have parts of themselves running on different machines; "Trojan horses" which appear to be one sort of program, but actually are doing damage behind the scenes; "logic bombs" which check for particular conditions and then execute when those conditions arise; and "bacteria" or "rabbits" which multiply rapidly and fill up the computer's memory.

Computer crimes, such as embezzlement or planting of logic bombs, are normally committed by trusted personnel who have permission to use the computer system. Computer security, therefore, must also be concerned with the actions of trusted computer users.

Another major risk to computer security is the so-called "hacker" who breaks into someone's computer system without permission. Some hackers intentionally steal data or commit vandalism, while others merely "explore" the system to see how it works and what files it contains. These "explorers" often claim to be benevolent defenders of freedom and fighters against rip-offs by major corporations or spying by government agents. These self-appointed vigilantes of cyberspace say they do no harm, and claim to be helpful to society by exposing security risks. However every act of hacking is harmful, because any known successful penetration of a computer system requires the owner to thoroughly check for damaged or lost data and programs. Even if the hacker did indeed make no changes, the computer's owner must run through a thorough investigation of the compromised system [Spafford, 1992].

Software Ownership

One of the more controversial areas of computer ethics concerns software ownership. Some people, like Richard Stallman who started the Free Software Foundation, believe that software ownership should not be allowed at all. He claims that all information should be free, and all programs should be available for copying, studying and modifying by anyone who wishes to do so [Stallman, 1993]. Others argue that software companies or programmers would not invest weeks and months of work and significant funds in the development of software if they could not get the investment back in the form of license fees or sales [Johnson, 1992, 1-8].

Today's software industry is a multibillion dollar part of the economy; and software companies claim to lose billions of dollars per year through illegal copying ("software piracy"). Many people think that software should be ownable, but "casual copying" of personally owned programs for one's friends should also be permitted. The software industry claims that millions of dollars in sales are lost because of such copying. Ownership is a complex matter, since there are several different aspects of software that can be owned and three different types of ownership: copyrights, trade secrets, and patents. One can own the following aspects of a program:

1. The "source code" which is written by the programmer(s) in a high-level computer language like Pascal or C++.
2. The "object code", which is a machine-language translation of the source code.
3. The "algorithm", which is the sequence of machine commands that the source code and object code represent.
4. The "look and feel" of a program, which is the way the program appears on the screen and interfaces with users.

A very controversial issue today is owning a patent on a computer algorithm. A patent provides an exclusive monopoly on the use of the patented item, so the owner of an algorithm can deny others use of the mathematical formulas that are part of the algorithm. Mathematicians and scientists are outraged, claiming that algorithm patents effectively remove parts of mathematics from the public domain, and thereby threaten to cripple science. In addition, running a preliminary "patent search" to make sure that your "new" program does not violate anyone's software patent is a costly and time consuming process. As a result, only very large companies with big budgets can afford to run such a search. This effectively eliminates many small software companies, stifling competition and decreasing the variety of programs available to the society [The League for Programming Freedom, 1992, 54-66].

Professional Responsibility
Computer professionals have specialized knowledge and often have positions with authority and respect in the community. For this reason, they are able to have a significant impact upon the world, including many of the things that people value. *Along with such power to change the world comes the duty to exercise that power responsibly.*

Computer professionals find themselves in a variety of professional relationships with other people, including:

employer — employee
client — professional
professional — professional
society — professional

These relationships involve a diversity of interests, and sometimes these interests can come into conflict with each other. Responsible computer professionals, therefore, will be aware of possible conflicts of interest and try to avoid them [Johnson, 1994, 37-57].

Professional organizations in the USA, like the Association for Computing Machinery (ACM) and the Institute of Electrical and Electronic Engineers (IEEE), have established codes of ethics, curriculum guidelines and accreditation requirements to help computer professionals understand and manage ethical responsibilities. For example, in 1991 a Joint Curriculum Task Force of the ACM and IEEE adopted a set of guidelines ("Curriculum 1991") for college programs in computer science. The guidelines say that a significant component of computer ethics (in the broad sense) should be included in undergraduate education in computer science [Turner, June 1991, 69-84].

In addition, both the ACM and IEEE have adopted Codes of Ethics for their members [Johnson, 1994, 165-73, 177]. The most recent ACM Code (1992), for example, includes "general moral imperatives", such as "avoid harm to others" and "be honest and trustworthy". And also included are "more specific professional responsibilities" like "acquire and maintain professional competence" and "know and respect existing laws pertaining to professional work." The IEEE Code of Ethics (1990) includes such principles as "avoid real or perceived conflicts of interest whenever possible" and "be honest and realistic in stating claims or estimates based on available data."

The Accreditation Board for Engineering Technologies (ABET) has long required an ethics component in the computer engineering curriculum. And in 1991, the Computer Sciences Accreditation Commission/Computer Sciences Accreditation Board (CSAC/CSAB) also adopted the requirement that a significant component of computer ethics be included in any computer sciences degree granting program that is nationally accredited [Conry, 1992].

It is clear that professional organizations in computer science recognize and insist upon standards of professional responsibility for their members.

The Future: Global Information Ethics

The above paragraphs provide a brief description of Computer Ethics — some of its history, some attempts to define it, and some sample areas of study. But that is the past. Computer Ethics is rapidly evolving into a broader and even more important field: *Global Information*

Ethics. Global networks like the Internet and especially the World-Wide-Web are connecting people all over the earth. As Krystyna Gor-niak-Kocikowska perceptively notes in her important paper, "The Computer Revolution and the Problem of Global Ethics" [Gorniak-Ko-cikowska, 1996], for the first time in history, efforts to develop mutu-ally agreed standards of conduct, and efforts to advance and defend human values, are being made in a truly global context. So, for the first time in the history of the earth, ethics and values will be debated and transformed in a context that is not limited to a particular geographic region, or constrained by a specific religion or culture. This may very well be one of the most important social developments in history. Consider just a few of the global issues:

Global Laws
If computer users in the United States, for example, wish to protect their freedom of speech on the Internet, whose laws apply? Well over one hundred countries are already interconnected by the Internet, so the United States Constitution (with its First Amendment protection for freedom of speech) is just a "local law" on the Internet — it does not apply to the rest of the world. How can issues like freedom of speech, control of "pornography", protection of intellectual property, invasions of privacy, and many others to be governed by law when well over a hundred countries are involved? If a citizen in a European country, for example, has Internet dealings with someone in a far-away land, and the government of that land considers those dealing to be illegal, can the European be tried by the courts in the far-away country?

Global Cyberbusiness
The world is very close to having technology that can provide elec-tronic privacy and security on the Internet sufficient to safely conduct international business transactions. Once this technology is in place, there will be a rapid expansion of global Cyberbusiness. Nations with a technological infrastructure already in place will enjoy rapid eco-nomic growth, while the rest of the world lags behind. What will be the political and economic fallout from rapid growth of global Cyber-business? Will accepted business practices in one part of the world be perceived as "cheating" or "fraud" in other parts of the world? Will a few wealthy nations widen the already big gap between rich and poor? Will political and even military confrontations emerge?

Global Education
If inexpensive access to the global information net is provided to rich and poor alike — to poverty-stricken people in ghettos, to poor nations in the "third world", etc.— for the first time in history, nearly ev-eryone on earth will have access to daily news from a free press; to

texts, documents and art works from great libraries and museums of the world; to political, religious and social practices of peoples everywhere. What will be the impact of this sudden and profound "global education" upon political dictatorships, isolated communities, coherent cultures, religious practices, etc.? If great universities of the world begin to offer degrees and knowledge via Internet courses and modules, will "lesser" universities be damaged or even forced out of business?

Information Rich and Information Poor

The gap between rich and poor nations, and even between rich and poor citizens in industrialized countries, is already disturbingly wide. As educational opportunities, business and employment opportunities, medical services and many other necessities of life move more and more into Cyberspace, will the gaps between rich and poor become even worse?

Conclusion

These are just a few of the many social and ethical issues that are bound to surface as the information revolution progresses. The above examples demonstrate that these issues are quickly becoming global in scope. The new field of Global Information Ethics, therefore, is now emerging as an important aspect of the Information Revolution.

NOTES

[1] This is an expanded version of a Polish-language article in Kocikowski, Andrzej, Terrell Ward Bynum and Krystyna Gorniak Kocikowska, *Wprowadzenie do etyki informatycznej*, Humaniora Press, Poland, (1997).

[2] For example, in 1995 the "Global Consortium on Computing and Social Values" was formed from three research centers, including one in England and one in Poland: The Research Center on Computing & Society. Southern Connecticut State University, USA, founded in 1987; the Centre for Computing and Social Responsibility, De Montfort University, UK, founded in 1995; and the Center for Business and Computer Ethics, Adam Mickiewicz University, Poland, also founded in 1995. These three research centers— through their publications, international conferences, research projects, World-Wide-Web pages, and international advisory boards— have stimulated cooperation and research among scholars around the globe. Especially noteworthy are three major conferences that brought together scholars from many countries and generated a diversity of publications, curriculum materials and video programs: The National Conference on Computing and

Human Values, 1991, Southern Connecticut State University, USA; ETHICOMP95, 1995, De Montfort University, UK; and ETHICOMP96, 1996, University of Madrid, Spain.

[3] See especially Wiener. (1948) *Cybernetics: Control and Communication in the Animal and the Machine.* Cambridge, MA: Technology Press, reprinted in 1961 by MIT Press; Wiener. (1950) *The Human Use of Human Beings: Cybernetics and Society.* Boston: Houghton Mifflin, reprinted in 1967 by Avon Books, NY; Wiener. (1964) *God and Golem, Inc.* Cambridge, MA: MIT Press; as well as the article, Wiener. (1960) "Some Moral and Technical Consequence of Automation", *Science,* 131: 1355-8.

[4] Comments by Donn Parker [Fodor and Bynum, 1992].

[5] See, for example, Donn Parker's publications: Parker, Donn. (1968) "Rules of Ethics in Information Processing," *Communications of the ACM,* 11: 198-201; Parker, Donn, Susan Nycum and Stephen S. Oura. (1973) *Computer Abuse: Final Report Prepared for the National Science Foundation.* Stanford Research Institute; Parker, Donn. (1976) *Crime By Computer,* Charles Scribner's Sons; Parker, Donn. (1979) *Ethical Conflicts in Computer Science and Technology.* AFIPS Press; Parker, Donn. (1979) *Computer Crime: Criminal Justice Resource Manual.* U.S. Government Printing Office. (Second Edition 1989); Parker, Donn. (1982) "Ethical Dilemmas in Computer Technology," Hoffman, W. and J. Moore, Eds. *Ethics and the Management of Computer Technology.* Oelgeschlager, Gunn, and Hain; Parker, Donn. (Summer 1988) "Ethics for Information Systems Personnel," *Journal of Information Systems Management,* 44-48; Parker, Donn, S. Swope and B.N. Baker. (1990) *Ethical Conflicts in Information & Computer Science, Technology & Business,* QED Information Sciences.

REFERENCES

Anderson, Ronald, Deborah Johnson, Donald Gotterbarn and Judith Perrolle. (February 1993) "Using the New ACM Code of Ethics in Decision Making," *Communications of the ACM,* 36: 98-107.

Conry, Susan. (1992) "Interview on Computer Science Accreditation," In Terrell Ward Bynum and John L. Fodor, creators, *Computer Ethics in the Computer Science Curriculum* (a video program). New Haven, CT: Educational Media Resources.

Fodor, John L. and Terrell Ward Bynum, creators. (1992) *What Is Computer Ethics?* [a video program]. Educational Media Resources, Inc.

Forester, Tom and Perry Morrison. (1990) *Computer Ethics: Cautionary Tales and Ethical Dilemmas in Computing.* Cambridge, MA: MIT Press.

Gorniak-Kocikowska, Krystyna. (1996) "The Computer Revolution and the Problem of Global Ethics." In Bynum and Rogerson, Eds. (1996) *Global Information Ethics,* Opragen Publications, 177-90.

Gotterbarn, Donald. (1991) "Computer Ethics: Responsibility Regained," *National Forum: The Phi Beta Kappa Journal,* 71: 26-31.

Gotterbarn, Donald. (1992) "You Don't Have the Right to Do It Wrong," *CIO.*

Johnson, Deborah G. (1992) "Proprietary Rights in Computer Software: Individual and Policy Issues," Bynum, Terrell Ward, Walter Maner and John L. Fodor, eds. (1992) *Software Ownership and Intellectual Property Rights.* Research Center on Computing & Society.

Johnson, Deborah G. (1994) *Computer Ethics.* Prentice-Hall, 2nd Edition, 1994. [First Edition 1985]

Kocikowski, Andrzej. (1996) "Geography and Computer Ethics: An Eastern European Perspective." In Terrell Ward Bynum and Simon Rogerson, Eds. (1996) *Global Information Ethics,* Opragen Publications, 201-10. (April 1996) *Science and Engineering Ethics.*

The League for Programming Freedom. (1992) "Against Software Patents," In Terrell Ward Bynum, Walter Maner and John L. Fodor, Eds. (1992) *Software Ownership and Intellectual Property Rights,* Research Center on Computing & Society.

Maner, Walter. (1996) "Unique Ethical Problems in Information Technology." In Bynum and Rogerson. (1996) 137-52.

Maner, Walter. (1980) *Starter Kit in Computer Ethics,* Helvetia Press (published in cooperation with the National Information and Resource Center for Teaching Philosophy).

Moor, James H. (1985) "What Is Computer Ethics?" In Terrell Ward Bynum, Ed. (1985) *Computers and Ethics.* Blackwell, 266-75. (October 1985 issue of *Metaphilosophy*).

Perrolle, Judith A. (1987) *Computers and Social Change: Information, Property, and Power.* Wadsworth.

Rogerson, Simon. (Spring 1996) "The Ethics of Computing: The First and Second Generations," *The UK Business Ethics Network News.*

Rogerson, Simon and Terrell Ward Bynum. (1995) "Cyberspace: The Ethical Frontier," *Times Higher Education Supplement*, The London Times, June 9, 1995.

Rogerson, Simon and Terrell Ward Bynum, Eds. (1998) *Information Ethics: A Reader*, Blackwell. This anthology contains articles from ETHICOMP95 and ETHICOMP96.

Sojka, Jacek. (1996) "Business Ethics and Computer Ethics: The View from Poland." In Bynum and Rogerson., Eds. (1996) *Global Information Ethics*, Opragen Publications, 191-200.

Spafford, Eugene. (1992) "Are Computer Hacker Break-Ins Ethical?" *Journal of Systems and Software*, January 1992, 17: 41-47.

Spafford, Eugene, et al. (1989) *Computer Viruses: Dealing with Electronic Vandalism and Programmed Threats.* ADAPSO.

Stallman, Richard. (1992) "Why Software Should Be Free." In Bynum, Terrell Ward, Walter Maner and John L. Fodor, Eds. (1992) *Software Ownership and Intellectual Property Rights*, Research Center on Computing & Society, 35-52.

Turkle, Sherry. (1984) *The Second Self: Computers and the Human Spirit.* Simon & Schuster.

Turner, A. Joseph. (June 1991) "Summary of the ACM/IEEE-CS Joint Curriculum Task force Report: Computing Curricula, 1991," *Communications of the ACM*, 34 (6): 69-84.

van Speybroeck, James. (July 1994) "Review of *Starter Kit on Teaching Computer Ethics*," by Terrell Ward Bynum, Walter Maner and John L. Fodor, Eds. *Computing Reviews*, 357-358.

Weizenbaum, Joseph. (1976) *Computer Power and Human Reason: From Judgment to Calculation*, Freeman.

HOW COMPUTERS EXTEND ARTIFICIAL MORALITY

PETER DANIELSON

Introduction

Artificial morality is a research program combining a substantive thesis about morality with a methodology for developing this thesis. The thesis is that important parts of morality are artificial cognitive and social *devices* that indirectly benefit the agent. The crucial test cases are social dilemmas, where we claim these devices allow cooperation unattainable otherwise. The methodology is computer-assisted generate and test. By constructing computer models of socially problematic situations and more and less morally constrained as well as amoral rational types of agents, we can test populations of programmed agents for instrumental success in social interaction. These tests have been successful; we have been able to isolate, refine, and improve some cognitive devices that make moralized interaction instrumentally justifiable. The computer's role in this methodology is the focus of the present paper.

Ethics is an unlikely subject to study using computers since it is one the last areas where appeal to intuition remains respectable. It is hard to see how we could build computer models of such subtle psychological phenomena when AI has so far failed to model better understood commonsensical notions. I agree, but I take this point in another way. Ethics is so charged with prejudice — intuition — that we need powerful tools to keep our theories honest and open to surprising — i.e. counter-intuitive — ideas. Ethics is an area where we should expect informal tools — such as the thought experiment — to be unreliable, because the equipment we run them on — our morally shaped minds, constrained by principle and norm — isn't up to the task of following out unwanted consequences. But even the formal tools that should suffice for studying instrumental morality may be unreliable, although for a different reason. Formal methods, like game theory, achieve their rigor by means of simplifying assumptions. The temptation for a formal approach to ethics is to bury ethical intuition in these simplifying assumptions (We shall see examples of this below in "A Test Case".). So *Artificial Morality* uses computers to try to weaken the pull of prejudice by mechanizing thought experiments on the one hand and weakening the assumptions of formal models on the other.

The goal is to generate new, surprising results. In this paper I shall review these methods and some results to argue that computer modeling has been both necessary and useful to the AM project.

Basic Artificial Morality

The Extended Prisoner's Dilemma

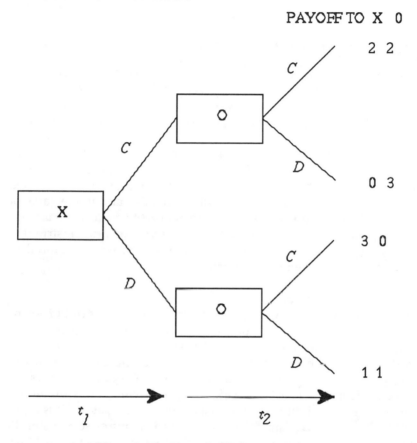

Figure 1. The Extended Prisoner's Dilemma

Consider the situation pictured in Figure 1. You are to move second in a one time, sequential game. If you are a straightforward maximizer of utilities, you consider the O outcomes only. Whatever first-moving X should do, you do better by choosing D. X can calculate this and also does best by choosing D. This is the familiar Prisoner's Dilemma, extended in time. Alternatively, consider the case where you commit yourself to the strategy of Conditional Cooperation (CC), following a C with a C and a D with a D. In this second case even a straightforward maximizer in role X will choose to cooperate, so long as it can predict your constrained choice (O's choice is constrained, because she must choose what is for her the worse outcome). The XPD is a situation where this ability to keep a promise — call it high fidelity — brings an immediate, although indirect, reward. But while less cognitively demanding than the simultaneous PD, none the less the XPD requires special — we might call them proto-moral — cognitive abilities. O needs to be able to communicate her constraint; X needs to be able to perceive this new sort of behavior.[1]

Computers in Artificial Morality

My book *Artificial Morality* [Danielson, 1992; hereafter *AM*] employed computer programs to argue that players could be designed for situations like this, and to show that even in small tournaments some unfamiliar types of player played important roles. In particular, although an obvious choice for a moral strategy, conditional cooperation is unlikely to be the choice for an instrumental morality, as a less restrictive strategy, reciprocal co-operation, (RC) does better. Second, *Artificial Morality* extended its argument to related problems, showing how CC and RC might work even in the simultaneous PD, and in the game of Chicken. The main job done by computers in *AM* was to serve as a filter on a possibility proof: to show that we could construct instrumentally successful morally informed strategies even when required to program a computer with these strategies.

Game Theory vs. Inductive Simulations

While *AM* deployed computer experiments, there are several reasons to think that the book's use of computers was not necessary. First, there are two methods in play in the book: game theory and computer simulation. Arguably, they are methods for doing the same sort of thing: predicting outcomes of interaction. But since game theory is analytically deeper, when both methods apply, we should prefer the game theoretic account to simulations, and drop the latter. This argument isn't conclusive. Game theoretic analysis requires strong simplifying assumptions about equal rationality and common knowledge,[2] so typically its methods don't apply to the very same model as exemplified by the computer simulation. Typically, variations in the players are flattened out. There is a good reason for this: variety is costly for the exhaustive search procedures upon which game theory depends; complexity of the model expands exponentially with the number of alternatives at each node. But sometimes we need more powerful generative methods to explore poorly understood terrain. Of course, while computer simulations can more readily be expanded to consider new possibilities, they remain *inductive*. One can always ask of the (ultimately) limited set of strategies considered, why this set (We return to this question in "Evolutiion")? So there are tradeoffs here; neither formal analytic nor more inductive methods are always better.

Critics of AM Didn't Need Computers
Nonetheless, there is additional evidence that one doesn't need computer simulations to make *AM*'s main points. Critics of the book, even while agreeing with various claims, support them without using the simulations.[3] For example Talbott [1996] uses an extension of game theoretic equilibrium analysis to argue that CC can be made into a coherent moral strategy in the single play PD. LaCasse and Ross [1996] argue that given the predictive and reactive strategies built into my XPD players, game theory suffices to select RC as the rational strategy. Neither needed computers to support their claims.

A Test Case
But these two criticisms do not sit well together: one wonders why the narrower RC strategy doesn't always dominate CC, even in the single play game? I don't have space properly to address my critics' arguments here, so I will take a shortcut and address my own (now obviously) weak argument on this point. In *AM* I introduced a player that used matching to solve the incoherence problem caused by predictive testing — SC who cooperates only with its clones and like RC benefits by exploiting unconditional cooperators. But (like Talbott) I dismissed this player because it was so specialized: "A substantively rational player must be able to cooperate with some dissimilar players as well as with players similar to herself" [Danielson, 1992, 218 n 28]. While it is true that requiring similarity imposes a cost (one fails to cooperate with would-be cooperators), there is no reason to assume that this cost will outweigh the two advantages of a narrower strategy: 1) the advantage of exploiting some unconditional cooperators, and 2) the cognitive advantages of simple similarity matching. We need a method to assess these different costs and benefits. Otherwise it is likely that our — mine and Talbott's — biases towards universality — both cooperative and cognitive — will determine our conclusions (Notice that assuming — as LaCasse and Ross do — that some (which?) strategies are available abstracts this sort of question away). In the next section I suggest that a computer model of the evolution of players can help answer these questions.

Evolution

Artificial Morality sees ethics are part of the social sciences — as social engineering, the technology of social improvement, to be precise. The subject matter of the social sciences is, most broadly, the unintended consequences of actions. So our general methodology inclines us always to look for the unintended consequences of our own designs —

such as the agents designed for *AM*: CC, RC and SC. Of course, in real social life, other people do this for us, by copying, mutating and re-using our principles and institutions.[4] Notoriously, it is hard to predict what this most complex of all processes will do to our designs. We resort of theories that idealize savagely: if all agents are rational and all strategies known to all in advance, game theory can identify equilibria outcomes. But we still should wonder about the prior question: what might happen when some new cognitive components and social devices enter our social life? This question is central to ethics, where we should know more about how a newly introduced moral standard — e.g. an eqalitarian idea — might alter existing family or corporate relations. We model this crudely by seeing what happens when the matching and testing principles introduced in *AM* are set loose. What sorts of agents and strategies might result from co-evolution in this now slightly richer conceptual and social soup?

Genetic Programming
Up until recently one would have said that this is just the sort of question that computers *won't* like help us with. The problem calls for entities that are so flexible that they remain workable after random mutation; computer programs are among the most *fragile* of structures. John Holland [1992, 66] makes the contrast well, "Mating or mutating the text of a FORTRAN program, for example, would in most cases not produce a better or worse FORTRAN program, but rather no program at all." But John Koza's [1992] remarkable development of evolutionary programming allows us to do just this.

To apply genetic programming to artificial morality we need to design functions (in Lisp) that, when mutated by cross-over, always produce working code, that is, well-formed functions that are strategies for the XPD. Of course, most of the offspring don't score very well in the XPD tournament, producing the variation in test results that drive an evolutionary process. We select the best, mutate them and test them in interaction again. To summarize work detailed in a series of papers [Danielson, 1994a, 1994b, 1994c, 1995c, 1996a], we design functions for straightforward selection of strategies in the Extended PD game: initial C or D, or C or D after the other's first more.[5] and for the AM extensions of the strategy set: C or D if the other's strategy matches one's own and C or D depending on the results of testing the other's strategy. As a sample of how these designs can tolerate mutation by cross-over, Figure 2 displays a (designed) Tit-for-Tat and a loopy CC player on top. Crossover applied to the second node of TFT and the first of loopy CC (the whole function) produce two children: a functional CC on the left and an unconditional cooperator on the right (This example is misleading as real crossover is much messier; see Figure 5.).

296

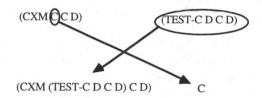

Figure 2. Crossover on Tit-For-Tat and Loopy CC

Notice how similar CC AND TFT are; where TFT moves C initially and then C for C and D for D, CC substitutes a test for the other player's response to C.[6]

Setup
All the tests used a population of sixty players in a co-evolutionary round-robin tournament. The first generation of players were generated by randomly constructing well-formed functions from a set of terminals {C, D} and the XPD strategy functors used in each test, such as {CXM, TEST-C, TEST-D, and MATCH}. Each player was paired with each of the others (but not itself) first playing role X and then playing role O in the XPD.[7] Using the total score to each player as the fitness measure, the best half of the population was retained unchanged in the next generation to provide continuity for the co-evolutionary model. Using the same measure, thirty parents were selected from the whole population. Crossover was applied to these parents in pairs to spawn thirty offspring. The standard run was forty generations, after which most runs were stable.

Calibration
We noted at the start that without predictive abilities, co-operation is not instrumental feasible in the XPD. So our evolutionary device shouldn't change this — or else it is an unreliable extension of AM. Our evolutionary device is a complex piece of software; we need to calibrate it. We do this by running a tournament with players consisting only of the CXM function, which allows no prediction. The bottom line in Figure 3 charts the best score in this population over the 40 generations. Notice first the initial bloom, as defectors exploit the randomly generated population which contains many cooperators, following by a crash to near universal defection. Our evolutionary device is reliable; it can model the "rational" failure of cooperation in the XPD. Notice second the unevenness of the path, as random mutation introduces (short-lived) exploitable agents. These two features are the

"signature" of our evolutionary device, forming the background against we can judge the influence of other changes. In particular, if we allow agents to test each other (via the TEST-C etc. functors) we get results of which the top line in Figure 3 is typical. After the bloom and bust we see a steady evolution of cooperation reaching (a noisy) stable optimum after about 30 generations. This shows that adding the devices of artificial morality allows the evolution of co-operation in the XPD, confirming AM's substantive thesis. The variety of co-operative agents (and their parasites) that do evolve adds to AM's content.

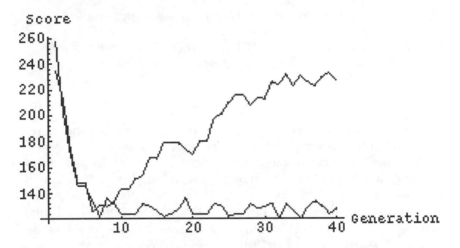

Figure 3. Evolution of Cooperation and Baseline

Results

From the perspective of using computers for philosophical research, there were three results that were counter-intuitive and methodologically interesting.

Recall from the section "A Test Case" that I saw SC as a logical curiosity — and with Talbott [1996] dismissed it as a special case. But in almost every evolutionary model that included matching functors, SC agents quickly saturated the population. We theorists might prize generality, but evolution goes for the effective quick fix here.[8]

A second surprising result was the persistence of Conditional Cooperation. Recall that AM, with the support of LaCasse and Ross' game theoretic analysis, predicts the demise of CC in favor of the nastier RC. But once we remove ingredients for attaining the much more readily evolved SC, CC most often does better than RC (meaning: no RC evolves or persists). One reason is that in these evolutionary simulations, information is not free, and RC needs much more information for its counterfactual strategy (CC need not know what the other player would do were CC not to cooperate). Evolved agents must pay for information, indirectly, in the number of generations it takes to evolve more complex code and the increased incidence of looping caused by RC's more complex tests. Another reason for CC's persistence takes us into territory unique to the evolutionary approach. Recall that CC's weakness is that it tolerates UC, so we predict that UC will drift into a CC population, allowing RC to invade. But this assumes that CC's will spawn some UCs. This is not an unlikely assumption, since a UC agent is the one of the two simplest kinds; it would be very difficult for a CC, chock full of "C"s, not to spawn some UC. But, surprisingly, stable CC populations do so rarely. Why? Consider Figure 4. The top line graphs the mean length over time of a typical CC population. Notice that these agents get very long, ending up at nearly 40 (lisp) atoms long (For comparison, the designed CC in Figure 2 is seven atoms long). So what? A complex CC will less likely spawn UC; cross-over's slicer will more likely choose larger chunks, which often happen to be more copies of CC (The three simplest are marked with bold type)!

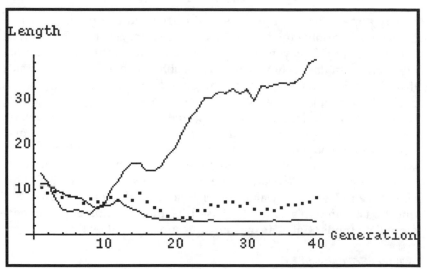

Figure 4. Length under Three Selection Regimes

(CXM(CXM (TEST-C D C (TEST-D C C D)) D (TEST-U (TEST-C D C D)
(TEST-C D C D) D))
(CXM D C D) (TEST-U (TEST-C D C (TEST-U (TEST-C D D D)(TEST-D C D D) D))
(CXM (TEST-C D C C) (CXM D C D)(TEST-U (TEST-C D C D) D D)) D))

Figure 5. CC with BS Tail (Evolved, gen 35)

299

Third, long-CC is a genetic strategy; it doesn't effect the outcome directly by a choice of strategy but indirectly, through determining the future population. This raises many issues but a caution stands out. An evolutionary framework exerts its own pressures; our agents' (reproductive) interests depend on two situations: the XPD and reproduction. Both are social interactions in our case but only the former is modeled as a game. This suggests that we bring the second interaction more explicitly into the game model.[9]

I conclude that evolutionary models of social interaction are fruitful and interesting and that computers are necessary for their construction and study. Sheer complexity makes computers necessary for these models. Even though our populations are small for evolutionary models[10] they require an enormous amount of computation: 60 agents x 59 others x 40 generations is 141,600 games of cc agents with mean length of 20 nodes.[11]

An External Problem

It may appear that evolutionary AM does need computers, but perhaps only to resolve problems of its own making, such as the evolved complexity of CC players, or the incentives introduced by evolutionary models. In this section I turn to a problem generated from outside the AM project, that suggests the independent value of our approach. Frohlich and Oppenheimer [1995b] report a surprising experimental result. When subjected to an external institution that gives incentives for choosing co-operatively in an N-player prisoner's dilemma, human subjects only cooperate while the incentives are altered; they behave worse when the incentives are removed than without the external incentive applied. These results raise many issues, some of which I have considered elsewhere [Danielson, 1995a, 1995b]. Here I discuss two questions: Can AM's computer based techniques supplement experimental methods? Can it answer any questions raised by them?

A Simplified GP model

Frohlich and Oppenheimer used an N-Person iterated PD as a game where moral dispositions may lead to cooperation. We have simplified the problem by using the XPD (2 person and not iterated) because this is a model for which we have developed a stable of agents. In this case we included "chunkier" components: one that included game tree look-a-head functions (ESM) and another partial matcher (GB). These components lead to quite rapid evolution of co-operation, as shown by the plain line (baseaver) in Figure 6. Notice that these agents learn to cooperate faster than those in Figure 2 (The curve is also smoother, but this is only because we used mean scores in these runs, for greater comparability with Frohlich and Oppenheimer's data).

300

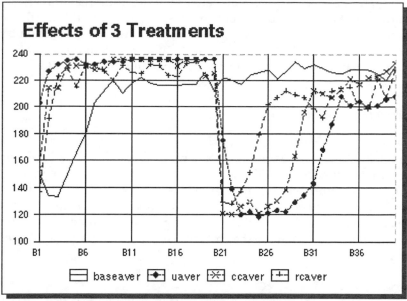

Figure 6. Three Training Regimes

We induce the Frohlich and Oppenheimer effect by changing the matrix in the first 20 generations, so that each player receives the average score of original PD matrix; CC and DD still pay 2 and 1, but CD and DC both pay 1.5. The uaver line marks the effect of this utilitarian transformation, agents learn to cooperate faster but then drop to universal defection and need to relearn to cooperate after the payoff matrix returns to the normal PD game. Notice that in this run they do not learn to play the normal PD as well after the impartial training session as they did in the baseline run without it.

Two conclusions

The first conclusion is that we can use our models to generate results very similar to those gotten — at greater effort, time and cost — running experiments on undergraduates. This can be read as giving empirical support for our models. Or it can be read more neutrally as a comparision (and contest) between *two simulation* techniques: computer models and highly artificial experimental regimes. I will leave this methodological question aside. In any case, this similarity of results suggests that the effect Frohlich and Oppenheimer observed wasn't due to a quirk of human psychology, but followed from more universal features of mechanisms adequate to learning moralized cooperation.

The second conclusion is that by varying the training regime, we can improve performance. The ccaver and rcaver runs were trained under CC and RC outcome matrices, respectively; see Danielson [1995a] for details. They each do better than the utilitarian (uaver) case studied by Frohlich and Oppenheimer. Of course, of all four, the no treatment base case does best, so the model throws some doubt on trying to train agents to be moral in morally less demanding situations (and we haven't factored in any costs to maintaining the initial situation).

Networked Collaboration

The Costs of Computer Based Research

In tracing how the AM project has evolved through a decade of computer intensive research, I've argued that computers have been necessary to my approach. But necessary doesn't mean good; to reach an evaluative conclusion we need to consider costs and benefits. So far, I have emphasized the benefits of building computer models of instrumental morality. What are the costs of using computers to do philosophy?

Babel?

The most obvious cost of computer models is the barrier they pose to critical communication. More precisely, computers create a double-sided barrier: they encourage communication among compatible systems and discourage it among incompatible systems. Two examples from the development of AM stand out. First, each of the four stages of the project has been implemented in a different computer language, each requiring a new family of hardware. So while the ideal of computer mediated theorizing is dropping an agent into a newly modeled situation and seeing what surprises result, the reality is that I could not even test the agents from the book's model (written in Prolog) in the evolutionary version (written in Common Lisp). Second, by requiring specialized and esoteric software, collaboration with others is undermined. In fact *no one* — outside of my seminars, where, significantly I have provided common software and compatible hardware — has ever answered my published calls to contribute new agents or situations to test. On the other side, within each project, it is easy to generate new agents. So the tendency of computerized models is *conservative:* to thoroughly — sometimes exhaustively — test the easily generated compatible cases and to neglect others.

These barriers to communication pose a threat to research programs. In their report of a detailed attempt to align two models, Axtell et al. [1996, 124] warn:

> Alignment [of computational models] is essential to support of two hallmarks of cumulative disciplinary research: critical experimentation and subsumption. If we cannot determine

302

whether or not two models produce equivalent results in equivalent conditions, we cannot reject one model in favor of another that fits data better; nor are we able to say that one model is a special case of another more general one.

Indeed, computer *models* pose a special temptation to idiosyncratic creation at the expense of critical dialogue. Quoting William Blake on the attractions of creating a system, they warn "But if these wonderful new possibilities of computational modeling are to become intellectual tools well-harnessed to the requirements of advancing our understanding of social systems, then we must overcome the natural impulse for self-contained creation and carefully develop the methodology of using them to 'Reason and Compare' " [Axtell et al., 1996, 136]. They recommend that incentives be offered by grantors and journals to researchers who facilitate model comparisons.

Adding Social and Critical Dimensions
I agree with Axtell et al about the need to reinforce the critical dimension of modeling. My own proposal is to make it easier for fellow researchers to work in a shared modeling environment. My project, Evolutionary Artificial Moral Ecologies (EAME) builds on the early work of Robert Axelrod [1978, 1994] in which he invited other researchers to submit players for an Iterated Prisoner's Dilemma Tournament. Recently the IIASA tournament [IIASA, 1995] has extended this model, by allowing researchers to contribute new situations (modeled as games) as well as players. We would like to extend this tendency in two dimensions.

First, by allowing researchers to modify existing players as well. To do this requires a software innovation: object oriented design allows independent design and replacement of parts. So, if you find my some component of existing "stock" players deficient — say they learn too locally, or are too restrictive in their conception of similarity, or discriminate friend and foe too crudely, etc., you can replace this module with your own design. Why not simply rewrite a player with your innovation? Because you are likely interested in what happens when your component becomes generally available in the stock of cognitive and social components.

Second, we would like to expand the environment in which agents can be tested. As we mentioned above, platform dependence is a problem here: we run different machines, so only the smallest core of a tournament, and a few sample players are worth the effort of recoding and re-implementation. But this has the bad effect of making these initial samples *salient* for later work. Consider how much is based on the arbitrary population of players contributed to Axelrod's tournaments. Our plan is to provide each contributor with a copy of the full tournament environment, including all the contributed players and modules, in a form that runs on her own machine. This depends on a second software innovation — actually a set of them: the WEB, the spread of compatible browsers, and the Java platform independent programming language [Gosling & McGilton, 1995]. EAME by connecting the simulations together, allows other people to act as a "reality check" on one's own cognitive and ethical fantasies. At the least, the results should become more robust, as further dimensions of diversity arise when others can add other elements to the situation. For example, others might "corrupt" your agents with some new "ideas" (cognitive or motivational elements), or disrupt your pre-established harmony with an awkward creature or problem.

Conclusion

I have argued that Artificial Morality has produced some surprising and interesting results, at least in part because of its use of computers. Computers have become more important as the project progressed. They served in the initial stages as a check on consistency and a push to explore new possibilities, but in the evolutionary extension of the program, they are strictly necessary to the research. Here we should note one qualification of this endorsement of computer-based theorizing: much of the complexity requiring computers here is created by our use of evolutionary methods, not the subject matter — social interaction — itself. Hopefully this will not turn out to be an irrelevant artifact of our methods; I conjecture that ethics crucially involves the evolution of its norms and cognitive devices. But our conclusion should note this reservation: if evolved complexity is part of the problem under study, computer based models will likely be useful. Finally, we sketched briefly our proposal for networked collaboratory models. Clearly computers are necessary for this sort of intensive communication and collaboration. Whether this further use of them is also beneficial, only trying it out will tell.[12]

NOTES

[1] To see why *both* are necessary for a robust instrumental morality, think through the fate of Tit-For-Tat, who, lacking one of these abilities, cooperates as X and plays CC as O.

[2] I have argued elsewhere [Danielson, 1992, section 1.4.3 ; 1991] that these assumptions are, ironically, too *friendly* to ethics. For example, Gauthier [1986], by extending the received framework minimally to include one type of moral agent to contrast with (straightforwardly) rational agents, ignores the possibility of conflict *between* his favored

conditional cooperator (CC) and more and less constrained agents (the unconditional and reciprocal cooperators, UC and RC, respectively).

[3] Indeed, none of the half dozen discussions of AM I have seen in print makes any use of its computer programs, nor has anyone responded to my invitation to contribute new agents to my tournaments. I comment further on this in section 4.

[4] See Danielson [1996b] for an application.

[5] The three argument function has this form: (CXM <initial move> <if-X-Cs> <if-X-Ds>).

[6] The test needs three arguments to provide an extra slot for cases where there is no response; this is a trap for looping tests.

[7] Therefore a maximum possible score was 2 (roles) times 3 (points) times 59 (co-players) = 354; universal cooperation with the whole population would yield 236 and universal defection 118.

[8] Of course this is not a conclusive argument in favor of matching.

[9] Cf. Epstein and Axtell [1996] for a more inclusive model that includes reproduction.

[10] Compared to the population of 300 used by Koza [1992, 434]'s co-evolution of strategies model.

[11] Each pair of CC agents is almost incomprehensible to human inspection — will the player in Figure 5 cooperate with itself?

[12] You are invited to try by visiting http://ethics.ubc.ca /eame.html.

REFERENCES

Axelrod, Robert. (1987) "The Evolution of Strategies in the Iterated Prisoner's Dilemma," in L. Davis, Ed. *"Genetic Algorithms and Simulated Annealing"*, Los Angeles: Morgan Kauffman, 32-41.

Axelrod, Robert. (1984) *The Evolution of Cooperation*, New York: Basic Books.

Axelrod, Robert. (1978) "Artificial Intelligence & the Iterated Prisoner's Dilemma," Ann Arbor: University of Michigan Institute of Public Policy Studies, No. 120.

Axtel, Robert, Robert Axelrod, Joshua Epstein and Michael Cohen. (1996) "Aligning Simulation Models: A Case Study and Results", *Computational and Mathematical Organization Theory* 1 (2): 123-141.

Danielson, Peter. (1996a) "Evolutionary Models of Cooperative Mechanisms," in P. Danielson, Ed., *Modeling Rationality, Morality and Evolution*, New York: Oxford University Press.

Danielson, Peter. (1996b) "Pseudonyms, MailBots, and Virtual Letter-heads: The Evolution of Computer Mediated Ethics," in Charles Ess, Ed., *Philosophical Perspectives on Computer Mediated Communication*, Albany, NY: State University of New York Press.

Danielson, Peter. (1995a) "The Ethical Aftermath of Incentive Compatible Devices," Computing & Philosophy Conference, Carnegie-Mellon University.

Danielson, Peter. (1995b) "From Rational to Robust," AAAI Fall Symposium on Rational Agency, MIT.

Danielson, Peter. (1995c) "Evolving Artificial Moralities: Genetic Strategies, Spontaneous Orders, & Moral Catastrophe," in Alain Albert, Ed., *Chaos and Society*. Amsterdam: IOS Press, 329 - 344.

Danielson, Peter. (1994a) "Growing Better Green Beards: Evolutionary Artificial Morality," Calgary: Canadian Philosophical Association.

Danielson, Peter. (1994b) "Artificial Morality & Genetic Programming," Computer Science Colloquium, Toronto: York University.

Danielson, Peter. (1994c) "Artificial Morality and Genetic Algorithms," Phil. Colloq., Edmonton: University of Alberta.

Danielson, Peter. (1992) *Artificial Morality: Virtuous Robots for Virtual Games*. London: Routledge.

Danielson, Peter. (1991) "Is Game Theory Good for Ethics?" Paper resented at a symposium on Game Theory at the American Philosophical Association Pacific Division meeting, San Francisco, March.

Epstein, Joshua M. and Robert L. Axtell. (1996) *Growing Artificial Societies*. Washington, DC: Brookings Institution.

Frohlich, N. and J. Oppenheimer (1995) "The incompatibility of Incentive Compatible Devices and Ethical Behavior: Some Experimental Results andInsights," *Public Choice Studies*, 25: 24-51.

Gauthier, David. (1986) *Morals by Agreement*, Oxford: Oxford University Press.

Gosling, James and Henry McGilton. (1995) *The Java Language Environment*, Mountain View, CA: Sun Microsystems.

Holland, John. (1992) "Genetic Algorithms," *Scientific American* 267(1): 66 - 72.

IIASA. (1995) "Announcement of the First Tournament of Learning to Play Games," Laxenburg, Austria: International Institute for Applied Systems Analysis.

Koza, John. (1992) *Genetic Programming,* Cambridge, Mass: MIT Press.

LaCasse, Chantale and Don Ross. (1996) "Morality's Last Chance," in P. Danielson, Ed., *Modeling Rationality, Morality and Evolution,* New York: Oxford University Press.

Talbott ,William J. (1996) "Why We Need a Moral Equilibrium Theory," in P. Danielson, Ed., *Modeling Rationality, Morality and Evolution,* New York: Oxford University Press.

COMPUTING AND CREATIVITY

MARGARET A. BODEN

Computing and creativity may seem to be very strange bedfellows. Indeed, many philosophers would say that they are inherently opposed. How could a computer program possibly generate creative ideas? How could it help us to understand what creativity is? How could it teach us anything about how people manage to be creative? And how could it help us to be creative? The very idea that any of these questions could be answered in a way favourable to computer technology is viewed by many people as absurd. I shall argue, to the contrary, that such answers can be given to all of them.

One cannot address these questions without adopting some account of what creativity is. This account should clarify the concept, exhibit the inner structure of creative phenomena, and show how it is possible for creativity to occur. A computational approach helps one to do all these things. Showing how creativity is possible has philosophical as well as psychological interest, not least because one of the puzzles about (some cases of) creativity is the apparent impossibility, or paradox, involved. A computational account of creativity would have a wider relevance too, for if artificial intelligence (AI) can help shed light on this seemingly unpromising phenomenon it should be able also to illuminate other areas within the philosophy of mind.

The concept of creativity is decidedly elusive. Philosophers offer conflicting accounts of it, and scores of different definitions have been published in the psychological literature (over 60 had been identified ten years ago [Taylor, 1988], since when more have appeared). This definitional diversity arises partly because of the paradoxical aspect mentioned above, partly because creativity is not a natural kind (it does not have only one scientific explanation), and partly because it is a many-sided phenomenon. Psychologists who study creativity ask very different questions about it, and construct their varying definitions accordingly. Some focus on its social and historical aspects, some on the psychometrics of originality, some on the role played by personality or birth-order, some on physiological and/or inheritable factors, and some on (some sub-class of) the mental processes that produce creative ideas. A comprehensive theory should recognize all these dimensions, and show how they are related [Boden, 1994a].

Computational approaches to creativity, my own included [Boden, 1990], stress the generative processes that make it possible. This is not to deny the importance of the other factors just listed, nor is it to pre-judge the question whether AI-programs could be genuinely creative (see below). But AI-insights can help us to refine our philosophical analysis of the concept. For example, they help to show that, although creativity is not a natural kind, several broad types of creativity can usefully be distinguished.

"Creative" and "creativity" can each be applied to ideas and also to people (In what follows, the context shows which type of use is intended; in some cases, both interpretations are admissible). The fundamental notion, in terms of which the others are defined, is that of a creative idea. An idea is creative if it is novel, surprising, and valuable. A person is creative — and a computer is at least apparently creative — if they sometimes produce creative ideas (For present purposes, we need not ask just how to interpret that "sometimes"). The person's creativity is their ability to produce creative ideas. And the creativity of an idea is its property of being creative, that is, of being novel, surprising, and valuable.

Three caveats arise immediately. First, creativity is not an all-or-none phenomenon. It is not even a matter of degree, for there is no single spectrum along which individual cases can be located. There are various ways in which an idea can be creative, so we should ask not whether it is creative, but in what respects. Moreover, an idea may be more creative than another in some ways, and less so in others: one may not wish to blur these distinctions by describing it simply as "more creative." Second, the term "idea" is being used very widely here. It includes things we commonly call ideas, such as concepts, hypotheses, and analogies. It also covers cultural and physical artifacts: poems, prose, music, and experimental designs; and tools, inventions, paintings, and sculptures. Third, and most important, each of my defining criteria — novelty, surprise, and value — needs elucidation.

An idea may be novel with respect only to the mind of the individual concerned or, so far as we know, with respect to the whole of human history. Let us speak of P-novelty and H-novelty respectively ('P' for psychological, 'H' for historical). There is no reason to suppose that the mental processes concerned in either case are fundamentally different, or that P-creativity (the generation of P-novelties) is inherently inferior to H-creativity. If your twelve-year-old daughter comes up with a good, and unexpected, idea while writing a poem or doing her physics homework, she has exercised her P-creativity whether or not she can be credited with H-creativity also. Would you really think her utterly uncreative merely because you happen to know that Keats, or Kelvin, had had the very same idea already?

Many discussions are bedevilled by confusions between P-creativity and H-creativity. In some contexts, one is more relevant than the other. For the purposes of the history of science, for example, H-creativity is crucial: your daughter's homework would be irrelevant there. But for our purposes here, P-creativity — which includes H-creativity as a special case — is the more important (I shall normally use the inclusive term 'creativity', without any letter-prefix).

As well as distinguishing two senses of novelty, we must also remark two senses in which an idea can be surprising. On the one hand, it may strike us as improbable, to a lesser or greater degree. In general, we regard an interesting idea as more creative, the more improbable it seems to be. It follows that if one can show that the idea was not so unlikely as we thought, then its creativity is downgraded also. On the other hand, the idea may strike us as, simply, impossible. Here, we are not just surprised, but astonished. We had assumed that no such idea was possible — or, more likely, we had never even envisaged the possibility of anything like it. The shock to our familiar way of thinking outstrips the surprise elicited by the most unexpected poetic image or graphic juxtaposition. This is not merely because impossibility trumps improbability, but because the shock seems to involve not just this one idea but a whole class of ideas, an entire thinking style.

A philosophical analysis of creativity should distinguish the apparently impossible creative ideas from the merely improbable ones, and a psychological theory should be able to explain how both types can be generated. If the distinction between impossibility and improbability, here, rests on differences in the generative processes involved, then the distinction between "philosophical" and "psychological" accounts of creativity is necessarily blurred. A computational approach can help us to ask these questions in a fruitful way.

Briefly (for more detail see [Boden, 1990]), we must distinguish three types of creativity: combinatorial, exploratory, and transformational. The first and third correspond roughly to the "improbable" and "impossible" cases mentioned above. The second, which is often overlooked, is closely related to the third.

Combinatorial creativity involves unfamiliar juxtapositions of individually familiar ideas. Examples include many cases of poetic imagery, and analogy in general. One might argue that many poetic images are close to analogies: the difference lies not in the nature of the juxtaposed ideas, but in the extent to which the structural basis of this novel association is deliberately and explicitly noted — perhaps for rhetorical effect or for scientific problem-solving. For both imagery and analogy, the more unexpected (improbable) the juxtaposition the more creative it is judged to be. However, some basis for the novel combination must be recognized: mere random coupling is not enough (Random coupling may occur within a wider context that provides significance: a writer may use randomness to highlight the relations between contingency and structure in human life, and some cases of

310

randomness — such as Mozart's aleatory music — fall clearly under exploratory creativity, discussed below).

Connectionist AI-modeling in general gives us some idea of how novel combinations of ideas are possible, and how they may arise from a variety of structural and associative bases. It helps us to understand, for instance, what psychological mechanisms could have generated Coleridge's imagery in "The Ancient Mariner" from various sources in his eclectic reading [Boden, 1990, ch. 6]. That such associations are possible has long been clear, of course. But just how they can happen has remained a mystery, and is still far from being fully understood.

As for analogy, the most interesting computational work has been done by Douglas Hofstadter and his colleagues [Hofstadter, 1995]. Unlike most AI-researchers, they stress the essential fluidity of all our concepts, and the close relation between conceptualization and perception. Their Copycat program, designed on broadly connectionist principles, can produce both wildly improbable and relatively plodding analogies, and can decide which features, among a host of possibilities, are most relevant in context. For instance, it recognizes that the two consecutive letters M in the strings AAFFMMPP and BCD-KLMMNOTUV are best described as a unit-pair in the first case and as parts of two different triples in the second. The closely related Letter Spirit project aims to model the perception and the self-critical creation of alphabetic style (as yet, only the perception has been implemented). The task is to design a 26-letter alphabet, given 1 or 2 sample letters — and to do this repeatedly, for very different sample letters. Analogies must exist at two levels: every A must be recognizable as an A, and within each font the A must be designed in the same spirit as all the other letters. These design constraints can exert opposing pressures: making a putative-A more obviously recognizable as an A may make it less similar to the Q, or the Z, in the same font. Work on Letter Spirit has raised, and clarified, many crucial questions about the sorts of analogy involved, and about the mechanisms by which such analogies could be created.

Combinatorial creativity requires some network of concepts with the potential for making associative links based (for example) on semantic structure, phonetic similarity, and cultural or personal history. Both exploratory and transformational creativity require more than this. They are possible only on the basis of some accepted style of thinking in the relevant domain [Boden, 1990, chs. 4 & 5].

Exploratory creativity, from which many people in arts and science earn a respected living, involves the production of novel (often H-novel) structures within a given thinking style. I call this style a conceptual space — partly to suggest the potential for exploration, and partly to recall the long-established AI notion of a problem-space. Conceptual spaces, like problem-spaces, are defined by a set of constraints that implicitly specify a range of potential positions within the space, and a set of generative rules for deciding which ones to visit. Someone who asks new (even H-new) questions within an accepted aesthetic or theoretical style is engaged in exploratory creativity, and may well come up with surprises. Many conceptual spaces are rich enough in their potential structure to include unexpected places. Much of what Thomas Kuhn [1962] called normal science involves exploratory creativity of this type, as does (for example) most jazz improvisation or choreography.

Most existing AI-models of creativity are concerned with exploring a conceptual space, sometimes with results that are not only H-novel but interesting to human beings. One example is AARON [McCorduck, 1991; Cohen, 1995], a program that produces individually unique — and aesthetically pleasing — line drawings (and, very recently, coloured paintings) in a particular graphic style. Another is a very early expert system called DENDRAL [Lindsay et al., 1980], which generates sensible molecular structures in a specific area of chemistry.

Unlike most AI problem-spaces, conceptual spaces (in programs or in human minds) are not rigidly defined once and for all, but are changeable in a variety of ways. Superficial tweakings may alter aspects such as numerical parameters, whereas fundamental transformations alter one (or more) of the structural dimensions defining the space. It can be easier to decide whether the space has been changed in a particular case than to judge whether the change is a tweaking or a transformation. This judgment is implicit in the nature of the surprise we experience on encountering the novel idea.

For example, consider the recent — and astonishing — discovery of Carbon-60. This H-creative idea effected a fundamental transformation in carbon chemistry, adding "Bucky-balls" to diamond and graphite as a third distinctive molecular structure. By contrast, the discovery of C-70, and the (continuing) synthesis of many different fullerenes, including "tubes" as well as "spheres," involve the deliberate tweaking and systematic exploration of this new chemical space. We can now ask how stable C-60 is, whether one can repeatedly remove two carbon atoms from it and still have a stable molecular structure, whether anything else can be "trapped" inside it, what side-chains can be added to it, and so on. All these creative questions were made possible by the conceptual transformation that generated the notion of carbon molecules that are spheres, not 2D/3D lattices.

The air of paradox and impossibility that attends examples of transformational creativity arises because these ideas simply could not have been reached by merely exploring the familiar conceptual space. For these new ideas to be possible, the space must have been transformed in some way. The transformation may be more or less fundamental, and more or less systematic. And the new space may be more or less promising, in terms of the scope it provides for further exploration and tweaking. Given the existing background of theoretical chemistry, it is not surprising that chemists immediately sensed the potential fecundity of C-60. That's not to say that they knew beforehand just what derivatives could arise, still less what their uses might be. Rather, it was immediately clear (to expert chemists) that a host of exploratory questions could be asked about the new molecule, many of which might turn out to have chemically interesting answers.

Transformational creativity, too, has been modeled in AI-terms. Examples include programs for generating H-novel coloured patterns [Sims, 1991], coloured 3D "sculptures" [Todd & Latham, 1992], the "bodily" anatomies of virtual creatures competing in a (simulated) physical world [Sims, 1994], and even the sensory-motor anatomy of autonomous robots [Cliff, Harvey, & Husbands, 1993]. In all these cases, the transformational principle is some sort of genetic algorithm (GA).

A GA enables a program to change (some of) its own rules at random, thereby generating structures which could not have been produced in the previous generation. The process is then repeated, perhaps hundreds of times, on a subset of the structures belonging to the most recent generation. In most GA-systems, the selection of that subset is done by the program itself. Sometimes, however, it is done by a human being. Some of the transformations involved are relatively superficial: the virtual sculptures, for example, bear a strong family resemblance because the random changes affect only parameters. Others are so fundamental that the ancestry may not be evident even from one generation to the next. This is true of the program that produces 2D patterns, because the GA concerned is able to make random changes not only to parameters but also to the very heart of the code, radically changing the structure of the image generation that occurs.

Clearly, then, GAs can generate new, previously impossible, ideas. To that extent, the paradoxical or impossibilist aspect of creativity is demystified. But this is not to say that it has been adequately explained. Human creativity may involve some random transformations, but it can also involve more deliberate ones. Current GAs mimic these only to a limited degree. Some GAs can protect the integrity of those subsets of code which have a high probability of producing useful results. But they cannot choose radical transformations (as opposed to superficial tweakings) that are especially likely to have fruitful results. As in other areas of the philosophy of mind, however, asking how one might model transformational creativity in computational terms helps one to think more clearly about the nature of the phenomenon concerned.

Some transformational programs, including the virtual sculptor mentioned above, cannot judge their own results. In these cases, the selection at each generation is done by a human being (so artists can use GAs without feeling that they have abandoned their own aesthetic voice). This brings us to the third criterion of creativity that needs elucidation, namely, value.

The problem, here, does not arise merely from the fact-value distinction. It arises also from two inconvenient truths relevant to the concept of creativity: that ideas are regarded as valuable for all sorts of reasons, and that these reasons themselves vary over space and time.

The reasons for valuing a novel idea as creative include many different general criteria of scientific or artistic worth. For instance: theoretical elegance or economy; humour, irony, or wit; associative richness; harmony of various types; unexpectedness, unorthodoxy, or even deliberate shock value. They also include more specific criteria, some of which are appropriate only to a particular style or theoretical approach. One may praise a sonnet for the subtlety of its rhymes, or criticize it for their obviousness or absence; but such considerations are not relevant in evaluating blank verse — or in assessing a new scientific theory. A general theory of creativity cannot mention specific criteria, such as rhyme or metre. At best, it can cite the more general notions listed above. More strictly, since even these general notions do not all apply in every case, it must rely on concepts such as interest, usefulness, or beauty. These concepts are notoriously vague. Just what is interesting, useful, or beautiful in the relevant domain must be decided in discussing the creativity of any particular idea.

A further difficulty in assessing the "value" of putatively creative ideas arises because the criteria deemed appropriate are both controversial and changing. The history of science and art, not to mention our everyday experience of consumer society, provide a wealth of evidence. Examples abound of people — and ideas — that have attracted popularity, even awe, at some times and scorn or neglect at others. Possibly, there are inborn dispositions to value certain types of idea: our evolutionary background may have disposed us to favour certain types of landscape, for example [Heerwagen & Orians, 1993; Orians & Heerwagen, 1992]. Even so, the evaluative aspect of creativity is overwhelmingly a matter of social judgment, which may vary across cultures, sub-cultures, and relatively exclusive peer groups [Schaffer, 1994].

None of this prevents our including positive evaluation within the concept of creativity. But it does mean that special difficulties arise with respect to crediting computers with creativity. These difficulties, however, are not quite what they are often assumed to be.

Normally, we expect the person who produced the valuable idea to recognize its value, or at least to have a hunch about it. If they do not, we may refuse to call them — or even the idea — creative. A schizophrenic's word-salad, for example, may include several valuable ideas: unusual juxtapositions of concepts, which others could exploit for their own creative purposes. But if the originator is incapable of distinguishing their potential, still less of developing it, and unable even to recognize their improbability, most people (followers of R. D. Laing excepted) would think twice before using the term "creative." In some cases, we are prepared to be generous to the "value-blind" originator, if (unlike the schizophrenic) they were engaged in a disciplined search for some artistic or scientific construction, and especially if they later realized (and developed) the value of their initially discarded idea [Boden, 1990, 83-84]. But we are more willing to use the vocabulary of creativity if the person concerned is able to recognize the value of their novel idea.

It follows that if a computer program is incapable of recognizing value, it is incapable of being creative in the full sense. It may be able (in ways outlined above) to produce novel, surprising, ideas. And if it can do this, it could be helpful to human beings in their attempts at creative thinking [Boden, 1994b]. But if it cannot also value its new ideas, it is not fully creative.

The question whether a computer could recognize value can be interpreted in two senses. First, we can ask whether (what we regard as) appropriate evaluative criteria could be provided to the program, and automatically applied by it to its own novel ideas. Second, we can ask whether the program itself could really, genuinely, appreciate the value.

The answer to the first question is a qualified "Yes." A variety of evaluative criteria have already been provided to computer models of creativity. Some are implicit in the generative process itself, others are applied post hoc to the system's novel products. It is easier to implement values in merely exploratory programs, because transformational programs — by definition — must transgress some accepted stylistic canons, and may also defy some wider evaluative criterion. This is especially likely if the transformations are fundamental in character, altering the core structure of the initial conceptual space. In principle, the relevant values can be implemented if they can be clearly expressed.

For this to be achieved in general, however, requires the solution of long-standing problems in aesthetics and the philosophy of science. Philosophers are well aware of the difficulty of identifying clear criteria in these areas. Sometimes, this difficulty can be sidestepped. For instance, a connectionist system could be shown a set of 2D patterns that (some relevant group of) humans find attractive, and another set which they regard as ugly, and could learn to categorize new examples with a high degree of plausibility. But much as the human beings might not be able to say just what evaluative criteria they were using, so the connectionist network would not necessarily make this explicit either. If it were connected to a transformational 2D-pattern generator similar to the one mentioned above [Sims, 1991], the program could judge the attractiveness of its own novel ideas. Indeed, given an appropriate feedback loop, the pattern generator might come to produce a higher proportion of "attractive" patterns as a result. But that assumes (what is not at present the case) that the program, or its programmer, could usually predict the likely results of a particular transformation.

It is sometimes said that programs cannot be creative because they cannot, like us, change their evaluative criteria. Admittedly, most current programs are locked into the evaluative attitude provided by the programmer. Random value-switching could of course be allowed, but the result in most cases would be judged by us to be inappropriate. Some programs, however, can develop new values, so that the criterion of what counts as interesting, or successful, changes intelligibly over time. This is not a matter of random value-swapping, but of the coherent development of new evaluative criteria based on the system's own creative activities. The cases I have in mind are GA-programs modeling co-evolution, such as the Tierra system [Ray, 1990] or the virtual fighting creatures mentioned above [Sims, 1994]. The most basic criterion of value is laid down by the programmer, and does not change: occupation of memory-space, for example, or pushing the opponent out of the designated area. But the fitness function used by the program at each generation for selecting "parents" likely to maximize this basic value does change. It evolves, and co-evolves, as the virtual creatures themselves are adaptively transformed.

The second interpretation of our question about computers and value was whether the computer itself could really, genuinely, appreciate value. As we've seen, a program could make "choices" or "decisions" based on evaluative criteria — but it would it know what it was doing? In other words, would it really be creative?

One might regard this question as one referring to a special case of AI-intentionality. It raises the problem of meaning, for we expect creators to understand their ideas. It also raises the problem of consciousness, for although people's novel ideas are often generated unconsciously, they are evaluated (and deliberately developed) consciously.

Alternatively, one might regard this as just another way of asking whether strong AI in general is possible. For creativity is not an isolated faculty of the mind, to be considered in isolation from all others. Nor is it the special preserve of a tiny human elite. On the contrary, it is a pervasive aspect of human thinking — not least in our ability to shift, compare, and transform our concepts continually [Boden, 1990, ch. 10]. As we have seen, some AI research emphasizes the fluidity of concepts and the ubiquity of creative analogy [Hofstadter, 1995]. But even this relatively human-oriented research is open to challenge as regards the philosophical coherence of strong AI.

This is not the place to rehearse the familiar arguments about strong AI, nor to launch into the philosophy of consciousness — which is why I omitted "Could a computer be genuinely creative?" from the

316

list of questions given at the outset of this paper. My own view is that, although the ascription of meaning and (especially) consciousness to computers are indeed problematic, the refusal to do either is less straightforward than is often assumed [Boden, 1990, ch. 11; Boden, forthcoming].

Irrespective of one's beliefs about "genuine" computer creativity, however, the positive answers to the four questions in the opening of this paper can stand. These answers do not assume the possibility of strong AI, so cannot be undermined by rejecting it. In sum: thinking in computational terms can help us to clarify our concept of creativity, and to understand how it is possible.

REFERENCES

Boden, M. A. (1990) *The Creative Mind: Myths and Mechanisms*. London: Weidenfeld & Nicolson. [1991 Expanded Ed.ition, London: Abacus.]

Boden, M. A., Ed. (1994a) *Dimensions of Creativity*. Cambridge, MA: MIT Press.

Boden, M. A. (1994b) "Agents and Creativity," in D. Riecken, Ed., *Communications of the ACM*, 37 (7): 117-121. [Special issue on Agents]

Boden, M. A. (forthcoming) "Consciousness and Human Identity: An Interdisciplinary Perspective." in J. Cornwell, Ed., *Consciousness and Human Identity*. Oxford: Oxford University Press.

Cliff, D., I. Harvey, and P. Husbands. (1993) "Explorations in Evolutionary Robotics," *Adaptive Behavior*, 2: 71-108.

Cohen, H. A. (1995) "The Further Exploits of AARON, Painter." Franchi, S. and G. Guzeldere, Eds. *Stanford Humanities Review*, 4: 141-160. [Special Issue on Constructions of the Mind: Artificial Intelligence and the Humanities.]

Heerwagen J. H., & G. H. Orians. (1993) "Humans, Habitats, and Aesthetics." Kellart, S. R. and E. O. Wilson, Eds., *The Biophilia Hypothesis*. Washington, DC: Shearwater Press, 138-172.

Hofstadter, D. (1995) *Fluid Concepts and Creative Analogies: Computer Models of the Fundamental Mechanisms of Thought*. New York: Basic Books.

Kuhn, T. S. (1962) *The Structure of Scientific Revolutions*. Chicago: University of Chicago Press.

Lindsay, R., B.G. Buchanan, E.A. Feigenbaum, and J. Lederberg. (1980) *DENDRAL*. New York: McGraw-Hill.

McCorduck, P. (1991) *Aaron's Code*. San Francisco: Freeman.

Orians, G. H., and J. H. Heerwagen. (1992) "Evolved Responses to Landscapes." in J. Barkow, L. Cosmides, and J. Toobey, Eds., *The Adapted Mind: Evolutionary Psychology and the Generation of Culture*. Oxford: Oxford University Press, 555-580.

Ray, T. S. (1990) "An Approach to the Synthesis of Life," in C. G. Langton, C. Taylor, J. D. Farmer, and S. Rasmussen, Eds., *Artificial Life II*. Redwood City, CA: Addison-Wesley. [Reprinted in M. A. Boden, Ed. (1996) *The Philosophy of Artificial Life*. Oxford: Oxford University Press, 111-145.]

Schaffer, S. (1994) "Making Up Discovery." in M. A. Boden., Ed., *Dimensions of Creativity*. Cambridge, MA: MIT Press, 13-52.

Sims, K. (1991) "Artificial Evolution for Computer Graphics," *Computer Graphics*, 25: 319-328.

Sims, K. (1994) "Evolving 3D Morphology and Behavior by Competition," *Artificial Life*, 1: 353-372.

Taylor, C. W. (1988) "Various Approaches to and Definitons of Creativity." in R. J. Sternberg, Ed. *The Nature of Creativity: Contemporary Psychological Perspectives.* Cambridge: Cambridge University Press, 99-121.

Todd, S., and W. Latham. (1992) *Evolutionary Art & Computers.* London: Academic Press.

PART II

THE IMPACT OF COMPUTING
ON PROFESSIONAL PHILOSOPHY

TEACHING PHILOSOPHY IN CYBERSPACE

RON BARNETTE

"A Classroom Without Walls," "The Electronic Agora," "The World-Wide Seminar," "A Global Classroom." Metaphors abound in attempts to describe education in cyberspace—that electronic medium known as the Internet. For the past several years, I have been engaged in helping structure a new medium for teaching philosophy, and I want to identify in this essay some central components in constructing and implementing a "virtual classroom" for the learning of philosophy. Like other fairly radical shifts away from traditional institutional procedures, in light of the Internet and particularly the World-Wide-Web, traditional procedures of the academy are likewise undergoing profound changes. It is thus important, I submit, to examine critically such shifts in direction, as we pioneer effective means for literally redefining the scope and nature of the academic department in the electronic, global arena. My aim here is to help articulate a new model for expanding teaching, consistent with new paradigms for engaging in the traditional components of the academic "holy trinity": teaching, research and service.

Technology IN the Classroom and Technology AS the Classroom

Technology-assisted teaching in the classroom has been with us for some time, be it through the use of film, video, overheads, computer-assisted learning, teleconferencing, or course information on the World-Wide-Web.[1] Terry Bynum (Southern Connecticut State University) demonstrated at the 1996 Pacific Division American Philosophical Association meeting what might be characterized as "levels of technology involvement" in integrating technology into the physical classroom.

Distinct from the incorporation of technologies *in* and *for* the classroom, however, is the use of information technology and Internet computing to literally *build* classrooms. In such courses, the teacher becomes an *architect* in the very design and delivery of the electronic philosophy class. Such a "classroom," once designed, can be thought of as owing its very *form* to computing technology, and as I hope to show, to a great extent, its course *content*.

PHICYBER—A Virtual Classroom: The Electronic Agora—A Totally Paperless Course

In 1993, as an educator and experimenter of sorts, I contemplated offering at Valdosta State University a "Special Topics in Philosophy" course during the summer term 1994 to be conducted entirely through the electronic medium. Utilizing the Internet to enable an asynchronous exchange of ideas, how would such a class—whose members know one another only through their thoughts written down and electronically exchanged—differ from the standard context, where a spatially/temporally coordinated co-presence is an integral part of communication and dialogue? How would library research projects fare in this medium where on-line resources available through an electronic source would be the essential research infrastructure? ...where individual critiques would be exchanged between classroom authors whose personal identities are shaped for others only by the written word..... where "you are what you write"?

After many discussions with colleagues and students, I planned, designed and launched (perhaps I was the first to do so) in summer 1994 a Philosophy in Cyberspace course—PHICYBER—accessible on-line twenty-four hours a day, seven days a week, for the ten-week term. Twenty-one participants made up the class, from physical locations in Georgia, Texas, New York, Illinois and North Carolina. Since then, PHICYBER has been offered in summer 1995 and summer 1996, and it will continue to be offered during summer terms at Valdosta State University. The growth, breadth and interest expressed have been remarkable. In 1996, one hundred eleven participants signed up for PHICYBER, from eleven countries representing five continents! Global, international, multicultural philosophical dialogue and debate were now happening, due entirely to computing technology. Unique classroom experiences were now a reality as students from around the globe discussed around the clock topics forged in a cyberspace community. They represented perspectives not otherwise realizable in the physical space of a university location, and it was apparent that space/time impediments to timely, ongoing multinational dialogue and opportunity could truly be transcended.

In such a course, all classroom discussion and dialogue are conducted through electronic mail, via a listserver—PHICYBER—to which all class members subscribe. Through our Philosophy Web site (http://www.valdosta.peachnet.edu/~rbarnett/phi) an electronic academic department is available to a world-wide philosophical community. PHICYBER participants make use of vast resources and materials through our Virtual Library, an electronic "doorway" to hundreds of philosophy works, journals, articles and resources. This growing collection in the Virtual Library is available thanks to materials on our own site as well as links to excellent philosophy Web sites around the globe. Collaboration and sharing are marvelous enablers, and it is truly an accomplishment by the greater philosophical community that such library resources are now on-line. In recent research, I discovered, much to my pleasure, that philosophers (in and out of academe) and departments of philosophy have consistently been leaders in providing academic materials through the Web.[2] By means of such cost-free resources, PHICYBER students pursue their research and develop their written projects and WWW home pages around philosophical themes, all of which are submitted in electronic form. The Electronic Agora is totally paperless.

For class discussion through the PHICYBER list, a topic and problem are assigned each week for discussion, accompanied by assigned readings and notes, which also are available through a PHICYBER home page on our Web site. As discussion progresses, it is rather uncanny to watch relationships develop, based only upon one another's ideas, developed, criticized, and expanded on-line. Participants address a discussion topic, defend their positions, raise critical objections, respond to challenges, and consider implied new directions for analysis and further critical thought. In this situation, an unusual learning community evolves and self-organizes through collaboration and interaction on topics like ethics, epistemology, historical problems, religious debates, and other traditional philosophical issues and questions.

An initial challenge that one faces in cyberspace is how to prompt such dialogue. Due in part to the novel forum, we all help to craft who we are through each word, and there are no slips of the tongue that are typically fast forgotten. As one student put it during a media interview about PHICYBER, "It is so different when you have to think through your ideas, put them in writing, and be prepared to back up your views, knowing that once expressed they are out there for the permanent record!" This student alludes here to the fact that all classroom work and discussions are placed in a course archive, and are available to the world for ongoing retrieval and review. One can think of the "in-class" portion of the course as a transcript. There are no voices or accents, no noises, nor distractions based on gender, race, ethnicity or age. Only ideas, and ideas about ideas, formulated, written and re-written, expressed and revisited. In fact, the ongoing discussion in the class *is* the class, and the class *is* the set of ideas expressed. A participant becomes, in a sense, a Platonist in cyberspace, instantiated by material objects and electricity!

Anonymity and Ethical Conduct

In addition to the question of how relative anonymity affects communication—which is a fascinating research program, and one in need of rigorous, thoughtful analysis—the question of how such invisibility might influence one's conduct was, and continues to be, a concern of mine and of others. While in cyberspace a person's presence and identity to others are known only through that person's words, so if one is on-line "silently," one's presence is known only to oneself. How does the so-called *lurker* tend to operate, when merely observing the goings on and only occasionally jumping into the discussion? Recall Plato's Myth of Gyges, which describes a scenario in which one finds a magic ring that renders one invisible and practically impervious to sanction. How is one prone to act in cyberspace when virtually invisible to others? How indeed?

Due in part to two elements in the Electronic Agora, I have found that anonymity engenders *more* civility and concern for others, not less. First, class members take very seriously just how they are regarded by others, as discussed above. They tend to *invest* in their work and in their discussion, so as to be understood as meant. Thus, they tend to go out of their way to clarify intent: "I hope you understand what I meant when I said ____," "Maybe I should further clarify ____," "Let me repeat what I meant by ____," "Please don't get the wrong idea, but ____," are often-repeated caveats and qualifiers, which are generally unnecessary, yet which are perceived as important metastatements by the discussants. The other reason for an almost hyperpoliteness (at times) might be that since part of my assessment of their work covers helpful, collaborative class involvement, it is prudent for them to learn good, constructive communication skills in this electronic social setting. There's nothing like a carrot and a stick! More seriously, though, I do maintain that a philosophy teacher's course objectives should stress the importance of learning to develop responsible academic and social skills in discussion and through constructive dialogue. To this end, I have coined a Kantian-like "PHICYBER E-Mail Golden Rule" that I expect all to follow:

> Click (or Enter) unto others as you would have them Click (or Enter) unto you.

And this cyberprescription seems to do the trick, in the main.

A friend and fellow pioneer in using cyberspace for on-line teaching of philosophy is Jon Dorbolo (Oregon State University), who uses an ethics component for teaching in cyberspace in his exciting learning model, *InterQuest* (http://www.cs.orst.edu:80/department/ instruction/phil202). At the August 1996 Conference on Computing and Philosophy at Carnegie Mellon University, Dorbolo presented a session on "Virtual Virtues," where he described on-line procedures for helping philosophy students become sensitive to ways in which interpersonal conflicts arise when one is engaged in computer-mediated communication. In that session, he described ways to prevent such insensitivities and conflicts from arising. His approach is refreshing, and thoroughly understandable to students, who are assigned tasks aimed at getting them to appreciate the value of reflective communication. Dorbolo's challenge to on-line teachers is commendable to initiate ethical education in this manner.

Assessment and Effectiveness

Like innovations in general, technology-based innovations in teaching need objective scrutiny and evaluation to the extent possible; for there is something gained and something lost, something enabled and something disabled. The central question is whether, on balance, teaching in cyberspace promotes academic and personal growth not otherwise available. Let me discuss a few issues related to these concerns and suggest some new directions for course assessment in the electronic frontier.

First, some obvious advantages:

1. Access to Library Resources
Not all students have access to physical library holdings of proportional quality. Electronic libraries and multimedia materials available on-line are fast becoming educational equalizers with respect to such access inequalities. In addition, they are allowing institutional collaboration on library and research budgets, making it possible for a cost-effective pool of inter-library holdings to be quantitatively and qualitatively enriched and made available to all, irrespective of physical locale. For example, the State of Georgia has initiated Project GALILEO (Georgia Libraries for Learning On-line) which serves all students and faculty in the state, providing library holdings and journals that are ever-increasing in number. (http://galileo.gsu.edu/ Homepage.cgi)

2. Personal Access
Not all students (or faculty members) are able to arrange and coordinate a common spatial/temporal meeting place, for a variety of reasons: non-traditional students, working students, those living in remote areas, those with temporary or permanent physical handicaps, to name but a few. In the "Virtual University," and through asynchronous communication, typical problems of place, time, distance, transportation, and physical well-being are all but eliminated.

Next, some less obvious advantages:

3. *Breadth of Contact*
A much wider context for discussing topics requiring multiple perspectives is available, when properly arranged, through the Internet
than is generally available in the physical university classroom. On-
line, regional and global similarities and differences tend to merge in
dialogue, and the volume of discussion reflects a much more mature
outlook on controversial topics than is typically the case among students in a standard setting. Participants in cyberspace don't perceive
themselves as "We the students— S/He the teacher." This
"democratization" helps to promote a much more robust sense of variation and exploration in thought.

4. *Depth of Study*
In addition, one can make a good case—though perhaps more controversial—that when the electronic classroom is properly planned and
offered to the appropriate group, the quality of student performance is
significantly higher than in the traditional physical classroom. I realize
that this is a strong claim, and it should be a focus for professional dialogue and assessment. But I have found that through asynchronous
discussion, ideas can be formulated and discussed with a far greater
degree of clarity and purpose, and this is made evident in critically
reviewing class discussions about readings, conflict resolution, and argumentation. Written work and research are exchanged, multiple
drafts are produced and discussed, and ideas are sharpened, all
around busy schedules and other demands on students' and faculty
members' time. The results and outcomes are, in general, of much
higher quality than standard large-course written works, which do not
proportionally reflect collaboration, ongoing discussion, and detailed
academic development.

5. *Student Attitude*
Students readily adapt to philosophy in cyberspace. The social dynamics of an expanding electronic culture might have a lot to do with explaining this phenomenon, but the fact is clear: The medium influences positively how students describe the class and how they characterize their educational experiences in their course evaluations. Responses to class topics and challenges are enthusiastic; time spent in
discussion reflects crisp, cheerful commentary; and questions about
additional on-line opportunities and development reveal an approach
to *doing* philosophy that enhances the student's own sense of educational growth. In a typical discussion class with a large population—
say, over thirty—it is not unusual for only a few students to "get into"
the class discussion, so to speak, while others recede, if not out of
sight, then clearly out of mind. Nothing of this sort occurs in cy-

berspace. Personal attitude matters greatly to course effectiveness and to the learning environment, and the electronic medium seems to enhance student attitude significantly.

Let's turn next to some disadvantages, before looking at assessment needs and new directions:

1. *Lack of Face-to-Face Contact*

It's a tautology to say that a cyberspace philosophy class omits physical interaction; and to the extent that this omission matters—which obviously it does—to that extent there's something missing in the Electronic Agora. Real-time, physical, interpersonal discussion is lacking, along with the quick timelines of traditional course activities. Yet, in spite of this lack of space/time sync, interpersonal contact, conflict resolution, and collaboration take place, albeit in a new context. In addition, the development of related interaction skills is promising in the electronic medium. It is a question of tradeoffs and balances, to be considered carefully, with a clear sense of desired outcomes and objectives.

2. *Educational Opportunities and Technology Access*

Not all students have ready access to requisite computing hardware and connectivity, especially off-campus people. One needs to be mindful of the risk of offering cyberspace learning opportunities only to those who are technology advantaged. The academy certainly doesn't need more divisions between those who can and those who cannot access educational opportunities. Fortunately, technology access is becoming more and more available and affordable. Yet the fact remains that not all can avail themselves of off-campus cyberspace opportunities.

3. *Faculty Teaching Loads*

Managing teaching time is very important to faculty, who also have many non-teaching responsibilities; so the prospect of having to tend to a huge amount of e-mail traffic and written commentaries on research drafts—for a class that literally runs around the clock—can be quite daunting indeed! How are reasonable teaching loads to be secured in cyberspace? How is enrollment to be managed? What new faculty development skills are needed, and how can one find time and assistance to learn the new pedagogy? These questions point squarely to issues of quality cyberspace course work discussed earlier, and they should be ongoing agenda items in departmental and university committee meetings. Further, I would recommend that professional organizations for philosophy teachers routinely schedule sessions devoted to such topics.

Other perceived pros and cons can be enumerated, to be sure; but, in light of the above issues, I want to conclude with the question of assessment of the new teaching technologies:

As mentioned above, I believe that there should be *widespread professional discussion,* on campuses and at professional meetings, of themes and experiences regarding on-line teaching. Collaboration and exchanges of ideas on these matters are essential if we are to move ahead responsibly in cyberspace. Similar dialogues should address, as well, the phenomena of *electronic publication and professional research:* issues of quality control, the use of electronic journals, appropriate peer review, and guidelines for promotion and tenure should all be topics discussed frequently. There are many materials related to these topics on the Web, and they should be examined and discussed routinely by professionals. After all, there is a significantly higher number of professional journals being launched *electronically* rather than in paper form, and professionals need to help shape quality.

Clear and precise *student learning outcomes* need to be formulated and stated, and course assignments and activities should be geared toward achievement of these ends. After all, in cyberspace *behavior and performance* are the measures of success, and teachers need to ask themselves *what the students should be able to do differently* as a result of their learning in the course. How can they *demonstrate* an understanding of Descartes' *Meditations,* say, or of problems and arguments on personal identity? Cyberspace activities can then be geared to these learning ends, as they evolve through dialogue and guided student performance.

Collaboration between teachers in cyberspace will enhance planning and teaching effectiveness, and provide students in the respective courses with an opportunity to discuss topics together, to share written work for critique and inter-class commentary. Cybercourses reflect what philosophers say they *do*: work together, debate the issues, present arguments and counterarguments, and the like. A tremendous opportunity exists in cyberspace for students to engage in the *activity* of philosophy along with their teachers. This can enhance significantly a student's appreciation of the field of study.

The *appropriate level of study* for students taking a course in cyberspace should be examined and discussed carefully, in light of various institutional cultures. At my institution, a junior or senior level philosophy course seemed appropriate, but this can and should vary with the institution and the student body in question. Here is where enrollment limits and teaching load calculations need to be clearly in focus as the course is being designed and planned.

Clear and precise student *assignments and expectations* should be formulated and reinforced throughout the course. In this way, varieties of written work can be appraised and commented upon in a consistent, helpful fashion. The key is to *engage* the student along the way, and to make this engagement *part of* the course, not a side activity.

As institutions, professional organizations, and accrediting agencies are expanding assessment efforts at colleges and universities, it is imperative that new ways of learning be able to show that the goals and outcomes of the learning design have been satisfied (in principle) by the details of the course delivery components. Thus, features such as class size will become a factor, proportionate to the time required to maintain and guide quality on-line discussion among class participants. As will clear and precise course syllabi, guidelines and instructional materials, given the heightened need in cyberspace to avoid miscommunication, throughout the course, over expectations and course objectives. And then there's the question of assessing 'cybertuition,' which appears to transcend traditional criteria for out-of-state, or international, fees generally brought to bear on students. Indeed, what do these concepts mean in the context of a global classroom? Many registrars even ask for inoculation evidence for course and college admission! Indeed, what are the differences to be expected from, and for, our new global student body?

The above considerations suggest elements in a needed model for assessment of on-line learning, for such a model would indeed benefit professors and administrators alike in the new era of technology and learning. Equally imperative, though, is for the teachers of philosophy to take an active role in the assessment design, and to provide their professional leadership in helping to forge quality learning experiments in cyberspace.

Concluding Remarks

The activities of teaching philosophy in cyberspace are as inspiring and rewarding as they are — often — frustrating and challenging. But the voyage — to borrow a line from Bill Uzgalis' *Great Voyages* — is clearly worth the effort. The Virtual Classroom model I sketched above should be examined critically as an exciting *supplement* to existing university life, *not* as a threatening replacement. And reasonable choices for academic alternatives on the electronic frontier can be made only after thoughtful, reflective balances are calculated. Given these qualifiers, I am convinced that Internet education experiments can bring out the best of what diversity in philosophy education can offer — some exciting approaches to learning philosophy in cyberspace.

331

NOTES

[1] Three excellent examples of using the Web for preparing philosophy course outlines, syllabi, assignments and information for on-campus students can be found in Bill Uzgalis' *Great Voyages for Modern Philosophy* (http://www.orst.edu/instruct/phl302) at Oregon State University; Cynthia Freeland's *Ancient Philosophy Homepage* (http://www.uh.edu/~cfreelan/courses/riceanc.html) at the University of Houston), and Valerie Hardcastle's *Philosophy of Mind Home Page* (http://mind.phi.vt.edu /www/mind .html) at Virginia Technical University.

[2] A very helpful Web site for ethics resources—probably the best on the Net—is Professor Lawrence Hinman's (University of San Diego) *Ethics Update* at http://www.acusd.edu/ethics. Hinman's resources provide outstanding materials for student projects, assignments and the like.

PHILOSOPHY TEACHING
ON THE WORLD WIDE WEB

JON DORBOLO

Philosophers tend towards the realm of the possible. Perhaps this is why philosophers are among the most active explorers of the educational potential of the World-Wide-Web (the Web.) We are dealing with a new and constantly changing medium. It is foolhardy to prognosticate in such circumstances, yet we explorers have sufficient experience with the Web to draw some conclusions about how it affects the conditions of philosophy education. A key supposition for what follows is that the consequences of technology cannot be recalled. We may be able to ignore, suppress, and minimize those effects, but we cannot unmake a potential once it has been supplied. The genie cannot be rebottled. This brief survey will consider how writing and teaching take on new characteristics through hypertext; how the traditional audience of philosophy education is diversifying; how discussion is reconstructed on the Web; how the Web functions to give students more autonomy and responsibility in the process of learning. My hope is that this synopsis will add some ideas to Web savants and peak interest among new explorers.

Writing The Web

What is commonly known as the World-Wide-Web appeared in February 1993 with the public release of Mosaic, a graphical interface browser. Mosaic offered both non-technical functionality (point and click) and true hypermedia capability. Images, texts, sounds, and videos are combined into complex documents. Any element of a Web document can be linked to another document. This linkage is the essence of hypertext (or hypermedia) and is what makes the Web philosophically significant, especially for educators.

A hypertext linked word has two uses in a text: 1) as a word in the text and 2) as a link to another text. The reader of a hypertext is presented with both the task of understanding the word in the expressed text and choosing whether to change texts by making a link. Even a primitive hypertext presents a nexus of meanings, double meanings, and hidden meanings from which the reader chooses paths of progression (digression, regression, etc.) Hypertext transforms the uses of a text in ways that have yet to be identified much less understood. The potential for philosophical investigation of these matters is rich.

Hypertext opens the way to new forms of writing and presenting. The technology of the written word in a period influences genres that develop in that period. Roman authors wrote to accommodate the limits of the roll. Typographic standardization and the encyclopedic ideal are connected. Contemporary speech writers fashion the sound-bite to carry the 10 to 30 second television spot. Hypertext presents a more radical departure from traditional writing than any of these. The roll, book, pamphlet, and TV spot all affect the context in which writing is produced and distributed. Hypertext affects not just the context but the word itself by extending its uses.

Linkage and connection are the primary problems of hypertext authorship because one is writing into the document the means and motive to leave that document. Serious writing often focuses on holding the readers attention. Hypertext writing must hold the attention and direct it away at the same time. For this reason it may not be possible to write a dynamic hypertext document and to predetermine the path of the reader. There may be some forms of order that cannot be rendered into a hypertext web, or the hypertext may inherently impose possibilities on a text. If so, we must be circumspect about rendering educational text into hypertext. Unintended effects may alter the presentation of the subject matter in undesirable ways.

The question of order is a serious matter for the hypertext author/educator. Creating an EdWeb means producing a nexus of texts, links, and connections. The educational Web site (EdWeb) determines how the student may receive the learning material and how they will experience the subject-matter. The EdWeb nexus provides a picture of the subject-matter which is revealed to the student as s/he acts on the links. The internal structure of an EdWeb says in effect; "this is how things hang together, these are relevant connections." How to use links to intentionally produce active learning is one of the important areas hypertext author/educators must investigate.

Population Growth

The Web allows philosophy educators to significantly expand their student population. Primary and secondary school students in the U.S. are rapidly gaining Web access. Distributed education by Web, which serves about 25 million users world-wide, is steadily moving into the mainstream of higher education [Kantor and Neubarth, 1996]. Philosophy is not among the topics traditionally offered at the primary and secondary levels. All this creates an optimum environment for philosophy educators to offer innovative learning resources to a previously unengaged student population.

In spring 1996 high school students enrolled in *InterQuest*, a Web-based introduction to philosophy class, for credit from Oregon State University. Being without synchronous class meetings and conducting all instruction on-line, the course was available to high schools students with Web access at school and/or home. The successful demonstration of high school enrollment in *InterQuest* SUITE (Seamless Uses of Internet Technology for Education) led to a pilot High School Outreach Program at Oregon State University to promote the secondary student enrollment in university distributed courses [Dorbolo, 1997]. Introducing high school students, and eventually primary levels, to philosophy by the Web is likely to increase interest in traditional philosophy offerings at colleges and universities.

Ron Barnette of Valdosta State University, Georgia has demonstrated how the internet may extend the population of philosophy learners. His course, PHICYBER, went on-line in summer 1994. In summer 1996 over 100 participants from 11 nations and five continents collaborated in the course. History shows that contact and exchanges among diverse cultures can have significant impact on the development of philosophy. The Web creates framework for cultural exchange on an unprecedented scale. The consequences for philosophy may be (and for philosophy education already are) momentous.

Though the graphical Web is only four years old, several philosophy educators have succeeded in different approaches to designing EdWebs. Robert Cavalier of Carnagie Mellon University produced an EdWeb site used in the classroom as part of his lecture presentation [Cavalier, 1996]. Lawrence Hinman of the University of San Diego provides a rich resource, "Ethics Updates," on the Web that may be used by other courses or as a stand alone learning resource [Hinman, 1996]. Bill Uzgalis, Oregon State University, offers "Great Voyages: The History of Modern Philosophy from 1492 to 1776." Using dynamic timelines and search capabilities, this course allows students to explore connections among events, ideas, and texts. This is just a sample of the varied approaches to Web use for philosophy education.

Discussion

A clear success of *InterQuest* is the high degree of student engagement through discussion. The 50 student class as a whole averages about 300 on-line exchanges per week in a ten week course. These exchanges include student-instructor messages as well as student-student exchanges. Picture a classroom-taught course largely devoted to discussion. The amount of time available for each student to express to the whole class (were all willing) is a function of the number of students and the time available. The on-line class does not have those limits. The ratio of expression to reception evens out as the rate of exchange increases. One student may write a comment to the class and be replied to by ten others the same day. The main limit to on-line discussion is the number of incoming messages students can handle. Strategies for discussion management are key to successful on-line teaching. *InterQuest* uses six discussion activity design models.

1) Peer-Peer Exchange: Pairs of students correspond with one another in a specified sequence of exchanges. This model produces large scale active participation with minimal impact on the instructor (as moderator, anyway.) Example: Dear Author [Dorbolo, 1997].

2) Inter-Group Exchange: The class is arranged into conversation sub-groups Groups may be designated by topics or desired group size. Each group member's work is broadcast to an entire group, but not the entire class. Example: Initial Impressions [Dorbolo, 1997.]

3) Extra-Group Exchange: The class is arranged into conversation sub-groups. The whole class is assigned the task of providing comments to sub-groups other than their own. This model can provide an impetus for a subsequent Inter-Group Exchange. Example: Framework Feedback [Dorbolo, 1997].

4) Intra-Group Exchange: Two (or more) mail groups exchange the results that each group produced in an Inter-Group activity. The key is to assign each group the task of fashioning a collective message to be sent to the other group. Example: Analysis Accord [Dorbolo, 1997].

5) Chain Exchange: A group of students performs a task sequentially passing messages along a chain. Starting the sequence with each individual allows all students to participate in all parts of the sequence. This model is effective for accentuating the articulation of a concept or process (e.g. an argument, a calculation, a sequence.) Example: Being In An Argument [Dorbolo, 1997.]

6) Global Exchange: What each student writes is broadcast to the entire class. This model is useful where everyone's concerns are at stake. Example: Class Constitution [Dorbolo, 1997].

I find the most effective place to start with on-line discussion activities is the Peer-Peer model. The most difficult to design and manage effectively is the Global-Exchange model. Interestingly, the later is typically the most used model for on-line class discussion by beginning Web educators. It is the simplest to set up technically. Perhaps this is a reason some faculty find their first experiences with on-line discussion disappointing.

These six types of activities may all be realized using a variety of Internet discussion methods. E-mail, listservers (e.g. Majordomo), threaded newsgroup clients (e.g. HyperNews), chat clients, are among the methods we have used in *InterQuest*. The difficulty with any method, however, is the complexity of instructions required for the students and level of maintenance required for the instructor. The more individuating a discussion strategy is, the more interdependent students become, and the higher the maintenance. For one thing many of the activities involve designated partners. If one partner fails to fulfill their role at any step of the activity, the other student's progress is blocked.

The instructor handles these instances by reassigning partners or filling the absent partner's role. Doing so is more maintenance than most instructors will want to assume for a single activity, no matter how pedagogically effective. Just creating and assigning the list of partners from a class of 50 is a fair amount of work. A management scheme is needed to allow the complex discussion activities to operate effectively for students and instructors.

The *InterQuest* SUITE solution to this instructoral dilemma (the more detailed the discussion activity, the greater the managerial workload) is the development of a Web Course management System. QuestWritertm is a full featured Web course management system including: on-line student registration, automatic mailing list subscription, gradebook creation, student authentication, individual student-accessible portfolios and grade reports, quiz tools (multiple-choice, true-false, fill-in, essay), reading activities, session entry and exit queries, conditional links for dynamic individualized content, and managed discussion activities.

The managed discussion activities employ a *lazy scheduling* method by which students are assigned discussion partners in order of completion of an activity step. The instructions for a single step appear on a web page with an editable writing space. The student completes that step and sends the result. When the partner complies (by a specified due date) they both advance to the next step. Only participating students become paired, so the problem of the inactive partner does not affect other students. If one partner stops participating part way into the activity, QuestWritertm sends alerts to the non-participant and the instructor, then regroups the active student with another active student. In its prototype trials, QuestWritertm discussion activities significantly reduced instructoral management of discussion activities in *InterQuest*.

QuestWritertm is a powerful example of educational technology being led by pedagogical theory and practice [Dorbolo, 1997].

On-line discussion is different from face-to-face discussion. On-line discussion is primarily written, asynchronous, and lacks the non-verbal aspects of face-to-face exchange (e.g. raised eyebrows and voices.) On-line discussion is closer to written correspondence than talking. Philosophy has a long tradition of discussion by correspondence. Writing letters is a powerful way of communicating and devel-

oping ideas. Just as a sustained exchange of letters between corespon-
dents reveals an intellectual relationship, an active exchange of philosophical writing on-line reveals an intellectual community. This is an
important phenomenon for educators concerned that on-line teaching
is impersonal and anti-individual. While powerful as an information
delivery system, the Web is vastly more meaningful as a communication medium. The communication power of the Web has the potential
to transform the character of education.

Guided Autonomous Learning

Hypertext allows students to choose diverse paths through the materials of a site. *InterQuest* makes use of this hypertext capacity by the
method of Guided Autonomous Learning. This strategy seeks to
match the course material and participants with the pre-existing philosophical commitments (beliefs, values, rehtorical moves) held by individual students. All introductory students have such philosophical
commitments. Few introductory students have any background education in philosophy or genuine initial interest in the discipline. Creating a curriculum for such students is a well known challenge in teaching philosophy. Guided Autonomous Learning seeks to engage indi-
vidusal students by directly addressing their pre-existing philosophical commitments. For discussion of the pedagogical basis of this strategy in the Socratic method and constructivist learning theory, see
"Guided Autonomous Learning" [Dorbolo, 1997].

The *InterQuest* project was launched in fall 1993 by Jon Dorbolo
and John Sechrest. It was first offered as a fully distributed Web course
(no class meetings, no textbook) in fall 1994 [Dorbolo, 1997, Sechrest,
1996.] In winter 1997, *InterQuest* enters its seventh term as a Web-
based course. Guided Autonomous Learning presents introductory
students with a number of Philosophical Frameworks, encapsulated
assertions of philosophical views. The current course provides alternatives of an egoist, holist, religious, relativist, and skeptic frameworks.
Students are directed to choose the framework that comes closest to
their genuine personal views. The class is arranged into groups based
on the student choices. Readings and activities are assigned with the
intent of promoting study and discussion of philosophical issues that
are relevant to each framework group. By selecting a philosophical
framework, each student charts a course of study relevantly connected
to her/his present views. Issues of common concern (the skills of discussion, argument, interpretation, analysis, and inquiry), common
texts, and directed intra-group discussion maintain exchanges among
students in different framework groups.

Guided Autonomous Learning has proven effective in augmenting
student motivation to learn and emphasizes the autonomy and responsibility of students for their learning. Evaluations, surveys, and

content-analysis assessment of *InterQuest* indicate the effectiveness of Guided Autonomous Learning as a pedagogy for introducing philosophy. It is important to note that Guided Autonomous Learning was a pedagogy in search of a technique. The Web turned out to be the effective technique. This sets a valuable precedent for the use of educational technology: the value of a technology is proportional to the need for that technology in achieving an educational objective. The technology of the Web alone adds no significant value to education. When combined with an appropriate teaching strategy, however, powerful educational opportunities arise.

Commencement

The technology of the Web has such powerful effects on writing, discussion, lesson design, and study that we must never take it's impact for granted. Neither can educators afford to eschew the potentials it allows. Through the system of distributed hypertext known as the World-Wide-Web diverse cultures are interacting, educators are collaborating, non-sequential writing is proliferating, and discussion about philosophical matters are ongoing. Making sense of such conceptual and social transformation is, after all, a traditional task of philosophy.

REFERENCES

American Philosophical Association. (December 1996) http://www.udel.edu/apa/

Barnette, Ron. (December 1996) *PHICYBER: The Virtual Classroom.* http://www.valdosta.peachnet.edu/~rbarnett/phi/phicyber/

Bush, Vannevar. (July 1941) "As We May Think," *The Atlantic Monthly.* http://www.csi.uottawa.ca/~dduchier/misc/vbush/as-we-may-think.html

Cavalier, Robert. (January 1997) *Home Page.* http://hss.cmu.edu/html/departments/philosophy/directory/Robert_Cavalier.html

Cavalier, Robert. (1996) "Making Mosaic Webs Work at a Course Level." http://cal.bemidji.msus.edu/english/Resources/Making Webs.html

Dorbolo, Jon. (January 1997) *InterQuest Projects.* http://osu.orst.edu/pubs/phoenix

Dorbolo, Jon. (November 1996) *InterQuest Pro-Ethics.* http://osu. orst.edu/pubs/phoenix

Dorbolo, Jon. (September 1996) *InterQuest.* http://osu.orst. edu/pubs/phoenix

Hinman, Lawrence. (November 1996) *Ethics Updates.* http:// www.acusd.edu/ethics

Sechrest, John. (June 1996) *PEAK, Inc.* http://www.peak.org/ ~sechrest/

Uzgalis, Bill. (January 1997) *Home Page.* http://www.orst.edu/ Dept/philosophy/uzgalis.html

Uzgalis, Bill. (December 1996) *Great Voyages.* http://www. orst.edu/instruct/phl302/

MULTIMEDIA AND RESEARCH IN PHILOSOPHY[1]

ROBERT CAVALIER

I

The term 'multimedia' is ubiquitous in today's computing environment, so much so that it may be as redundant to speak of 'multimedia computing' as to speak of 'Graphical User Interface Computing.' Computers naturally combine diverse forms of media such as text, graphics, sound and digital video. But it was not always thus. Multimedia, in its current, computer-based meaning, had its technological forerunner in the interactive videodiscs of the 1970s and 80s.

Videodiscs are based upon analog video. Transferred onto 12-inch platters, the video, in its interactive form, is essentially sectored into 54,000 discrete segments, accessed by a computer program, and displayed on a TV monitor. Configurations for such systems involve a videodisc player and either a separate monitor or special graphics boards for converting the analog video into digital video. More complex systems use special boards to overlay the analog video with graphics such as buttons or various kinds of screen layouts.

Just as the technology of multimedia can be traced to the 70s and 80s, so too may the development of multimedia programs for Higher Education. Of particular interest are a number of projects sponsored by schools participating in the Inter-University Consortium for Educational Computing (ICEC) [Cavalier and Dexheimer, 1989]. MIT's Project Athena explored the development of 'visual computing' and Brown's Intermedia Project implemented early versions of hypermedia.[2] But work of immediate relevance to philosophy came out of Carnegie Mellon's Center for Design of Educational Computing (CDEC) and its flagship multimedia efforts under the aegis of Project THEORIA. Beginning in 1987, the center developed two interactive videodisc projects that eventually led to EDUCOM awards for Best Humanities Software.[3]

The acronym "THEORIA" stands for : Testing Hypotheses in Ethics/ Esthetics: Observation, Reason, Imagination, and Affect. It is intended to play off of the origins of both 'theory' and 'theater' in the ancient Greek verb *theorein:* to see, to view, to behold. One stimulus for the project was Derek Bok's claim that while computers may be useful in areas of data and calculation, they are ill-equipped to handle the often open-ended areas of the humanities. CDEC was to take up his charge by showing that if you shifted the paradigm of 'computing' away from the command screen terminal to a system that could display all kinds of information, including visually rich information, computers could indeed address some important issues in the humanities, including puzzling cases in aesthetics and hard cases in ethics. The reason for this lies in the ability of 'video' to convey 'rich data' in the form of, for example, art images and personal narratives. The goal of Project THEORIA thus became focused on the task of designing compelling, interactive simulation environments for testing hypotheses and theories of the arts and morals — among the most difficult and disputed of human value domains.

II

In the area of aesthetics, this goal focused on what Preston Covey called the Three A's: Access, Attention, and Analysis. An interactive multimedia environment should provide convenient *access* to both information about the artworks in question ("external" evidence) as well as the relevant works themselves ("internal" evidence), close *attention* to the primary data, the details and features of visual artworks themselves (the "internal" evidence for aesthetic judgments and attributions) and critical *analysis* of both the evidence and the evidentiary issues pertinent to the inter-related judgments of attribution and aesthetic value [Covey, 1992, foreword].

Art or Forgery? The Strange Case of Han van Meegeren implements these criteria with a pedagogical ploy revolving around a famous case of alleged Vermeer forgeries. Han van Meegeren, an artist whose credentials had declined in the eyes of art critics, was accused of collaborating with the Nazis in the acquisition of a heretofore undiscovered Vermeer masterpiece: *Christ and the Adulteress*. At his trial shortly after the Allied victory, van Meegeren claimed to have painted the work himself. Was he telling the truth or was he risking the charge of forgery rather than face the more serious charge of collaboration?

The critics had praised the work as an authentic Vermeer. How much weight should their views hold? Is a work praised by the Art World no longer valuable if the Art World changes its mind — reducing a former Vermeer to a mere forgery of a Vermeer? In this context, the topic of forgery touches upon some key issues in the philosophy of art.

Working from puzzles to principles, the case of van Meegeren stimulates discussions of attribution and worth, the relation of internal (art comparison) to external (art composition) evidence, and the very nature of value theory itself.[4]

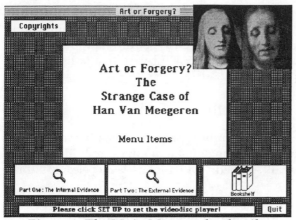

Copyrights

Art or Forgery?
The
Strange Case of
Han Van Meegeren

Menu Items

Part One: The Internal Evidence | Part Two: The External Evidence | Bookshelf

Please click SET UP to set the videodisc player! | Quit

Figure 1. The Main Menu and a detail comparison of the paintings Christ at Emmaus and Christ and the Adulteress. Both paintings, it turns out, were van Meegeren forgeries.

But to do justice to these discussions, it is critical to have access to the images and to attend carefully to the relevant data as many ways as possible. Traditionally, one way of doing this kind of analysis is the slide comparison. Calling up images of the painting in question and comparing it (wholely or in part) with other images was the very essence of analyzing internal evidence. Videodisc technology allowed CDEC to provide an extensive database and the computer driven program allowed users to explore this database in a relevant fashion. While certainly dated by today's wholly digital environment, the program represented a serious R&D attempt to integrate technology into the curriculum of art history.

The program also served to stimulate thinking about the deeper relationship between technological advance and aesthetic theory. In an article entitled "Theoretical and Practical Perspectives on Technology and the History of Art History," David Carrier argued that changes in the ways that art can be mechanically reproduced and displayed have affected the very way that we think about art and art history. Referring to Trevor Fawcett's history of the slide lecture, Carrier notes that the sequential, visual comparisons of art historian Heinrich Woelfflin *presupposed* the availability of two simultaneous images and that, indeed, "the entire system of teaching he developed early in this century, and the books he wrote, depended upon a system of left screen/right screen comparisons," [Cavalier and Carrier, 1989, 245].

If technology now allows for new and more flexible representations of art, perhaps new ways of teaching Art History and new ways of thinking about Art History will come into play. In the 1920s Aby Warburg imagined a 'picture atlas' called *Mnemosyne* upon which he could pin photographs and rearrange them according to relevant content and emerging themes. Today, programs like Extensis Corporation's Fetch allow users to customize an image database, giving each picture a catalogue depth that enables open-ended searches and rich displays. Art History CD-ROMs such as Planet Art provide copyright free use of, for example, collections of the Dutch Masters while projects like Microsoft's Corbis are setting new standards in high quality digital imaging. If someone like Heinrich Woelfflin had today's *Mnemosyne* at his disposal, we might well look forward to a radical change in our approach to art history.[5]

III

At the 1993 meeting of the Computing and Philosophy conference, Preston Covey, speaking about the domain of ethics, provided the following abstract for his talk entitled: "Of Balloons & Bicycles, Multimedia & Ethics"

> Ethical wisdom is formed in that crucible of moral experience in which ethical theory is tested. Ethical judgment requires more than a capacity for skilled ratiocination; *inter alia:* the vivid representation of the interests of others; empathic skills and a rich imagination; practiced confrontation with complex facts, unforeseen consequences, and strong feelings; active deliberation under the duress of emotion, hard choices, and irreducible uncertainties. Ethics education must therefore afford students the opportunity to experience the rigors of judgment under the duress of these conditions as well as the opportunity for studious reflection. Interactive multimedia can simulate these conditions, stimulate the moral imagination, present both the affecting realities of 'real life' situations and the reflective opportunities that should be afforded by academic study, and thereby enhance two complementary modes of ethical inquiry: engagement and detachment. I assume that the *integration* of emotion and reflection is a higher-order, more complex requirement than dispassionate analysis by the lights of ethical theory alone. Borrowing a metaphor from Albert Jonsen, I argue that ethics education requires sweaty bicycle tours as well as lofty balloon rides over the terrain of moral experience.

Covey's summary provides one of the theoretical backgrounds for the development of *A Right to Die? The Dax Cowart Case*. This interactive CD-ROM program investigates a burn patient's request to be allowed to die. The case relates the story of a 25-year-old man who received second and third degree burns over two-thirds of his body. At the time that we encounter Dax in treatment, his injuries have left him severely scarred, his hands are badly deformed, and the sight in his one remaining eye is at risk. As a patient, he undergoes daily treatments in an antiseptic tank – tankings that are so painful to him that he has persistently asked the doctors to stop his treatment. Dax feels that the length of his projected treatment and the quality of life that he can ex-

344

pect to regain do not warrant the torment he must suffer. The doctors know that if they continue his treatment, he will live; if they stop his treatment, he will surely die. A basic question posed at this point of impasse between Dax and his care givers is: Does Dax have a right to die? And, if so, what does this mean?

Traditional approaches to this kind of case study often rely on a four or five paragraph case study. The study is treated as an example to be discussed within the framework of prior readings and is used to test the analytical skills of the student and to explore the relation between the general and the particular. But one pressing problem with a 'case summary' is the discrepancy between its description and its reality.[6] The palpable complexity of real life situations seems to recede in the text book overview of such cases – hence the attempt to introduce reality into the context of case studies through the thoughtful use of interactive multimedia.

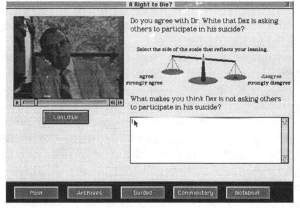

The CD-ROM provides flexible navigation through the central, and often competing, issues of the case. In the Guided Inquiry section, the users take a semi-Socratic tour from the bare facts to a confrontation with the patient, the doctors and the other principals over the issues of Medical Professionals' Obligations, Pain of

Figure 2. After listening to a doctor's perspective on one aspect of the case, the user is queried as to his or her opinion and reasons for agreeing or disagreeing with the stated position.

Treatment, Quality of Life, and Patient's Rights and Capacities. At the end, a decision must be made as to whether Dax should have his request or not. Final sequences are determined on the basis of this recommendation.

An Archive section contains video sections on the principals and main issues as well as descriptions of other cases (e.g. Karen Quinlin) and recent State and Federal court decisions on issues like physician-assisted suicide.

The program on Dax's case serves as an example of the kind of mediated, yet engaged environment that goes beyond the simple case summary and allows one to explore perspectives and issues that are involved 'at ground level.' In doing so, it provides a counterbalance to a curriculum often over loaded with theory and exemplars incapable of coming to terms with the reality of, for example, the conflicts of persons and principles that can arise in today's hospital environment. The program thus touches the very core of how we might go about teaching ethics and argues that we need these 'sweaty bicycle rides' along with our cooler reflections from on high.[7]

As with many innovations in curricular design, a new approach in one area can lead to new approaches in other areas. One of the recent changes in ethical theory advocates a 'conversational turn' in moral decision making. It explores a 'dialogical' approach to dealing with hard cases and changing societal structures. With echoes of John Dewey's pragmatism, writers such as Habermas and Rawls speak of the 'public use of reason' as evidenced in an open and informed conversation by diverse members of a community. Norms and policy procedures need as many perspectives as possible to ensure the fairness of decisions and such perspectives need to be rich with detail to ensure that justice is done to the voices that are heard or represented. In this regard, the richness of the CD-ROM fits nicely with the emerging richness of Web-based communication environments. In fact, Carnegie Mellon's Center for the Advancement of Applied Ethics is creating multimedia web-pages for case-based moral reasoning. These pages will include a network-based, hypermedia page on the Case of Dax Cowart and built-in communication links (for postings and commentary). The page will form part of a hypermedia course syllabus and will expand upon the meaning and use of the World Wide Web as a 'laboratory for moral reasoning.' It is hoped that other case studies from around the world would be 'added' to these pages to form a radial taxonomy of 'hard cases' in Medical Ethics. Such an environment would facilitate the ability to gain experience ('clinical rounds in ethics') in ways that traditional methods preclude. Theoretical foundations for this use of interactive multimedia include works by Jonsen and Toulmin (*The Abuse of Casuistry*) and Mark Johnson (*Moral Imagination: Implications of Cognitive Science for Ethics*).

A history of logic, broadly construed, branches off from two sources in Aristotle. His *Categories, On Interpretation,* and the *Prior* and *Posterior Analytics* form the foundation for a 'technical logic' that culminates in the advances of mathematical logic during the 19th and 20th centuries. His *Topics, On Sophistical Refutation,* and the *Rhetoric* form the foundation for an informal logic that reached its early height in the works of Cicero. The Roman orator, in his *Topica* and *De inventione,* emphasized the role of reason and argument in forensic dispute and with that the need to grasp how an argument is constructed and what both its weak and strong points are. Stephen Toulmin's *Uses of Argument* marks a 20th Century philosophical appreciation of this move in 'informal logic.' In his Introduction he writes:

"Logic is concerned with the soundness of the claims we make – with the solidity of the grounds we produce to support them, the firmness of the backing we provide for them...Logic (we may say) is generalized jurisprudence. Arguments can be compared with law-suits, and the claims we make and argue for in extra-legal contexts with claims we made in the courts, while cases we present in making good each kind of claim can be compared with each other," [Toulmin, 1958, 7].

Roger Schank's recent work at the Institute for the Learning Sciences builds upon this branch of logic with multimedia projects in "Evidence-Based Reporting." The strategy of the project is to create a goal-based scenario in which students are given the task of an 'advisor' in a complex and evolving social policy situation [Schank, 1994a, 429-453]. The user must construct a report that will analyze the situation and take into account the conflicting views of a panel of experts. For example, one project places the user in the midst of a "Crisis in Kosova" (modeled upon Bosnia). In the course of the investigation, a panel of experts can be called upon to offer opinions, opinions that differ from one another and that are cross-linked in a hypermedia database. The student must weigh the opinions and evidence under the pressure of offering concrete advice to the President. The program utilizes various kinds of tools to aid the user in composing the report and has a diagnostic utility which can evaluate quality of evidence used in support of the advice given.[8]

In one scenario, a student might claim that the 'Full Court Press' option will have a negative effect on the World Stability goal. He has collected some evidence for this from Madeline Robbins, one of the advisors, who thinks the Full Court Press option violates the UN Charter and that violating the UN Charter is bad in the long run. But another advisor, Michael Pritzker, disagrees with this position by saying that the 'Full Court Press' option is actually good for world stability because it punishes aggression. The student must now weigh the claims against one another and suggest a course of action.

347

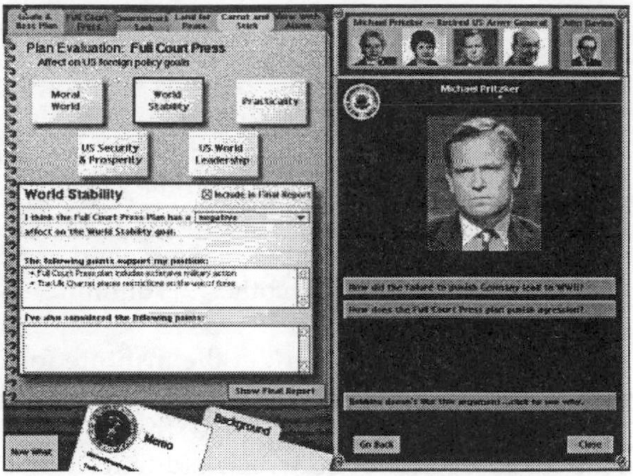

Figure 3. This example shows a number of features in the program. One item, a memo, lists foreign policy goals that the student uses to rate each policy option. Advisors can speak up when they disagree with something the student has said.

The software behind this program utilizes indexed hypermedia and a query program based on the metaphor of ' conversation with a group of experts.' As such, the program comes close to modeling real-world decision making in a manner that might prove useful to future 'critical reasoning' applications.

IV

It might be helpful to note some general themes that run through the three examples given. Each project combines experience with narrative: the experience of artworks and art puzzles with the story of Han van Meegeren; the experience of a hospital ward and moral conflict with the story of Dax Cowart; and the experience of a political crisis with the story of 'Kosova.'

Each of these situations combines a topical area with *interactive* engagement in real decision-making and each relies on a *multimedia* horizon in which stories play a pivotal role. Each does so, furthermore, in a manner that focuses on argument, experience, and narrative.

With emphasis on the narrative strand, Walter Fisher writes that "the narrative paradigm can be considered a dialectical synthesis of two traditional strands that recur in the history of rhetoric: the argumentative, persuasive theme and the literary, aesthetic stream. The narrative paradigm implies that human communication should be viewed as historical as well as situational, as stories or accounts competing with other stories or accounts purportedly constituted by good reasons, as rational when the stories satisfy the demands of narrative probability and narrative fidelity, and as inevitably moral inducements," [Fisher, 1987, 58].

Mark Johnson, arguing for a 'cognitive science of moral understanding,' states that "there is abundant empirical evidence that narrative is a fundamental mode of understanding, by means of which we make sense of all forms of human action....Narrative is not just an explanatory device, but is actually constitutive of the way we experience things," [Johnson, 1993, 11]. For Johnson, 'stories are our most basic contact with rational explanation' and thus form a key role in our ability to reason well about the matters before us.

In Martha Nussbaum's work, this narrative strand is tied to Aristotelian *phroneisis* and to the belief that education in the fullest sense must cultivate 'citizens who are perceivers.' "Where the teaching of moral reasoning itself is concerned, the Aristotelian conception will strongly endorse recent American efforts to make this a central part of education in medicine, law, business, and in undergraduate education more generally....The sort of moral reasoning course recommended by Aristotle will be clear, well argued, theoretically rich. But it will also make large demands on upon the imagination and the emotions. It will be very far from a course in formal decision theory....At every stage," she continues, "the student would continue to refine her abilities to reflect and perceive in and about concrete cases..." [Nussbaum, 1990, 103-104].

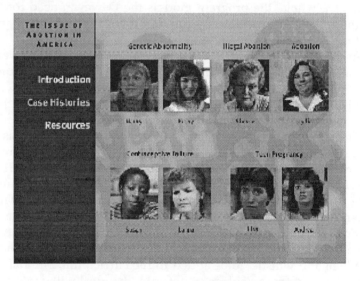

Figure 4. Menu to an archive of case studies.

One of the most significant points about philosophical research into multimedia is that it has been able to combine and extend recent work in rhetoric, cognitive science, and ethics. For as Nussbaum completes her sentence above with the phrase "perhaps again through continued contact with the works of literature and history," we may now add 'and philosophically grounded works of interactive multimedia.'

349

The "call of stories" that runs through the comments by Fisher, Johnson and Nussbaum is explicitly sought in the program, *The Issue of Abortion in America* [Routledge, 1997/98]. Extending Roger Wertheimer's request to understand the argument of abortion from within the viewpoints held by the various interlocutors of the debate,[9] this program uses interactive multimedia to capture those Rortyan 'thick descriptions' that underscore the personal struggles behind the political rhetoric of the abortion controversy.

Starting with a taxonomy of circumstances conditioning the possibility of terminating a pregnancy (such as rape, failed contraception, fetal abnormality), the program enters the life histories of individuals and couples struggling with their decisions. Through detailed analysis of the various positions that people hold, the user experiences the complex nature of the problem as part of the process of coming to a reasoned opinion about each of the general circumstances. The program also contains sections on the historical, legal, and medical dimensions of the issue as well as overviews of religious and philosophical perspectives and positions in Common Ground movements. Taken as a whole, the program models the Deweyan need for 'open and informed' conversations by providing both factual detail and access to the experiences of others.

As 'formal logic' became the first area of philosophy software, so 'informal logic' has become the first area for interactive multimedia work in philosophy. Certainly more areas will appear (e.g., vision models in android epistemology), but, as for now, multimedia has already made its mark by expanding the field beyond its standard textbook recitation of argument identification and argument analysis.

Just as the interplay between casuistical methods and principled responses requires the kinds of programs like *A Right to Die? The Dax Cowart Case*, more generally speaking, the interplay that warrants our move from data to claim requires a sensorium rich with detail and human complexity. Indeed, this is precisely the kind of 'theater' that practical reason demands if it is to be realistically honed and tested. Viewed in light of the requirements of practical reason, multimedia is not a 'bell and whistle' to be added to the curriculum, but a *necessary augmentation* of those fields in philosophy that deal with areas such as ethics, aesthetics, and critical thinking.

NOTES

[1] An outline for this chapter was presented at the Central Division meeting of the APA [April, 1996]. Part of this piece first appeared in Syllabus Magazine [September, 1996].

[2] The phrase 'interactive videodisc' has given way to terms like 'interactive multimedia' and 'hypermedia.' The latter refers to the 'multimedia links' that now exemplify the cyberspace of the World Wide Web. Ideas for hypertext and hypermedia go back to Ted Nelson's quixotic *Computer Lib*. First published in 1974, the book has been reissued by Microsoft Press, Redmond WA [1987].

[3] In the late 1980s EDUCOM (a consortium of colleges and universities advocating the use of technology) sponsored a number of national competitions in support of educational computing. The two awards that CDEC won were for *A Right to Die? The Case of Dax Cowart* [1989] and *Art or Forgery? The Strange Case of Han van Meegeren* (1990). A CD-ROM version of Dax's Case is now published by Routledge.

[4] This is the pedagogical premise behind *Puzzles About Art: An Aesthetics Casebook*.

[5] In preparing this videodisc for publication, we confronted the troublesome task of copyright acquisition. While no museum of the 16 that we contacted prohibited our use of an image, many had vastly different criteria for the use of their images. The bureaucratic detail was most time consuming and poses, perhaps, the greatest impediment to any project that seeks an art image database involving more than 50 sources.

[6] See K. Danner Clouser [1993]: "Trying out one's theory on real situations, thick with details, is very different from the philosopher's typical hypothetical case, which, if not simply invented, is so highly abstracted from real circumstances that only enough details remain to defend selectively the particular point the philosopher wants to make thereby. His or her use of cases is much more to *illustrate* theory than to test it. But when *solving* the moral problem is the main point, the relentlessness of the details becomes readily apparent. There is no refuge; there is one quagmire after another; retreating to the theory is not a viable option."

[7] Extensive bibliographic support for this thesis is included in the Teacher's Guide that accompanies the multiple user version of the Dax Cowart CD. In regard to the case-based approach of the program, see Kevin Ashley and Matthew Keefer [1996, 483-488].

[8] An authoring tool is being developed by ILS to facilitate others in creating hypermedia goal-based scenarios. See Same Architecture New Domain (SAND): An Alternative Methodology for Building High-Quality Reusable Tutoring Systems (contact: Menachem Jona <jona@ils.nwu.edu>). Also note the recent work in creating 'intelligent' multimedia indexing at CMU's the Infomedia Project (presented by Scott Stevens at the 1996 CAP conference): URL = http://www.informedia.cs.cmu.edu/.

[9] "By an argument I do not mean a concatenation of deathless propositions, but something with two sides that you have with someone, not present to him; not something with logical relations alone, but something encompassing human relations as well. We need to understand the argument in this fuller sense, for if we don't understand the human relations, we won't understand the logical ones either," [Roger Wertheimer, 1971, 67].

REFERENCES

Ashley, Kevin and Matthew Keefer (1996) "Ethical Reasoning Strategies and Their Relation to Case-Based Instruction: Some Preliminary Results," *18th Annual Conference of the Cognitive Science Society*, July 1996.

Battin, Fisher, Moore and Silvers. (1989) *Puzzles About Art: An Aesthetics Casebook*. St. Martin's Press.

Cavalier, R. and Carrier (1989) *Leonardo*, 22 (2).

Cavalier, R. and Dexheimer (1989) "ICEC: A Collaborative Effort to Ad-vance Educational Computing, 1983-1989," *Academic Computing*, November 1989.

Clouser , K. Danner (1993) *Hastings Center Report*, Special Supplement, 25 (6): S11.

Covey, Preston (1992) *Art or Forgery?* Intellimation. Foreword to the Manual.

Fisher, Walter (1987) *Human Communication as Narration: Toward a Philosophy of Reason, Value, and Action*. University of South Carolina Press.

Johnson, Mark (1993) *Moral Imagination: Implications of Cognitive Science for Ethics*. University of Chicago Press.

Nussbaum, Martha (1990) "The Discernment of Perception: An Aristotelian Conception of Private and Public Rationality," *Love's Knowledge*. Oxford University Press.

Schank, R.C. (1994a) "Goal-Based Scenarios: A Radical Look at Education," *The Journal of the Learning Sciences*, 3. [Special thanks for Michael Korcuska who gave a presentation on this project at the Eastern Division APA, April 1996.]

Toulmin, Stephen (1958) *The Uses of Argument*. Cambridge University Press.

Wertheimer, Roger (1971) "Understanding the Abortion Argument", *Philosophy & Public Affairs*, 1 (1): 67-95.

TEACHING PHILOSOPHY WITH MULTIMEDIA

JOHN L. FODOR

Introduction

In the following paper, I offer some comments on multimedia; suggest how to integrate multimedia into philosophy classes; and provide a criterion for selecting pedagogical multimedia software.

General Comments on Multimedia

Despite the current hype, the press attention, and promises of epiphany over computer-based interactive multimedia, we should not succumb to the idea that multimedia is a new phenomenon. Indeed, multimedia has been with us for quit some time — since before recorded history! Take, for example, the cave paintings of Lascaux; these paintings were produced as part of an elaborate multimedia ritual. Some cultures are steeped in multimedia to this day. Traditional dance in Bali, for example, makes use of costumes, masks, music and choreography in a complex story-telling/teaching process.

Modern technology, therefore, has not created multimedia; rather, modern technology has redefined it. Modern technology has also provided us with new media, such as audio recordings, photographs, movies, video, CD-ROMs, and Virtual Reality. And modern technology has broadened our access to an increasing number of multimedia events.

Teaching Philosophy with Multimedia

Let me suggest a few ways of using multimedia to teach philosophy. For my examples, I will draw from the CD-ROM *Introduction to Computer Ethics* [Bynum and Fodor, 1996] and my experiences with it when I taught computer ethics (The classroom I used was equipped with four large monitors which were connected to a computer).

1. Multimedia as a "Teaser"
At the beginning of a class, I would select a short piece — such as a few minutes of a video clip — in order to introduce the students to a problem. Most often, such a dramatic introduction will hold their at-

354

tention and allow them to fix upon the subject. For example, on the day I taught professional responsibility, I started class by showing a video clip (featuring Donald Gotterbarn) which highlighted the events surrounding the Aegis Radar disaster. This example pinpointed the problems of professional responsibility, while the extreme tragedy surrounding the incident held the students' interest.

This idea of using multimedia as a "teaser" can be expanded to other classes. If the medium you choose is current, and something with which the students are familiar, then the results are even more powerful. For example, if you are about to discuss love in your ethics class, you may consider briefly listening to a selection from Julee Cruise's *The Voice of Love* CD. Or, if you are teaching political philosophy and are about to discuss social equity, you may consider briefly listening to Labi Siffre's *Nothing's Gonna Change*. And so on.

2 Multimedia for Conceptual Clarity

Often it is difficult to verbally convey a sense of large areas, topics, or fields. Multimedia allows you to expand the presentation of your ideas, as well as providing for conceptual clarity. For example, it was easy for me to show the students what areas we were going to cover during the entire semester by merely clicking on the "map" feature of the CD-ROM. At this point in the CD, all of the various topics were displayed. I used the graphical map from the CD as a conceptual map for the students to follow.

You can use overhead projectors, slides, chalkboards, videos to achieve similar results. By using a variety of pedagogical technologies in your class, you also allow students with different learning styles to grasp materials. This is particularly true with younger students. Perhaps as a result of MTV, students now are more visually oriented than before. By introducing visuals into your curriculum, you may make it easier for them to understand the teaching goals.

3. Multimedia to Bring Experts to Class

Few of us are leading authorities on all the topics we teach. However, with multimedia, we can bring experts into the classroom, at our convenience. Ideas can be developed by such experts recorded on some medium. For example, early in the semester, when I focused on the history of computer ethics, I used a video clip from the CD-ROM which featured Walter Maner. Maner was the person who coined the term *computer ethics*. The video clip showed him discussing what went through his mind at the time he came up with the term.

This classroom experience was valuable because it provided a primary source of information. The students could hear straight from Maner what issues and concerns vexed him as he developed a curriculum and coined the term "computer ethics".

Of course by using experts in such a way, I am not undermining the role or importance of the teacher in the classroom. Rather, such media merely offer the teacher extensive repositories of information. And if used wisely, they can complement one's teaching style.

Integrated Media not Multimedia

Given that there are so many kinds of media available from which to choose, one should be guided by the following maxim:

> Multimedia should be integrated media.

(Integrated media, as defined by Art Johnson of Harvard University Graduate School of Education) In other words, the media that you choose should be coordinated in such a way that all of the parts work together toward the instructional objective(s). The mere combination or juxtaposition of media elements does not guarantee successful transfer of knowledge. This suggestion goes hand in hand with the way(s) in which you are going to use the media .(See below)

Settings for Multimedia

There are at least four ways in which media can be used.

1. Class Lecture
The first, I have described above; namely, as part of a class lecture.

2. Class Supplement
Next, media — such as the CD-ROM *Introduction to Computer Ethics* — can be used as class supplements. For example, you may want the students to consult various portions of the CD on their own, as homework.

3. Independent Study
Elsewhere I have discussed the interesting intersection of artificial intelligence, virtual reality, and good pedagogical software [Fodor, 1996]. I described such a confluence as providing the ingredients for a *Virtual Learning Environment.* In such a place, education would be tailored to the learning style of the individual user. Furthermore, in such an environment, information would be provided, thoughtful practice elicited, informative feedback given, and motivation generated [I draw these four points from Perkins, 1992, Ch. 3].

But even now, before virtual learning environments are fully developed, good software can be used for independent study. Students can learn at their own pace. Furthermore, students with various disabilities can use programs that are universally accessible (Such programs allow persons with various disabilities to access them).

4. Research Tool
Not only students, but scholars and researchers too can use good multimedia. For example, good integrated media will have repositories of references, articles, bibliographies, glossaries and live links to the World-Wide-Web. These tools will be invaluable to scholars and researchers.

Success of Multimedia in Teaching

Even though the prospects of pedagogical media are inviting, there is much debate over the effectiveness of multimedia in learning. This debate will be settled when enough empirical data has been collected and analyzed. Then, I believe, we will find that the media one uses *are* crucial in determining learning effectiveness. I agree with Donald Norman who says,

> technology poses a mind-set, a way of thinking about it and the activities to which it is relevant, a mind-set that soon pervades those touched by it, often unwittingly, often unwillingly. The more successful and widespread the technology, the greater its impact upon the thought patterns of those who use it, and consequently, the greater its impact upon all of society [Norman, 1993, 243].

Consequently, careful attention should be paid to selecting multimedia for class use. Multimedia should be evaluated in terms of its ability to create thinking environments where *retention* of knowledge is targeted, and where the *active* use of knowledge is elicited (i.e., knowledge about the subject matter which is generated by the user). A good litmus test — when considering multimedia — is to ensure that the knowledge which is transferred by the multimedia instrument will not, "just sit there but [will] function richly in people's lives to help them understand and deal with the world." [Perkins, 1992, 5]

An important collateral goal, in evaluating educational multimedia products, is that they provide sufficient motivation for the user to move beyond the content provided in the multimedia instruments.

As educators, our relationships to new technologies in general — and to multimedia in particular — will depend on how we see education. We can view education as a regulation of the process of coming to share in the social consciousness, as described by John Dewey; or as the idea of following one's interests passionately until they expand into ever widening adjacent fields, as described by Alvin Johnson; or as any one of countless other perspectives. The theory we adopt, will

357

determine whether or not we incorporate multimedia into our curricula.

Choosing to use multimedia as part of our pedagogy, then, depends very much on how we see our roles as educators. To a large measure, this means defining where we stand ideologically on the didactic-constructivist continuum. To use — or not to use — multimedia, depends, in part, on whether we see ourselves as a sage on the stage, or as a guide on the side.

REFERENCES

Bynum, Terrell Ward and John L. Fodor (1996) *Introduction to Computer Ethics.* Research Center on Computing and Society. Southern Connecticut State University.

Fodor, John L. (1996) "AI, Virtual Reality and Good Pedagogy" presented at the American Philosophical Association Central Division Meetings in Chicago, IL, April 1996.

Norman, Donald. (1993) *Things that Make us Smart.* New York: Addison-Wesley .

Perkins, David. (1992) *Smart Schools.* New York: The Free Press.

RESOURCES IN ETHICS ON THE WORLD WIDE WEB

LAWRENCE M. HINMAN

The last few years have brought an explosion of material available on the World-Wide-Web. Some of this relates directly to ethics, while other ancillary material offers invaluable support for those interested in contemporary moral issues. Let's begin by looking at some of the resources that relate directly to ethics, and then turning to a consideration of other, supplementary resources. I will conclude with a few remarks on how these resources can be utilized in teaching contemporary moral problems courses.

Ethics Centers

Ethics centers on the World Wide Web typically offer a rich set of resources that combine the specific concerns of the center with the advantages of the web. Here are a few examples which typify the possibilities of the web-oriented center. This survey is by no means exhaustive, and new site are continuing to come on-line.

One of the most extensive sites for ethics on the web is to be found at the *Centre for Applied Ethics* at the University of British Columbia. The web site has been set up by Chris MacDonald, a graduate student at UBC. The site features working papers from the Centre, schedules for lectures, information about the Centre, and — most extensive of all — a guide to applied ethics resources on the web, divided into sections on Biomedical & Health Care Ethics, Business Ethics, Com-puter & Information Ethics, Environmental Ethics, Ethical/Moral Decision Making, Media Ethics, Professional Ethics, Science and Tech-nology Ethics, and Miscellaneous. There is also an extensive list of codes of professional ethics. This is one of the most helpful guides on the web, and the best place to start a research project on any of the topics covered by this site. There is also a section on "Featured Applied Ethics Web Sites," which highlights and describes a particular web site at irregular intervals.

The *Center for the Advancement of Applied Ethics* [http://www. lcl.cmu.edu/CAAE/Home/CAAE.html] at Carnegie Mellon University is "a research and development environment that focuses on teaching people practical methods for analyzing and responding to real ethical problems. The Center's members combine knowledge and experience from different areas: interactive multimedia, business and professional ethics, and conflict resolution." It contains information about Project THEORIA and other multimedia interactive projects for experiential learning in ethical issues. Of particular interest is the link to "A Right to Die? Case of Dax Cowart," [http://www.lcl.cmu.edu/CAAE/Home/Multimedia/THEORIA.html][1] an interactive CD-ROM by David Andersen, Robert Cavalier, and Preston K. Covey.

The *Center for Bioethics* [http://www.med.upenn.edu/~bioethic/] at the University of Pennsylvania is a rich and very well structured resource. Its opening screen offers visitors options to learn more about the Center, to learn about its faculty, to see an introduction to bioethics by Glenn McGee and Art Caplan and other resources in "Bioethics for Beginners," to connect to the Global Conversation on Ethics and Genetics, the AMA, and to a "Fireside Chat: Genetics and Ethics Internet Course". This site also contains an excellent list of journals, networks, and bioethics associations in the U.S. and Canada. The papers which are available on the Ethics and Genetics page are strong philosophical pieces with solid and incisive commentaries. This is a superb site, exceptionally well presented and rich with content.

The *MacLean Center for Clinical Medical Ethics* [http://ccme-mac4.bsd.uchicago.edu/CCME.html] at the University of Chicago offers ethics consultation and ethics education for the University of Chicago Medical School and its hospitals as well as the larger community. In addition to this, it has a superb set of links to bioethics resources, end of life issues, medical resources, legal resources, and health care reform. Anyone researching any of these topics can save countless hours by beginning with this site.

The *National Center for Genome Resources* [http://www.ncgr.org/gpi/Index.html] (NCGR) in Santa Fe, New Mexico offers an excellent selection of resources. This includes "Genetic Odyssey: A Monthly Exploration of Genetic Topics." Past topics include Biotechnology and Food Production, Colon Cancer, Diabetes, Genetic Cloning, Genetic Privacy, Breast Cancer and BRCA 123, and Alzheimer's Disease and Genetics. It also contains an extensive set of educational resources, including links to some of the Kennedy Institute's Scope Notes Series and its Bibliography of Bioethics, and guides to other web sites dealing with genetic research and applications. There is also an excellent collection of links to resources dealing with the social implications of genetic technologies.

Ethics Center for Engineering and Science [http://web.mit.edu/ethics/www/], directed by Caroline Whitbeck at MIT, hosts a very interesting and well-developed web site that offers extensive resources in research ethics, engineering ethics cases, moral leaders, ethics in a corporate setting, ECSEL Information and Resources for Reducing the

Barriers to Minorities & Women in Engineering, Ethics Codes and Guidelines, selected on-line essays, and instructional resources. Although this site only began in 1996, it is already very "deep" in the sense that there are several layers of material present under each major heading.

Supported by an NSF grant, the Ethics Center has as its mission "to provide engineers, scientists, science and engineering students with resources useful for understanding and addressing ethically significant problems that arise in their work life. The Center is also intended to serve teachers of engineering and science students who want to include discussion of ethical problems closely related to technical subject as a part of science and engineering courses, or in free-standing subjects in professional ethics or in research ethics for such students."

One of the hallmarks of the site is the use of the case-study method. The Research Ethics section, for example, contains five subdivisions, and there are ten excellent case studies and scenarios under just one of those subdivisions.

Perhaps the most innovative feature of this site is its section on "Moral Leaders." Although at present there are only three profiles here — Rachel Carson, Roger Boisjoly, and William LeMessurie — this promises to be an excellent set of case studies in what one might call "the virtuous scientist." The Center also publishes an on-line Newsletter at irregular intervals.

The *Center for Environmental Philosophy* [http://www.cep.unt.edu/] at the University of North Texas is the home of the journal *Environmental Ethics*. Under the leadership of Eugene C. Hargrove, the Center publishes both *Environmental Ethics* and a book series entitled Environmental Ethics Books. It also runs workshops and conferences and promotes graduate and postgraduate work in environmental ethics. On the Web, it makes information about its programs available and provides the tables of contents for all issues of *Environmental Ethics* and gives short descriptions of the books in its series. Also at the University of North Texas is *the International Society for Environmental Ethics* [http://www.cep.unt.edu/ISEE.html]. Its Newsletter is available on-line, and it offers an excellent collection on bibliographical resources. There is a section on "Selected Books and Articles," which contains pages on anthologies, systematic works, ecotheology, and other subject bibliographies. The ISEE Bibliography is fully searchable and very well constructed. This is a superb resource. It also has a Syllabus Project, containing numerous links to several dozen environmental ethics courses and environmental philosophy courses.

The *Markkula Center for Applied Ethics at Santa Clara University* provides an excellent example of how a web site can be used to bring together various campus activities and link them to a larger national context. The site contains the full collection of *Issues in Ethics*, the quarterly publication of this Center. Several case studies are presented, and visitors are given the opportunity both to make comments on the cases and to read the comments of others. It also has a very good set of links to other sites, including very helpful reviews of their content. There is also plenty of information about SCU's course offerings on ethics, conferences, etc. This is a very well done model of how a web site can be used to pull together a number of different aspects of a campus's concern for ethics. All of this is presented in an excellent format with a very well crafted web interface.

Ethics Updates [http://ethics.acusd.edu].[2] This is a site which I established in 1995 simply to keep the bibliographical essays in a couple of my ethics books up-to-date. One thing led to another, as it usually does on the Web, and gradually it has developed into a set of web-based resources on a series of contemporary moral issues (abortion, euthanasia, death penalty, etc.) and on topics in moral theory (utilitarianism, Kant, Aristotle, etc.). In organizing material, I have continually asked myself what students (and, secondarily, instructors) would find helpful in approaching a given topic. I have tried whenever possible to provide links to web-based resources of very high quality. In addition, there are resources on journals in ethics, on-line books, syllabi, etc. Most recently, I have added a series of Ethics Discussion Forums, which I hope to use as a forum for international discussions of contemporary moral issues.

Codes of Ethics. For a good collection of codes of ethics as well as material on a variety of areas in applied ethics (including military ethics, movie and TV ethics, sports ethics, governmental ethics), see *Ethics on the World Wide Web* [http://www5.fullerton.edu/les/ethics_list.html] at the School of Communications at California State University, Fullerton. For codes of ethics relating to engineering and science, see those collected at *the Ethics Center for Engineering and Science at MIT* [http://web.mit.edu/ethics/www/index.html. The codes themselves are at http: //web.mit.edu /ethics/www/codes. html]. *The MacLean Center for Clinical Medical Ethics* at the University of Chicago site maintains an excellent collection of clinical codes, physician codes and oaths, nursing codes and oaths, and other professions' codes of ethics [http://ccme-mac4.bsd.uchicago.edu/ CCMEPolicies/index# codes]. It also contains resources on religious bioethics in Islam, Buddhism, Judaism and Christianity.

On-Line Journals

Since 1994 several journals have appeared on-line. Some are electronic versions of their printed counterparts; some are new creations that happen to be on the web but are still traditional in their structure and format; and a few are web-based creations that utilize the unique strengths of the web to do things that would not have been possible in traditional print media.

The Advantages of Web-Based Publishing

What possibilities are available on web-based journals that are not available in the traditional print medium? Web-based journals have several possible advantages. First, because there are no paper or printing costs, the costs of production are significantly less. Production costs are basically no more than the costs of producing a computer file.

Second, distribution is faster and cheaper. Electronic versions of journals may either be distributed by e-mail or else posted on a web site where the articles can be read or downloaded. If they are sent out by e-mail, the cost is exceedingly low — simply the cost of an e-mail account. If the journal is posted on a web site, then there is the additional cost of maintaining a web site (including a twenty-four hour a day Internet connection). In actuality, these associated costs are usually absorbed by the universities hosting the journal. The distribution of electronic journals is also faster, since there is no printing time or mailing time (which can be considerable with fourth class postage). Once a computer file of a journal issue is finished, publishing it takes only a few minutes or, at most, hours.

Third, length of articles is no longer a major issue. It's unclear whether this should be listed as an advantage or a disadvantage, but there is little doubt it is both. Text occupies very little room, in contrast to graphics, audio, or video. When the entire OED was put on CD-ROM, the text occupied less than half the disk — the search engine took up the other half.

Fourth, articles can have more robust links to other resources. As resources become increasingly available on the web, it is possible to replace traditional footnotes with hyperlinks which, when clicked, take the reader to the source to which the footnote refers. Thus a footnote to Plato's *Apology*, for example, might take a reader to the full text of Plato's dialogue, highlighting the relevant passage. If the reference is to the superb Perseus Project at Tufts University, the reader merely has to click to switch from the English translation to the Greek text. Similarly, a reference to death penalty statistics can take the reader to a site, such as the one at Northern Illinois University, which contains a full set of such statistics. Then, as those statistics are updated, the reader will see statistics on the same issue that have appeared even after the original article was written.

Fifth, articles can contain discussion groups for each article that has been written. Ideally, when an article is available on a web site for a journal, there would be a link to a discussion forum that will allow readers to post commentaries on the article. For an excellent model of how this would work, see the articles available on Glenn McGee's Ethics and Genetics site [http://www.med.upenn.edu/~bioethic/ genetics.html]. Each article available there contains a discussion group for commentaries and rejoinders to that particular article.

Sixth, articles that are available in electronic form are easily stored and searched. Programs are available that quickly search an entire subdirectory (or an entire drive) for a specific word, making retrieval of important references very easy and quick. For example, for the past year I have been reading three newspapers — *The New York Times*, the *Los Angeles Times*, and the *Washington Post* — on-line. I save any interesting articles on a number of different topics such as abortion, the death penalty, right to die, and the like. If, for example, I want to find anything on Australia's right to die law, I simply search my hard drive's subdirectory on euthanasia for the word "Australia" and immediately have a list of all files that refer to Australia. Simple, efficient, and there's no printing ink on your fingers from clipping articles.

Finally, articles may contain links to the authors. Philosophers are increasingly developing their own home pages, and it is easy to put in a link to those. If an author does not have a home page, a simple link to an e-mail allows readers to send authors queries quickly and efficiently. Although there are some authors who would find it necessary to restrict the flow of such mail, most of us — myself included — do not have to worry that the volume of mail generated by our publications would be overwhelming! Such technology, however, does open up an important dimension for our work, for it allows authors to receive many more reactions to their work than would otherwise occur.

The Financial Issues

Although I have specified several of the ways in which web-based publishing saves money, the obvious problem here is that journals could well lose crucial revenue if their publications are distributed for free on the web or by e-mail. This is rarely a matter of reducing profits —journals in philosophy don't make profits — but of undermining the minimal funds necessary to keep the journal alive. Without financial support for editorial staff, offices, copying, mailing, etc., journals simply cannot function.

There are, I think, several ways in which the financial stability of a journal can be preserved while at the same time the benefits of web-based publishing can be realized. Let me sketch out two possible scenarios in this regard.

First, the danger of publishing a journal electronically is that no one will pay for it. One way of avoiding the resulting financial catastrophe would be to allow individuals to have an option for subscribing to a journal. Take, for example, a journal such as *Ethics*. An individual subscription costs $28 per year for APA members. Offer readers the option of an electronic subscription which would allow them to receive an e-mail version of the journal for a price equal to the regular price minus the actual cost of printing and postage. For the sake of the example, let's say that printing and postage costs equal fifteen dollars; then the cost of an e-mail subscription would be $13. In an arrangement such as this, the journal's revenues would not be decreased and individuals would be allowed to choose which medium they prefer. Furthermore, there may be individuals who would choose to subscribe by e-mail at the lower rate who do not presently subscribe at the higher, printed rate. If this is the case, revenues would actually increase.

Second, journals may be available on web sites that are password protected. Subscriptions could then just give a password which would allow individual access to the web site. To make this more appealing, one could have the web site provide tables of contents, perhaps even abstracts, available to all visitors and the full text available only to subscribers. This might even attract more subscriptions. Subscriptions could be handled either on an individual basis, as described earlier, or by institutions. Just as a university library now subscribes to a journal which is places on its shelves for access by all members of its community, so too a university could pay for web access to a journal for its members. Then anyone whose e-mail address ends in, for example, "acusd.edu" could have access to the journal site when that university (the University of San Diego) pays for an institutional subscription.

Both of these proposals allow possibilities for illegal distribu- tion — e-mail can be passed along, return e-mail addresses and even passwords can be faked or illicitly shared. It's an empirical question to determine how many people are trying to get free copies of ethics journals, but my hunch is that they're not clambering at the gates. Furthermore, the possibility of unauthorized reproduction is already present, though less convenient, through Xeroxing.

Example Journals

Journal of Buddhist Ethics [http://www.cac.psu.edu/jbe/jbe.html], which is co-edited by Charles Prebish and Damien Keown with Wayne Husted as Technical Editor, is an outstanding example of how well an on-line journal can be presented. The *Journal* contains original articles, book reviews, and assorted announcements. It is possible to subscribe to on-line delivery, or to read the journal on its web site. In addition to current and back issues of the *Journal*, the site contains scholarly resources on Buddhism, the Pali canon on-line, on-line conferences, and assorted other resources. The on-line conferences, which can last up to two weeks, are excellent examples of scholarly exchanges. The 1995 conference on "Buddhism and Human Rights" contained ten papers and probably several hundred messages. This is an excellent example of how a web site and e-mail can be used to coordinate a virtual conference.

Online Journal of Ethics [http://condor.depaul.edu/ethics/ethg1. html], edited at DePaul University's Institute for Business and Professional Ethics, is devoted to business and professional ethics. Typical articles include "Macro and Micro: The Emerging Field of Organizational Ethics," by Charles M. Horvath; "Teaching Business Ethics Through Literature," by Jon M. Shepard, Michael G. Goldsby & Virginia W. Gerde; and "The Ethics of Handwriting Analysis in Pre-Employment Screening," by Daryl Koehn. Currently fewer than a dozen articles are available on-line.

Electronic Journal of Analytical Philosophy [http://www.phil.indiana.edu/ejap]. The first issue of the EJAP was published in 1993, and it was the first electronic journal in philosophy. The journal is edited by Craig de Lancey at Indiana University. Although it is not directly primarily toward ethics, it is a true web-based journal that provides full text of all articles on the web. Issue 3 (Spring, 1995) is devoted to the topic of justifying value in nature, and contains several articles that deal with issues in ethics.

Science and Engineering Ethics [http://www.cableol.co.uk/ opragen/]. Edited by Stephanie J. Bird (MIT) and Raymond Spier (Surrey University), this journal is published in paper format but tables of contents and abstracts are available on the web. The journal began in 1995, and provides very high quality articles on topics in engineering ethics and in teaching ethics to scientists and engineers.

BEARS

Philosophy, Plato taught us, is a conversation, and BEARS shows some of the potential that the web has for encouraging that conversation. When this conversation occurs in printed journals, however, the conversation usually proceeds at a snail's pace. It often takes a year or more for a reply to appear in a print journal, and the rejoinder may appear one or two issues after that. The promise of web-based communications has been that it could drastically reduce the amount of time between each contribution to the discussion.

BEARS, the Brown Electronic Articles Review Service in Moral and Political Philosophy [http://www.brown.edu/Departments/Philosophy /bears/ homepage.html], is edited by David Estlund and James Dreier at Brown University's Department of Philosophy. Initially, BEARS just provided on-line reviews of articles that had appeared in print journals. The reviews are of very high quality, and they focus on important articles. Bryan Van Norden, for example, has a review of Julia Annas's "Prudence and Morality in Ancient and Modern Ethics;" Paul Weithman reviews Cheshire Calhoun's "Standing for Something;" and Mark van Roojen has a review of Frank Jackson and Philip Pettit's "Moral Functionalism And Moral Motivation." Frank Jackson then provided a reply to van Roojen. The original article by Jackson and Pettit appeared in the January, 1995 issue of *The Philosophical Quarterly*; van Roojen's review appeared in March of the same year, and Jackson's reply in September. The is a good example of the way in which a web-based publication can facilitate philosophical dialogue.

This year the editors have taken this a step further, presenting several symposia on articles. In November, 1996, BEARS published a symposium on Ronald Dworkin's "Objectivity and Truth: You'd Better Believe It," which had appeared in *Philosophy & Public Affairs* in Spring 1996. The commentators were Simon Blackburn, Michael Otsuka, Nicholas Zangwill. In August, 1996, BEARS presented a symposium on Thomas Hurka's "Monism, Pluralism, and Rational Regret" [*Ethics,* April 1996] with contributions from Richard Brook, Brad Hooker, Robert Johnson, Michael Stocker, and Alison McIntyre. An added feature of this conversation is that a link is given to each participant's e-mail address so that the conversation can be continued on an individual basis.

A Model Website

Ethics and Genetics: A Global Conversation [http:// www. med. upenn .edu/~bioethic/genetics.html]. Glenn McGee, at the Center for Bioethics at the University of Pennsylvania, has led the way in creating a model web site, one that shows the true potential of this medium. McGee designed the first U.S. philosophy department web site while at the University of Massachusetts liberal arts college at Dartmouth, then convinced the University of Chicago to include an early version of the "ethics and genetics" experiment in the ENIAC of web philosophy, The Chicago Philosophy Project. At Penn, the ethics and genetics site has grown to be the best known of a ten-part bioethics/ philosophy of biology web program that includes a student section (Bioethics for Beginners), two list-servers (PHILCLUB, the international undergraduate philosophy list; and FIRESIDE CHAT, a new web-based philosophy of biology chat room), and a virtual library complete with direct access to all major philosophy search engines on the web. In the "ethics and genetics conversation," the dialogue model of philosophy emerges most clearly through the skillful use of web-based technology. This site is part journal, part discussion group — and combines the best of both. The full text of articles is available on-line for all to read (Currently there are eight articles available). Simply click on the title to see the full text of the article. Authors are listed, and a click on an author's name take you to that individual's home page, usually with an e-mail link, a list of publications, and even ordering information for that person's books. Finally, there is a discussion group for each article. Click on each and you can see the comments that participants have made on that particular article. There is an e-mail link for each contributor to the discussion, so a single click allows one to send e-mail to that person as well. One of the dangers of completely open discussion groups is that the level of knowledge of the participants can vary greatly. The Ethics and Genetics project has struck a nice balance in this regard. "Those with documented writing and research interests in genetics are encouraged to join the group's discussion faculty; students and others may serve as associate discussants." Thus anyone gets to read the discussion; many can be on the list server; and those with an appropriate background can participate. The "conversation" has so far served as the basis of or part of more than a dozen courses in the U.S., Australia, Israel, Great Britain, and Croatia. Special arrangements for web courses are available by contacting the Penn Center for Bioethics.

On-Line Philosophical Texts and Resources on Philosophers

One of the best collections on on-line philosophical texts is to be found at Carnegie-Mellon University. The Virtual Library of the University of Bristol maintains a collection of electronic texts [http://www.bris.ac.uk/Depts/Philosophy/VL/etexts.html]. Valdosta State University's index of Philosophy electronic texts [http://www.bris.ac.uk/Depts/Philosophy/VL/etexts.html]. Mary Mallery maintains a Directory of Electronic Text Centers at Rutgers University [http://www.ceth.rutgers.edu/info/ectrdir.html].

For those interested in classical Greek philosophy, the *Perseus Project* at Tufts University provides an incomparable resource and a model for how to do critical editions on the web. For any text available, readers can see an English translation, a transliteration of the original Greek, or — after downloading the appropriate font — the Greek text in the original characters. Clicking on a Greek word takes the reader to the Liddell-Scott Intermediate Greek Lexicon, an excellent classical Greek dictionary for scholars. Clicking on hyperlinks in the English translation takes the reader to a classical encyclopedia, which contains about three hundred articles written expressly for the Perseus Project as well as about 3,500 entries from Herodotus and Apollodorus and the Frazer edition of Pausanias. Where appropriate, the link will also take the reader to maps, sculpture, vases, coins, and architectural sites.

I hope that eventually there will be similar sites for other texts in the history of moral philosophy. For example, it would be wonderful to have a similar bilingual edition of Kant's works in moral philosophy, with a German critical edition and a look-up feature for any German word that not only gave standard German meanings (a la Duden or Wildhagen) but also indexed all other uses of that word by Kant. The English text could be linked so that a click on a word would show the reader what the original German term was, and hyperlinks to key secondary literature would provide readers with useful commentary. References given in footnotes to Kant's various works in article in *Kant-Studien* and in the *Ergnzungshefte*. Commentaries, such as

Wolff's and Paton's, could also be coordinated. Such a project would be massive but of great value to scholars.

Example resources include:

Aristotle

- *Eudemian Ethics,*[3] Perseus Project, Tufts University. English with Greek links.
- *Nichomachean Ethics,*[4] Hypertext at Perseus.
- *Nichomachean Ethics,*[5] W. D. Ross, trans. ASCI.
- *Politics,*[6] Hypertext. Perseus Project, Tufts University.
- *Politics,*[7] Jowett, trans. ASCI.
- *Rhetoric,*[8] Hypertext. Perseus Project, Tufts Univesity
- *Rhetoric,*[9] W. Rhys Roberts, trans. ASCI.
- *Virtues and Vices,*[10] Hypertext. Perseus Project. Tufts University.

Epictetus

- *The Discourses*[11]

Marcus Aurelius

- *Meditations,*[12] Long, trans.

Augustine

- *Confessions,*[13] Text, HTML, and pdf formats. Wheaton College.

Thomas Aquinas

- *Summa Theologica,*[14] Maintained by the English Dominican Province

Montaigne

- *Essays,*[15] Charles Cotton, trans. ASCI.

Hobbes

- *The Leviathan,*[16]

Locke

- *Second Treatise of Government,*[17]
- *A Letter Concerning Toleration,*[18] translated by William Popple

Hume

.. *Essays on Suicide & the Immortality of the Soul,*[19] Unauthorized
1783 Edition.

.. *An Enquiry Concerning Human Understanding,*[20]

.. *The Natural History of Religion,*[21]

.. *My Own Life,*[22]

John Stuart Mill

.. *On Liberty,*[23]

.. *The Subjection of Women,*[24]

.. *Utilitarianism,*[25]

.. *Autobiography,*[26]

.. "Speech in Favor of Capital Punishment,"[27]

Mary Wollstonecraft

.. *Vindication of the Rights of Woman,*[28] 1792

Kant

.. *Critique of Practical Reason,* Abbott translation,[29]

.. *Fundamental Principles of the Metaphysics of Morals,* Abbott
translation,[30]

.. *Introduction to the Metaphysic of Morals,* Hastie translation[31]

.. *The Science of Right,* Hastie translation[32]

.. *Metaphysical Elements of Ethics,* Abbott translation[33]

.. *The Critique of Aesthetic Judgment,* hypertext edition[34]

.. *Critique of Judgment,* Meredith translation[35]

.. "What Is Enlightenment?"[36]

Steven Palmquist's site, "Kant on the Web," [http://www.hkbu.
edu.hk/~ppp/Kant.html] is an invaluable source of web-based Kant
resources, including electronic texts, lexical aids, Plamquist's own
Kant essays, syllabi of Kant courses, and links to other Kant-related
sites. The North American Kant Society maintains a web page with information on Kant-related conferences, etc [http://funnelweb.utcc.
utk.edu/~philosop/naks.html]. The University of Marburg also maintains a Kant site [http://www.fb03.uni-marburg.de/~kant/ welcome.
html].

Syllabi

Having an electronic syllabus for a course can be simply silly. There's
nothing more annoying that having to click on a computer and log
onto a network in order to look at a schedule that you could otherwise
consult if you simply opened a file folder or notebook in your briefcase

(Of course, this presumes that you can find the folder — all too often a false assumption in my own case!). If an electronic syllabus is to be genuinely useful, it must offer several improvements not available with the standard paper syllabus.

What might these advantages be? I see several possibilities. First, the syllabus might contain (through hyperlinks) the actual reading assignments themselves, not just a mention of what they are. Second, the syllabus might contain (again, through links) additional resources that could fall into the traditional category of "recommended readings," the kind of materials we often place on room reserve in the library for a particular course. Third, the syllabus might contain (again, through links) computer-based activities that are part of the course. In logic, links to specific computer-based homework exercises would be an obvious example. Fourth, the syllabus can also contain a link to a grade sheet, with students listed either by an alias or a student number. Finally, syllabi can contain links to discussion forums. Indeed, an assignment can be posting a position paper on a class discussion forum and responding to two other such position papers that have already been posted.

Stephen Darwall's Not-Yet-Cool Home Page [http://www-personal.umich.edu/~sdarwall] contains several syllabi which provide excellent examples of how ethics courses can be presented on the web. For example, Phil. 361, a course in Philosophical Ethics [http://www-personal.umich.edu/~sdarwall/Phil361.html], contains links to major works in ethics that are available on-line and on on-line course schedule [http://www-personal.umich.edu/~sdarwall/ Phil361.html] that not only contains the course assignments, study guides, etc., but also the outline of Darwall's lectures. In his course on Contemporary Moral Issues, Darwall has numerous links to web resources on specific topics (such as abortion and affirmative action) that supplement required readings. There is even an on-line version of the Prisoners' Dilemma that you can play in either cooperative or competitive mode [http://serendip.brynmawr.edu/~ann/pd.html] — a good example of the way a syllabus can integrate an activity. For another example of a syllabus in Political Philosophy that also builds in links to the course lectures and the readings, see James Schmidt's PO291: Introduction to Political Philosophy [http://software.bu.edu/POLISCI/JSCHMIDT/ PO291syl.html] at Boston University.

Additional Helpful Resources

In addition to the resources discussed above, which relate directly to ethics, there are a number of other resources on the Web that provide excellent supplementary materials to anyone working on contemporary moral issues. Here are a few of the most useful.

Court Decisions

Supreme Court. Most court decisions are easily available on the web. Supreme Court decisions since 1990 are available at the Cornell School of Law site [http://supct.law.cornell.edu/supct/], as well as 300 historic decisions (such as Roe v. Wade) prior to 1990. Many earlier decisions (7,400) are now on-line from FedWorld [http://www.fedworld.gov/supcourt/index.htm]. Both sites offer searches accord-ing to topic as well as case name or number. The Cornell site offers far better html formatting than the FedWorld site. FindLaw now offers all Supreme Court decisions back to 1937 [http://www.findlaw.com/].

In addition to the text of the Supreme Court decisions, audio recordings of the oral arguments are now available from Oyez Oyez Oyez [http://oyez.at.nwu.edu/oyez.html], a superb web site maintained at Northwestern University through a grant from the National Endowment for the Humanities. Students can hear the "give and take" of arguments before the Court in a way that had previously been either impossible or very difficult. The site uses RealAudio, a streaming audio server that plays at the same time that it downloads. Thus there is no need to wait a long time for a large file to download—just click and it will begin playing as it continues to download additional material. The RealAudio player, which works with most major web browsers, is available for free downloading. Listeners only need a sound card and a 14.4 connection for AM radio quality sound, 28.8 for CD quality sound. Further enhancements to this site are planned in the near future.

Several of these sites also contain additional resources on the court, such as biographical information about the Justices. In addition to these sources, the Washington Post maintains an excellent set of resources on the Court, especially its "Inside the Supreme Court" [http://www.washingtonpost.com/wp-srv/interact/longterm/horiz on/100996/court1.htm] by Joan Biskupic, the Post's legal correspondent.

U.S. Circuit Courts of Appeal. Recent U.S. Circuit Courts of Appeal decisions are also available on the web, although each circuit maintains its own decisions. A comprehensive list of links to the particular circuits is available from the Federal Judicial Center [http://www.fjc.gov/WWWlinks/govlinks.html]. The Federal Court Locator at Villanova University provides a map that displays the various federal districts [http://www.law.vill.edu/Fed-Ct/fedcourt.html]. Indeed, the Villanova Center for Information Law and Policy contains an excellent collection of government-related resources and links [http://www.law.vill.edu/].

Legislation

The best source of information about legislation on the national level is Thomas, the Web site of the United States Congress. It offers easy searching facilities, a topics index for the present and previous session of Congress, the full test of the Congressional Record since 1993, committee reports, and a few historical documents. In addition to this, it not only contains links to other branches of the federal government, but also state and local government information. Although it may not give you all the information you need, Thomas will probably point you in the correct direction.

News reports

Several of the major daily newspapers are now available on line, including the *New York Times* [http://www.nytimes.com/] the *Washington Post* [http://www.washingtonpost.com/], and the *Los Angeles Times* [http://www.latimes.com/HOME/]. In addition to this, *Time Magazine* [http://pathfinder.com/@@0Xu*CAYAeZjs1NWk/time/], CNN [http://www.cnn.com], and various other news organizations maintain web sites.

Among the monthly magazines, the *Atlantic Monthly* stands out in a class by itself. It provides a model of what web-based publishing should be like. Drawing on over a century of high quality articles, the editors of the on-line version of the Atlantic have put together a site of amazing strength. For example, it has a superb collection of original articles on race and related issues by Booker T. Washington, W. E. B. Du Bois, Frederick Douglass, Martin Luther King, Jr., as well as more recent articles by Claude Steele, Robert Coles, Daniel Moynihan, Nicholas Lemann, Elijah Anderson, Stanley Fish, Juan Williams, and Thomas Edsall.

The Boston Review, edited by Joshua Cohen, is now available on the Web (http://www-polisci.mit.edu/bostonreview/), and it is a superb resource for those interested in contemporary moral issues and contemporary social and economic policy. The Review regularly publishes very high quality pieces by first-rate philosophers on pressing moral issues, and those articles have the added advantage of being directed toward a general, well-educated audience instead of being written primarily for philosophers. In the summer, 1997 issue, for example, Frances Kamm has a typically well-argued piece on euthanasia, "A Right to Choose," and it is accompanied by Vivian Rotherstein's "Beyond The Call of Duty," a first person piece on the meaning of her mother's suicide. Judith Thomson had an excellent piece on abortion, and the Review-as it often does-has a number of replies, in this case by Philip L. Quinn, Donald Regan, Douglas Laycock, Drucilla Cornell,

Peter de Marneffe, and a rejoinder by Judith Jarvis Thomson. This is an excellent dialogue, and a model for students of reflective grappling with a difficult moral issue. A number of other excellent symposia are available on topics such as race, the responsibility of intellectuals, economic inequality, welfare and the like.

One of the best news resources on the web these days is Ray Suarez's "Talk of the Nation" on National Public Radio. Suarez offers the most intelligent talk radio program on national radio today. Many of his topics touch on contemporary moral issues such as the right to die, capital punishment, abortion, and gay rights. He often has philosophers as guests. For example, he has had three recent shows on euthanasia and physician-assisted suicide, and guests have included Margaret Battin, Ira Bylock, Dr. Timothy Quill, and Dr. Stephen Jamison; shows on reproductive technologies and cloning have included Art Caplan, Ruth Macklin and Glenn McGee. Again, these are available on RealAudio.

Finally, PBS's series *Frontline* has complemented its television programs with a series of web sites that contain both materials from a particular show and other, supplementary web-based resources. It has sites on Kevorkian and physician-assisted suicide, capital punishment and "Dead Man Walking," breast implants, the Holocaust, "Murder on 'Abortion Row'" the Tailhook issue and gender equity in the Navy, adoption, and smoking and the tobacco industry. All offer excellent complements to traditional text-based materials in a moral problems course.

Putting It All Together in the Classroom[37]

Taken together, these resources provide a powerful array of sources to complement traditional textbook materials. They can be employed like room-reserve materials have been used in the past, and students can be directed to them just as they used to be directed toward the reserve desk in the library.

Imagine you are offering a course in contemporary moral problems, and next week you intend to discuss the issue of euthanasia and end-of-life decisions. You would probably want to have your students read some court decisions. Both the appellate court and the Supreme Court decisions, *Quill v. Vacco* and *Compassion in Dying v. State of Washington* are available on the web as is the so-called "Philosophers' Brief" by Dworkin, Rawls, Nozick, Thomson and Scanlon, the brief by George Annas et al., and several other friend of the court briefs. Frances Kamm's "A Right to Choose," which contains an insightful analysis of the argument by Dworkin et al., is also available on the Boston Review site.[38] Or you might want your students to read a classic case such as *Cruzon v. Director, Missouri Department of Health* [1990]. On the web, student can even hear the oral arguments with Kenneth

Starr and William Colby as the principal attorneys. Legislative information is easily available, including the text of things such as the Oregon Death with Dignity Act and transcripts of hearings and the final report [June, 1995] of the Senate Special Committee on Euthanasia and Assisted Suicide. Statistical information about American attitudes toward physician-assisted suicide is also easily available. Various religious documents, including papal encyclicals, are also on-line. Codes of ethics, include religious codes for Islam, Buddhism, Christianity, and Judaism, are available from the MacLean Center for Clinical Medical Ethics at the University of Chicago. *Talk of the Nation* shows, hosted on NPR by Ray Suarez, are available on physician-assisted suicide, and include as guests Dr. Ira Bylock, Professor Margaret Battin, Dr. Herbert Hendin, and Dr. Stephen Jamison—all on RealAudio. *Frontline*, the PBS documentary series, has an excellent Web-based segment on Kevorkian, including RealAudio recordings from Kevorkian and three people who eventually were assisted in their death by him; there are also interviews with Dr. Timothy Quill and Professor Arthur Caplan. Ezekiel Emanuel's "Whose Right to Die?", which just appeared in *The Atlantic Monthly* in March, 1997, is also available in full-text for students to read on the web. Perhaps one of the readings in your course is from Ronald Dworkin's *Life's Dominion*; if so, you might well want to direct your students to read the review of that book by Laurence Tribe in the *New York Times Book Review*.[39]

The web is particularly useful for late-breaking issues. For example, when the case of Dolly the cloned sheep hit the news, I was able within two days to put on virtual reserve an extensive set of resources for students in my contemporary moral problem course.[40] In addition to several articles in The Washington Post, I was able to provide links to two *Talk of the Nation* Shows, which include interviews with Arthur Caplan, Director, Center of Bioethics and Trustee Professor of Bioethics, University of Pennsylvania; Gladys White, National Board of Ethics and Reproduction; Dr. Thomas Murray, Center for Bioethics at Case Western Reserve; Dr. Ruth Macklin, Albert Einstein College of Medicine; and Glenn McGee, University of Pennsylvania Center for Bioethics. In addition to this, I could post a link to an extensive bibliography on cloning at the Georgetown University Kennedy Center for Ethics as well as to several other articles dealing with cloning. A few days later, I could add a link to the *Time Magazine* issue on cloning, which included half a dozen different articles on cloning.

All of this takes time, of course, but it also takes time to Xerox the same material and bring it over to the library and put it on reserve. Moreover, the quality of what one is able to provide, especially the color photographs and the RealAudio recordings, are beyond what one could usually provide with Xerox copies. However, the mechanics of developing web pages have become increasingly easy, and now it is not much more difficult than word processing. Nor do such web pages have to be beautiful. They can simply consist of a title and a series of links. Many editors, such as Microsoft's FrontPage, even make this an easy task. As more material is placed on the Web, this will become an increasingly powerful tool.

NOTES

[1] This is a superb example of the power of CD-ROM-based interactive technology in teaching. Dax Cowart was a young man who suffered third degree burns over a large percentage of his body —and who pleaded to be allowed to die and to be helped in the process, since he was physically unable to end his own life. Instead, he underwent nine months of incredibly painful burn therapy, which saved his life but was accomplished against his will. David Andersen, Robert Cavalier, and Preston K. Covey has created this CD-ROM, and it is a felicitous collaboration. It is philosophically sophisticated and also technically well done.

There are several impressive and important aspects of the Dax CD-ROM. First, students are able to navigate their own course through this material, choosing the material they want to pursue in greater detail. Second, this format allows the authors to provide plenty of background material, including relevant case law and legislation. Third, students are encouraged to log their responses to key questions and also to keep a journal that accompanies their investigation of this case. This is a very nice way of focussing the student's attention and structuring the student's journey through the material.

The fourth and final characteristic of this medium is perhaps the most important. It contains video and audio interviews with key participants in this case, including Dax at several stages in his life, his nurse, his physician, his attorney, and his wife. For those of us who believe that moral reflection must confront the detail and complexity of real-life situations, this format is a great step forward over anything previously available. To see Dax, to hear his pain, is crucial to understanding this case, and that is hardly possible without the type of detail this CD-ROM provides.

[2] For more information on this site, see my "The Virtual Seminar Room," available at http://ethics.acusd.edu/Virtual_Seminar_Room. html.

[3] http://www.perseus.tufts.edu/cgi-bin/text?lookup=aristot.+eud. +eth.+1214a

[4] http://www.perseus.tufts.edu/cgi-bin/text?lookup=aristot.+nic. +eth.+1094a

[5] gopher://english.hss.cmu.edu/00ftp%3AEnglish.Server%3A

philosophy%3AAristotle%3AAristotle-Nicomachean%20Ethics.

[6]http://www.perseus.tufts.edu/cgi-bin/text?lookup=aristot.
+pol. +1252a

[7]gopher://english.hss.cmu.edu/00ftp%3AEnglish.Server%3
Aphilo sophy%3AAristotle%3AAristotle-Politics

[8]http://www.perseus.tufts.edu/cgi-bin/text?lookup=aristot.
+rh. +1354a

[9]gopher://english.hss.cmu.edu/00ftp%3AEnglish.Server%3A
philosophy %3AAristotle%3AAristotle-Rhetoric

[10]http://www.perseus.tufts.edu/cgi-bin/text?lookup=aristot.+vir.
+1249a

[11] gopher://gopher.vt.edu:10010/02/80/1

[12] gopher://gopher.vt.edu:10010/02/38/1

[13] http://ccel.wheaton.edu/augustine/confessions/confessions.html

[14] http://www.knight.org/advent/summa/summa.htm

[15]gopher://english.hss.cmu.edu/00ftp%3AEnglish.Server%3
Aphilo sophy%3AMontaigne-Essays

[16] gopher://gopher.vt.edu:10010/02/98/1

[17] http://wiretap.spies.com/ftp.items/Library/Classic/locke2nd.txt

[18] gopher://gopher.vt.edu:10010/02/116/2

[19]gopher://english.hss.cmu.edu/00ftp:English.Server:Philosophy:
Hume-Suicide%20and%20Immortality

[20]http://www.knuten.liu.se/~bjoch509/works/hume/
human_underst.txt

[21]gopher://unix1.utm.edu/00/departments/phil/hume/writings/
nhr.txt

[22]gopher://unix1.utm.edu/00/departments/phil/hume/writings/
life.txt

[23] gopher://wiretap.spies.com/00/Library/Classic/liberty.jsm

[24] gopher://wiretap.spies.com/00/Library/Classic/women.jsm

[25] gopher://gopher.vt.edu:10010/02/122/3

[26]http://www.knuten.liu.se/~bjoch509/noframes/philosophers/
intros/mill/mil-intro.html

[27] http://ethics.acusd.edu/Mill.html

[28] gopher://gopher.vt.edu:10010/02/161/1

[29] gopher://gopher.vt.edu:10010/02/107/6

[30] gopher://gopher.vt.edu:10010/02/107/5

[31] gopher://gopher.vt.edu:10010/02/107/3

[32] gopher://gopher.vt.edu:10010/02/107/4

[33] gopher://gopher.vt.edu:10010/02/107/1

[34] http://www.music.qub.ac.uk/~walker/KantCritJudgement.html

[35] gopher://gopher.vt.edu:10010/02/107/2

[36] http://eng.hss.cmu.edu/philosophy/kant/what-is-enlightenment.txt

[37] For further discussion of using the web in the classroom, see my "The Virtual Seminar Room," *Teaching Philosophy*, Vol. 19, No. 4 (December, 1996), 319-29. It is available in a hypertext version at http://ethics.acusd.edu/Virtual_Seminar_Room.html.

[38] Links to all these resources are available on my site at http://ethics.acusd.edu/euthanasia.html.

[39] http://search.nytimes.com/books/search/bin/fastweb?getdoc+book-rev+book-rev+15735+1++euthanasia

[40] All of the resources discussed in this paragraph are available at http://ethics.acusd.edu/reproductive_technologies.html#Cloning.

THE APA INTERNET BULLETIN BOARD
AND WEBSITE

SAUL TRAIGER

The American Philosophical Association (APA) made its foray into Internet publishing in the fall of 1989, well before the Internet had become a household name. As we harness continually evolving computing and networking technologies and assess their application to scholarship and teaching in philosophy, the development of Internet resources for APA members has been and remains an exciting adventure with no end in sight. The importance of APA's Internet projects go far beyond technology and computing. I argue that such projects concern the very mission of the APA. In this paper I will provide a brief history of the APA's Internet efforts, the issues and problems faced by the national organization along the way, and offer recommendations for the future.

The First Five Years: 1989-1993

At the August, 1989 Computers and Philosophy Conference at Carnegie-Mellon University I met with Robert Cavalier, who had located an electronic, on-line bulletin board system or "BBS" running on a computer owned and operated by the Advanced Technology Laboratory (ATL), housed in the administrative offices of California State University in Seal Beach, California. Cavalier made preliminary arrangements for the APA to use the ATL system for a pilot electronic bulletin board. I volunteered to meet with the ATL staff and learn about the capabilities of the system. After an initial meeting in Seal Beach in October, I set up and began the administration of the new APA Bulletin Board. The Bulletin Board quickly became the most popular of several electronic boards running at ATL. As many as 4,000 logins were recorded in a single month, even in those early days of limited Internet access.

Access to the APA Bulletin Board was achieved by a Telnet connection to the ATL computer over the Internet. Once connected to the ATL computer, the user logged in as "apa" and was immediately presented with a menu of nine items. These include choices such as "News from the Divisions," "E-mail Addresses of the Membership," and "Philosophical Calendar." When the user selected one of these items, she was presented with another menu of up to nine items. Selecting one of these items revealed scrolling text. For example, beginning at the top menu one might select the Philosophical Calendar, then at the next menu, the item entitled "January/February", and then a text file with information about conferences in January and February. Users could also send an electronic mail message to the administrator.

The coming into existence of the Bulletin Board raised a host of technological, institutional and editorial issues, many of which persist to this day. The most fundamental issue was the question of content. What information belongs on an electronic bulletin board system? How does the electronic medium differ from conventional paper publications and how can those differences be exploited to serve the membership? Should the APA repeat print publications in electronic form, or is doing so redundant and unnecessary?

The newness of the electronic medium made it impossible to settle these issues by appeal to precedent or custom, and it added other dimensions to the problems. In 1989, access to the Internet was not enjoyed by all institutions of higher education. In particular, it was virtually impossible for non-academically affiliated philosophers to connect to the Internet. Anything published electronically, therefore, would only reach a portion of the membership. Nowhere was this issue more important than with the matter of the electronic publication of job information.

In the late 1980s computers were being used by philosophers typically to accomplish tasks more quickly and efficiently, rather than to do new things, such as to search electronic texts. One of the tasks which many members of the APA had to accomplish is the tedious process of applying for positions in philosophy, working from printed issues of *Jobs for Philosophers* (*JFP*) to produce letters of applications to many institutions. It seemed to me that one of the principle benefits of an online service would be to distribute *JFP* data in electronic form, enabling job applicants to import such information directly to their computers, thereby automating one of the most tedious aspects of the job application process. Given the importance of job placement in the profession, I argued that placing *JFP* online would be a compelling use of the new computer technology.

The APA's National Office and then the APA Board of Officers was unwilling to make *JFP* or any other print publications available through the Internet. Their decision was based on several reasons, first among them a concern about access and fairness. It was feared that an electronic *JFP* would privilege those job candidates with access to computers and the Internet and handicap those without those tools. If electronic publication meant that some job candidates would receive notice of available positions sooner than others, that would be unacceptable. At about this time a rumor circulated among some graduate departments that job information was available on the Electronic Bulletin Board and several departments contacted the National Office to express their concern.

The National Office and the APA Board feared that the open electronic publication of *JFP* and other print publications would have a detrimental effect on membership. The Bulletin Board was accessible to anyone with Internet access. That meant that individuals who were not members of the APA would be able to view materials intended for members' eyes only. Would APA members abandon the organization if publications such as the *Proceedings of the APA* and *JFP* were placed on the Internet?

The APA's concern about the role of new technology in academic philosophy were natural and understandable, and to some extent, legitimate. Computers and the Internet had raised new questions about how to manage and run a professional organization, and no one had the answers, in part because no one knew where this technology was headed. Would electronic communication over networks be a passing fad? Would new technologies help solve the fairness issues and the access-limiting issues? No one knew, and there was speculation that the Bulletin Board, and with it these issues, would eventually fade away.

Indeed, some of the difficulties outlined above were a function of the early stage of computer use by philosophers and the newness of the Internet. It has already been noted that in 1989 many campuses did not have Internet access. While some philosophers were using e-mail, many, perhaps the majority, were on campuses using the Bitnet network, which did not support Internet protocols such as Telnet and FTP. The APA's first Internet accessible bulletin board, then, was not available to all or even most philosophers. Many philosophers did not have access to computers at all, and thus were not comfortable with the idea that professional information might be transmitted through them.

The Internet itself presented a challenge in handling the APA's concern about access by non-members. The impediments to restricting access were both technological and cultural. The Bulletin Board was not password protected. Anyone who knew the Internet address could establish a Telnet connection. The Bulletin Board gained notoriety through other online services. Early Internet 'surfers' created their own Telnet sites with categorized lists of Internet resources. The first Internet books began appearing in bookstores, and the APA Bulletin Board was one of the first academic sites listed in them.

Middle Years: 1992-1994

In the early 1990s the Internet, and with it the APA's presence on it, began a period of rapid change. During the summer of 1993 the Ford Foundation supported the work of Occidental College senior cognitive science major Jan Panero, under my supervision, to develop a 'gopher' server replacement for the APA bulletin board. A gopher server is a menu-driven information delivery system, installed on a computer connected to the Internet. On the surface it is similar to the bulletin board system running the APA Bulletin Board. In our case, Panero installed a gopher server on a Sun workstation at Occidental College. She moved and then reorganized the information from the old APA bulletin board to the more flexible and powerful menu system of the gopher server. For example, instead of breaking up the list of e-mail addresses of the membership into nine submenus, arranged alphabetically, the gopher server allowed the user to search for a desired name or e-mail address through an easy to use interface. Instead of grouping all the items in the Philosophical Calendar for August together in one long scrolling file, each item could now appear in its own menu listing.

The gopher server was an advance over the bulletin board because it emerged as a standard for Internet-based information systems, and it facilitated the seamless integration of Internet resources. Other academic societies and institutions developed gopher servers and those gopher servers which were of interest to APA members were selectable as menu items on the APA gopher server. There were links to the gophers of such publications and organizations as the Chronicle of Higher Education, the American Mathematical Society, and the History of the Philosophy of Science Working Group (HOPOS). Files maintained by users on remote machines were also accessed through the APA gopher. For example, David Chalmers' extensive bibliography in the philosophy of mind, originally placed on the Internet in an anonymous FTP site, was linked from the APA gopher. Internet sites which maintained electronic versions of full length works, including philosophical works, were linked as well. The idea of a web of interconnected, locally maintained but globally linked Internet resources was born, before almost anyone had heard of the World-Wide-Web.

A demonstration of the APA Gopher was presented at the Eighth Annual Computing and Philosophy Conference at Carnegie Mellon University, August 12, 1993. The conference was sponsored by the APA Committee on Computer Use in Philosophy. The demonstration illustrated the improvement in the user interface and functionality achieved with the gopher server.

The gopher system was accessed through the Internet, as was the Bulletin Board. Unlike the Bulletin Board, however, for which one needed the Telnet capability, gopher required software called a "gopher client." Most central academic computers at U.S. colleges and universities had gopher client software up and running. Users easily made the transition from the Bulletin Board to the new system. The strength of the gopher system was in its openness.

The new gopher server changed the nature of information delivery to APA members. On the old system, the user had access only to files placed on the system directly. With gopher, the selections available to the user included hypertext links to other gopher sites, FTP sites, and remote text and binary files. The APA Bulletin Board quickly became a central access point for philosophers looking for profession-related material on the Internet. As other Internet resources evolved, APA members were introduced to them through the APA's site.

The Rise of the Web: 1994-1996

Although the World-Wide-Web had been in use since 1990, it wasn't in widespread use until the middle 1990s, largely because most web clients were still text-based. In 1990 there were only about 500 websites on the Internet. During the next few years, however, researchers at the University of Illinois and Cornell University developed the now ubiquitous graphics-enabled web browsers for popular platforms like Windows and the Macintosh. The number of websites increased dramatically.

What is the Web and why is it so well suited for organizing and distributing content? The World-Wide-Web is really just two standards for formatting and distributing files stored on computers. The formatting standard is called the HypertText Markup Language. (HTML) Adhering to HTML insures that documents have the same appearance and function, regardless of the computer which is accessing that document. The features available under HTML keep growing, but they include standard text formatting features, the ability to include graphics in documents, and the ability to make any part of a document a link to another document, so that by selecting the link (usually by clicking on it with a mouse) the user retrieves the linked document. The standard for distributing documents on the Web is called HyperText Transfer Protocol. (HTTP) This standard controls how documents are stored and retrieved over a network. Typically HTML documents are stored as files on personal computers, workstations, and mainframe computers and retrieved over the Internet. What makes the Web 'world-wide' is the fact that HTTP allows any one who is using a computer connected to the Internet to retrieve and view documents stored on any other computer on the Internet.

HTTP and HTML don't distinguish between local and remote documents. That means that it really doesn't matter to a student or professor whether a document is located on a computer in Tokyo or

Topeka. Documents can be selected by their relevance. Further, because documents are digital and networked, they may be found by search engines which comb and index the vast holdings of the Web. Finally, computer users are still discovering that computers can, in principle store and display any information which can be represented digitally, from the Mona Lisa to the sound of John Coltrane's 'A Love Supreme.'

The World-Wide-Web platform brought with it significant enhancements to the APA's Internet offerings. It enabled formatted text, including italics, boldfacing, and variable font sizes. It became possible to embed graphic images, and later tables, into web documents. Hypertext links can occur anywhere in a web document. Hence images, words, and maps could serve as navigation points for readers.

The HTML and HTTP formats make it easy for users to provide information to the APA through the use of forms. Web pages were developed with specific fields to be filled in by the user for the submission of information to the National Office, or as a request for information from the National Office. HTTP departs from the unrestricted access of gopher servers by providing security for web documents. Access to documents may be restricted through password protection or user address, or a combination of the two.

The importance of the web has less to do with the its technological advances over earlier Internet solutions than it does with the brute fact that it has become extremely popular in the general population as well as in the academic community. The ease of use and the ease of creating and publishing web documents has led philosophers to embrace the Internet as never before. The new widespread use of the World-Wide-Web means that APA's web resources are connected to a huge corpus of web-based materials developed by philosophers for other philosophers. The accessibility of the APA's website by nonmembers provides a visibility to the APA's activities not previously enjoyed.

Some APA print publications are moving to the Web. In 1995 the APA began imposing a fee for subscription to the APA Newsletters. At the same time, those newsletters were made available on the Web. It seems likely that the Web version will ultimately replace the print version altogether.

Transition to National Office Control

To many of those philosophers who have explored the use of computing technology in philosophy, it has been clear for a long time that the APA's presence on the Internet would not be temporary. Through the entire development period there was continual discussion with the National Office about matters of policy, support, and editorial judgment. Through this period the National Office itself faced many issues

384

involving computer technology. The day to day tasks of that office, from membership maintenance to the publication of the *Proceedings*, had become increasingly dependent on computers. In the fall of 1995 the APA Board of Officers authorized the National Office to create a half-time position for a Coordinator of Information Resources, with responsibility for the APA's Internet resources and general office automation at the National Office.

The Coordinator of Information Resources position was filled in the late spring of 1996 and the APA's website was moved to the University of Delaware a few months later. Some of the benefits of the move are already apparent. The website now makes extensive use of forms. Users can submit requests for information, e-mail addresses and home-page addresses through forms. Individuals may also request a membership application or update membership information. Although the APA has been slow to move its publications to the Web, the fact that the National Office itself now manages and updates its Internet resources should make it easier for APA publications to migrate to the Web in the future.

The Future of the APA's Internet Resources

The APA's website is now an established service. Members increasingly look to the APA's Internet resources, rather than to its print publications, for the latest information. What can we reasonably expect for the future?

Print publication and regular mail distribution remains the norm at the present time. As the cost of this traditional distribution form rises, and the ease of use and wide availability of electronic media and network distribution increases, the APA will, in my view, begin moving its publications to the Web or its successor. Most of the APA's publications are time-sensitive. They contain deadlines for paper submissions, the programs of upcoming conferences, announcements of position vacancies, grant opportunities and the like. The Web is the natural place for such information. Web pages can be augmented, updated, and items can be replaced on a daily basis. Some of the updating of information can be automated. The costs associated with traditional printing and mailing can be reduced or eliminated.

What of the APA's reluctance to place materials such as *Jobs for Philosophers* online? In my view, the arguments against electronic publication are no longer cogent. The facts about access have changed dramatically. The cost of a computer with Web browsing capabilities is less than the cost of an electric typewriter was 20 years ago, in real dollars. Internet access is a fact of life in most institutions of higher learning, but more importantly, any individual can connect to the Internet at a low cost through a commercial Internet provider. Even job candidates without a computer could access the *JFP* at their local library, and enjoy immediate delivery of the most up-to-date information. Access to a Web-based *JFP* and other publications can easily be restricted to APA members in good standing. Most importantly, a Web-based *JFP* would be a valuable service for job candidates, enabling them to search for jobs by category, to cut and paste addresses and other items from the electronic documents directly into letters of application, and to have such information in a timely manner.

Other membership services should make their way to APA members through the Web. Membership dues, now payable only by check through normal post, could be collected using credit cards or electronic fund transfers. As the evidence of commercial websites makes obvious, the technology is already in place. Marcia Homiak, with the assistance of myself and Christ Bender of Rice University, has developed a relational database of Women in Philosophy which is being ported to the Web under the auspices of the Committee on Women in Philosophy. This is a searchable, regularly updated database.

I've already noted that the APA's electronic publications have reached a wider audience than the print publications. The responsible promotion of philosophy is clearly in the scope of the APA's activities. The APA's presence on the Web should be a welcoming one, designed to answer some of the questions of laypersons about the profession and the discipline. One way to achieve this is to have an 'Ask a Philosopher' website, staffed weekly or monthly by several philosophers who agree to monitor incoming questions and respond.

The APA could help enhance the quality of philosophical discussion at its divisional meetings by placing papers, or at least longer abstracts, on the web, in advance of the meetings, with the cooperation of authors, of course. Attendees could then participate in sessions with some antecedent understanding of the author's position and arguments.

NOTES

My work on the APA's Internet Resources could not have been carried out without collaboration with many individuals and institutions. Robert Cavalier, of Carnegie Mellon University, provided the initial impetus and constant encouragement and advice over the entire project. The Executive Directors of the APA, first David Hoekema and currently Eric Hoffman, have shown leadership and a sincere interest in using computers to enhance the services provided to members, and in doing so, to support the practice of philosophy in the United States.

David Axeen, Dean of the Faculty at Occidental College, and Thomas Slobko, Vice President for Computing and Information Services, have placed Occidental College's substantial computing resources at the service of the APA over a period of almost seven years. Paul Hubbard, of Occidental College's Computer Center, made the computers work. Support for student participation on the project was made possible through the Ford Foundation.

USING COMPUTING TECHNOLOGY FOR PHILOSOPHICAL RESEARCH: AN APA REPORT

ROBERT CAVALIER

The use of the computer for research in philosophy has been growing yearly for the last decade. Today it forms a part of what Leslie Burkholder calls the "computational turn" in philosophy.[1] In order to get an empirical snapshot of the use of computers in this area, the following survey questions were distributed to departments across the country:

1. How many Philosophy faculty members are in your department?

2. How many of your faculty members use "routine" computing, such as Internet searches and database searches, to find writings and other resources for philosophical research?

3. In addition to these "routine" uses of computing, some Philosophers have begun to use computing for "new" kinds of research. Please check any of the following uses that apply to at least one person teaching Philosophy in your department.

   Using computers to develop or test philosophical models of some sort (for example: models of the mind, of reasoning, of logical proof, of rational decision-making, etc.).

   Using computers to explore philosophical concepts (for example: creativity, distributive justice, perception, belief, etc.).

   Other. Please explain briefly.

4. What is the total number of faculty members in your department using computing resources beyond the routine activities described in question 2?

5. How many student theses or dissertations during the past five years have significantly involved consideration of some aspect of computer technology?

There were 270 responses to this questionnaire. The total number of faculty in the responding departments were 2,025. Of those, 1,178 were using the computer for some form of philosophical research and 263 were using the computer beyond the scope of question #2. Approximately 120 student dissertations involved some form of philosophical research involving computing.

The survey results show that, of those responding, more than half of the faculty (58%) were using the computer for some form of research and 13% were using the computer for more advanced forms of research. From the "comments" part of the survey, many of those responding were using the computer in 'routine ways' such as a tool to search for information, a tool for correspondence and a tool for materials preparation. Many were using the World-Wide-Web for accessing electronic texts, articles and other resources as well as using e-mail for sharing drafts and discussing issues.[2] Comments from these groups include:

"Obtaining contemporary problems type material for use in ethics classes"

"Software development for critical thinking tutorial"

"Exploring impact of computer programming on conceptual and doxastic roles and organization"

"Designing a computer program to explore social evolution with prisoner's dilemma game."

"...working on a multimedia CD-ROM to teach information ethics (focusing on a case study)"

"Plan to adopt no textbook henceforth that has no software for research, reading, etc. accompanying it."

"A proof-checking program is used to help students in symbolic logic courses."

"Using Stella II to explore systems thinking in social and political theory."

"Research into finite automata theory"

"Neural net modeling"

Other activities discovered by searching URLs submitted by the respondents include: development of an Internet Encyclopedia of Philosophy [www.utm.edu:80/research/iep/], on-line courses [www.orst.edu/Dept/philosophy/wproj.html and www.valdosta.peachnet.edu/~rbarnett/phi], and several sites dealing with Ethics. The latter sites range from Larry Hinman's Ethics Updates [www.acusd.edu/ethics/], R. Cavalier's Introduction to Ethics [caae.phil.cmu.edu/CAAE/80130/Syllabus.html], and Peter Danielson's Artificial Morality [www. ethics.ubc.ca:80/~pad/] (*a la* game theory) to the Center for the Advancement of Applied Ethics' dialogical approach to contemporary moral problems [www.lcl.cmu.edu /CAAE /Home /Forum /ethics. html].

But perhaps the most far reaching conclusions that can be drawn from a survey like this come from the way that a number of departments describe themselves. In this regard, the Philosophy Department at Carnegie Mellon [hss.cmu.edu/HTML/departments /philosophy/philosophy.html] may indicate certain kinds of changes that the profession will see in the near future. Excerpts from its Mission Statement speak to its interest in "contemporary and applied areas [such] as automated theorem proving, machine learning, language technology, game and decision theory....This emphasis arises from our commitment to refine philosophical insights of the past through confrontation with problems of the present. The teaching and learning of this material is supported by appropriate technology (computer tutors, interactive multimedia software)..."

Pointers from its research and faculty pages reveal, along side traditional areas, the following kinds of areas of specialization: Game Theory, Belief Revision in Expert Systems, Interactive Media, Cognitive Science, Formal Learning Theory, Distance Learning of Ethics, Multimedia Education, Proof and Decision Theory, Cognitive Psychology, Graphical and Statistical Modeling of Causes, Artificial Intelligence, Interactive Systems.

Along with CMU, a number of departments submitted URLs that indicate a significant curricular trend. This trend, perhaps not unlike that which happened during the 17th Century, marks a paradigm shift wherein philosophy appears in the newly forming constellation of 'Cognitive Science.' At SUNY-Binghamton [www.paccs.binghamton.edu /index.html][3], for instance, the following announcement appears:

With the cooperation and assistance of the Computer Science, Psychology and Systems Science Departments, the Philosophy Department of SUNY-Binghamton offers an innovative, interdisciplinary MA/PhD program in Philosophy. This program is designed to integrate the disciplines of philosophy, cognitive science, artificial intelligence, computer science and systems science.

If we place these department configurations next to recent publications at both the introductory and graduate level, at least one aspect of the discipline, viz., 'theory of knowledge,' seems to be undergoing a profound, even revolutionary change.

Clark Glymour's introductory philosophy text, *Thinking Things Through*, [Glymour, 1992] is a particularly good example of a book that prepares the undergraduate student for serious and sustained work within the new demands of contemporary epistemology. Its chapters on Proofs, Knowledge, and Minds provide not only discussions of the issues, but rigorous excursions into the mathematical, scientific and statistical contexts in which many current problems are explored. And *Android Epistemology*, a collection of articles dealing with many facets of the computer's impact on philosophy, offers the graduate student a glimpse into the kind of conference presentations and course offerings that may very well form a natural part of 'doing philosophy' in the 21st Century. In the book's Introduction, the Editors write:

> Android epistemology is not a methodology or a discipline. The very idea of a disciplinary methodology -- that there is one proper, professional way to do things -- is by nature exclusionary....Android epistemology violates all kinds of traditional disciplinary boundaries in science, bringing together engineering and the life sciences, placing mathematical linguistics in the heart of electrical engineering and requiring moral philosophers to understand computation theory. University deans, forced to work within the old hierarchies, weep with frustration...We live in interesting times, [Ford, Glymour, and Hayes, 1995].

Interesting times, indeed. The very appearance of these publications highlights the potential need for a change in undergraduate philosophy curricular. Many students now taking up the field of philosophy will be well advised to include core courses in the social and cognitive sciences along with the more traditional liberal arts. I believe that such backgrounds for philosophy undergraduates, backgrounds that build upon statistical analysis and computer programming, will be an excellent way to prepare these students for the new research agenda in the field -- an agenda that we are only beginning to glimpse through the results of surveys such as these.

NOTES

[1] See *Philosophy and the Computer* [Burkholder, 1992]. This book contains chapters growing out of presentations at the annual Computing and Philosophy Conference.

[2] From one respondent: "We have established a 'philosophy e-mail group' to exchange day-to-day diatribes, dialectic and discussion of on-going topics. About 6 to 10 of us exchange one to five group-wide messages weekly; there are also a number of ongoing 2 or 3 party exchanges going on. May I recommend this super simple step into computer literacy to one and all? I have found this medium for philosophical reflection surprisingly novel and stimulating."

[3] At the University of California at San Diego (www.ucsd.edu/philosophy), the "department is affiliated with both the Science Studies Program and the Interdisciplinary Cognitive Science Program."

REFERENCES

Burkolder, Leslie, Ed. (1992) *Philosophy and the Computer*. Westview Press.

Ford, Glymour, and Hayes, Eds. (1995) *Android Epistemology*. Cambridge: MIT Press.

Glymour, Clark. (1992) *Thinking Things Through*. Cambridge: MIT Press.

USING COMPUTER TECHNOLOGY FOR TEACHING PHILOSOPHY: AN APA REPORT

RON BARNETTE

The following report is based on results submitted either in hard copy to the offices of the American Philosophical Association at the University of Delaware, or in electronic form through the APA website established for the survey. The survey was conducted during the summer and fall, 1996, and was mailed to some 2000 departments of philosophy, to be completed by a department chair or designee for providing departmental information. Departmental faculty did not submit individual responses; each response represents a summary of departmental information for purposes of the survey.

I have included a sample survey form which will serve as a point of reference for the results, as summarized below.

Sample Survey:

Using Computing Technology While Teaching Philosophy
Instructions: Please answer the follow questions. Your time is greatly appreciated.

University or College:
Name:
Title:
If your department has a Web page, please include it here:
http://
Please provide us with the name and e-mail address of the most computer-savvy department member:
Name:
E-mail:

1. How many Philosophy faculty members are in your department?

2. How many of your faculty members use "routine" computing, such as word processing and data entry to do any of the following?

prepare lectures, handouts, assignments, exams, etc.
keep grades, attendance, and other traditional records
make overhead transparencies for classroom use.

3. In addition to these "routine" uses of computing, some Philosophy faculty members have begun to use computing for other aspects of teaching. Please check any of the following uses that apply to at least one person teaching Philosophy in your department.

   A. Using computers in class to generate multimedia materials, such as graphics, video clips and sound-bites, during Philosophy lectures (for example, using PowerPoint slides or Astound).

   B. Using computer-assisted instruction to help students learn Philosophy.

   C. Using e-mail to consult with students about course-related issues.

   D. Using Web pages or other network resources as sources of information for students to access.

   E. Using network/Web resources as "places" for students to submit their course work.

   F. Using virtual "chat rooms" or other computer generated "locations" for students to "meet" with each other and/or faculty.

   G. Using Web pages or other network "places" to conduct entire credit bearing courses in Philosophy.

   H. Other. Please explain briefly.

4. What is the total number of faculty members in your department using computing resources beyond the routine activities described in question 2?

5. If any members of your department have plans to use computing technology for other teaching activities in the near future, please briefly describe those plans here, or provide an electronic address where we can acquire relevant information:

6. Please list any computer-related courses offered by your department, such as Artificial Intelligence or Computer Ethics:

Summary of Results

Number of departments responding to survey:

310 (approximately 16% of those surveyed)

Number of departmental websites reported:

135 (or 44% of those responding)

Based on Questions 1 and 2-
Number of departments reporting a high percentage of faculty members who use 'routine' computing, as defined in the survey (for this purpose I considered greater than 50% of the faculty to constitute a 'high percentage'):

294 (or 95% of those responding)

Based on Question 3-
Number of departments reporting faculty who use computing in addition to 'routine,' as described by each of the following survey items:

A:	87	E:	62
B:	147	F:	65
C:	238	G:	16
D:	191	H:	26[1]

Based on Questions 1 and 4-
Number of departments reporting a high percentage of faculty members who use computer resources beyond 'routine' (again, 'high percentage' = greater than 50%):

90 (or 29% of those responding)

Based on Question 5-
Number of departments expressing plans for using computing technology in their teaching activities:

93 (or 30% of those responding)[2]

Based on Question 6-
Number of departments who listed computer-related courses offered:

80 (or 26% of those responding)[3]

Plans are currently underway to utilize these helpful results in such a manner as to assist philosophy teachers with their computer-related projects, and to facilitate an exchange of information pertinent to philosophy teaching with computer resources. Permission from individual respondents will need to be secured, however, before further databases can be shared publicly.

NOTES

[1] H: WWW/distance education connections, neural net modeling, online philosophy databases for research, CD-ROM collections, electronic class journals, specialized logic programs, student web pages, bioethics network, self-paced courses on disks or CD-ROM, course evaluations, class materials for student exchanges, doctoral dissertation research and discussion, conference planning and registration, file transfer for exchanging student projects, daily posting of lecture notes and commentary.

[2] Plans for Computer-related Teaching Activities: Off-campus teaching, department and individual webpages, posting coursework online, multimedia presentations, logic coursework, library CD-ROM access, e-mail correspondence with students and off-campus teaching faculty, computer simulations, Internet course development, use of Bulletin Boards for course dialogue, interactive conferencing, Java Script development, high tech classroom development, critical thinking team-teaching over the Internet, logic lab setup, student presentations, chat rooms, course listservers, class demonstrations.

[3] Computer-related Courses Offered: Complete online courses, online graduate program, logic courses, AI courses, Virtual Reality coursework, writing hypertext, mind/machine courses, computer ethics, philosophy of mind courses, ethics and technology class, coursework in science, technology and society, logic programs, philosophy of computing, automated reasoning project, mathematical logic, learning theory and epistemology, philosophy of communication, technology and the future.

USING COMPUTING TECHNOLOGY FOR PROFESSIONAL COOPERATION: AN APA REPORT

LAWRENCE M. HINMAN

In the summer of 1996, the APA Committee on Philosophy and Computing undertook a survey of APA members and their involvement with various facets of computing. This article offers a report and analysis of the responses to the third issue considered by the Committee: the use of computer technology for professional cooperation. I will begin by reproducing the survey which was sent to APA members, and then provide a tabulation of the results. After that, I will turn to an analysis of the significance of these results.

The Survey Form

Instructions: Please answer the follow questions. Your time is greatly appreciated.

University or College:
Name:
Title:
E-mail:
Telephone:

1. How many Philosophy faculty members are in your department?

2. How many of your faculty members use "routine" computing, such as e-mail, LIST servers, and philosophical bulletin boards to gather information or carry on philosophical conversations with other philosophers?

3. In addition to these "routine" uses of computing, some philosophers have begun to use computing for other kinds of professional activities. Please check any of the following uses that apply to at least one person teaching Philosophy in your department.
    A. Using computer networks to register for philosophical conferences.
    B. Using computer networks to plan philosophical conferences.

C. Using computer networks to participate "virtually" in philosophical conferences.

D. Using computer networks to work as a member of a professional committee (for example: the APA Committee on the Status and Future of the Profession).

E. Using computer networks to submit papers for publication.

F. Using computer networks to submit works for publication in electronic journals.

G. Other. Please explain briefly.

4. What is the total number of faculty members in your department using computing resources beyond the routine activities described in question 2?

5. If any members of your department have plans to use computing technology for other professional cooperation in the near future, please briefly describe those plans here, or provide an electronic address where we can acquire relevant information:

6. Please list any electronic addresses where we can acquire information about any of the above activities in your Department:

The Results

The response to this questionnaire was very good: we received 307 responses, 202 of which were submitted on paper by traditional mail and 105 of which were submitted electronically through the APA web site. In tabulating these results, I have initially separated the paper replies from the electronic replies. They have then been combined in a weighted total, since there are almost twice as many paper replies as electronic ones.

The differences between the paper and electronic responses are interesting in themselves. First, we are obviously still a paper-oriented group, if the 2:1 ratio of paper to electronic responses is any indication. Second, and not surprisingly, departments that responded electronically overall show a higher level of computer involvement in almost all categories covered in this survey. Intuitively, one suspects that there is a higher level of involvement in departments that file electronically, but there are undoubtedly other variables at work here. Departments that filed electronically, for example, were larger on average than those that did not.

There is a discrepancy in these results when we compute the average percentage of a department that uses routine computing, which can be done in three possible ways. First, one can divide the average number of individuals by the average number of department members. (In the paper responses, this is 5.9/7.0=84.4%.) Second, one can add up the total number of department members given, then add up

398

the total number of those who use routine computing, and divide the latter by the former. Each individual is, as it were, given one vote (In the paper responses, this would be 1034/1406.25=73.5%.) Finally, one can compute the percentage of those who use routine computing within each department, and then average those percentages. Each department, as it were, gets one vote. The most reliable number here is the average of raw numbers, which suggests that just under three fourths of the surveyed members in use "routine computing," which in this questionnaire is defined as "as e-mail, LIST servers, and philosophical bulletin boards to gather information or carry on philosophical conversations with other philosophers."

Question Number	Question Content	Paper	Electronic	Total
1	Number of department members	7.0	8.3	7.4
2	Number who use routine computing	5.9	6.2	6.0
	Percentage analysis			
	Averaging summary numbers	84.4%	75.5%	81.4%
	Averaging raw numbers	73.5%	74.8%	74.0%
	Averaging departmental percentages	70.4%	77.7%	72.9%
3-A	Use networks to register for philosophical conferences	35.6%	43.8%	38.4%
3-B	Use networks to plan philosophical conferences	32.7%	42.9%	36.2%
3-C	Virtual participation in conferences	12.4%	29.5%	18.2%
3-D	Use networks as member of a professional committee	29.2%	38.1%	32.2%
3-E	Use networks to submit papers for publication	27.7%	39.0%	31.6%
3-F	Submit works to electronic journals	15.8%	22.9%	18.2%
3-G	Other	11.4%	19.0%	14.0%
4	Total number beyond routine uses			
	Percent of department that goes beyond routine uses described in Question #2	25.7%	31.9%	27.8%
	Number of respondents:	202	105	307

Analysis

The overall picture presented by this survey is one in which approximately 75% the surveyed members of the profession use computers in routine ways, such as e-mail and list-servers. Percentages drop off considerably when we look at participation in other network-based computer technologies that involve professional cooperation.

Response 3-A: Using Networks to Register for Philosophical Conferences. In *Response 3-A*, we see that only 38% of those surveyed use networks to register for philosophical conferences. This is hardly surprising. Some conferences, such as Carnegie Mellon's Computing and Philosophy (CAP) Conference offer on-line registration, but the APA still does not. On-line registration is somewhat more difficult to set up than paper-based registration since it usually involves knowing something about CGI scripts, and security (for on-line payment of conference registration fees) is still an issue.

Response 3-B: Using Networks to Plan Philosophical Conferences, which deals with the use of networks to plan philosophical conferences, reveals an overall average participation rate of 36%. This number may, however, be misleading, since there is no base number specifying how many respondents are currently involved in planning philosophical conferences. It simply specifies the percentage of departments that have at least one person who uses networks to plan philosophical conferences. My hunch is that a high percentage of people who are currently planning philosophical conferences use the Internet as part of that process. Certainly this is regularly true of APA program committees and many conference notices contain e-mail address and web site addresses for additional material.

Response 3-C: Participation in On-Line Conferences. A relatively small percentage of members participate in on-line conferences. Of the departments responding on paper, only 12.4% had at least one member who had participated in an on-line conference; of the departments responding electronically, almost 30% had at least one department member who participated virtually in a conference. These results are not surprising, in part because such conferences are still comparatively rare.

Response 3-D: Using Networks to Participate in Professional Committees. A somewhat higher percentage of members use networks to participate in professional committees. Again, it is important to note here exactly what the figures mean. Of the departments responding on paper, 29% had at least one member who used networks to participate in professional committees; the figure for those departments that responded electronically was 38%, nine points higher. Once again, this is not calculated against a base of the total number of individuals participating in professional committees. I would suspect that, of those participating in professional committees, a high percentage use e-mail to coordinate with committee members on other campuses.

Response 3-E: Submitting Papers Electronically for Publication. The responses to this question, which deals with submitting papers electronically for publication, were approximately the same at responses to the previous question: 27% and 39%, respectively, for paper and electronic departmental responses. This number actually seems high to me, but that may be due to an ambiguity in our wording of the question. Many journals require a paper submission, as does the APA, and I would be surprised if there are many non-electronic journals that accept submissions that are only electronic without any paper copy. However, many journals welcome— and some strongly desire— that accepted pieces be accompanied by a disk copy of the article. This facilitates the printing process. Also, there is another barrier to electronic submissions. Transmitting complex word processing files electronically is often frustrating for both the sender and the recipient. Many computer users still find it difficult to attach a file to an e-mail message, and even experienced users may find it difficult to decode the attachment and load it in the proper program. Of course, one can use snail mail to send an electronic file without a paper copy, but there is something incongruous about this. Furthermore, many editors and reviewers are use to marking up paper manuscripts, and the transition to electronic submissions — which requires that reading be done at the computer screen — can be a considerable inconvenience. There are, of course, advantages as well, and these will increase as more sophisticated software is developed for document sharing. Reviewers will then be able to mark up electronic copies of manuscripts and editors can see all the comments together in a single file. Yet right now this is cutting edge technology that depends on everyone having the same software and easy access to a good Internet connection. Eventually all this will come to pass, and electronic submissions will eventually become the standard. At present, however, we are far from this state.

Response 3-F: Submitting Works to Electronic Journals. Electronic journals are still in their infancy. The first, *The On-Line Journal of Analytical Philosophy*, was first published in 1993; *The Journal of Buddhist Ethics* began publication in 1994. The responses indicate that 16% of the surveyed departments have at least one person who has submitted work to an electronic journal; the number for those responding electronically was 23%. This number will undoubtedly increase as the number of electronic journals increases, but it is not clear how quickly that number will increase. Electronic journals are much cheaper than their paper counterparts, but currently they bring in no revenues. Moreover, although they are high quality publications, they presently have less established status than older, traditional print-based journals and face an up-hill road for recognition.

Response 3-G: Other. The response rate here was fairly low, since the previous questions had covered many of the standard ways in which computing is used to enhance professional cooperation: 11% and 19%, respectively, for paper and electronic responses.

The interesting material here, of course, lies not in the numbers but in the comments. In addition to one general comment about "no computer and proud of it!", the paper respondents mentioned the following activities: co-editing electronic journals, corresponding with department members, discussing editorial board policy of an on-line journal, web pages for course materials, international communication, co-authoring papers, co-authoring grant proposals, distributing drafts of papers for comments, web pages for professional organizations, refereeing for journals, publicizing conferences, planning conferences, book publication, participating in electronic discussions of humanities sponsored by NEH, submitting and accepting referees' reports, managing a listserver on C. S. Pierce, participating in an electronic chat room, participating in on-line meetings, contributing to on-line encyclopedias and databases, communicating with publishers about manuscripts, desktop publishing, distance education, grading tests, multimedia preparation of K-12 teachers' guide (Some redundancies have been eliminated).

The electronic respondents added the following comments: For statewide and national collaboration, several listservers have been established to facilitate fast, timely communication between colleagues who share interests, but not physical proximity; Using the WWW to make pre-prints available to others; Using computers & networks to edit and compile publications such as encyclopedias with multiple authors; We use a distribution list with high school philosophy teachers, and I can use the list to pass messages to them, arrange conferences, etc.; Call for papers for our publication: *Horizons philosophiques*; as editor of journal; Use of the WWW and e-mail for discussion and collaboration among philosophers and classes for dialogue and critical exchanges; Exchanges of research and teaching information, announcements of conferences, and helpful resources are continually being exchanged — in fact, our department has established such electronic collaboration as a key feature of its departmental mission for faculty and students; Using computer networks to survey courses, faculty, and departments on the web; Colleagues now routinely share drafts by email (e.g. conference commentators); Use email to advise and stay in touch with students who have transferred to colleges and universities where they are currently majoring in Philosophy; our "Academic Dialogue on Applied Ethics" which seeks to use the Web as a conversation medium in a way that improves upon face-to-face conference panels; Using computer networks to do surveys as part of research, to engage in discussions and get information on issues in applied ethics; advertising vacant position; help produce a WWW page for a professional society; Download papers from web page constructed for conference. Again, some redundancies were eliminated.

Conclusion

The overall picture that we see from this survey is of a group that makes extensive use of computers for such routine tasks as e-mail and one which, as opportunities for more extensive use of computers increase, is gradually becoming involved in more ambitious forms of network-based collaboration. Obviously, had this survey been taken ten years ago, the response would have been almost non-existent.

The intriguing thought is to imagine what the results will be ten years from now. One of the most promising areas for the enhancement of professional cooperation lies in web conferencing. It is now possible to broadcast a regular conference live over the Internet, with live video as well as audio. The hardware requirements for those on the receiving end are reasonable: Win95 or NT, a sound card, and a 28.8 or better Internet connection. With that configuration, people can both hear and see live conferences on the web. The software, Microsoft NetMeeting, is free. The hardware requirements for broadcasting conferences without video are not substantially greater. The conference room must have a live internet hook-up (dial-up is ok), and the conference room microphone must feed into the computer's sound card. If video is being broadcast, then the hardware requirements become more intensive. The broadcasting computer must at least have a video camera attached, a real-time video capture card, and sufficient RAM and high-speed hard drives to handle the translation of the video for output. However, this is hardware that many universities already have, even if they have only one or two such machines. Again, the software is free — the same software as those who are receiving the signal.

The really amazing thing about this emerging technology, however, is that it is not just like a live TV broadcast. It is truly interactive in two senses. First, it is easy for interaction to occur between the physical conference and the virtual attendees. Virtual participants need only have a microphone on their home computer in order to be able to ask questions that can be broadcast in real time over the conference-room speakers. They can also hear the replies and respond to them. In addition, virtual participants can pop up a whiteboard (a virtual blackboard) and this can be projected on the conference projector, if that projector is hooked up to the internet computer. Indeed, virtual participants can even present before the whole conference, managing a software presentation (for example, in PowerPoint) remotely from their home computer, hearing and responding to questions, and the like. All virtual participants need is a good microphone connected to their computer's soundboard. Second, it is possible for the virtual attendees to interact with one another in several ways. If, as is still unlikely, they have a video camera attached to their computer, they can broadcast a live video to other participants. If they have a microphone, they can talk back and forth to those who also have microphones and are virtual participants in the conference. All virtual participants may draw and type on a whiteboard, and they may also enter chat rooms to send typed messages back and forth. Finally, they may even share applications on one another's computers.

This technology should not eliminate conferences in real time and space — there is usually no need or desire for them to do so. For many of us, one of the principal reasons we attend conferences is for the face-to-face human interaction. Instead, it offers a virtual supplement to those conferences, allowing the attendance and participation of those who would otherwise be unable to be present. My own site, Ethics Updates, is now available to host the live broadcast of ethics conferences on the Web, and I will continue to post information about this emerging technology on the site at http://ethics.acusd.edu/ netmeeting.html. This promises to be one of the most exciting areas for enhancing professional cooperation in the near future.

NOTES

I am indebted to Leeanna Cummings, the Philosophy Department secretary at the University of San Diego, for data entry of the paper responses to this survey.

404

INDEX OF NAMES

407

Landau, D. P.   132
Landauer, R.   118, 131
Langley, Pat   50, 58, 60, 64, 76, 77
Langton, C. G.   135, 150-152, 318
Latham, W.   313, 319
Laycock, Douglas   374
Lederberg, J.   60, 76, 77, 318
Ledgard, Henry E.   253, 255, 273
Leibniz, Gottfried   2, 8, 118, 171
Lejeune, A.   120, 132
Lemann, Nicholas   373
LeMessurie, William   361
Lenat, Douglas B.   199, 200, 208, 211, 212
Lenz, Michael   113
Leong, Mun-Kew   116
Leslie, J.   132
Levi, Isaac   41, 46
Levine, Joseph   171
Levy, A. Y.   209, 212
Levy, David   215, 229
Lewis, D.   123, 124, 130, 132
Lewis, Harry   248, 251
Lilly, J. C.   118, 132
Lindsay, Robert K.   53, 60, 64, 76, 77, 312, 318
Lippman, R. P.   170
Lipton, Richard   253, 254, 256, 257, 259, 271
Locke, John   370
Loebner, Hugh   222, 223, 225, 227, 228
Long, Douglas   177-181, 186, 187, 190
Loving, Steve   113
Loui, Ronald P.   46
Ly, Eric   113
Lycan, William   6, **171-192**

MacDonald, Chris   359
MacDonald-Ross, G.   118, 132
Macklin, Ruth   374, 375
Maes, P.   149
Makinson, David C.   39, 46
Maner, Walter   277-279, 289, 290, 291, 355
Marcotty, Michael   253, 255, 273
Marcus Aurelius   369
Margolus, N.   120, 128, 133
Marsoobian, Armen   14

Matthews, Gareth   186, 191
Maull, Nancy   70, 73, 75
Maurer, James   256, 257, 260, 263
Mavrovouniotis, M.   53, 60
Mayo, Deborah G.   63, 77
McCarthy, John   118, 126, 132, 194, 201, 206, 208, 209-211, 268
McIntyre, Alison   366
McClelland, J.L.   133, 136, 152
McCorduck, P.   312, 318
McGee, Glenn   360, 364, 366, 374, 375
McGilton, Henry   304, 307
McNaughton, Robert   245, 249, 251
McShea, Daniel W.   146, 151
Melnyk, Andrew   185, 191
Melo, F.   133
Mendelson, Elliot   238, 251
Merleau-Ponty, Maurice   200, 202, 206, 207, 209, 212
Metcalfe, Janet   156, 170
Meulen, Alice   251
Meyer, Bertrand   268
Meyer, J. A.   190
Michalski, R. S.   150
Mill, John Stuart   51, 279, 370
Minsky, Marvin   118, 119, 132
Mitchell, T. M.   150
Mittal, Sanjay   71, 74
Moberg, Dale   67, 74, 75, 77
Montaigne   369
Moody, J.   170
Moor, James H.   **1-14, 213-230**, 274, 277, 279, 280, 290
Moore   352
Moore, J.   288
Moore, J. Strother   273
Morgan, T. H.   62
Morrison, Perry   282, 289
Moses, Yioram   46
Moynihan, Daniel   373
Mozart, W. A.   311
Muller, Harald   259, 263, 273
Mullins, Atty   113
Murray, Pete   113
Murray, Thomas   375

Nagarajan, Satish   74, 75
Nagel, Ernest   141, 151